The History of
Australian Exploration

by
Ernest Favenc

Contents

PREFACE.

A complete history of the exploration of Australia will never be written. The story of the settlement of our continent is necessarily so intermixed with the results of private travels and adventures, that all the historian can do is to follow out the career of the public expeditions, and those of private origin which extended to such a distance, and embraced such important discoveries, as to render the results matters of national history.

That private individuals have done the bulk of the detail work there is no denying; but that work, although every whit as useful to the community as the more brilliant exploits that carried with them the publicity of Government patronage, has not found the same careful preservation.

To find the material to write such a history would necessitate the work of a lifetime, and the co-operation of hundreds of old colonists; and, when written, it would inevitably, from the nature of the subject, prove most monotonous reading, and fill, I am afraid to think, how many volumes. The reader has but to consider the immense area of country now under pastoral occupation, and to remember that each countless subordinate river and tributary creek was the result of some extended research of the pioneer squatter, to realise this.

Since the hope of finding an inland sea, or main central range, vanished for ever, the explorer cannot hope to discover anything much more exciting or interesting than country fitted for human habitation. The attributes of the native tribes are very similar throughout. Since the day when Captain Phillip and his little band settled down here and tried to gain the friendship of the aboriginal, no startling difference has been found in him throughout the continent. As he was when Dampier came to our shores, so is he now in the yet untrodden parts of Australia, and the explorer knows that from him he can only gain but a hazardous and uncertain tale of what lies beyond.

FAVENC

But, in this utter want of knowledge of the country to be explored, where even the physical laws do not assimilate with those of other continents, lies the great charm of Australian exploration. It is the spectacle of one man pitted against the whole force of nature--not the equal struggle of two human antagonists, but the old fable of the subtle dwarf and the self-confident giant.

When the battle commenced between Sturt and the interior, he was, as he thought, vanquished, though in reality the victor.

In the history of exploration are to be found some of the brightest examples of courage and fortitude presented by any record. In the succeeding pages I have tried to bring these episodes prominently to the fore, and bestow upon them the meed of history.

In compiling this book I have had the sympathy of many gentlemen, both in this and the neighbouring colonies, and my best thanks are due to them, especially as, owing to it, I have been able to make the work perfectly authentic, and I trust, a thoroughly reliable work of reference.

Sydney, 1888.
ERNEST FAVENC.

Introduction - Part I

Rumours of the existence of a Southern Continent in the Sixteenth Century--*Jave* and *Jave la Grande*--Authentic Discoveries and visits of the early Navigators--Torres sails between New Guinea and Terra Australis--Voyage of the *Duyfhen* in 1606--Dirk Hartog on the West Coast, his inscribed plate--Restored by Vlaming--Afterwards by Hamelin--Nuyts on the South Coast--Wreck of the *Batavia* on Houtman's Abrolhos--Mutiny of Cornelis--Tasman's second voyage--Dampier with the Buccaneers--Second Voyage in the *Roebuck*--Last visit of the Dutch--Captain Cook--Flinders; his theory of a Dividing Strait--Plans for exploring the Interior--His captivity--Captain King--Concluding remarks.

The charm of romance and adventure surrounding the discovery of hitherto unknown lands has from the earliest ages been the lure that has tempted men to prosecute voyages and travels of exploration. Whether under the pretext of science, religion or conquest, hardship and danger have alike been undergone with fortitude and cheerfulness, in the hope of being the first to find things strange and new, and return to civilized communities with the tidings.

In the days of Spain's supremacy, after the eyes of Europe had been dazzled with the sight of riches brought from the New World, and men's ears filled with fairy-like tales of the wondrous races discovered, it was but natural that the adventurous gallants of that age should roam in search of seas yet to be won.

Some such hope of finding a land wherein the glorious conquests of Cortes and Pizarro could be repeated, brought De Quiros on a quest that led him almost within hail of our shores. What little realization of his dreams of cities rich with temples, blazing with barbaric gold, inhabited by semi-civilized people skilled in strange arts he would have found in the naked nomads of Terra Australis, and their rude shelters of boughs and bark we now know; and perhaps, it was as well for the skilful pilot that he died with his mission unfulfilled, save in fancy. His lieutenant, Torres, came nearer solving the secret of the Southern Seas, and, in fact, reports sighting hills to the southward, which--on slight foundation--are supposed to have been the present Cape York, but more probably were the higher lands of Prince of Wales Island. In all likelihood he saw enough of the natives of the Straits to convince him that no such rich pickings were to be had, as had fallen to the lot of the lucky conquerors of Mexico and Peru. He came across none of the legendary canoes from the land of gold, deep laden with the precious metal, nor sandy beaches strewn with jewels, to be had for the gathering. He puts on record what he thought of the islanders in the few terse words, that they were "black, naked and corpulent," beyond that, they do not seem to have impressed him.

Apparently they, on their part, were not impressed at being informed that they were thenceforth subjects of the King of Spain, for their dislike to Europeans appears to have increased as the unfortunate Dutch captains, Carstens and Poole, afterwards found to their cost. Even the gracious act of His Holiness the Pope in partitioning these unknown lands between Spain and Portugal did not meet with the favourable consideration at their hands that it deserved.

The jealousy with which the maritime nations of Europe guarded their discoveries from each other has been the means of putting great difficulties in the way of tracing out the early traditions of the great South Land. The domineering Spaniard looked upon the Portugese navigator as a formidable rival in the race for trade; and the sturdy Hollander they regarded as a natural enemy and a rebel. The generous emulation of fellow-workers in the cause of scientific discovery was unknown, and the secrets of the sea were scrupulously kept.

On behalf of Dutch reticence, it may be said that the cause of the merited hatred they bore to Spain was still too fresh in their memory to allow them to divulge anything that might possibly benefit a Spaniard.

Sir William Temple, ambassador at the Hague in the time of Charles II., gives it as his opinion that "a southern continent has long since been found out." He avers that, according to descriptions he has gathered," it is as long as Java, and is marked on the maps by the name of New Holland, but to what extent the land extends either to the south, the east, or the west, none know." He states, that he has heard it said among the Dutch that their East India Company "have long since forbidden, and under the greatest penalties, any further attempts at discovering that continent, having already more trade than they can turn to account, and fearing some more populous nation of Europe might make great establishments of trade in some of these unknown regions, which might ruin or impair what they already have in the Indies."

But although no documentary evidence has been brought to light, proving beyond all doubt the certain discovery of the South Land in the sixteenth century, we find on the old charts of the world various tracings indicating a knowledge of the existence of this continent, which would appear to have been derived from other than fabulous sources.

A shadowy claim to the honour of being the first discoverer of Terra Australis has been advanced on behalf of the Frenchman Gonneville, who sailed from Honfleur in 1503, on a voyage to the East Indies. He is said to have doubled the Cape of Good Hope, and being driven by stress of weather into an unknown sea, found a land inhabited by friendly people, with whom he stayed some time, being accompanied back to France by one of the king's sons who was desirous of studying the precepts of Christianity. The general belief, however, is that it was probably Madagascar whereon De Gonneville landed.

Another claim, based upon the authority of an ancient map, is put forward for the noted Portugese navigator Magalhaens, when in the service of the Emperor Charles V. of Spain; but there is little appertaining to the arguments advanced on behalf of this belief to render it credible.

In some of the old charts, dating back to the middle of the sixteenth century, a large country south of Java is portrayed, which from its position appears to be intended for the conjectural South Land. In all these maps the outlines of this terra incognita are so nearly identical that it is evident various hydrographers drew their inspirations from the same sources. The annexed tracing is a copy of a portion of one of the most ancient of these maps; the original was presented to the British Museum by Sir Joseph Banks in 1790. It is most carefully drawn, the coast line being elaborately filled in with names in French, and it is embellished with drawings of animals and men, being also ornamented with two shields bearing the arms of France. The map is undated, but was probably designed in the latter part of the reign of Francis I, for his son, the Dauphin, afterwards Henry II.

It has been alleged that Captain Cook was guided by these charts to the eastern shore of New Holland, and the similarity of some of the names thereon, such as Coste des Herbaiges, and Coste Dangerouse, to names given by him, has been pointed out. This allegation, however, will not stand criticism. Botany Bay, for instance, is about the last place that any one would select to bestow such a name on as Coste des Herbaiges, which name would signify a rich and fertile spot, certainly not such a desolate place as Botany Bay was in Captain Cook's time. Captain Tench, one of the survey party sent there in 1789, writes in his journal:--"We were unanimously of the opinion that had not the nautical part of Mr. Cook's description been so accurately laid down, there would exist the utmost reason to believe that those who have described the contiguous country had never seen it. On the side of the harbour, a line of sea coast more than thirty miles long, we did not find two hundred acres which could be cultivated." Any approximation then in position between Botany Bay and the fabulous Coste des Herbaiges must be considered as accidental.

The generally received opinion of this and the other charts is, that Java (Jave) is fairly well laid down, and that Great Java stands for the supposed South Land. Plausible as this theory reads, it is, however, open to objection. If it be accepted, and the narrow strait the river Grande be looked upon as that portion of the Indian Ocean dividing Java from the north-west coast of Australia, any resemblance to the present known shape of our continent is very hard to trace, unless after a most distorted fashion. If, however, we make the necessary allowances for the many errors that would creep in from one transcription to another, and look upon Jave and Jave la Grande as one continent intersected by a mediterranean sea, we have a fair, if rude, conception of the north coast of Australia. Moreover, let the reader imagine a south coast line drawn from Baye Perdue on the east to Havre de Sylla on the west, doing away with the conjectural east and west coast continuations south of those points; the deep inlet between Jave and Jave la Grande standing for the Gulf of Carpentaria, a very passable outline of the whole continent is obtained. And it is more than probable that this view was originally suggested by this map, and from it sprang the belief current, even to the beginning of this century, that an open passage existed from the west coast, either into the Gulf of Carpentaria, or to the head of Spencer's Gulf. The other maps give no more information than this one, and the identity of their origin is obvious. One, however, has been found in the British Museum the features of which are different. It is a rough copy of an old map showing the north west portion of a continent to the south of "Java Major." It bears a legend in Portugese, of which the following is a translation:--"Nuca Antara was discovered in the year 1601 by Manoel Godinho Eredia, by command of the Viceroy Ayres de Soldanha." This would point to a Portugese discovery of Australia immediately preceding the Dutch one.

In Cornelius Wytfliet's "Descriptionis Ptolemaicae Augmentum," Louvain, 1598, the following passage is to be found:--
"The Australis Terra is the most southern of all lands; it is separated from New Guinea by a narrow strait; its shores are hitherto but little known, since, after one voyage and another, that route has been deserted, and seldom is the country visited unless when sailors are driven there by storms. The Australis Terra begins at two or three degrees from the equator, and is maintained by some to be of so great an extent that if it were thoroughly explored it would be regarded as a fifth part of the world."

The above is so vague and suppositious that it would scarcely be worth quoting, were it not for the singular mention of the narrow strait separating Australis Terra from New Guinea; for at this time Torres had not sailed through the straits, nor was the fact of his having done so known to the world until the end of the eighteenth century, when Dalrymple discovered his report amongst the archives of Manila, and did justice to his memory.

In 1605, Pedro Fernandez de Quiros, having for his second in command Luis Vaez de Torres, sailed from Callao with two well-armed vessels and a corvette. After the discovery of several islands, they came to a land which Quiros supposed to be the continent he was in search of, and therefore named it Australia del Espiritu Santo. "At one hour past midnight," says Torres, in his account of the voyage, "the Capitana" (Quiros' vessel) "departed without any notice given to us, and without making any signal." This extraordinary conduct was supposed to be the result of discontent and mutiny amongst the sailors, an outbreak having already taken place which was not quelled quite so firmly as Torres advocated. After vainly waiting for many days, Torres set sail, and first ascertaining that it was only an island where they had been anchored, he made his way by the dangerous south coast of New Guinea to Manila, where he arrived in 1607.

Up to the preceding year popular knowledge concerning the South Land must be looked upon as being mixed up with much that is both doubtful and hazardous. We now, however, reach the period which may be regarded as the beginning of the authentic history of the discovery of New Holland. In 1606 the yacht Duyfhen sailed from Bantam, and, coasting along the south-west shore of New Guinea, her commander unknowingly crossed the entrance of Torres Straits, and continued his voyage along the eastern side of the Gulf of Carpentaria, under the impression that it was part of the same country. They sailed nearly to latitude 14 degrees south, when want of provisions and other necessaries compelled them to turn back. Cape Keer-Weer (Turn Again) they named the furthest point reached by them. Their report of the country was most unfavourable. They described it as being "for the greatest part desert, but in some places inhabited by wild, cruel, black savages, by whom some of the crew were murdered, for which reason they could not learn anything of the land or waters as had been desired of them."

The name of the captain of the Duyfhen--the Columbus of the south--has not been preserved. Ten years after this visit, in 1616, Captain Dirk Hartog, in command of the ship Endracht, from Amsterdam, discovered the west coast of Australia. He left a tin plate on an island in Dirk Hartog's Roads bearing the following inscription:--

"Ao 1616, den 25sten October, is hier vangecommen het schip de Endracht van Amsterdam, den Oppercoopmen Gilles Mibais van Luyck; schipper Dirk Hartog, van Amsterdam, den 27sten, dito t' zeijl gegaen na Bantam, den Ondercoopman Jan Stoyn, Opperstierman Pieter Dockes, van Bil, Ao 1616."

[Translation.--On the 25th October, arrived here the ship Endraght of Amsterdam; the first merchant, Gilles Mibais, of Luyck; Captain Dirk Hartog; of Amsterdam; the 27th ditto set sail for Bantam; undermerchant Jan Stoyn, upper steersman, Pieter Dockes, from Bil, Ao, 1616.]

Captain Vlaming, of the ship Geelvink, found this plate in 1697, and replaced it with another, on which he copied the original inscription, and added to it as follows:--

"1697. Den 4den Februaij is hier vangecommen het schip de Geelvink van Amsterdam, den Commandeur schipper, Williem de Vlamingh, van Vlielandt, Adsistent Joan van Bremen, van Coppenhage; Opperstierman Michiel Blom van Estight, van Bremen. De Hoecker de Nyptang, schipper Gerrit Collaert van Amsterdam; Adsistent Theodorus Heermans van de; d`Opperstierman Gerrit Gerritz, van Bremen, 't Galjoot t' Weseltje, Gezaghabber Cornelis de Vlamingh van Vlielandt; Stierman Coert Gerritz, van Bremen, en van hier gezeilt met ons vloot den 12do voorts net Zuijtland te ondersoecken en gedestineert voor Batavia."

[Translation.--On the 4th of February, 1697, arrived here the ship Geelvinck, of Amsterdam; Commandant Wilhelm de Vlamingh, of Welandt; assistant, Jan van Bremen, of Copenhagen; first pilot, Michiel Bloem van Estight, of Bremen. The hooker, the Nyptangh,

Captain Gerrit Collaert, of Amsterdam, Assistant Theodorus Heermans, of the same place; first pilot, Gerrit Gerritz, of Bremen; then the galliot Weseltje, Commander Cornelis de Vlaming, of Vlielandt; Pilot Coert Gerritz, from Bremen. Sailed from here with our fleet on the 12th, to explore the South Land, and afterwards bound for Batavia.]

In 1801, the boatswain of the Naturaliste found this plate half buried in sand, lying near an oaken post to which it had been nailed. Captain Hamelin, with rare good taste, had a new post made, and the plate erected in the old spot. Another outward bound ship, the Mauritius, touched on the west coast in 1618, and discovered and named the Willems River, near the Northwest Cape, probably the present Ashburton. The Leeuwin (Lioness), visited the west coast in 1622, and the well-known reef of Houtman's Abrolhos was so-called after Frederick Houtman, a Dutch navigator of distinction who, however, never personally visited Australian shores. The next navigator to the South Land met with an untimely end. In the year 1623, Governor Coen dispatched two yachts, the Pera and the Arnhem, on a voyage of discovery. Landing on the coast of New Guinea, Captain Jan Carstens, of the Arnhem, and eight of his crew were murdered by the natives, but the vessels proceeded, and touched upon the north coast of New Holland, west of the Gulf of Carpentaria, still known as Arnhem's Land. A river, the Spult, is here laid down in the old charts, in the vicinity of the present Liverpool River, and there is also another opening marked the "Speult," on the eastern side of the Gulf, since determined to be the Endeavour Strait of Captain Cook,

At Arnhem's Land the yachts parted, the Pera continuing the voyage alone. Crossing the head of the Gulf she followed the course of the Duyfhen, and passing Cape Keer-Weer, made as far south as 17 degrees, where the Staaten River is laid down. Their report was also unfavourable, and is summed up in the official dispatches of the company, thus:--"In this discovery were found everywhere shallow waters and barren coasts, islands altogether thinly peopled by divers cruel, poor, and brutal nations, and of very little use to the Dutch East India Company." Pera Head, in the Gulf, is another memorial of this voyage.

Now came the turn of the south coast of New Holland. In 1627, Captain Pieter Nuyts, in his ship the Gulde Zeepard, accidentally touched on the south coast. He followed it along for seven or eight hundred miles, and bestowed on it the name of Pieter Nuyts' Land. The Vianen sighted the west coast in 1628, and kept in sight of it for some two hundred miles, reporting "a foul and barren shore, green fields; and very wild, black, barbarous inhabitants."

FAVENC

The wreck of the Batavia on Houtman's Abrolhos, in 1629, is one of the most tragic incidents in early Australian history. The Batavia, commanded by Commodore Francis Pelsart, was separated from her consorts by a storm, and during the night of the 4th of June struck on the rocks of Frederick Houtman. The crew and passengers were landed on one island, and two small islets in the neighbourhood, and the ship broke up. No fresh water was found, and Pelsart sailed in one of the boats in search of some on the mainland. He was unsuccessful, and finally steered for Batavia. Meanwhile, a terrible scene of riot and murder was enacted. Jerome Cornelis, the supercargo, headed a mutiny, and those refusing to join his band were in part cruelly assassinated. One company however, on one of the islets, in charge of Weybehays defended themselves valiantly, finally taking Cornelis prisoner. Fresh water was found, and the two hostile camps awaited the reappearance of Pelsart. The design of the mutineers had been to surprise Pelsart on his return, capture his vessel, and sail away on a piratical cruise. The determined front shown by Weybehays and his party, who, although unarmed, had twice defeated them with some slaughter, disarranged their plans.

When the Sardam, with Pelsart on board, hove in sight of the Abrolhos, the smoke rising from the islands assured the captain, who was naturally tormented with anxiety, that some, at any rate survived. To their surprise, a boat came off to meet them, pulled by men dressed in rich uniforms, made from the silks and stuffs that had formed part of the Batavia's cargo. Pelsart's suspicions were at once aroused, knowing as he did, that insubordination had &hewn itself even before his departure. These men were ordered to come on board unarmed, with the alternative of being sunk, and Weybehays coming off at the same time, they had no choice but to obey, and the whole of the mutineers were soon in irons. After recovering most of the treasure, with the exception of one chest, containing eight' thousand rix dollars, a consultation was held as to the fate of the murderers. It was unanimously decided that, having in view the overcrowded state of the ship, and the temptation presented by the recovered treasure, the presence of such turbulent spirits on board would be dangerous to the safety of the company. Therefore, it was thought best to try the offenders there and then, instead of taking them to Batavia. This was done, and the sentences at once carried into effect. Two men, however, were condemned to the more lingering punishment of being marooned on the mainland, there to meet a cruel death at the hands of the savages. These two blood-stained criminals were the first Europeans to leave

10

their bones in Australia, an unhappy omen of the future. According to the instructions issued to Tasman, on his second voyage, he was directed to "enquire at the continent thereabout" (i.e., the neighbourhood of the Abrolhos) "after two Dutchmen, who, having by the enormity of their crimes forfeited their lives, were put on shore by the Commodore Francisco Pelsart, if still alive. In such case, you may make inquiries of them about the situation of those countries, and if they entreat you to that purpose, give them passage thither." He was also instructed to recover, if possible, the chest of rix dollars. Unfortunately Tasman's journal has never been discovered, and it is not known how he fared on his mission.

Captain Gerrit Tomaz Poole sailed from Banda in 1636, with the yachts Klyn, Amsterdam, and Wesel, to meet his death on the New Guinea coast, in the same place that had been fatal to Carstens, and in a like manner. The supercargo took charge, and prosecuted the voyage, revisiting Arnhem's Land.

A name familiar to all is that of Abel Janz Tasman. In 1644, after his discovery of Van Dieman's Land, he was sent out on a second voyage of exploration. His instructions were: "To discover whether Nova Guinea is one continent with the Great South Land, or separated by channels and islands lying between them, and also whether that New Van Dieman's Land" (Arnhem's Land) "is the same continent with these two great countries, or with one of them." He was also directed to search for the strait between New Guinea and New Holland, in a large opening said to exist in that locality. Apparently, this portion of his instructions was, for some reasons, not thoroughly carried out.

Although Tasman's journal of this voyage has never been found, we have pretty good evidence that he safely accomplished it. Dampier, in his volume of voyages, mentions having in his possession a chart laid down by Tasman, and an outline copy of the same was inlaid in the floor of the Groote Zaal, in the Stadhuys in Amsterdam. The annexed tracing is from a fairly authenticated copy of Tasman's map, with the discoveries of former navigators attached, soundings being given along that portion of the north-west coast that would have embraced Tasman's proposed track. Many of the names still retained in the Gulf of Carpentaria are significant of Tasman's visit. Vanderlin Island, after Cornelis Van der Lyn; Sweer's Island, after Salamon Sweers; Maria Island, after his supposed sweetheart, Maria Van Dieman; and Limmen Bight, after his ship, the Limmen. This chart may be looked on as being the first one to give a reliable and good outline of the Australian coast as then known--namely, from Endeavour Strait, in the extreme north, to the eastern limit of Pieter Nuvt's Land, on the south. The two placer, where "Ffresh" water is marked would be the Batavia River, near Cape York, and the present Macarthur River, at the head of the Gulf, the well defined headlands shown there having been resolved by Captain Flinders into a group of islands, now known as the Sir Edward Pellew Group. Tasman's ships were the Limmen, the Zeemeuw, and the tender De Brak.

The first Englishman to land on New Holland was William Dampier in 1688. In very bad company, namely, a crew of buccaneers who left Captain Sharpe and travelled across the Isthmus of Darien, he visited the west coast of New Holland, where they remained over a month refitting and cleaning their ship. Dampier does not seem to have been on the best of terms with his shipmates, for some difference of opinion arising as to the final destination of their voyage, he "was threatened to be turned ashore on New Holland for it, which made me desist, intending, by God's blessing, to make my escape the first place I came near." His notes on this occasion refer chiefly to the natives seen, whose personal appearance and habits he considers alike equally disgusting and repulsive.

Towards the end of the year 1696, William de Vlaming, in search of the Ridderschap, a missing ship supposed to have been wrecked on the coast of New Holland, came to the Great South Land. He found and named the Swan River, this being the first mention ever made of black swans, two specimens of which were captured and taken to Batavia. At Dirk Hartog's Road, he found, as before-mentioned, the tin plate left by that captain, and after a careful examination of the coast so far as the North-west Cape, left for Batavia.

Dampier now reappears on the scene in charge of the Roe-buck--a ship sent out by the English Government in 1699. His account of his voyage is very minute and circumstantial, but he still retains his aversion to the unfortunate natives, of whom he always speaks with the greatest scorn. Some of his statements are slightly doubtful, to say the least of it, as, for instance, one concerning the capture of a large shark, "in which we found the head and bones of a hippopotamus, [Note, below] the hairy lips of which were still sound and not putri-fied, and the jaw was also firm, out of which we pluckt a great many teeth, two of them eight inches long and as big as a man's thumb, small at one end and a little crooked, the rest not above half so long."

[Note: M. Malte Brun calls him "the learned and faithful Dampier," and, in corroboration of the hippopotamus story, mentions that Bailly, when exploring the Swan River, "heard a bellowing much louder than that of an ox from among the reeds on the river side, which made him suspect that a large quadruped lay somewhere near him." It is remarkable that in the several accounts of the early Dutch visits to the northern coast no mention is made of alligators, although they are so common to all the inlets and rivers of that region, the name Crocodils Eylanden on one old chart being the sole exception.]

Dampier disputes the accuracy of the "draught of Tasman's" that he had with him in many particulars, and constantly advances his theory of the existence of a strait dividing New Holland into two parts, probably taking this idea, as before indicated, from the old map of the Dauphin.

In 1705, the ships Vossenbach, Wayer, and Nova Hollandia were sent out to investigate the north coast, under the command of Martin van Delft. The journals of the voyage have not been found, although a report of the notable events that happened was laid before the Governor-General of the East India Council. This was the last voyage of exploration undertaken by the Dutch, and closes the history of the early discovery of New Holland. The existence of the Southern Land was definitely established, and it remained for the English and French nations to determine its size and formation with accuracy, and fill up the gaps on the coast line.

Sixty-five years passed before Captain Cook sailed through the Endeavour Strait, finally settling the question of the separation of this continent from New Guinea, and during that period New Holland, so far as we know, was unvisited.

The association of Captain Cook with this continent is too well-known to need more than a passing reference in this introduction. He proved the insularity of the South Land, and examined the long-neglected east coast.

In. 1777, Mons. de St. Alouarn anchored near Cape Leeuwin, but no details of his visit have been preserved.

In 1791, Captain George Vancouver touched on the south coast, and gave the name of King George's Sound to that well-known harbour; thence he sailed eastward. In the following year Rear-Admiral Bruny D'Entrecasteaux, in search of the hapless La Perouse, who so narrowly missed appropriating New Holland for the French, made an elaborate survey of part of our south coast.

Before the close of the century, Bass and Flinders--fit companions--had commenced their daring exploits in the little Tom Thumb, and finally, with the sloop Norfolk, established the existence of the strait named after the enterprising young surgeon.

13

In the year 1799, Flinders went north in the Norfolk sloop, and followed up Cook's discoveries in Moreton Bay. In 18oi he was appointed to the Investigator (formerly the Xenophon), and sailed from Spithead on the voyage which was to render him one of the leading figures in Australian history.

Reaching Cape Leeuwin he commenced his survey of the south coast, discovering and naming the two Gulfs of Spencer and St. Vincent. The former he at one time thought would lead him through the continent into the Carpentarian Gulf. He reached Port Jackson in May, the year after he left England, and active preparations were soon afterwards commenced to prepare the ship for her long northern cruise.

In July, 1802, the Investigator, with the Lady Nelson as tender, left Sydney Cove; the object of the voyage being to thoroughly survey the eastern and northern coasts. Flinders rounded Cape York, and after a close examination of the Gulf of Carpentaria, which, like Spencer's Gulf in the south, deluded him for a time with the false hope of affording an inlet into the interior, brought his work to an end at Cape Wessel, in consequence of the rotten state of his ship. He called at Coepang in Timor, whence, after obtaining some supplies, he made for Port Jackson by way of the west coast.

Throughout this cruise it is evident that Flinders was much impressed by the notion advanced by Dampier, that New Holland (meaning the north-west portion) was separated from the land to the south by a strait opening north of Shark's Bay. "Unless," says Dampier, "the high tides and indraught thereabout should be occasioned by the mouth of some large river, which hath often low lands on each side of the outlet, and many islands and shoals lying at its entrance; but I rather thought it a channel or strait than a river." To quote the words of Flinders:--

"This opinion he supports by a fair induction from facts, and the opening of twelve miles wide, seen by Vlaming's two vessels, near the same place, and in which they could find no anchorage, strongly corroborated Dampier's supposition."

Later information had demonstrated that the supposed strait could not lead into the great ocean eastward, as the English navigator (Dampier) had conjectured, but it was thought possible that it might communicate with the Gulf of Carpentaria, and even probable that a passage existed from thence to the unknown parts of the south coast beyond the Isles of St. Francis and St. Peters.

"In the case of penetrating the interior of *Terra Australis*, either by a great river, or a strait leading to an inland sea, a superior country, and perhaps, a different race of people might be found, the knowledge of which could not fail to be very interesting, and might prove advantageous to the nation making the discovery."

This was the goal of Flinders' ambition, the vision that haunted him always--the discovery of a mediterranean sea.

There being no ship in Port Jackson fit to continue the survey work left uncompleted by the Investigator, Flinders determined to return to England, and obtain a suitable vessel from the Admiralty. He and twenty-two of his men and officers embarked as passengers in the Porpoise, and left Port Jackson in company with the Batavian-bound ships Cato and Bridgewater.

They sailed on the 10th of August, 1803, and on the night of the 17th, the Porpoise and Cato struck on a reef, and became complete wrecks. The crews escaped to a sand-bank adjoining the reef, and here they were left to their fate by the third ship, the Bridgewater, the captain of which vessel sailed away to Batavia, without any attempt being made to save them.

Discipline and order were, however, maintained on Wreck Reef Bank, as it was called, and Flinders, who took command after the vessel struck, proceeded to Sydney in the cutter, to obtain assistance for the remainder of the crews, who were to employ the time in constructing two decked boats from the timbers of the Porpoise. This perilous voyage in an open boat, Flinders accomplished safely, and returned in six weeks, with two colonial schooners, the Cumberland and the Francis, and the ship Rolla, bound for Canton. The shipwrecked men were taken off the bank, and Flinders started for England in the Cumberland, a small schooner of but twenty-nine tons. On his way homeward he was forced to put into the Mauritius, to refit his little craft, before venturing round the Cape of Good Hope; and on the pretext that the passport he carried did not afford safe conduct to the Cumberland, having been made out for the Investigator, he was detained a prisoner in the Isle of France for over six years.

The conduct of General de Caen in this matter has been severely commented on, as it was entirely due to his personal pique and jealousy in the affair that this indignity was put upon Flinders. The generous hospitality extended by the British settlement to the French navigators at Port Jackson found no response in this rough specimen of a soldier of the revolution, who throughout the period of Flinders' detention, treated him with studied rudeness and unnecessary harshness.

For three months Flinders was kept close prisoner as a spy, and for twenty months as an ordinary prisoner of war. Still during his captivity in the Isle of France, his thoughts were constantly busied with projects for the further exploration of the great southern continent he had lately left. In addition to the chafing weariness of prolonged detention and enforced inactivity, he was constantly haunted by the dread that the French would, after examination of his papers, step in and forestall him in the matter. In a letter to Sir Joseph Banks, dated March 20th, 1806, [See fac-simile of original letter (not included in this eBook)] he mentions this fear, and adding, that disappointment and deferred hope of release have in no way damped his ardour in the cause of science, advances for consideration a scheme for exploring the interior of Australia. Though now, after more than eighty years of discovery have given us an intimate knowledge of the nature of the difficulties he would have encountered, we may smile at the somewhat crude notions of the daring navigator, we cannot refuse to recognise that a good deal of thoroughness was mixed up with his plan, simple as it reads. An incursion of five hundred miles north and south, respectively, would without doubt, if possible, have done much towards an earlier knowledge of the interior.

His dream of sailing up a deep estuary--some great water way--leading to more fertile lands than those of the coast inhabited by a superior race of natives, had vanished. As the shores of the Gulf of Carpentaria rounded his course from south to west, and from west to north, so the picture his fancy had painted faded; and he found himself compelled to fall back upon the conception of a mode of transit patriarchal in its simplicity.

He writes:--

"With five or six asses to carry provisions (and they can be obtained here), expeditions might be made into the interior of Australia from the head of the Gulph of Carpentaria in 18 deg., and from the head of the great gulph on the south coast in 32 deg., until the courses should nearly meet, five hundred miles each way would most probably be sufficient, since the country does not appear to be mountainous: a view of my general chart will exemplify this. In case of being again sent to Australia, I should much wish that this was a part of my instructions."
[Note: Referring to Flinders' scheme for exploring Australia, it may be amusing to the reader to contrast it with one projected some years later by M. Malte Brun. In his case, the amount of material the eminent geographer considered necessary for the expedition is as excessive as that of Captain Flinders' was simple. His method for exploring the continent is this: "In order to determine these questions" (namely the different theories propounded as to the nature of the interior) "it has

been proposed to send an expedition to penetrate the country from Spencer's Gulf. For such an expedition, men of science and courage ought to be selected. They ought to be provided with all sorts of implements and stores, and with different animals, from the powers and instincts of which they may derive assistance. They should have oxen from Buenos Ayres, or from the English settlements, mules from Senegal, and dromedaries from Africa or Arabia. The oxen would traverse the woods and the thickets; the mules would walk securely among rugged rocks and hilly countries; the dromedaries would cross the sandy deserts. Thus the expedition would be prepared for any kind of territory that the interior might present. Dogs also should be taken to raise game, and to discover springs of water; and it has even been proposed to take pigs, for the sake of finding out esculent roots in the soil. When no kangaroos and game are to be found the party would subsist on the flesh of their own flocks. They should be provided with a balloon for spying at a distance any serious obstacle to their progress in particular directions, and for extending the range of observations which the eye would take of such level lands as are too wide to allow any heights beyond them to come within the compass of their view. The journey might be allowed a year or eighteen months, which would be only at the rate of four or five miles per day. . . . The author of the present work" ("Universal Geography") "has discoursed this project in conversation with the enlightened and indefatigable traveller, M. Péron, who saw no insuperable obstacle to its probability, except the existence of an immense ocean of sand occupying the whole of the interior of the continent, which to him appeared extremely probable."]

But Flinders was never fated to see the interior of Terra Australis, either from the deck of a ship, or from any point of vantage; he surveyed its shores, suggested the name it now bears--Australia, and left the work of discovery, not even to this day quite completed, to other hands. But though the name of Flinders has not received the world-wide recognition that has been bestowed upon that of Cook, in Australia it should be equally honoured. The land that witnessed his long labours and heroic courage ought not to repay him with forgetfulness.

The crazy state of the Investigator having compelled Flinders to terminate his voyage abruptly, a considerable space of coast line was still left on the north, and north-west, that had not been minutely examined. Lieutenant Phillip King, between the years 1818 and 1822, completed the survey left unfinished by Flinders, and the work of marine exploration temporarily ceased.

In looking back over the early history of Australia, the apparently careless manner in which the English became possessed of the whole of the continent is very noticeable. Although the Dutch had so long been acquainted with our shores, and the neighbourhood of their possessions in Java would have afforded them greater facilities for exploration than were held by any other nation, no attempt at colonisation was ever made by them. The apparent poverty, both of the country and the natives, offered the East India Company no inducement to extend their operations. Still, in a vague kind of way, the Dutch claim to the western portion of Australia was recognized. In the patent to the first governor at Port Jackson, the western limit of New South Wales is fixed at 13.5 deg. E. longitude, a position approximating to the boundary of New Holland as fixed by the Dutch, whereby the country was divided into New Holland and Terra Australis. This line of demarcation would bisect the present colony of South Australia. In the early part of this century, the French evidently considered that they had a well-founded claim, both to the discovery and possession of the south coast, west of Nuyts' "Island of St. Peters." The name of "Terre Napoleon" was given to it, Spencer's Gulf becoming "Golfe Bonaparte," and the Gulf of St. Vincent "Golfe Josephine." Malte Brun remarks:--
"The claims of the English have no fixed boundaries; they seem desirous of confounding the whole of New Holland under the modern name which they have given to the east coast, which was minutely explored by Captain Cook. It is worthy of remark that the French geographers had, from a comparison of the tracks navigated by Abel Tasman, previously concluded on the existence and direction of this coast itself."

But neither Dutch nor French claims were ever seriously advanced, and the whole of the continent and adjacent islands were ceded to the English in much the same happy-go-lucky fashion that we recently let slip a large portion of New Guinea. One cause of the apathy displayed was without doubt the forbidding nature of the reports published by all the navigators. The coast line had been examined, and the various inlets followed up without any important or navigable river having been brought to light, and the absence of fresh water streams in such a large continent naturally led thinking men to the conclusion that the inland slope was nothing but an arid desert, parched beneath a rainless sky. The hot winds that had been experienced on the southern coast aided this belief, and the natives when interviewed professed no knowledge beyond the limits of their tribal hunting grounds. The little colony clustered around Rose Hill, and on the shore of Sydney Cove, was shut in by the gloomy gorges and unscaleable precipices of the

Caermarthen Hills, that stayed all progress to the westward, and the same frowning barrier had been found to extend north and south.

Men's imaginations were exhausted in picturing the physical appearance of the mysterious interior. Some thought it a vast level plain, where the few and sluggish rivers were lost in shallow lakes, to disappear by evaporation; others again, believed it to be an immense bed of sand where no rivers formed, and the thirsty sands absorbed the scanty rainfall; and many imagined an inland sea connected with the ocean by subterranean outlets: one and all agreed in its inhospitable nature.

There was nothing hopeful nor inspiriting in the outlook to induce men to attempt to penetrate this silent desert, save the love of adventure, and the gratification of a laudable curiosity.

The convicts, who in efforts to regain their liberty, from time to time made desperate attempts to escape, either perished miserably or, daunted by the sterile nature of the land and the hostility of the natives, returned to give themselves up, before reaching any distance from the settlement. The work of exploration was toilsome and difficult, from the lack of beasts of burden. Each member of the party had a heavy pack to carry, and when to that was added the cumbrous firearms and ammunition of those times, a day's journey was no light labour. The weary system of counting the paces all day must have considerably added to the monotony of the march. Two thousand and two hundred paces over good ground were allowed to a mile. When too, nature had barred the way with an apparently insurmountable range, it is not to be wondered at that the area of explored country was not very widely extended during the first twenty years of settlement.

In striking contrast to other portions of the world's surface that have been slowly explored and examined by the European nations, Australia has throughout retained a character of its own. From the coastal formation of most lands, fair indications could be obtained of the character of the interior. Large rivers gave evidence of a defined system of drainage, the crests of snow-topped mountain ranges in the distance were proof of whence these rivers sprang. The native tribes were of higher intelligence, had a partial knowledge of what lay beyond their immediate ken, and could show articles of barter and commerce that they had obtained from more inland residents.

Australia was a silent and sullen blank, and for a century of exploration nature has resisted, step by step, the encroachments on her stronghold, making the invaders pay toll with many a gallant life.

Introduction - Part II

The Continent of Australia--Its peculiar formation--The coast range and the highest peaks thereof--The coastal rivers--The inland rivers--Difference of vegetation on the tableland and on the coast--Exception to the rule--Valuable timber of the coast districts--Animals common to the whole continent--Some birds the same--Distinct habits of others--The Australian native and his unknown origin--Water supply--Upheaval.

It was comparatively at a late period in the world's history when Australia was opened up as a field for geographical research; but, notwithstanding that the accumulated knowledge of centuries was thus brought to bear upon it, the characteristic and unique formation of the country set at naught all the approved deductions and theories of the scientific world. A paradox, or, as a clever writer recently put it, "a surviving fragment of the primitive world," with a nature contradictory and inconsistent, as compared even with itself, cut off from the rest of the globe, and left to work out the problem of its existence alone; no wonder it was only after successive generations had toiled at it, that Australia was, even in part, understood.

The interior of Australia is, as is well-known, an immense plain, having an average height of fifteen hundred to two thousand feet, with a decided tilt, or slope, towards the south-west. Round the foot of this tableland, is a terrace of lower country, varying greatly in width. The river systems of the coastal lands, lying between the sea and the foot of the tableland, were easily understood and traced, that of the interior was far more difficult.

Starting from Cape York, in the extreme north, and following down the eastern coast, the edge of the tableland is formed of ranges, often of considerable height, the gullies and spurs of which are mostly clothed with scrub and jungle of tropical growth and luxuriance; amongst the peaks of this range there are Distant Peak, 3,573 feet;

Pieter Botte Mountain, 3,311 feet; Grey Peak, 3,357 feet; and the Bellender Kerr Hills, 5,433 feet high. Further south, the level is more uniform; the isolated peak of Mount Elliott--which attains a height Of 4,075 feet--forming the exception, until further south again the elevations approach to 4,250 feet. An average height of a little over two thousand feet is then maintained until the border line of Queensland is reached, and here--in Mount Lindesay--5,500 feet is met with. The New England Range maintains this altitude in many peaks, including Mount Seaview--from which point Oxley sighted the ocean-6,000 feet high. Still to the south, the mountains on the border of the plateau keep up an average of between three and four thousand feet until, at the south-east extremity of our continent, the greatest height is attained in Mount Kosciusko, falling some 700 feet short of the limit of perpetual snow, its elevation being 7,308 feet.

To the westward, many of the peaks reach altitudes of over 5,000 and 6,000 feet, until the large depression is encountered through which the great body of interior waters find their way to the sea by means of the Murray Channel.

West of this gap, the edge of the tableland is broken, and depressed, the highest crests of the coastal range rarely reaching to 3,000 feet in height. and along the shore line, facing the Great Australian Bight, it is almost non-existent.

On reaching the south-west corner of Australia, the elevated edge reforms in the Russell and Darling Ranges, and trending northward, skirting the coast, culminates in Mount Bruce, 4,000 feet above sea level. From hence, the range following the sea line is broken, rugged and precipitous, but of inconsiderable height, and when the centre of the Gulf of Carpentaria is reached, it falls away into highlands and slopes, joining the eastern ranges.

On the great plateau encircled by this range, no elevations of any moment are to be found; a kind of chain traverses the centre from north to south, but though in places presenting a bold formation, the highest altitude attained is in the Macdonnell Ranges--4,000 feet.

From the coastal range, the edge of the tableland, flow the rivers that run direct to the sea on the seaward face; but in many instances a false tableland occurs, the streams that drain which unite in forcing their way through deep gorges to the lowlands of the coast. This false tableland is conspicuous in the valley of the Upper Burdekin River on the east coast, and on the head waters of the Fitzroy, The country drained by the top tributaries of these rivers being only divided from the real tableland by a gentle ascent, whereas the descent to the coast

21

is steep and abrupt. Most of the northern rivers, too, take their rise in a plateau that is almost on a level with the great plain, but cut their way down to the sea through gorges, instead of being lost in the interior.

It follows then, that the drainage and character of the terrace surrounding the continent, keeping to natural and known laws was at once understood, but the drainage of the plateau was more difficult to comprehend, and it is now known to be confined to two river systems only, first, that of the Darling and Murray, which rivers receive all the waters flowing to the westward of the eastern coast range, and secondly, the lake system further to the westward; the great salt lakes to the north of Spencer's Gulf receiving Cooper's Creek and its many tributaries, and also the Diamantina and Herbert; their waters being dissipated by soakage and evaporation. Westward, again, there is little doubt that no system exists, the level nature of the country and intermittent rainfall shortening the existence of the creeks before they have time to unite their flood waters in one large permanent channel.

The rivers of the eastern coast are the Kennedy, the Endeavour, the Barron, the Burdekin with its many tributaries, the Clark, the Perry, the Star, the Keelbottom, the Fanning, the Suttor (which last brings down the united waters of the Cape and Belyando), and finally after passing through the Leichhardt Range the Bowen, and the Bogie. The Fitzroy, another river of many tributaries, the Mackenzie, the Isaacs, the Nogoa, and the Dawson. Then come the Boyne, the Kolan, the Burnett (which receives another Boyne), the Mary, the Brisbane, all in the Colony of Queensland. On this coast in New South Wales, come next the Tweed, the Richmond, and the Clarence; the Macleay, the Hastings, and the Hunter. The Hawkesbury the Shoalhaven and the Clyde. The Snowy River, though rising in New South Wales, discharges itself into the sea in Victorian waters; thence we come to the Latrobe and the many minor streams that flow into the ocean instead of into the great receiver the Murray. The Glenelg and the Wannon. Then comes the Murray, the outlet of the inland waters. Westward, the rivers of the coast become smaller and less frequent, until at last they cease to exist; but on the western shore--where the coast range once more reasserts itself--we find in Western Australia, the Swan, the Irwin, the Greenough, the Murchison, and the Gascoyne, the Ashburton, the Fortescue, the De Grey, and another Fitzroy. On the north coast, we meet with the Victoria, the Daly, the Adelaide, the Alligator, the Liverpool, the Roper, the Limmen Bight, the Macarthur, the Robinson and the Calvert, the Albert--which is the outlet for the Nicholson and the Gregory--the Leichhardt and the Flinders, the Norman, the Gilbert, the Einesleigh, the Mitchell, the Archer, the Jardine, and the Batavia, which brings us back to our starting point at Cape York.

Now come the inland arteries, the streams running through the tableland and feeding the Darling and the Murray. These are the Murrumbidgee, which equals the Murray almost in importance, the Lachlan and the Darling, which brings down the waters of a hundred streams, the Macquarie, the Castlereagh, and the Bogan, the Namoi and Gwydir, the Dumaresque, the Condamine, the Maranoa, the Moonie, and the Warrego. And falling into the Murray itself, from the south are, the Ovens, the Goulburn, the Mitta Mitta, the Campaspe and the Loddon.

The other rivers of the inland slope are the Barcoo and Thomson, forming Cooper's Creek, the Diamentina, the Burke and the Hamilton, the Herbert or Georgina, and Eyre Creek, all these end in the flats and shallows of the Great Salt Lake District.

The remaining watercourses to the westward cannot be classed in any way, their course is apparently determined by local inequalities of the surface, and although some are very considerable in appearance, their flow is so brief that it is impossible to consider them as at all forming parts of one system; the longest and most important is Sturt's Creek.

The coast country, meaning the land watered by the rivers first enumerated, has the advantage over the tableland in the matter of rainfall, and the rivers therefore possess more of the characteristics of running streams, than the chains of isolated ponds that are known as rivers in the inland slope. The climatic influence is especially noticeable in the indigenous grasses and herbage of the two regions. Mr. George Ranken, in one of his essays on Australian subjects ["The Squatting System of Australia," by "Capricornus."] draws an excellent picture of the reclamation and transformation of the forest primeval.
"The first comers in 1788, found before them, as their ships came to anchor, sandstone bluffs covered with scraggy trees and heath-like plants, with a bright blue sky above, and an elastic, buoyant atmosphere around. As they went inland, they found an endless open forest, the ground being clothed with a light, tufty grass, but it was the starved outline of European woodland scenery, for the trees rose bare and branchless from a thirsty soil, and the grass covered only half, the surface of the earth. Except the grass, and that was thin enough, though it grew everywhere, the country seemed poor in products, and looked as if it were involved in a constant struggle between droughts and floods. They would have judged it to be poor in capability also, if, on further

experience, a vitality had not appeared which seemed to electrify the soil on the touch of colonisation. Imported animals, trees, and plants lived and flourished among the dingy forests, which barely yielded food enough for a few wandering savages.

"The farther they went, the greater contrast appeared, more drought and better country; and in later times, as the last of enigmas, a change of vegetation and climate seemed to follow the settler with his flocks and herds. After a few years' feeding with stock, water has been found permanently standing in country where it never stood before, and sometimes the tufty herbage has changed into a sward. The flats that used in one season to show a succession of swamps, and in another a surface of bare dusty soil, rifted with yawning cracks, has often become good level turf, intersected with runnels cut by the hoofs of the sheep and cattle."

The first invasion of the new territory across the range led to a terrible feeling of disappointment; true, that on at once crossing the crest of the watershed country was found, which being partly within the influence of the heavier fall of rain, approached in every way the perfection dreamt of by the explorers; but as progress inland was made, a change was found to take place, and, above all, the familiar indigenous grasses were lost, and replaced by what the settlers took to be nothing but worthless weeds. All the now prized edible shrubs, such as the many kinds of saltbush, the cotton-bush, &c., were amongst these despised plants; and even the very stock did not take to them, until some years of use had rendered them familiar. These drought-resisting plants were at first supposed to be confined to the inner slope of the range, but the extended exploration of the continent shows us that where the coast range loses its character of a pronounced range, and is only represented by an insignificant rise, the characteristics of the plain are continued right down to within a short distance of the sea.

This is notably the case on the north, where the Flinders River and its tributaries drain country that bears all the distinctive growth of the interior. On the south coast, west of the Murray, this is also the case, and in these parts, through the depression of the range, the climate is much drier. On the eastern coast, however, the distinction between the uplands and lowlands is strongly marked both in Queensland and New South Wales, even in those cases where the rivers rise in uplands approaching in elevation to the level of the tableland. The eastern coast of northern Queensland is, from its situation and the superior height of the coast range combined, the tropical garden of Australia, the luxuriant growth of vegetation, taking the form of dense scrubs and jungles springing from a deep, rich soil. These scrubs, of slightly varying character, form a characteristic of the whole length of the eastern seaboard, and amongst them we find much valuable timber. The cedar tree is one important feature, and the kauri pine is found in one small tract in the north of Queensland.

Further south, however, the trees grow to an enormous height in the elevated forest lands. Victoria and Western Australia are particularly noted for the giant growth of some of their trees. In Victoria the white gum (eucalyptus amygdalina) has been found growing to a height of over four hundred feet; the red gum (eucalyptus rostrata), and the blue gum (eucalyptus globulus) also attain a great size in our southern colonies. In Western Australia the jarrah (eucalyptus marginata) and the karri (eucalyptus diversicolor) have become noted in the world as being most valuable hardwoods.

Right through the continent, from east to west, the box tree (eucalyptus malliodora) is to be found. On the tableland the timber is altogether of a different growth. The giants of the slopes of the seaward range are replaced by low, stunted, and crooked trees, some of them, however, possessing edible foliage. Most of the acacias are of this kind--the acacia pendula or myall, the brigalow, the mulga, and yarran. The caesariansae common all over Australia, under the name of the oak tree.

The difference between the products of the interior upland and the coastal lowland is mainly induced by the difference of climate, those grasses and herbs growing on the tableland, while repellent in appearance and colour, compared to the richer herbage of the coast, possess qualities that render them invaluable as fodder plants. Once let the grasses of the coast lose their moisture from drought, and they become sapless and worthless, but it is not so in the tableland. Months of dry weather have no effect upon the fattening properties of the shrubs; the stock, however, have to become used to feeding on them before their full value is attained.

Amongst the fauna of Australia the distinction between coast and tableland is not so well marked, most of the well-known species ranging indifferently over the whole continent. In the kangaroos, differences in size, colour and appearance can easily be detected in widely separated localities, but they do not amount to anything very noticeable to the ordinary observer. The smaller kinds, the wallaby and kangaroo rat, are common everywhere on the continent. In birds, however, the difference is great, the seeds and fruit on which some birds exist being only found in either the coastal scrubs or lowland country, whilst many of the parrots and pigeons of the interior could not live on the coast. So sharply is the line drawn in some places, that on the dividing watersheds of the east coast flocks of galar parrots and plain-pigeons will be found feeding on the western slope of a ridge, but never by any chance crossing on to the eastern.

Australia is rich in waders, and they are found all over the continent. The beautiful jabiru, or gigantic crane, is equally at home in some lonely waterhole in the far west and at the head of a coast swamp; so, too, the grus Australis, or native companion, and the quaint and rich-plumaged ibis. The familiar laughing-jackass is to be found everywhere, but his peculiar note differs somewhat in different parts; a blackfellow from the south says that the laugh of the northern bird makes him feel sick, whilst the northern native says the same of the southern kingfisher. The great inland plains are the haunt of the flock-pigeon; in countless myriads, these beautiful birds come at some seasons of the year, and in the morning when flying in to the water they look like distant clouds.

The fish of the tableland differ greatly from those of the coast. In some of the inland lakes and permanent lagoons they are so fat as to be almost uneatable, and at times so plentiful and easily caught that the blackfellows scarcely trouble to get them, which is rarely the case elsewhere. The Australian native is a man with an unknown history whether he is an improvement on his remote ancestors or a degenerate descendant it is impossible to form any idea.

Whoever they were they left nothing behind them, except this wandering savage, and he has neither traditions nor customs that tell us anything of the past. The language is a perfect confusion of tongues, and dialects, words of similar sound and meaning are often found in places hundreds of miles apart; in distinct tribes wherein the rest of the language is altogether different. Their physique does not differ greatly. Perhaps in the north an admixture of Malay blood gives a handsomer cast to the features in individual cases, but the Australian native is unmistakable wherever you meet him, north, south, east or west.

The geological formation of Australia is, as is well-known very old, one third of the continent being desert sandstone with no marine fossils, but although, scantily supplied with water on the surface, there is little doubt of the immensity of the subterranean supply.

Water has been struck by boring five hundred and seventy-two feet, and risen to within ten feet of the surface, and on the Kallara run at one hundred and forty-four, where it rose twenty-six feet above the surface. Water then, will probably be found almost anywhere at a depth of six hundred feet, and a vast portion of the lightly watered plains of the interior will be worked up to their fullest capabilities by means of boring.

It is generally supposed that the first portion of Australia that rose above the sea was the south-east corner where the largest and probably the most active of our volcanoes existed; the rise of the whole continent which subsequently took place would have then left the interior a shallow inland sea, girt round with a broken chain of more or less active volcanoes. In time, these grew extinct, the sea evaporated and we were left with our present coast range, with its now lifeless peaks, and our depressed inland plateau, with its saline flats and lakes.

Chapter I

Expeditions of Governor Phillip--Mouth of the Hawkesbury found in Broken Bay--Second expedition and ascent of the river--Expedition of Captain Tench--Discovery of the Nepean River--Lieutenant Dawes sent to cross the Nepean, and to try to penetrate the mountains-- Attempt by Governor Phillip to establish the confluence of the Nepean and Hawkesbury-- Failure--The identity settled by Captain Tench-- Escaped convicts try to reach China--Captain Paterson finds and names the Grose River--Hacking endeavours to cross the Blue Mountains--The lost cattle found on the Cow Pastures--Bass attempts the passage of the range--Supposed settlement of a white race in the interior--Attempt of the convicts to reach it-- James Wilson--His life with the natives--Discovery of the Hunter River by Lieutenant Shortland.

As may be well supposed, the men who arrived in Australia in charge of the first party of convicts had more pressing work on hand than devoting their time to scientific exploration. Separated by half the world from the source of their supplies, in charge of a body of criminals of the most dangerous type, Arthur Phillip and his officers had no light task to perform, and every credit must be given to the little band of pilgrims who, beset by danger from within and without, brought the colony through its infancy without any tragedy happening. Apparently, these early adventurers were no whit behind travellers of the present day in bringing back wonderful tales of their discoveries whenever they essayed a trip into the unknown. One of the officers writes:--
"We found the convicts particularly happy in fertility of invention and exaggerated descriptions; hence, large fresh-water rivers, valuable ores, and quarries of limestone, chalk, and marble were daily proclaimed soon after we had landed. At first we hearkened with avidity to such accounts, but perpetual disappointments taught us to listen with caution, and to believe from demonstration only."

Amongst these gentry was a convict named Daly, afterwards banged for burglary, who distinguished himself by instigating the first gold prospecting party in Australia. Having broken up a pair of brass buckles, he mixed the fragments with sand and stones, and represented the result as specimens of ore he had found. A party was sent out under his guidance to examine the locality, but, needless to say, failed in the endeavour, the perpetrator of the hoax confessing to it in the end, and suffering the punishment common at that period.

The discovery of the Hawkesbury River, in the year following the settlement, may be looked upon as the first effort emanating from the colony to push exploration to any appreciable distance.

On the 6th of June, 1789, Governor Phillip, accompanied by a large party in two boats, proceeded to Broken Bay. After spending some time without result, they pulled into an inlet, and suddenly found themselves at the entrance of a fresh-water river, up which they rowed twenty miles in a westerly direction, but provisions failing, they turned back.

A second expedition was then undertaken, and this time the boats penetrated between sixty and seventy miles, inclusive of the windings of the river. Further progress was stayed by a fall. The party examined the surrounding country, but opinions differed greatly as to its value; some reporting rich and beautiful land, others low-lying flats subject to floods. A hill close by the fall was ascended, and christened Richmond Hill, and the river was named the Hawkesbury.

On the 26th of the same month, Captain Tench, then in charge of the newly-formed outpost of Rose Hill, started on an expedition to the westward. He was accompanied by Mr. Arndell, assistant-surgeon of the settlement, Mr. Lowes, surgeon's mate of the Sirius, two marines, and a convict. His relation of his trip is interesting, as being the earliest record of land exploration, and also as containing the account of the discovery of the Nepean River. An extract from his journal runs as follows:--

"I left the redoubt at daybreak, pointing our march to a hill distant five miles, in a westerly or inland direction, which commands a view of the great chain of mountains called the Caermarthen Hills, extending from north to south farther than the eye can reach. Here we paused, surveying 'the wild abyss, pondering over our voyage.' Before us lay the trackless, immeasurable desert in awful silence. At length, after consultation, we determined to steer west and by north by compass, the make of the land indicating the existence of a river. We continued to march all day through a country untrodden before by an European foot. Save that a melancholy crow now and then flew croaking over-head, or a kangaroo was seen to bound at a distance, the picture of solitude was complete and undisturbed. At four o'clock in the after-noon we halted near a small pond of water, where we took up our residence for the night, lighted a fire, and prepared to cook our supper-that was to broil over a couple of ramrods a few slices of salt pork, and a crow which we had shot. At daylight we renewed our peregrination, and in an hour after, we found ourselves on the banks of a river nearly as broad as the Thames at Putney, and apparently of great depth, the current running very slowly in a northerly direction. Vast flocks of wild ducks were swimming in the stream, but, after being once fired at, they grew so shy that we could not get near them a second time. Nothing is more certain than that the sound of a gun had never before been heard within many a mile of this spot."

A short description of the hunting practices of the natives here follows, and the explorer then continues:--

"Having remained out three days, we returned to our quarters at Rose Hill with the pleasing intelligence of our discovery. The country we had passed through we found tolerably plain, and little encumbered with underwood, except near the riverside. It is entirely covered with the same sort of trees as grow near Sydney; and in some places grass springs up luxuriantly; other places are quite bare of it. The soil is various; in many places a stiff, arid clay, covered with small pebbles; in other places, of a soft, loamy nature; but invariably in every part near the river it is a coarse, sterile sand. Our observations on it (par-ticularly mine, from carrying the compass with which we steered) were not so numerous as might have been wished. But, certainly, if the qualities of it be such as to deserve future cultivation, no impediment of surface but that of cutting down and burning the trees exists to pre-vent its being tilled.

"To this river the Governor gave the name of Nepean (after Captain Nepean, of the New South Wales corps). The distance of the part of the river which was first hit upon from the sea coast is about thirty-nine miles, in a direct line, almost due west."

In December, 1789, Governor Phillip dispatched a party, un-der Lieutenant Dawes, of the Marines, accompanied by Lieutenant Johnson and Mr. Lowes, to cross the Nepean and try to penetrate the range beyond. They discovered a ford in the river, and crossing, pro-ceeded in a westerly direction. So rugged and difficult, however, did they find the country that in three days they had only covered fifteen miles. At a bill that they called Mount Twiss they turned back, having penetrated fifty-four miles in a direct line from the sea coast.

In August, 1790, Messrs. Tench, Dawes, and Morgan explored south and west of Rose Hill. They struck the Nepean higher up, nearer its source than on the former occasion, and remained out seven days, penetrating to a considerable distance in a south-west direction. Near the end of the same month, the same party made an excursion to the north-west of Rose Hill, and traced the Nepean to where it was first discovered by Tench's party in 1789.

In April, 1791, Governor Phillip, attended by a large company, numbering in all twenty-one persons, including two natives, set out on an expedition from Rose Hill to determine the identity, or not, of the Nepean and the Hawkesbury. On the 12th of the month they struck the river, and followed it down for some distance, but did not accomplish the object they had in view.

In the following month, however, Messrs. Tench, Dawes, and two soldiers, again went out, and settled the vexed question.

About this time, although scarcely to be included in the tale of exploration, a number of convicts made a desperate attempt to proceed overland to China. They, however, only managed a very short stage of the journey--namely, to Broken Bay. Here they were attacked by the natives, and returned in a demoralised condition to Rose Hill and gave themselves up.

The impression these deluded men set out under was, that at a considerable distance to the northward there was a large river which separated this country from China, and when it was crossed they would find themselves amongst a copper-coloured people, who would receive and treat them kindly.

In 1793, Captain Paterson, who had already had some experience as an African traveller, started on an expedition to the Caermarthen Hills (by this time beginning to be known as the Blue Mountains), intending, if possible, to cross the range, or at any rate, penetrate some distance into it, He was accompanied by Captain Johnstone, and Messrs. Palmer and Lang. The party was well equipped, and provisioned for six weeks. Pulling up the Hawkesbury, they left the heavy boats at the fall that had formerly stayed the progress of Governor Phillip, and taking two light ones with them, they tried to ascend higher up the river. They managed to reach ten miles beyond the furthest point ever before visited, and then, their boats having suffered some damage, and there being a slight fresh in the river, they returned. The highest part of the river where they were they

31

named the "Grose," and Paterson, who was a botanist, discovered several new kinds of plants.

Another determined effort to cross the range that seemed to defy all the attempts of the colonists was made by quarter-master Hacking, in 1794. The party succeeded in pushing out twenty miles further than any European had been, but their report was unfavourable. They reached the foot of the range, and after climbing over some eighteen or twenty ridges, formed of little else but precipitous rocks, they saw before them nothing but the same savage and inaccessible country. Tier after tier of ranges rose in view, divided by abrupt and impassable chasms and gorges. The only natives they saw fled at their approach, and, saving for the presence of some large red kangaroos, little sign of animal life was met with. Away to both north and south, the same iron range could be traced, showing no prospect of gap or pass, and they returned dispirited. The colonists now began to look upon the Blue Mountains as their western limit, and the extension of settlement in that direction was regarded as chimerical.

The cattle that had escaped from the settlement had, with their usual instinct, wandered on until they had found suitable grazing land on the Nepean, and there had settled down. When discovered they had thriven well, and increased into a small herd. By the Governor's direction they were left unmolested, being but occasionally visited, and their run became known as the Cow Pastures.

Mr. Bass, the bold explorer of Bass Strait, in company with some other gentlemen, visited these pasture lands in 1797, and from Mount Taurus, on the Nepean River, took a straight course to the coast, where a whale boat was sent to meet them. Their .experience was of the usual kind. After leaving the fertile grazing lands appropriated by the cattle, they crossed a succession of barren ridges, gradually growing worse and worse until the sea was reached.

Bass had, before this, attempted to cross the range in 1796. His attempt was of the same character as all the others, failure and disappointment attending his steps, although the endeavour to obtain success was carried through, as might be expected, with his usual untiring energy and contempt for danger. It is sad to think that a career that opened so brilliantly should have been doomed to close miserably in the mines of South America.

Having become partially convinced that there was no high road to be found between Port Jackson and the Chinese Empire, some of the convicts (principally the Irish prisoners) became possessed with the notion that a colony of white people existed three or four hundred miles in the interior, south-west of the settlement. This tale, highly embellished, was sufficient to inflame the imaginations of men condemned to servitude, and panting for liberty. The existing rumour being found out by the authorities, it proved on investigation that so far had this preposterous legend gained ground that written instructions had been issued for guidance to this Arcadia, accompanied with a paper having the figure of a compass drawn on it. The Governor, wishing to save these foolish dupes from the punishment and probable loss of life that would necessarily ensue in carrying out such a wild project, wrote to a magistrate at Parramatta the following instructions. He was to go to Toongabbie, where most of these infatuated men were employed, and, knowing how impossible it would be to reason them out of their belief, he was to inform them that four picked men would be allowed to start out and satisfy themselves of the impossibility of any show of success attending their search, and that in order to ensure their safe return three experienced men would be sent as guides with them.

On receipt of this information so many assembled that stricter measures had to be taken, and sixteen of the number were arrested and sent to Sydney for punishment. Four men were then selected by the malcontents themselves, and were about to depart in search of the supposed colony when a treacherous plot was discovered. A scheme was on foot for a stronger party of convicts to abscond, and these meeting the explorers at a pre-arranged spot, should there murder the guides, and having possessed themselves of their weapons, the prisoners would be at liberty to prosecute their researches alone. Four soldiers were added to the party to resist any attempt of this sort, and on the 14th January, 1798, they left Parramatta in search of El Dorada.

Amongst the men chosen to act as guides was one James Wilson, who had for some time previously been living in the bush with the natives, and had even submitted to his body being marked and scarred after their fashion. On his return from this nomadic existence, he stated that he had traversed the country for nearly one hundred miles in every direction around the settlement, and discoursed at length upon having seen large tracts of open country, and many strange birds and animals, unknown to the settlers. His stories were for the most part discredited, but it was thought that his experiences would be most useful to the party, and he was therefore selected.

Ten days after the explorers left, the soldiers returned with three of the delegates. On reaching the foot of the mountains, where it was arranged that the soldiers were to leave the party and return home, these three men were so thoroughly tired of their quest, and convinced of their folly, that they had begged to be allowed to go back.

On the 9th February the remainder of the expedition reached Prospect Hill more dead than alive. Wilson alone had kept heart, and managed to sustain the flagging spirits of his companions sufficiently to enable them to stagger in to the settlement.

Their report of the surroundings of the colony contained little more than what was already known or guessed at. They described the country passed over as alternating between barren, rocky ridges and spacious meadows. Running creeks had been crossed, and they turned back on the bank of a river which they described as being as large as the Hawkesbury, with level country in view on the opposite side.

They had seen but few natives, and those they saw were clothed in skins from head to foot. Amongst other novelties they had noticed the blue-gum trees, the mountain wallaroo, which had drawn their attention from being larger and fatter than those formerly familiar to them, a kind of pheasant, as they described it, now known as the lyre-bird, a specimen of which the brought back with them, and a kind of mole, the modern wombat, one of which formed their last meal before reaching the settlement. These accounts corroborated the former reports made by Wilson. This expedition was, however, of not much service from a geographical point of view, from the unreliability of the course kept.

The party also reported coming across a hill of salt, and in the month of March, Henry Hacking was sent out to inspect it. He was accompanied by Wilson and another man, who were supplied with provisions and directed to penetrate as far into the country as their supplies would permit. Hacking found that several veins of salt existed, and the two men stated that they had succeeded in getting 140 miles S.W. by W. from Prospect Hill. During their journey they had travelled over many varieties of country, crossing a number of narrow creeks and rivers with which the land was intersected. They passed through much promising country and much that was unpromising. From the summits of some of the higher hills that they ascended, they had extensive views to the westward, and as usual, saw mountain rising upon mountain in that direction. They brought back another specimen of the lyre-bird.

In the year '97 preceding this trip, some convicts had boarded and seized a colonial-built boat, called the Cumberland, during her passage to the Hawkesbury. The crew were landed at Pitt Water, and making their way from there overland gave information of the piracy.

Two boats under Lieutenant Shortland started in pursuit. One returned in a few days, but Shortland with the other went as far north as Port Stephens without, however, seeing anything of the pirates. His voyage was not by any means destitute of result, as on his return he found a river; "into which he carried three fathoms of water in the shoalest part of its entrance, finding deep water and good anchorage within. The entrance of this river was but narrow, and covered by a high rocky island, lying right off, so as to leave a good passage round the north end of the island between that and the shore. A reef connects the south part of the island with the south shore of the entrance of the river. In this harbour was found a very considerable quantity of coal of a very good sort, and lying so near the water's side as to be conveniently shipped; which gave it, in this particular, manifest advantage over that discovered to the southward. Some specimens of this coal were brought up in the boat." In the foregoing description, the Hunter River and the present harbour of Newcastle will be easily recognised.

In July, of the year '99, Flinders was instructed by the Governor to examine the two large openings marked by Cook on the east coast, namely, Glass House Bay and Hervey Bay. Glass House Bay-- now Moreton Bay--was so called after some remarkable peaks that were visible on the north side. These peaks Captain Flinders made an excursion to examine, and from the summit of one obtained an extended view over the surrounding country, nothing novel, however, being seen. At Hervey's Bay, too, the only additional information gained, was of a nautical character, the natives seeming to be the most interesting objects met with.

Wilson, whose career amongst the natives, and as an explorer is most notable, now met his death in a sufficiently tragic, if appropriate, manner. This man had served the term of his transportation, and both as a convict and a free man had passed a great part of his time wandering through the bush with the aboriginals. He had been suspected, justly or unjustly, of prompting the blacks to attack the settlers; aiding them with his knowledge of the habits of the whites, and the best season for carrying out their designs. At any rate, his long intercourse with the natives had rendered him careless of consequences, and a flagrant violation of their customs led to his being speared.

During the governorship of Captain King, Ensign Barraillier came to the front as an explorer. He was notably an accurate and painstaking surveyor, and although his expeditions were circumscribed by the ever present barrier of the Blue Mountains, he was evidently an indefatigable worker in the cause of science. From a letter of Governor

King's, addressed to Sir Joseph Banks in May, 1803, we learn something of Barraillier, and also of the petty private squabbles that prevailed amongst the colonists, even in the highest quarters. Governor King writes:--

"As our maritime surveying is now turned over to Captain Flinders, who has the *Lady Nelson* with him, by the Admiralty's direction, I had begun making discoveries in the interior by means of Ensign Barraillier. He has been one journey, and went twenty miles from the first range of hills, till his further course was interrupted by a river running north, which is a curious circumstance, being in the mountains. He described it as wide as the Thames at Kingston. Some native iron he found, and also an imperfect limestone, and the dung of an unknown animal. Samples of everything he there found will be sent by the *Greenwich* (whaler), and I did hope to have been able to add something farther from another journey he was about undertaking, and for which purpose I had established a chain of depôts of provisions, to further his return.

"Cayley is just gone on an excursion, and you will see by his letters he is undertaking a still longer one. As he keeps all his knowledge to himself, I am hopeful you are benefited by it, and I hope much good will result from his journeys, which he is now determined on persevering in. I informed you of the refusal he gave me and Mr. Brown to his going in the Investigator."

George Cayley was a botanist sent out by Sir Joseph Banks to collect for Kew Gardens. He was industrious and painstaking in his vocation, but sadly overburdened with vanity. He made one important journey to the Blue Mountains, with the usual result. He erected a cairn of stones at the furthest point he reached, which Governor Macquarie afterwards christened "Cayley's Repulse."

To return to Barraillier. Governor King, in the same, letter, further writes:--

"I have informed you in my several letters of the great use Ensign Barraillier, of the New South Wales Corps, was to me and the public. First, in going to the southward, and surveying the coast from Wilson's Promontory to Western Port, next, in surveying. Hunter's River, where he went twice, and since then in making useful observations about the settlement, and in making a partial journey to the mountains, which was introductory to his undertaking the journey he afterwards performed, but which I was obliged to effect by a ruse, as Col. Paterson had very ill-naturedly informed me that officers being at all detached from their regimental duty was contrary to some instructions he had from the Duke of York. In consequence I was obliged to give up his services after this unhandsome claim, but claimed him as my *aide-de-camp*, and that the object of discovery should not be relinquished, I sent him on an embassy to the King of the Mountains."

This idea of an embassy to the King of the Mountains is about as unique an incident in the history of exploration as can be imagined. Whether Barraillier reached this fancied potentate or not we are left in ignorance. Governor King says:--

"He was gone six weeks, and penetrated one hundred and thirty-seven miles among the mountains beyond the Nepean. His journal being wrote in such an unintelligible hand, I have not been able to get it translated or copied, but have sent it open under your address to Lord Hobart. . . . I have not had time to decipher and read it, but am satisfied from what M. Barraillier has done and seen, that passing these barriers, if at all practicable, is of no great moment to attempt any further at present, as it is now well ascertained that the cattle have not, nor cannot, make any progress to the westward, unless they find a passage to the northward or southward of those extensive and stupendous barriers. I intend sending M. Barraillier to Port Jarvis very soon, to penetrate into the interior from thence, if Col. Paterson is not advised to prevent it."

From this it will plainly be seen how completely the colonists had given themselves up to the dominion of the overshadowing range that stayed their western progress. It required the stern hand of necessity to compel them to at last force that "stupendous barrier," as King terms it.

Meanwhile, the presence of the French ships under Baudin, had created uneasiness in Governor King's mind, rumour and gossip had magnified their intentions into a sinister claim being about to be established upon Van Dieman's Land or the south coast of New Holland. In 1802, King had sent home to Sir Joseph Banks his idea of the importance of King's Island, and the adjacent harbour of Port Phillip.

"Port Phillip is also a great acquisition, and as I have urged the fixing of a settlement in the latter place, I am anxious to begin it, but unfortunately I have no person I can send there equal to the charge. Policy certainly requires our having a settlement in these Straits."

No lack of zeal for the future supremacy of the British flag in these seas can be charged upon the founders of the colony, in fact, Governor King sent a small schooner under command of a midshipman after M. Baudin, with secret orders to watch their movements, and, if necessary, hoist the King's colours and land a corporal's guard at any place where the French appeared likely to make a demonstration.

Port Phillip was discovered by Lieutenant Murray, of the Lady Nelson, in 1802. Surveyor-General Grimes went there with him, and during the survey he made, is reported to have camped on the spot where Melbourne now stands. The port was discovered three times independently in the same year. First by Murray, next by Baudin, and again by Flinders. Colonel Collins, formerly of Norfolk Island, was dispatched in the year that Governor King wrote his letter (1803) to found a township. He at once declared the country unfit for settlement, with scarcely any examination; and it was immediately abandoned in favour of Van Dieman's Land.

The results of efforts at inland discovery were now but slight. Flinders on the south coast had sailed up Spencer's Gulf, and from Mount Brown at the head a fine view was obtained, but nothing more. "Neither rivers nor lakes could be perceived, nor anything of the sea to the south-eastward. In almost every direction the eye traversed over an uninterruptedly flat, woody country; the sole exceptions being the ridge of mountains extending north and south, and the water of the gulph to the south-westward."

Compared with the great size of the island continent, it will be seen that but an insignificant portion had, by the end of the eighteenth century come under the sway of colonisation. The rivers Hawkesbury, Nepean, and Grose, with other minor tributaries in the neighbourhood of Sydney. To the north, the river Hunter, and to the south, the district now known as the Illawarra. This was the sum total of the known country inside the coastal line; and with all the wish to extend their knowledge of their wide domain, the administrative demands of the little colony pressed too heavily on the authorities to permit them to devote much time to extended exploration.

Chapter II

The great drought of 1813--The development of country by stocking—Second expedition under Evans--Discovery of the Lachlan River--Surveyor-General Oxley explores the Lachlan--Finds the river terminates in swamps--Returns by the Macquarie--His opinion of the interior--Second expedition down the Macquarie--Disappointment again--Evans finds the Castlereagh--Liverpool Plains discovered--Oxley descends the range and finds Port Macquarie-- Returns to Newcastle-Currie and Ovens cross the Morumbidgee--Brisbane Downs and Monaroo--Hume and Hovell cross to Port Phillip--Success of the expedition.

The first ten years of the present century were singularly devoid of excursions inland. The strip of country between the range and the sea, sufficing for the immediate wants of the settlers, and the discovery of the Hunter River having opened so much new country for their use, no actual necessity compelled them at this period to go further a-field. This lack of urgent need, combined with the bad success that had attended all efforts to penetrate the mountains, had somewhat damped the ardour of the colonists.

But throughout these years the stock steadily increased, and the severe drought in 1813 led some of the settlers to make another attempt to find out new pasture lands.

The victory that at last crowned the struggle may be said to have at once inaugurated a new phase of exploration The days of expeditions on foot, when each man carried his own supply of provisions, and the limit of their journey only extended a little over a hundred miles, were past. Horses were now destined to play an important part in the outfit of the explorer, and take their share of sacrificing their lives in the cause.

The results gained by these first journeys were far from promising; always hoping to find a navigable river, or rivers, through the interior, the colonists found themselves most unexpectedly baffled. Having discovered the head waters of large streams flowing on a western course, with a sufficient depth of water for boat navigation, it appeared conclusive that to follow them down would in course of time lead the party doing so to the sea; the only probable obstacle which would come in the way would be falls. But the rivers led them into shallow stagnant swamps, with no limit within ken; the outskirts, so they deemed, of an inland sea.

Across here Oxley wrote, desert; unfitted ever to sustain settlement, and in doing this he did not err more glaringly than many later pioneers. It must be borne in mind that the characteristics of the inland plain were all new to the travellers who first ventured to enter its confines. They had not won the key of the desert; the fashion in which nature adapted herself to climatic decrees was a lesson still to be learnt. Oxley spoke honestly when, in bitter disappointment, he prophesied the future of the great plain to be that of an unprofitable waste, wherein the work of men's hands and the cunning of their brains would avail nothing; but he spoke hastily and almost thoughtlessly. The great plain had its glorious mission to fulfil, but the secret, like all things worth knowing, was one that took time and labour to solve; not in one or two generations was it to be done.

There was one great factor in the reclamation of the desert that Oxley could not take into his calculations--for he did not know its power--the sure, if gradual change wrought by stocking. Under the ceaseless tread of myriad hoofs, the loose, open soil was to become firm and hard, whilst fresh growths of herb and grass followed the footsteps of the invading herds. The shaking bogs and morasses were to become solidified, and the waters that permeated them to retreat into well defined chains of ponds and lagoons. This the first explorer could not foresee, he was disheartened by what he found, and unwitting of the change that was to follow he gave a hostile verdict. But although it did not fall to his lot to trace out the great system of the Murray watershed, he had, at any rate, the proud satisfaction of achieving the first stage.

Governor Macquarie, whose name has been sown broadcast over so much of New South Wales, was a man bent on the development of the colony as rapidly as possible, and although the defects in his administration have been severely criticised, exploration received at his hands every encouragement, and during his tenure of office, the first steps were taken to open up the vast field of inland discovery. We must now remember that the adaptability of the country to pastoral occupation was fully recognised. The days when famine was imminent if the fleet from England did not duly arrive had passed away. The future of the colony was assured, provided fresh outlets could be opened up.

In 1813, the prolonged drought to which the little settlement had been subjected, led to a most serious view being taken of the future. The stock had now attained dimensions, when the yearly increase was something considerable, compared to the narrow strip of grazing lands that supported the herds. It was an evident necessity to find fresh territory speedily, or great loss would inevitably ensue. Three of the settlers interested in stock-breeding, made another attempt to cross the range during this year. They were: William Charles Wentworth, whose name is so familiar to Australians, Lieutenant Lawson, of the Royal Veteran Company, and Mr. Gregory Blaxland. They crossed the Nepean at Emu Plains, and attempted to follow up a main spur forming the watershed of the Grose, and for a time successfully pursued its twists and windings, keeping to the crown of the ridge. At last, like all their predecessors, they began to get entangled in the intricate network of deep gullies that rendered straightforward travelling so difficult in this region. Like them, they commenced to think advance impossible, and to speak of turning back. Passages had to be cut through the thick brushwood for their pack horses, circuitous roads found around steeps too precipitous to scale, and the purpose of the journey seemed hopelessly lost. They had succeeded in crossing the first outwork of the mountains, but the Main Range had yet to be won. At length they fortunately hit upon a dividing spur, leading to the westward, and this they perseveringly followed, until they were rewarded by reaching the summit, and seeing below them a comparatively open valley, and beyond, chains of hills, broken it is true, but only trifling compared to what they had passed over. It was a work of time and much labour to gain access to this valley. The mountain they had ascended was steep and rugged, and great care had to be exercised in descending. But fatigue was not much thought of with their hopes so happily fulfilled.

At the bottom of the valley they found a running stream and good pasture, beyond this point they proceeded about six or eight miles in order to ascertain the extent of their discoveries, and then returned, having been absent one month.

The creek found by Blaxland and party was one of the tributaries of the Nepean, so that granted that a range had been crossed, access had been only obtained to the higher waters of a coast river. But although this important journey fell short of one of the great aims of western exploration, namely the discovery of a river flowing to the west, it was the immediate cause of the expedition being undertaken that led to the finding of the Macquarie.

George William Evans, Deputy-Surveyor of Lands, can certainly claim the honour of first discovering an Australian inland river; but Blaxland and his companions led the way across the hardest portion of the course.

As may well be believed, the tidings brought back by the exploring party created great excitement in the small community. No longer would the mountainous barrier frown defiance at them; for over thirty years it had successfully resisted all their attempts, but its time had come; the march to the west had at last commenced. On receipt of the news, Governor Macquarie sent out Mr. Evans with a party to at once follow up this discovery and find out what lay beyond. Evans crossed the Nepean on the 20th of November, and in six days arrived at the spot where the last party had turned back. Striking westward, he found a broken, hilly country, which was, however, well grassed and watered, presenting little hindrance to his progress, and on the 30th of the month, he struck the head of a stream holding a distinctly western course. Following this down, he found it joined by another from the south, and below the junction he gave the new found river the name of the Macquarie.

So promising was the country that he continued his course until the 18th December, when finding the river, now of a fair magnitude, still flowing steadily north-west, and not being prepared for a very prolonged absence, he turned back and retraced his steps, arriving at the Nepean on the 8th January, 1814. Strange to say, during the whole time of his absence in this hitherto untrodden waste, the only natives seen by the party were four women and two children.

This most successful termination of the work. commenced by Messrs. Blaxland, Lawson, and Wentworth. and the confirmation of the hopes that had been entertained, led to more active steps being at once initiated.

Mr. Cox was entrusted with the superintendence of the work of constructing a public road across the range, following much the same route as that taken by the first explorers; and this work was completed early in the year 1815, and on the 26th April of the same year the Governor and a large staff set out to visit the new territory, and arrived there on the 4th May.

Meantime, Mr. Evans was again sent out to the south-west, and once more he was successful, returning with tidings of the discovery of the Lachlan River. He was absent nearly a month, and met the Governor and suite on their arrival at Bathurst Plains.

The course of the Lachlan being nearly due west, it was selected as the most likely river of the two to lead immediately to the navigable waters of the interior, which everybody now firmly believed in; but a delay of nearly two years occurred before an expedition was formed to carry into effect the purpose of following it down with boats.

Meantime, the settlers took every advantage of this new outlet for their energies. Cattle and sheep were pushed out, and some of the land put under tillage. Buildings rapidly sprang up, and, favoured by a beautiful site, the township of Bathurst soon presented an orderly appearance. Private enterprise had also been at work elsewhere, and the early pioneer graziers were now making south from the settlement towards the Shoalhaven River and the intermediate country. It was down here that young Hamilton Hume, the first native-born explorer to take the field, was then gaining his bushcraft. Hume was a son of the Rev. Andrew Hume, who held an appointment in the Commissariat Department, and came to the colony in the Lady Julian.

The future explorer was born at Parramatta in 1797, so that he was but seventeen when, in 1814, he made his maiden effort in the country around Berrima, in company with his brother and a black boy; and-in the year following he again made an excursion in this district. In 1816 his father conducted Dr. Throsby to new country that the energy of his sons had discovered; and in March, 1817, at the time when Oxley was about starting on his Lachlan expedition, Hume, at the request of Governor Macquarie, went with Mr. Surveyor Meehan and Mr. Throsby on an expedition as far as the Shoalhaven River. Here, in consequence of some dispute with Mr. Meehan, Mr. Throsby left the party, and, accompanied by a black boy, made his way to Port Jarvis.

Meehan and Hume continued their journey, and discovered Lake George, Lake Bathurst, and the country called Goulburn Plains.

But the trip undertaken by Mr. Oxley at this time, leading as it did to such unexpected results, claims our first attention. As the party were to take boats with them, boat builders were sent up to Bathurst, thence to proceed to the river and build the necessary craft. A depôt having been formed on the Lachlan River, on the 6th of April, 1817, Mr. Oxley left Sydney to join his party there, and arrived at this depôt on the 25th of the same month, having been detained a short time at

Bathurst. On the 1st of May, Mr. Oxley reached the limit of Mr. Evans' journey in 1815, a small creek which they christened Byrne Creek; from here the work of exploration commenced.

The following is a list of the men comprising, this, the first most important expedition in the annals of exploration:--

"John Oxley, chief of the expedition; George William Evans, second in command; Allan Cunningham, King's botanist; Charles Fraser, colonial botanist; William Parr, mineralogist; George Hubbard, boat builder; James King, 1st boatman and sailor; James King, 2nd horse-shoer; William Meggs, butcher; Patrick Byrne, guide and horse leader; William Blake, harness mender; George Simpson, for chaining with surveyors; William Warner, servant to Mr. Oxley."

They had with them two boats and fourteen bât (pack) and riding horses.

Following the bank of the river the party met with no obstruction to their progress for twelve days, save the usual accidents and delays incidental to travelling in an unexplored region. Oxley's opinion of the value of the new district had, as is evident from his journal, been steadily decreasing since leaving the depôt. The flatness of the country, the numerous branches of the river and the want of height visible in its banks, seemingly depressed him very much. On the 6th of May he writes:--

"I have reason to believe that the whole of the extensive tract of country, named Princess Charlotte's Crescent" (about 130 miles west of Bathurst), "is at times drowned by the overflowing of the river; the marks of floods were observed in all directions, and the waters in the marshes and lagoons were all traced as being derived from the river. During a course of upwards of seventy miles, not a single running stream emptied itself into the river on either side; and, I am forced to conclude, that in common seasons this whole tract is extremely badly watered, and that it derives its principal, if not only supply, from the river within the bounding ranges of Princess Charlotte's Crescent. There are doubtless many small eminences which might afford a retreat from the inundations, but those which were observed by us were too trifling and distant from each other to stand out distinct from the vast level surface which the crescent presents to the view. The soil of the country we passed over was a poor and cold clay; but there are many rich levels which, could they be drained and defended from the inundations of the river, would amply repay the cultivation. These flats are certainly not adapted for cattle; the grass is too swampy, and the bushes, swamps, and lagoons are too thickly intermingled with the better portions, to render it a safe or desirable grazing country. The timber is universally bad and small; a few misshapen gum trees on the immediate banks of the river may be considered as exceptions."

On the 12th of May, their, as yet, uninterrupted course down the river received an abrupt check.

"We had scarcely proceeded a mile from the last branch before it became evident that it would be impossible to advance farther in the direction in which we were travelling. The stream here overflowed both banks, and its course was lost among marshes, its channel not being distinguishable from the surrounding waters.

"Observing an eminence about half a mile from the south side, we crossed over the horses and baggage" (by aid of the boats) "at a place where the water was level with the banks, and which, when within its usual channel, did not exceed thirty or forty feet in width; its depth even now being only twelve feet.

"We ascended the hill, and had the mortification to perceive the termination of our research, at least down this branch of the river. The whole country from the west, north-west, round to the north, was either a complete marsh or lay under water, and this for a distance of twenty-five or thirty miles in those directions. To the south and south-west the country appeared more elevated, but low, marshy grounds lay between us and it, which rendered it impossible for us to proceed thither from our present situation. I therefore determined to return back to the place where the two branches of the principal river separated, and follow the south-west branch as far as it should be navigable. Our fears were, however, stronger than our hopes, lest it would end in a similar manner to, the one we had already traced, until it became no longer navigable for boats.

"In pursuance of this intention we descended the hill, which was named Farewell Hill, from its being the termination of our journey in a north-west direction, at least for the present, and proceeded up the south bank of the stream."

The investigation of the south-west branch proving equally unsatisfactory, Oxley determined to leave the river and strike for the coast in the neighbourhood of Cape Northumberland, anticipating that on this course he would intersect any river rising in these marshes and falling into the sea between Spencer's Gulf and Cape Otway. The boats were hauled up on the south bank and secured, together with such articles as they could not take with them; and at nine o'clock on May 18th, the journey to the coast commenced.

From having too much water the party now found themselves straitened for want of it, and the journey, too, began to tell upon the horses. Thick scrubs of eucalyptus brush, overrun with creepers and prickly acacia bushes, soon helped to bar the way, and when they at last reached the point of a range, which they named Peel Range, Oxley reluctantly abandoned his idea of making for the coast in a south-west direction, and turned north. Wearily he writes:--

"June 4. Weather as usual fine and clear, which is the greatest comfort we enjoy in these deserts abandoned by every living creature capable of getting out of them. I was obliged to send the horses back to our former halting place for water, a distance of near eight miles this is terrible for the horses, who are in general extremely reduced but two in particular cannot, I think, endure this miserable existence much longer.

"At five o'clock, two men whom I had sent to explore the country to the south-west and see if any water could be found, returned after proceeding six or seven miles; they found it impossible to go any farther in that direction or even south, from the thick bushes that intersected their course on every side; and no water (nor, in fact, the least sign of any) was discovered either by them or by those who were sent in search of it nearer our little camp."

"June 5. From everything I can see of the country to the south-west, it appears, upon the most mature deliberation, highly imprudent to persevere longer in that direction, as the consequences to the horses of want of grass and water might be most serious; and we are well assured that within forty miles on that point the country is the same as before passed over. In adopting a north-westerly course, it is my intention to be entirely guided by the possibility of procuring subsistence for the horses, that being the main point on which all our ulterior proceedings must hinge. It is, however, to be expected that as the country is certainly lower to the west and north-west than from south-east to south-west, there is a greater probability of finding water in this latter direction. In our present perplexing situation, however, it is impossible to lay down any fixed plan, as (be it what it may) circumstances after all must guide us. Our horses are unable to go more than eight or ten miles a day, but even then they must be assured of finding food, of which, in these deserts, the chances are against the existence.

"Yesterday being the King's birthday, Mr. Cunningham planted under Mount Brogden acorns, peach and apricot stones, and quince seeds, with the hope, rather than the expectation, that they would grow and serve to commemorate the day and situation, should these desolate plains be ever again visited by civilised man, of which, however, I think there is very little probability.

"June 6. A mild pleasant morning: set forward on our journey to the westward and north-west, in hopes of finding a better country."

"June 8th. The whole country in these directions, as far as the eye could reach, was one continued thicket of eucalyptus scrub. It was physically impossible to proceed that way, and our situation was too critical to admit of delay; it was therefore resolved to return back to our last station on the 6th, under Peel's Range, if for no other purpose than that of giving the horses water. I felt that by attempting to proceed westerly I should endanger the safety of every man composing the expedition, without any practical good arising from such perseverance, It was therefore deemed more prudent to keep along the base of Peel's Range to its termination, having some chance of finding water in its rocky ravines, whilst there was none at all in attempting to keep the level country."

We have now seen how Oxley, prevented from following the river down by an overflow amongst the marshes, turned south-west, only to be driven back by impenetrable scrubs and general aridity. He struck north, with the hope of shortly regaining the too well watered country he had left. The fixed idea of the utterly useless nature of the country is ever present in his mind as he proceeds. On the 21st June he writes:--

"The farther we proceed north-westerly the more convinced I am hat for all the practical purposes of civilised man the interior of this country, westward of a certain meridian, is uninhabitable, deprived as it 5 of wood, water and grass."

A sweeping and hasty condemnation this, considering that he threshold of the interior had been scarcely more than crossed.

On the 23rd of June the travellers suddenly and unexpectedly came upon the river again, an incident, as the leader says, little expected by any one.

The next day they started once more to follow down the stream, with brighter hopes of better success, until, on the 7th of July, progress was once more arrested, and Oxley turned back recording in his journal:--

"It is with infinite regret and pain that I was forced to come to the conclusion that the interior of this vast country is a marsh, and uninhabitable."

The party now retraced their steps to the eastward, disgusted with the want of success that had attended their efforts, and the dreary monotony of their surroundings.

"There is a uniformity in the barren desolateness of this country which wearies one more than I am able to express. One tree, one soil, one water, and one description of bird, fish, or animal prevails alike for ten miles and for one hundred. A variety of wretchedness is at all times preferable to one unvarying cause of pain or distress."

On the 4th of August, being then satisfied of their position on the river, and knowing that a further course along its bank would only lead them amongst the swamps that had stayed their downward journey, it was determined to strike to the northeastward, in order to avoid this low country and, if possible, reach the Macquarie River and follow it up to the settlement of Bathurst. After experiencing some difficulty in manufacturing a raft out of pine logs, whereby to cross their baggage over, Oxley and his party left the Lachlan.

They endured for some time a repetition of their struggles in the south for grass and water, and then the explorers reached fertile and well-watered country; and, on the 19th of August, halted on the bank of the Macquarie, which river Oxley found to equal his fondest hopes. They now turned their steps homeward, and arrived at Bathurst on the evening of the 29th of August.

Convinced that, in the Macquarie, he had now discovered the highway into the interior, Oxley writes:--

"Nothing can afford a stronger contrast than the two rivers, Lachlan and Macquarie; different in their habit, their appearance, and the sources from which they derive their waters, but, above all, differing in the country bordering on them; the one constantly receiving great accession of water from four streams, and as liberally rendering fertile a great extent of country, whilst the other, from its source to its termination, is constantly diffusing and diminishing the waters it originally receives over low and barren deserts, creating only wet flats and uninhabitable morasses, and during its protracted and sinuous course, is never indebted to a single tributary stream."

Oxley having successfully carried through the Lachlan expedition, was at once selected to command a similar one down the Macquarie, on which, now that the former river had so disappointed expectations, men's hopes were fixed. Oxley seems to have been particularly unhappy in his deductions, every guess hazarded by him as to the future utility of the country he passed over, or the probable nature of the farther interior, was incorrect; and now the Macquarie was to refuse to bear his boat's keel to the westward; after the same manner as the Lachlan.

In those days men had not yet mastered the idea that the physical formation of Australia was not to be worked out on the same lines as that of other countries; they looked vainly for a river with a wide and noble opening, and none being found on the surveyed coast, conjecture placed it far away in a few leagues of unexplored shore line on the north-west. The constancy with which the southern coast had been examined, precluded all idea from men's minds that the entrance to this long sought river was there. No, it must be yet undiscovered to the westward. Wentworth says:--

"If the sanguine hopes to which the discovery of this river (the Macquarie) has given birth, should be realised, and it should be found to empty itself into the ocean on the north-west coast, which is the only part of this vast island that has not been accurately surveyed, in what mighty conceptions of the future greatness and power of this colony, may we not reasonably indulge? The nearest distance from the point at which Mr. Oxley left off, to any part of the western coast, is very little short of two thousand miles. If this river, therefore, be already of the size of the Hawkesbury at Windsor, which is not less than two hundred and fifty yards in breadth, and of sufficient depth to float a seventy-four gun ship, it is not difficult to imagine what must be its magnitude at its confluence with the ocean: before it can arrive at which it has to traverse a country nearly two thousand miles in extent. If it possess the usual sinuosities of rivers, its course to the sea cannot be less than from five to six thousand miles, and the endless accession of tributary streams which it must receive in its passage through so great an extent of country will without doubt enable it to vie in point of magnitude with any river in the world."

It may, therefore, well be imagined that it was in a most sanguine spirit that Oxley undertook his second journey.

As before, a party had been sent ahead to build boats, and get everything in readiness, and, on the 6th June, 1818, he started on his second expedition into the interior. He had with him, as next in command, the indefatigable Evans, Dr. Harris, who volunteered, Charles Frazer, botanist, and twelve men, eighteen horses, two boats, and provisions for twenty-four weeks.

On the 23rd of the month, having reached a distance of nearly 125 miles from the depôt in Wellington Valley, without the travellers experiencing more obstruction than might have been expected, two men, Thomas Thatcher and John Hall, were sent back to Bathurst with a report to Governor Macquarie, as had been previously arranged.

No sooner had the two parties separated, one with high hopes of their future success, the others bearing back tidings of these confident hopes, than doubt and distrust entered the mind of the leader. In his journal, written not twenty-four hours after the departure of his messengers, he says:--

"For four or five miles there was no material change in the general appearance of the country from what it had been on the preceding days, but for the fast six miles the land was very considerably lower, interspersed with plains clear of timber, and dry. On the banks it was still lower, and in many parts it was evident that the river floods swept over them, though this did not appear to be universally the case. . . .

"These unfavourable appearances threw a damp upon our hopes, and we feared that our anticipations had been too sanguine."

In his after report to the Governor, forwarded by Mr. Evans to Newcastle, he writes:--

"My letter, dated the 22nd June last, will have made your Excellency acquainted with the sanguine hopes I entertained from the appearance of the river, that its termination would be either in interior waters or coastwise. When I wrote that letter to your Excellency, I certainly did not anticipate the possibility that a very few days farther travelling would lead us to its termination as an accessible river."

So short-lived were the hopes he had entertained.

On the 30th June, after, for many days, finding the country becoming flatter and more liable to floods, Oxley found himself almost hemmed in by water, and had to return with the whole party to a safer encampment, where a consultation was held. It was decided to send the horses and baggage back to Mount Harris, a small elevation some fifteen miles higher up the river, whilst Oxley himself, with four volunteers and the large boat, proceeded down the river, taking with them a month's provisions. During his absence, Mr. Evans was to proceed to the north-east some sixty miles, and return upon a more northerly course, this being the direction the party intended taking if the river failed them.

Let us see how Oxley fared.

"July 2. I proceeded down the river, during one of the wettest and most stormy days we had yet experienced. About twenty miles from where I set out, there was, properly speaking, no country; the river overflowing its banks, and dividing into streams, which I found had no permanent separation from the main branch, but united themselves to it on a multitude of points. We went seven or eight miles farther, when we stopped for the night, upon a space of ground scarcely large enough to enable us to kindle a fire. The principal stream ran with great rapidity and its banks and neighbourhood as far as we could see, were covered with wood, inclosing us within a margin or bank, vast spaces of country clear of timber were under water, and covered with the common reed, which grew to the height of six or seven feet above the surface. The course and distance by the river was estimated to be from twenty-seven to thirty miles, on a north-west line.

"July 3rd. Towards the morning the storm abated, and at daylight we proceeded on our voyage. The main bed of the river was much contracted, but very deep, the waters spreading to a depth of a foot or eighteen inches over the banks, but all running on the same point of bearing. We met with considerable interruption from fallen timber, which in places nearly choked up the channel. After going about twenty miles we lost the land and trees: the channel of the river, which lay through reeds, and was from one to three feet deep, ran northerly. This continued for three or four miles further, when although there had been no previous change in the breadth, depth, and rapidity of the stream for several miles, and I was sanguine in my expectations of soon entering the long sought for Australian sea, it all at once eluded our further search by spreading on every point from northwest to northeast, amongst the ocean of reeds that surrounded us still running with the same rapidity as before. There was no channel whatever amongst these reeds, and the depth varied from five to three feet. This astonishing change (for I cannot call it a termination of the river), of course, left me no alternative but to endeavour to return to some spot on which we could effect a landing before dark. I estimated that on this day we had gone about twenty-four miles, on nearly the same point of bearing as yesterday. To assert positively that we were on the margin of the lake or sea into which this great body of water is discharged might reasonably be deemed a conclusion which has nothing but conjecture for its basis; but if an opinion may be permitted to be hazarded from actual appearances, mine is decidedly in favour of our being in the vicinity of an inland sea or lake, most probably a shoal one, and gradually filling up by immense depositions from the higher lands, left by the waters which flow into it. It is most singular that the high lands on this continent seem to be confined to the sea coast or not to extend to any distance from it."

Satisfied that to the westward nothing more could be done in the way of exploration, Oxley returned to Mount Harris, where a temporary depôt was formed. Mr. Evans immediately started on a trip to the north-east; he was absent ten days, during which time he discovered the Castlereagh River.

The weather had set in wet and stormy, the rivers kept rising and falling, and the level country was soft and boggy, excessively tiring to their jaded horses; moreover, in consequence of the boats being now left behind, the packs were greatly increased in weight.

On the 20th July, the whole of the party bade adieu to the Macquarie, which they had once trusted to so fondly, and commenced their journey to the eastern coast, making in the first place for Arbuthnot's Range. Before leaving, a bottle was buried on Mount Harris, containing a written scheme of their proposed route and intentions, with some silver coin.

On July 27th, they reached the bank of the Castlereagh, after a hard struggle through the bogs and swamps. The river was flooded, and must have risen almost directly after Mr. Evans crossed it on his homeward route. It was not until the 2nd of August that the waters fell sufficiently to allow them to cross. Still steering for the range, their course lay across shaking quagmires, or wading through miles of water; constantly having to unload and reload the unfortunate horses, who could scarcely get through the bog without their packs. Before reaching the range, the party camped at the small hill, previously ascended by Mr. Evans. Here they found the compass strangely affected: on placing it on a rock the card flew round with extreme velocity, and then suddenly settled at opposite points, the north point becoming the south. A short distance from the base of the hill the needle regained its proper position. This hill received the name of Loadstone Hill.

Crossing Arbuthnot Range round the northern base of Mount Exmouth, the explorers, although still terribly harassed by the boggy state of the country, found themselves in splendid pastoral land. Hills, dales, and plains of the richest description lay before them, and from the elevations the view presented was of the most varied kind; this tract of country was called by Oxley Liverpool Plains. On Mount Tetley, and many of the hills about, the same variations of the compass were observed as had formerly been noticed on Loadstone Hill. Through this beautiful district the party now had a less arduous journey than before, and their horses were able to regain some of their lost strength.

On the 2nd of September, they crossed a river which they named the Peel River, and here one of their number narrowly escaped drowning. Still pushing eastward, and continuing to travel through beautiful grazing country Oxley was suddenly stopped by a deep glen running across his track:--

"This tremendous ravine runs near north and south, its breadth at the bottom does not apparently exceed one hundred or two hundred feet, whilst the separation of the outer edges is from two to three miles. I am certain that in perpendicular depth it exceeds three thousand feet. The slopes from the edges were so steep and covered with loose stones that any attempt to descend even on foot was impracticable. From either side of this abyss, smaller ravines of similar character diverged, the distance between which seldom exceeded half-a-mile. Down them trickled small rills of water, derived from the range on which we were. We could not, however, discern which way the water in the main valley ran, as the bottom was concealed by a thicket of vines and creeping plants."

This barrier turned them to the south, and afterwards to the west again; on the way, they met with a grand fall one hundred and fifty feet in height, which they named Becket's Cataract. At the head of the glen they found another fall which they estimated at two hundred and thirty feet in height; crossing above this cataract, which was called Bathurst's Fall, the eastern course was once more resumed, and tempests and storms found them wandering amongst the deep ravines and gloomy forests of the coast range, seeking for a descent to the lower lands.

On the 23rd of September, Oxley, accompanied by Evans, ascended a mountain to try and discover a practicable route, and from there caught sight of the sea.

"Bilboa's ecstasy at the first sight of the South Sea could not have been greater than ours when, on gaining the summit of this mountain, we beheld Old Ocean at our feet: it inspired us with new life: every difficulty vanished, and in imagination we were already home."

Now commenced the final descent, and a perilous one it was:--

"How the horses descended I scarcely know; and the bare recollection of the imminent dangers which they escaped makes me tremble. At one period of the descent I would willingly have compromised for a loss of one third of them to ensure the safety of the remainder. It is to the exertions and steadiness of the men, under Providence, that their safety must be ascribed. The thick tufts of grass and the loose soil also gave them a surer footing, of which the men skilfully availed themselves."

They were now on a river running direct to the sea, which was named the Hastings River, and which the party followed down with more or less trouble until they reached a port at the mouth of it, which the explorer, after the fashion of the day, immediately dubbed Port Macquarie. It is an unfortunate thing for New South Wales that such an absence of originality with regard to naming newly discovered places was displayed by the travellers of that time.

On the 12th of October, the wanderers made a final start for home, commencing a toilsome march along the coast south. Stopped and interrupted for a time by many inlets and creeks, they at last came upon a boat buried in the sand, which had belonged to a Hawkesbury vessel, lost some time before; this boat they carried with them as far as Port Stephens, where they arrived on the 1st of November, using it to facilitate the passage of the salt water arms. During the latter part of this wearisome journey, they were much harassed by unprovoked attacks by the natives, and one of the men, William Black, was dangerously wounded, being speared through the back and in the lower part of the body.

Oxley had thus, after innumerable hardships and dangers, brought his party, with the exception of the wounded man, back in safety to the settlements. True he had not fulfilled the mission he was dispatched on, but he had discovered large tracts of valuable land fit for settlement; he had crossed the formidable coast range far away to the north, and established the fact that communication between his newly discovered port and the interior was practicable. Oxley's expeditions were both well equipped and well carried out, he also had the assistance of able and zealous coadjutors, each or any of them being capable of assuming the leadership in case of misfortune. His travels may be said to inaugurate the series of brilliant exploits in the field of exploration that we are about to enter on.

In 1819, Messrs. Oxley and Meehan, accompanied by young Hume, made a short excursion to Jarvis Bay, Oxley returning by sea, his companions overland.

The era of the pioneer squatter had now commenced henceforth exploration and pastoral enterprise went hand in hand. North and south of the new town of Bathurst, the advance of the flocks and herds went on; Oxley's report may have somewhat checked a westerly migration, but the stay in that direction was not doomed to last long. Northward, to and beyond the Cugeegong River and the fertile valley of the Upper Hunter, southward, towards the mysterious Morumbidgee, which was now reported as having been found by the settlers, pressed the pioneers. It is not known who was the first discoverer of this river. Hume, in company with Throsby, must have been close to it during their various excursions, and in 1821 Hume discovered Yass Plains, almost on its bank. It was, however, destined to be the future highway to the undiscovered land of the west.

In 1822 Messrs. Lawson and Scott attempted to reach Liverpool Plains, Oxley's great discovery, from Bathurst; they were, however, unable to penetrate the range that formed the southern boundary of the Plains, and returned, having discovered a new river at the foot of the range, which they named the Goulburn.

In 1823, Oxley, Cunningham, and Currie were all in the field in different directions.

On the 22nd of May, Captain Mark John Currie, R.N., accompanied by Brigade-Major Ovens, and having with them Joseph Wild, a notable bushman, started on an exploratory trip south of Lake George. On the 1st of June, they came to the Morumbidgee, as it was then called, and followed up the bank of it, looking for a crossing. The day before they had caught sight of a high range of mountains to the southward, partially snow-topped. In their progress along the river they came to fine open downs and plains, which, with the singularly bad taste, which still, unfortunately, holds sway, Currie immediately named after the then Governor, "Brisbane Downs;" although but a short time before they had learnt from the aborigines the native name of Monaroo. Fortunately, in this instance, Monaroo has been preserved, and Brisbane Downs forgotten.

On the 6th June they crossed the river, and found the open country still stretching south, bounded to the west by the snowy mountains they had formerly seen, and to the east by a range that they took to be the coast range. Their provisions being limited, they turned back, and reached Throsby's farm of Bong-Bong on the 14th of the same month.

Cunningham, meantime, during the months of April, May, and June, was busily engaged in the country north of Bathurst. He had two purposes in view--his pursuit as a botanist, and the discovery of a pass through the northern range on to Liverpool Plains, which Lieutenant Lawson had been unable to find. On reaching the range he searched vainly to the eastward for any valley that would enable him to pierce the barrier, and had to retrace his steps and seek more to the west. Here he came upon a pass, which he called Pandora's Pass, [See Appendix.] and which he found to be practicable as a stock route to the plains. He returned to Bathurst on the 27th of June.

In October, Oxley started from Sydney on a very different kind of expedition to those lately undertaken by him. His mission now was to examine the inlets of Port Curtis, Moreton Bay, and Port Bowen, with a view to forming penal establishments there. On the 21st of October, therefore, 1823, he left in the colonial cutter Mermaid, accompanied by Messrs. Stirling and Uniacke. At Port Macquarie, Oxley had the pleasure of seeing the settlement that had so rapidly sprung up on his recommendation of the suitability of the port. Further on, they discovered and named the Tweed River. On the 6th November, the Mermaid anchored in Port Curtis. Here the party remained for some time, and found and christened the Boyne River. Oxley's report was unfavourable.

"Having," he says, "viewed and examined with the most anxious attention every point that afforded the least promise of being eligible for the site of a settlement, I respectfully submit it as my opinion, that Port Curtis and its vicinity do not afford such a site; and I do not think that any convict establishment could be formed there that would return either from the natural productions of the country, or as arising from agricultural labour, any portion of the great expense which would necessarily attend its first formation."

As it was too late in the season to examine Port Bowen, the Mermaid went south, entered Moreton Bay, and anchored off the river that Flinders had christened Pumice Stone River, heading from the Glass House Peaks. Here a singular adventure occurred:--

"Scarcely was the anchor let go," writes Mr. Uniacke, "when we perceived a number of natives, at the distance of about a mile, advancing rapidly towards the vessel; and on looking at them with the glass from the masthead, I observed one who appeared much larger than the rest, and of a lighter colour, being a light copper, while all the others were black."

This light-coloured native turned out to be a white man, one Thomas Pamphlet. In company with three others he had left Sydney in an open boat, to bring cedar from the Five Islands, but, being driven out to sea by a gale, they had suffered terrible hardships, being (so he stated) at one time twenty-one days without water, during which time one man had died of thirst. Finally they were wrecked on Moreton Island, and had lived with the blacks ever since--a period of seven months. Pamphlet informed them that his two companions were named Finnegan and Parsons, and that they had started to make for Sydney, overland, but, after going some fifty miles, he (Pamphlet) returned, and shortly afterwards was joined by Finnigan, who had quarrelled with Parsons. The latter was never heard of.

Next day Finnegan turned up, and both he and Pamphlet, agreeing that at the south end of the bay there was a large river. Messrs. Oxley and Stirling started the following morning in the whale boat to look for it; taking Finnegan with them. They found the river, and pulled up it about fifty miles, being greatly satisfied with the discovery. Not being provided for a longer trip, Oxley turned back at a point he named Termination Hill, which he ascended and from which he obtained a fine view of the further course of the river. Still haunted by his inland lake theory, and as usual drawing erroneous deductions, he writes:--

"The nature of the country, and a consideration of all the circumstances connected with the appearance of the river, justify me in entertaining a strong belief that the sources of the river will not be found in mountainous country, but rather that it flows from some lake, which will prove to be the receptacle of those interior streams crossed by me during an expedition of discovery in 1818."

This river Oxley named the Brisbane, and taking with them the two rescued men, the Mermaid set sail for Sydney, where the party arrived on December 13th. With regard to the shipwrecked men, it may be here mentioned that their conviction at the time they were found was, that they were to the south of Sydney, somewhere in the neighbourhood of Jarvis Bay.

Oxley's work and his life too were now almost at a close. He died at Kirkham, his private residence, near Sydney, on the 25th of May, 1828. He had been essentially a successful explorer, for although he had not in every case attained the issue aimed at, he had always brought his men back in safety, and had opened up vast tracts of new country. [See Appendix.]

The journey made by Messrs. Hume and Hovell across to Port Phillip has a character of its own, being the first successful trip undertaken from shore to shore, from the eastern to the southern coast. The expedition originated from a somewhat wild idea that entered the head of that unpopular governor Sir Thomas Brisbane.

Surveyor-General Oxley, not having determined the question as to whether any large rivers entered the sea between Cape Otway and Spencer's Gulf, excepting to his own satisfaction, Sir Thomas Brisbane bit upon the scheme of landing a party of prisoners near Wilson's Promontory, and inducing them, by the offer of a free pardon and a land grant, to find their way to Sydney overland; and that they should have a better chance of eventually turning up, it was recommended that an experienced bushman should be put in charge of them.

The flattering, if somewhat dangerous, offer of this position was made to Mr. Hume, who, on consideration, declined it; he, however, offered to conduct a party from Lake George, then the outermost station, or nearly so, to Western Port, if the Government provided necessary assistance. The Government accepted h is offer, but forgot to provide the assistance. This caused much delay and vexation, and Mr. Hovell, offering to join the party and find half the necessary men and cattle, the Government agreed to do something in the matter. This something amounted to six pack-saddles and gear, one tent of Parramatta cloth, two tarpaulins, a suit of slop clothes each for the men, two skeleton charts for tracing their journey, a few bush utensils, and the following promise: a cash payment for the hire of the cattle should any important discovery be made. This money was refused on the return of the party, and Mr. Hume states that he had even much difficulty in obtaining tickets-of-leave for the men, and an order to select 1,200 acres of land for himself. Mr. Hovell was a retired shipmaster, who had been for some time settled in Australia. Each of the leaders brought with them three men, so that the strength of the expedition was eight men in all. They had with them two carts, five bullocks, and three horses.

On October 14th, 1824, the party left Lake George. On reaching the Murrumbidgee they found it flooded, and after waiting three days, and the river continuing the same, an attempt was made to cross, and by means of the body of a cart rigged up as a punt with a tarpaulin, they succeeded.

On the south side of the river they found the country broken, and somewhat difficult to make good progress through, but it was all well grassed and adapted to grazing purposes. Here, as might have been anticipated, they soon had to leave their carts behind, and pack their cattle for the remainder of their journey. Following the Murrumbidgee, after a short distance they left it for a south-west course, which still led them through hills and valleys rich with good grass and running water.

On November 8th, they were destined to enjoy a sight never before witnessed by white men in Australia. Ascending a range, in order to get a view of the country ahead of them, they suddenly came in front of snowcapped mountains. There, under the brilliant sun of an Australian summer's day, rose lofty peaks that might have found a fitting home in some far polar clime, covered as they were for nearly one-fourth of their height with glistening snow.

Skirting this range, which was called the Australian Alps, the travellers, after eight days wandering through the spurs of the lofty mountains they had just seen, came on a fine flowing river, which Mr. Hume named after his father the "Hume," destined to be afterwards called the Murray when visited lower down.

Failing to find a ford, a makeshift boat was constructed by the aid of the useful tarpaulin, and the passage of the Hume safely accomplished. Still passing through good available country watered by fine flowing streams, on the 24th they crossed the Ovens River, and on the 3rd of December they came to another river, which they called the Hovell (now the Goulburn), and on the 16th of the same month reached the sea shore, near where Geelong now stands. Two days afterwards they commenced their return, and on the 18th January arrived at Lake George.

This exploration had a great and lasting bearing on the extension of Australian settlement. A few years after one of the highest authorities then in the colony had deemed the western interior, beyond a certain limit, unfitted for human habitation; and expressed his opinion that the monotonous flats over which he vainly looked for any rise, extended almost to the sea coast--snow-clad mountains, feeding innumerable streams, were discovered to the south of his track.

The successful and arduous expedition led by the young native-born explorer, had the twofold effect of exposing Oxley's fallacies, and teaching a lesson of caution to future explorers not to indulge hastily in general condemnation. This lesson, however, has not been heeded; the history of Australian exploration being a history of conclusions drawn one year, to be falsified the next. Hume's journey to Port Phillip at once added to the British-Colonial Empire millions of acres of arable land watered by never-failing rivers, with a climate calculated to foster the growth of almost any species of fruit or grain.

It is a pity that in concluding the review of an expedition, fraught with so much benefit to the colony, and carried out with so much courage, hardihood, and facility of resource. that it cannot also be said, and marked with the same cheerful spirit that pervaded those of Oxley's, but unfortunately, the evil feeling of jealously that would arise from the presence of two leaders, showed plainly throughout in petty and undignified squabbles, which, in after days, led to paper warfare between the two explorers. It is painful, if amusing, to read of the disagreement as to their course in very sight of the lately discovered Australian Alps, and how, on agreeing to separate and divide the outfit, it was proposed to cut the tent in half, and the only frying-pan was broken by both parties pulling at it.

Thomas Boyd, the only survivor of the party in 1883, who was then eighty-six years old, was the first white man to cross the Murray, which he did, swimming it with a line in his mouth. In the year named he signed a document, giving the credit of taking the party through in safety to Hume. Boyd himself was one of the most active members of the expedition, and always to the front when there was any work to be done.

The training that Hume received in this, and his former journey, admirably qualified him to become the companion of Sturt in his first expedition when he discovered the other great artery of the Murray system, the Darling. The young explorer was thus singularly fortunate in having his name connected with the discovery of two of the most important rivers in Australia. In the trip just narrated he and his companion, Hovell, had arrested the hasty conclusion that was being formed as to the aridity of the interior. The result of their expedition held out high hopes for any future explorer, and the report they brought in was afterwards fully confirmed by Major Mitchell.

Chapter III

Settlement of Moreton Bay--Cunningham in the field again--His discoveries of the Gwydir, Dumaresque, and Condamine Rivers--The Darling Downs, and Cunningham's Gap through the range to Moreton Bay--Description of the Gap--Cunningham's death--Captain Sturt--His first expedition to follow down the Macquarie--Failure of the river--Efforts of Sturt and Hume to trace the channel--Discovery of New Year's Creek (the Bogan)--Come suddenly on the Darling--Dismay at finding the water salt--Retreat to Mount Harris--Meet the relief party--Renewed attempt down the Castlereagh River--Trace it to the Darling--Find the water in that river still salt--Return--Second expedition to follow the Morumbidgee--Favourable anticipations--Launch of the boats and separation of the party--Unexpected junction with the Murray--Threatened hostilities with the natives--Averted in a most singular manner--Junction of large river from the North--Sturt's conviction that it is the Darling--Continuation of the voyage--Final arrival at Lake Alexandrina--Return voyage--Starvation and fatigue--Constant labour at the oars and stubborn courage of the men--Utter exhaustion--Two men push forward to the relief party and return with succour.

In 1824, in consequence of the favourable report of Surveyor Oxley, a penal settlement was formed at Moreton Bay, but it was speedily removed to a better site on the Brisbane River, where the capital of Queensland now stands. The natives bestowed upon the abandoned settlement the name of "Umpie Bong," [Literally, dead houses] which name is still preserved as Humpybong.

In 1825 Major Lockyer made a long boat excursion up the Brisbane River, and the stream being somewhat swollen by floods, he was able to penetrate, according to his own account, nearly one hundred and fifty miles.

He was much taken with the promising nature of the country, both on the Brisbane and its tributary, the Bremer, and great hopes, happily fulfilled, were entertained of the success of the new settlement. During this year Mr. Cunningham had undertaken another journey to Liverpool Plains. Threading the pass he had formerly discovered and named Pandora's Pass, he crossed the plains, and ascended and examined the table land to the north, returning to Bathurst.

In 1827 this explorer, whose industry never flagged, started on the most eventful trip he ever made, destined to considerably affect the immediate progress of the new colony established at Moreton Bay. On the 30th of April he left Segenhoe Station, on the Upper Hunter, and on crossing Oxley's 1818 track to Port Macquarie, at once entered on the unexplored northern region. On the 19th May, after traversing a good deal of unpromising country, a fertile valley was entered, which led the travellers on to the banks of the Gwydir River, one of Cunningham's most important discoveries. He next found and named the Dumaresque River, and finally emerged on the beautiful plateau, thenceforth known as the Darling Downs, where the Condamine River received its name, after the Governor's aide-de-camp. Cunningham's description of this tract of pastoral country is very glowing:--
"Deep ponds, supported by streams from the highlands immediately to the eastward, extend along their central lower flats. The lower grounds thus permanently watered present flats which furnish an almost inexhaustible range of cattle pasture at all seasons of the year; the grass and herbage generally exhibiting in the depth of winter an extreme luxuriance of growth. From these central grounds rise downs of a rich black and dry soil, and very ample surface; and as they furnish abundance of grass and are conveniently watered, yet perfectly beyond the reach of those floods which take place on the flats in a season of rain, they constitute a sound and valuable sheep pasture."

Here Cunningham halted for some time, with the view of ascertaining the practicability of a passage across the range to Moreton Bay.

In exploring the mountains immediately above the tents of the encampment, a remarkably excavated part of the main range was discovered, which appeared likely to prove available as a pass. Upon examination, the gap was found to be rugged and broken, partially blocked with fallen masses of rocks, and overgrown by scrub and jungle. Beyond these impediments, which could soon be removed, the gap now known as Cunningham's Gap was apparently available as affording a descent to the lower coast lands. Relinquishing any further attempts for the present, either through the mountains or to the western interior, Cunningham returned to the Hunter, crossing and re-crossing his outward track. He was absent oil this expedition thirteen weeks.

The following year the discoverer of the Darling Downs, accompanied by his old companion, Charles Frazer, Colonial Botanist, proceeded by sea to Moreton Bay with the intention of starting from the settlement and connecting with his camp on the Darling Downs by way of Cunningham's Gap. In this attempt he was also accompanied by the Commandant, Captain Logan. The party followed up the Logan River, and partly ascended Mount Lindsay, a lofty and remarkable mountain on the Dividing Range. They were, however, unsuccessful in finding the Gap on this occasion. Cunningham, however, immediately started from Limestone Station on the Bremer, now the town of Ipswich, and this time was quite successful. On the 24th Of August he writes:--

"About one o'clock we passed a mile to the southward of our last position, and, entering a valley, we pitched our tents within three miles of the gap we now suspected to be the Pass of last year's journey.

"It being early in the afternoon, I sent one of my people (who, having been one of my party on that long tour, knew well the features of the country lying to the westward of the Dividing Range) to trace a series of forest ridges, which appeared to lead directly up to the foot of the hollow-back of the range.

"To my utmost gratification he returned at dusk, having traced the ridge about two and a-half miles to the foot of the Dividing Range, whence he ascended into the Pass and, from a grassy head immediately above it, beheld the extensive country lying west of the Main Range. He recognised Darling and Canning Downs, patches of Peel's Plains, and several remarkable points of the forest hills on that side, fully identifying this hollow-back with the pass discovered last year at the head of Miller's Valley, notwithstanding its very different appearance when viewed from the eastern country."

The next day, accompanied by one man, Cunningham ascended the pass that bears his name. Following the ridges, they arrived in about two and three-quarter miles to the foot of the Gap.
Immediately the summit of the pass appeared broad before us, bounded on each side by most stupendous heads, towering at least two thousand feet above it.

"Here the difficulties of the Pass commenced. We had now penetrated to the actual foot of the Pass without the smallest difficulty, it now remained to ascend by a steep slope to the level of its entrance. This slope is occupied by a very close wood, in which red cedar, sassafras, palms, and other ornamental inter-tropical trees are frequent. Through this shaded wood lye penetrated, climbing up a steep bank of a very rich loose earth, in which large fragments of a very compact rock are embedded. At length we gained the foot of a wall of bare rock, which we found stretching from the southward of the Pass.

"This face of naked rock we perceived (by tracing its course northerly) gradually to fall to the common level, so that, without the smallest difficulty, and to my utmost surprise, we found ourselves in the highest part of the Pass, having fully ascertained the extent of the difficult part, from the entrance into the wood to this point, not to exceed four hundred yards."

In this comparatively easy manner was the main range crossed, and access at once obtained from the coastal districts to the rich inland slope--a startling result when compared with the years of labour and baffled hope wasted on the Blue Mountains before victory was won.

In the following year (1829) Cunningham went on his last expedition, to the source of the Brisbane River, and this work concluded ten years of constant and unceasing labour in the cause of exploration. He died in Sydney ten years afterwards, on the 27th of June, leaving behind an undying name, both as a botanist and ardent explorer. During his own travels, and whilst sailing with Captain King, he had seen more of the continent than any man then living.

Captain Charles Sturt, of the 39th Regiment! What visions are conjured up when this name comes on the scene! Cracked and gaping plains, desolate, desert and abandoned of life, scorched beneath a lurid sun of burning fire, waterless, hopeless, relentless, and accursed: that is the picture he draws of the great interior. He had followed up Oxley's footsteps and exposed the fallacies into which that explorer had fallen, and erred just as egregiously himself. True, like Oxley, he was the sport of the seasons. Oxley had followed the rivers down when, year after year, the regular rainfall had made them navigable for his boats, and had finally lost them in oceans of reeds. Sturt came when the land was smitten with drought, and the rivers had dwindled down to the tiniest trickle.

"In the creeks weeds had grown and withered, and grown again and young saplings were now rising in their beds, nourished by

the moisture that still remained; but the large forest trees were drooping and many were dead. The emus, with outstretched necks, gasping
for breath, searched the channels of the rivers for water, in vain; and
the native dog, so thin that he could hardly walk, seemed to implore
some merciful hand to dispatch him."

Such was Sturt's description of the state of the country.

In 1828, the year that witnessed his first expedition, no rain
had fallen for two years, and it seemed as though it would never fall
again. The thoughts of the colonists turned to that shallow ocean of
reeds to the westward wherein Oxley had lost the Macquarie, and it
was thought that now would be the time to verify its existence or find
out what lay beyond. Captain Sturt was appointed to take command,
and with him went Hamilton Hume, who had so successfully crossed
to Port Phillip. The party consisted, besides, of two soldiers and eight
prisoners of the crown, two of whom were to return with dispatches.
They had with them eight riding and seven pack horses, two draught
and eight pack bullocks. They had also with them a small boat rigged
up on a wheeled carriage.

It would be uninteresting to follow the party over the already
known ground to Mount Harris where Oxley had camped in 1818; this
place Sturt and his men reached on the 20th December, 1828.

"As soon as the camp was fixed, Mr. Hume and I rode to
Mount Harris, over ground subject to flood and covered for the most
part by the polygonum, being too anxious to defer our examination of
the neighbourhood even a few hours. Nearly ten years had elapsed
since Mr. Oxley pitched his tents under the smallest of the two hills
into which Mount Harris is broken. There was no difficulty in hitting
upon his position. The trenches that had been cut round the tents were
still perfect, and the marks of the fire places distinguishable; while the
trees in the neighbourhood had been felled, and round about them the
staves of casks, and a few tent pegs were scattered. Mr. Oxley had selected a place at some distance from the river on account of its then
swollen state. I looked upon it from the same ground and could not
discern the waters in the channel, so much had they fallen below their
ordinary level. On the summit of the great eminence which we ascended, there remained the half-burnt planks of a boat, some clenched
and rusty nails, and an old trunk; but my search for the bottle Mr. Oxley had left was unsuccessful.

"A reflection arose to my mind, on examining these decaying
vestiges of a former expedition, whether I should be more fortunate
than the leader of it, and how far I should be enabled to penetrate be-

yond the point which had conquered his perseverance. Only a week before I left Sydney I had followed Mr. Oxley to the tomb. A man of uncommon quickness and of great ability. The task of following up his discoveries was not less enviable than arduous; but, arrived at that point at which his journey may be said to have terminated and mine only to commence, I knew not how soon I should be obliged, like him, to retreat from the marshes and exhalations of so depressed a country. My eye turned instinctively to the north-west, and the view extended over an apparently endless forest. I could trace the river line of trees by their superior height, but saw no appearance of reeds save the few that grew on the banks of the stream."

Satisfied, after consultation with his companion Hume, that there was no obstacle to their onward march, they left their position, intending, as Sturt says, "to close with the marshes."

The night of the first day found them camped amongst the reeds, which they came upon sooner than they expected, and the next day they halted for the purpose of preparing the dispatches for the Governor. On the morning of the 26th, the journey was resumed, the two messengers leaving for Bathurst, the rest proceeding onward until checked by finding themselves in the great body of the marsh, which spread in boundless extent around them.

"It was evidently," says the leader, "lower than the ground on which we stood; we had, therefore, a complete view of the whole expanse, and there was a dreariness and desolation pervading the scene which strengthened as we gazed upon it."

Under the circumstances, an advance with the main body of the party was considered unwise, and it was determined to launch the boat, and try and follow the course of the river, whilst a simultaneous attempt was made to penetrate the reed bed to the north. Accordingly Sturt, with two men, started in the boat, and Hume and two more struck north.

Sturt's boating expedition came very quickly to a close. In the afternoon of the day he started:--

" . . . the channel which had promised so well, without any change in its breadth or depth, ceased altogether, and while we were yet lost in astonishment at so abrupt a termination of it the boat grounded."

All search was fruitless, and mysteriously and completely baffled as Oxley had been, so was his successor, and there was nothing for it but to return to camp.

Hume had been more successful. He reported finding a serpentine sheet of water to the northward, which he did not doubt was the channel of the river. He had pushed on, but was checked by another of the seemingly inevitable marshes.

On the 28th the camp was shifted to this lagoon, and the boat was launched once more; without result. The new-found channel was soon lost in reeds and shallows. Forced to halt again, Hume went to the north-east to scout, and Sturt went north-west, each accompanied, as before, by two men. They left the camp on the last day of the year.

After sunset on the first day, Sturt struck a creek of considerable size leading northerly, having good water in its bed. The next day, after passing through alternate plain and brush for eighteen miles, a second creek was found, inferior to the first both in size and the quality of the water; it too ran northerly. Crossing this creek, after a short halt, they travelled through stony ridges and open forest, and at night camped on the edge of a waterless plain, after a hot and thirsty ride; here one of the men, noticing the flight of a pigeon, found a small puddle of rain water that just sufficed them. Next day, the country steadily improving in appearance, they made west by south for an isolated mountain with perpendicular sides, from the top of which Sturt trusted to see something hopeful ahead. He was disappointed, the country was monotonous and level, and no sign of a river could be seen. They camped that night at a small swamp, and next morning Sturt turned back, like Oxley, coming to the conclusion that:--

"Yet upon the whole, the space I traversed is unlikely to become the haunt of civilised man, or will become so in isolated spots, as a chain of connection to a more fertile country; if such a country exist to the westward."

Hume had not returned when the party reached the main camp on the 5th of January; the next day he made his appearance. He reported having travelled, on various courses, about thirty miles N.N.W. over an indifferent country. He had anticipated meeting with the Castlereagh, but had been forced to conclude that that river had taken a more northerly course than Mr. Oxley had supposed. He went westward, and across fine far-stretching plains, but saw no sign of the Macquarie River having re-formed, crossing nothing but small 'reeks or chains of ponds.

Most of the men, including Hume, complaining of sickness, he camp was shifted four miles to the north, on to a chain of ponds reported by Hume. This creek they followed down, when it disappointed them by disappearing in the marsh. Without water, they continued skirting the low country until fatigue compelled them to stop, when, by digging shallow wells in the reeds, they obtained a small supply. From here they made their way by a different route to the hill that had terminated Sturt's late trip, and which he had christened Oxley's Tableland. Here they rested a few days, and Sturt and Hume, with two men, made another excursion westward, but without result.

Their only resource now was to make north to a creek that they had followed down on their way to Oxley's tableland, and see where it would lead them.

On the 31st January they came upon this creek, which was called by them New Year's Creek, now the Bogan, and the next day they suddenly found themselves on the brink of a noble river:--

"The party drew up upon a bank that was from forty to forty-five feet above the level of the stream. The channel of the river was from seventy to eighty yards broad, and enclosed an unbroken sheet of water, evidently very deep, and literally covered with pelicans and other wild fowl. Our surprise and delight may better be imagined than described. Our difficulties seemed to be at an end, for here was a river that promised to reward all our exertions, and which appeared every moment to increase in importance to our imaginations. Coming from the N.E. and flowing to the S.W., it had a capacity of channel that proved that we were as far from its source as from its termination. The paths of the natives on either side of it were like trodden roads, and the trees that overhung it were of beautiful and gigantic growth.

"The banks were too precipitous to 'allow of our watering the cattle, but the men descended eagerly to quench their thirst, which a powerful sun had contributed to increase; nor shall I ever forget the cry of amazement that followed their doing so, or the looks of terror and disappointment with which they called out to inform me that the water was so salt as to be unfit to drink. This was indeed too true. On tasting it, I found it extremely nauseous, and strongly impregnated with salt, being apparently a mixture of sea and fresh water. . . Our hopes were annihilated at the moment of their apparent realisation. The cup of joy was dashed out of our hands before we had time to raise it to our lips."

Finding fresh feed lower down the river, the party halted for the benefit of the cattle, who, unable to drink the water, soaked their bodies in it. Meantime, although the tracks of the natives were abundant, they looked in vain for any of them. Fortunately, that night Hume found a pond of fresh water, and the party were refreshed once more. The phenomena of the salt river was puzzling to Sturt, though too familiar now to excite wonder; the long continued drought having low-ered the river so that the brine springs in the banks preponderated over the fresh water, was of course the explanation, and it is a common characteristic of inland watercourses. The size of the river and the saltness of its water, however, partly convinced Sturt that he was near its confluence with an inland sea; so for six days they moved slowly down the river, finding, however, no change in its formation, until the discovery of saline springs in the bank convinced the leader that the saltness was of local origin.

Leaving the party encamped at a small pool of fresh water, Sturt and Hume pushed ahead to look for more, but without success. Before leaving they were startled, one afternoon, by a loud report like a distant cannon, for which they could in noway account, as the sky was clear and without a cloud. [These strange reports have since been frequently heard, often at the same moment, at places more than a hundred miles apart. The cause is generally ascribed to atmospheric disturbances.]

The advance was now checked, no fresh water could be found on ahead, and their animals were weak and exhausted. Sturt christened the river the Darling, and gave the order to retreat.

As they again approached Mount Harris on the Macquarie, where they expected to find a relief party with fresh supplies, fears began to be entertained regarding the safety of those who might be awaiting them at the depôt. The reed beds were in flames in all parts, and the few natives they met displayed a guilty timidity, and one was observed with a jacket in his possession. Their fears were, however, fortunately vain, the natives had made one attempt to surprise the camp, but it had been frustrated, and the relief party had now been some three weeks awaiting the return of the explorers.

Sturt rested for some days, during which time Hume made a short western trip.. to the south of the marsh land. He reported that for thirty miles the country was superior to anything they had yet seen, and exceedingly well watered; beyond that distance the plains and brush of the remote interior again resumed their sway.

On the 7th March the party struck camp and made for the Cas-tlereagh, the relief going back to Bathurst. On the 10th they reached the Castlereagh, and found it apparently without a drop of water in its bed. From here downwards the old harassing hunt for water com-menced once more, and as they descended the river they were further puzzled by the intricate windings of its course and the number of channels that intersected the depressed country they were travelling through. On the 29th they again struck the Darling, ninety miles above the spot where they had discovered it:

"This singular river still preserved its character so strikingly that it was impossible not to have recognised it in a moment. The same steep banks and lofty timber, the same deep reaches, alive with fish, were here visible as when we left it. A hope naturally arose to our minds, that if it was unchanged in other respects, it might have lost the saltness that rendered its waters unfit for use; but in this we were dis-appointed-even its waters continued the same."

Fortunately the adventurers were not this time in such un-happy straits for water as before, so that the disappointment was less intense. Knowing what they might expect if they followed the Darling down south, the party at once halted. It was evident that to the east and north-east, the rigorous drought had put its mark on the land, from the fact that large bodies of natives driven in from that direction were congregated round the few permanent waters left. A reconnoitring ex-pedition across the Darling to the N.W. was accordingly determined on, to see if any advance into the interior was possible, and after a camp had been formed Sturt and Hume started on the quest. No en-couragement to proceed resulted. By four p.m. they found themselves on a plain that stretched far away and bounded the horizon.

"It was dismally brown, a few trees only served to mark the distance. Up one of the highest I sent Hopkins on, who reported that he could not see the end of it, and that all around looked blank and deso-late. It is a singular fact that during the whole day we had not seen a drop of water or a blade of grass.

"To have stopped where we were would, therefore, have been impossible; to have advanced would probably have been ruin. Had there been one favourable circumstance to have encouraged me with the hope of success I would have proceeded. Had we picked up a stone, as indicating our approach to high land, I would have gone on; or had there been a break in the country, or even a change in the vege-tation; but we had left all traces of the natives behind us, and this seemed a desert they never entered--that not even a bird inhabited. I could not encourage a hope of success, and therefore gave up the point, not from want of means, but a conviction of the inutility of any further efforts. If there is any blame to be attached to the measure it is I who am in fault; but none who had not like me traversed the interior at such a season would believe the state of the country over which I had wandered. During the short interval I had been out, I had seen riv-ers cease to flow before me and sheets of water disappear, and had it

70

not been for a merciful Providence should, ere reaching the Darling, have been overwhelmed by misfortune.

"I am giving no false picture of the reality. So long had the drought continued that the vegetable kingdom was almost annihilated, and minor vegetation had disappeared."

Once more the order to retreat from the inhospitable Darling was given, and the weary march home recommenced. On their way they traced and followed a defined channel, or depression, formerly crossed by Hume, and ascertained it to be the outflow of the Macquarie Marshes. On the 7th of April, 1829, they reached Mount Harris.

The mystery of the Macquarie was now, to a certain extent, cleared up, but there still remained another riddle to solve in the course and outlet of the Darling. Sturt, the discoverer of this river, was destined to find the answer to this problem as well.

We have now traced the gradual extension of exploration to the westward, and seen a river system growing up, as it were, piece by piece, as the result of these expeditions; it may, therefore, be as well to continue to follow up Captain Sturt's expeditions, and note how the Murray and its tributary streams were gradually elaborated, before touching upon events at this time occurring afar on the south-west coast of the continent.

The desire to ascertain the course of the Darling naturally became a subject of great interest so soon as the result of Captain Sturt's expedition was known; and the Macquarie and Lachlan rivers having failed to afford a means of reaching the interior, it was determined to try the Morumbidgee. The fact that this river derived its supply from the highest known mountains, and was independent, to a large extent, of the periodical rainfall, was a great inducement to hope for success.

Almost exactly a year after he had started on his journey down the Macquarie, Captain Sturt left Sydney, on his Morumbidgee expedition, on the 3rd of November, 1829.

Hume, was not, on this occasion, able to accompany the party, his own affairs on his farm needing his attention; doubtless in spirit he was often with them, and it would have been but fitting had the discoverer of the Murray or Hume, been one of the party to first trace its downward course. In Hume's place went George M'Leay, the son of the then Colonial Secretary, Alexander M'Leay; with them also went Harris, Hopkinson, and Fraser, members of the Macquarie expedition,

To our modern eyes the appearance of the troop that marched out of Sydney, early that summer morning, would have looked strange indeed.

71

FAVENC

"At a quarter before seven the party filed through the turnpike gate, and thus commenced its journey with the greatest regularity. I have the scene even at this distance of time, vividly impressed upon my mind, and I have no doubt the kind friend who was with me on the occasion bears it as strongly on his recollection. My servant Harris, who had shared my wanderings, and had continued in my service for eighteen years, led the advance with his companion Hopkinson; nearly abreast of them the eccentric Frazer stalked along, wholly lost in thought. The two former had laid aside their military habits, and had substituted the broad-brimmed hat, and the bushman's dress in their place, but it was impossible to guess how Frazer intended to protect himself from the heat or damp, so little were his habiliments suited for the occasion. He had his gun over his shoulder, and his double shot belt as full as it could be of shot, although there was not a chance of his expending a grain during the day. Some dogs Mr. Maxwell had kindly sent me followed close at his heels, as if they knew his interest in them, and they really seemed as if they were aware that they were about to exchange their late confinement for the freedom of the woods. The whole of these formed a kind of advanced guard. At some distance in the rear the drays moved slowly along, on one of which rode the black boy; Robert Harris, whom I had appointed to superintend the animals generally, kept his place near the horses, and the heavy Clayton, my carpenter, brought up the rear."

It will be needless to follow the progress of the party through the settled districts that now extended to the banks of the Morumbidgee: on the 27th, we find them preparing to start from Mr. Whaby's station, the last outpost of civilization. From thence they followed the river down, maintaining constant and friendly intercourse with the natives on the banks. For some time they passed through rich available country, and at one point they made a slight excursion to the north to connect with Oxley's most southerly limit; although they did not actually verify it, Sturt was of the opinion that they were within at least twenty miles of the range seen by Oxley. Still following the river they now found its course leading them amongst the plains and flat country with which they were so well acquainted, and naturally travelled in the constant dread of the stream conducting them to the lame and impotent conclusions of the Macquarie and Lachlan.

"Our route was over as melancholy a tract as ever was travelled. The plains to the N. and N.W. bounded the horizon; not a tree of any kind was visible upon them. It was equally open to the south, and

72

it appeared as if the river was decoying us into a desert, there to leave us in difficulty and in distress."

Sturt now was constantly haunted with the thought of once more finding himself baffled and perplexed in some vast region of flooded country, without a defined system of channels. Every time he looked at the river he imagined that it had fallen off in appearance, feeling certain that the flooded spaces over which he was travelling would soon be succeeded by a country overgrown with reeds. The flats of polygonum stretched away to the N.W., and to the S., and the soil itself bore testimony to its flooded origin. Some natives here met with spoke of the Colare, a name which Sturt had beard before, and which he took to mean the Lachlan, from the direction in which the blacks pointed. These men indicated that they were but one day's journey from it. Sturt and M'Leay, therefore, rode to the north to examine the country; they found a creek of considerable size, and from its appearance and the nature of the surrounding flats, deemed it to be a similar channel from the Lachlan marshes to the Morumbidgee, as the one Sturt and Hume had formerly noticed to the north, leading from the great marsh of the Macquarie to the Darling. In point of fact they actually crossed the Lachlan, and went some distance beyond it, passing close to Oxley's lowest camp, as the natives afterwards testified to Major Mitchell.

The extract from the Major's journal bearing on the subject runs thus:--

"The natives further informed me that three men on horseback, who had canoes (boats) on the Murrumbidgee, had visited the Lachlan thereabouts since, and that after crossing it, and going a little way beyond, they had returned."

Sturt mentioned seeing the fires of the natives during this trip, but he did not see them, although it was evident that they had a good look at him.

On the 26th of December, it seemed that their gloomiest hopes were to be realised. Traversing plains like those described before, Sturt says:--

"The wheels of the drays sank up to their axle-trees, and the horses above their fetlocks at every step. The fields of polygonum spread on every side of us, like a dark sea, and the only green object within range of our vision was the river line of trees. In several instances the force of both teams was put to one dray, to extricate it from the bed into which it had sunk, and the labour was considerably increased from the nature of the weather. The wind was blowing as if through a furnace, from the N.N.E., and the dust was flying in clouds, so as to render it almost suffocating to remain exposed to it. This was the only occasion upon which we felt the hot winds in the interior. We were, about noon, endeavouring to gain a point of a wood at which I expected to come upon the river again, but it was impossible for the teams to reach it without assistance. I therefore sent M'Leay forward with orders to unload the pack animals as soon as he should make the river, and send them back to help the teams. He had scarcely been separated from me twenty minutes, when one of the men came galloping back to inform me that no river was to be found--that the country beyond the woods was covered with reeds as far as the eye could reach, and that Mr. M'Leay had sent him back for instructions. This intelligence stunned me for a moment or two, and I am sure its effect upon the men was very great. They had unexpectedly arrived at a part of the interior simi-lar to one they held in dread, and conjured up a thousand difficulties and privations. I desired the man to recall Mr. M'Leay; and, after gain-ing the wood, moved outside of it at right angles to my former course, and reached the river, after a day of severe toil and exposure. at half-past five. The country, indeed, bore every resemblance to that around the marshes of the Macquarie, but I was too weary to make any further effort; indeed it was too late for one to undertake anything until the morning."

The following day, accompanied by his friend, Sturt pro-ceeded to examine the river. He found it still running strong, without any sign of diminution in its flow, but the reedy flats were so dense and thick that no passage for the teams was practicable. At noon the leader halted, and announced his intention of returning to camp. He had come to the determination to construct the whaleboat he had with him in sections, to send the teams back, and, with six men and Mr. M'Leay, to start down the river, and follow it wherever it went; whether ever to return again or not was for the future to determine.

Clayton, the carpenter, was at once set to work upon the boat, or boats, for a tree was felled, a sawpit rigged up, and a small boat half the size of the whaleboat built. Everybody worked hard, and in seven days the boats were afloat, moored alongside a temporary wharf, ready for loading. Six men were then chosen to form the crew, who were about to undertake one of the most eventful and important voyages in Australia's history. They were Clayton, the carpenter, Mulholland and Macnamee, the three soldiers, Harris, Hopkinson and Fraser, the leader, and M'Leay--eight in all. The remainder of the party, under Robert Harris, were to remain stationary one week, in case of accident, then to proceed to Goulburn Plains and await instructions from Sydney.

On the 7th of January, 1830, the voyagers started, towing the smaller boat, the men all in high spirits at the wide prospect of adventure before them.

Going with the stream they made rapid progress, using only two oars, but the first day did not suffice to carry them clear of the reeds, in fact, at night when they landed to camp, they could scarcely find room to pitch their tents. On the second day, an accident happened to the skiff they were towing; she struck on a log, and immediately sank with all the valuable cargo she carried. Two days were spent in recovering the things, as the boat had gone down in twelve feet of water, and during the time they were so employed, the blacks robbed the camp of many articles.

Once more on the move, they found the river still winding its way through a flat expanse of reeds, and threatening to end as the other rivers had done. On the afternoon of the next day a change for the better took place; the reeds on both sides of the river terminated, and the country became more elevated, and bore the appearance of open forest pasture land; a tributary creek of considerable size joined the river from the S.E., and the spirits of the voyagers rose again. More tributaries now came in from the south-east, and the dangers of navigation increased, the river being full of snags and fallen timber, and the utmost care had to be used to keep the boat clear. On the second day of this distressing work, they were destined to meet with a surprise.

"About one we again started. The men looked anxiously ahead, for the singular change in the river had impressed on them the idea that we were approaching its termination, or near some adventure. On a sudden the river took a general southern direction, but, in its tortuous course, swept round to every point of the compass with the greatest irregularity. We were carried at a fearful rate down its gloomy and contracted banks, and in such a moment of excitement, had little time to pay attention to the country through which we were passing. It was. however, observed that chalybeate springs were numerous close to the water's edge. At three p.m., Hopkinson called out that we were approaching a junction, and in less than a minute afterwards we were hurried into a broad and noble river.

"It is impossible to describe the effect of so instantaneous a change upon us. The boats were allowed to drift along at pleasure, and such was the force with which we had been shot out of the Morumbidgee, that we were carried nearly to the bank opposite its embouchure, whilst we continued to gaze in silent astonishment on the capacious channel we had entered; and when we looked for that by which we had been led into it, we could hardly believe that the insignificant gap that presented itself to us was indeed the termination of the beautiful and noble stream whose course we had thus successfully followed."

Sturt had now succeeded beyond his hopes--his bold adventure had been rewarded even sooner than he could have expected. He felt assured that at last he floated on the stream destined to bear him to the sea. The key to the river system of the south-east portion of the continent was in his grasp, and all former fallacies and fanciful theories were answered for good. The voyage down the Murray, as this river was named, after Sir George Murray, then the bead of the Colonial Department, now continued free from some of the difficulties that had beset them in the Morumbidgee. The natives again made their appearance, and were constantly seen every day, some betraying great timidity, others appearing more curious than frightened. Four of these natives accompanied them for two days, during which time the explorers narrowly suffered wreck in a rapid in the river.

They now approached the confluence of the Darling, although of course they were not then able to verify the supposition that it was their old friend, and at this point one of the most singular adventures ever narrated in the intercourse with native tribes happened.

The wind was fair, and with the sail set, the boat was making rapid way when, at the termination of a long reach, they observed a line of magnificent trees, of green and dense foliage. A large number of blacks were here assembled, and apparently with no friendly intentions, armed, painted, and shouting defiance. Anxious to avert hostilities, Sturt steered straight for them, thinking to make friends; but when almost too close to avoid a meeting, he could see that the matter was serious. The blacks had their spears poised for throwing, and their women were behind with a fresh supply. The sail was lowered and the helm put about, and the boat passed down the stream, the natives running along the bank, keeping pace with them, shouting and attempting to take aim.

To add to their danger the river shoaled rapidly, and a sandspit appeared ahead, projecting nearly two thirds of the way across the channel, and on this spit the blacks now gathered with tremendous uproar, evidently determined to make an assault on the boat as she ran the gauntlet through the narrow passage. Amongst the four blacks who had accompanied them for two days was one of superior personal strength and stature. These men had left the camp of the whites the night before, and it was believing in their presence in the crowd before them that led Sturt to disregard the hostile demonstrations.

A battle now seemed inevitable. Arms were distributed to the crew, and orders given how to act when the emergency arose.

We will let Sturt tell his own story:--

"The men assured me they would follow my instructions, and thus prepared, having already lowered the sail, we drifted onwards with the current. As we neared the sand-bank, I stood up and made signs to the natives to desist, but without success. I took up my gun, therefore, and cocking it, had already brought it down to a level; a few seconds more would have closed the life of the nearest savage. The distance was too trifling for me to doubt the fatal effects of the dis-charge; for I was determined to take deadly aim, in hopes that the fall of one man might save the lives of many. But at the very moment when my hand was on the trigger, and my eye was along the barrel, my purpose was checked by M'Leay, who called to me that another party of blacks had made their appearance upon the left bank of the river. Turning round, I observed four men at the top of their speed. The foremost of them, as soon as he got ahead of the boat, threw him-self from a considerable height into the water. He struggled across the channel to the sandbank, and in an incredibly short space of time stood in front of the savage, against whom my aim had been directed. Seiz-ing him by the throat, he pushed him backwards, and forcing all who were in the water upon the bank, he trod its margin with a vehemence and an agitation that were exceedingly striking. At one moment point-ing to the boat, at another shaking his clenched hand in the faces of the most forward, and stamping with passion on the sand; his voice, that was at first distinct, was lost in hoarse murmurs. Two of the four na-tives remained on the left bank of the river, the third followed his leader (who proved to be the remarkable savage I have previously no-ticed) to the scene of action. The reader will imagine our feelings on this occasion; it is impossible to describe them. We were so wholly lost in interest at the scene that was passing, that the boat was allowed to drift at pleasure.

"We were again aroused to action by the boat suddenly strik-ing upon a shoal, which reached from one side of the river to the other. To jump out and push her into deep water was but the work of a mo-ment with the men, and it was just as she floated again that our attention was withdrawn to a new and beautiful stream, coming apparently from the north. . . . A party of about seventy blacks were upon the right bank of the newly discovered river, and I thought that by landing amongst them I might make a diversion in favour of our late guest, and in this I succeeded. The blacks no sooner observed that we had landed than curiosity took the place of anger. All wrangling ceased, and they came swimming over to us like a parcels of seals . . . It was not until after we had returned to the boat, and had surveyed the multitude on the sloping bank above us that we became fully aware of the extent of our danger, and of the almost miraculous intervention of Providence in our favour. There could not have been less than six hundred natives upon that blackened sward."

After presenting their friend who had acted so effectively on their behalf, and whose energetic conduct and prompt interference to preserve peace is unparalleled in native annals, with suitable gifts and refusing them to the other chiefs, the boat's crew proceeded to examine the new river they had discovered at such a critical moment.

Pulling easily up for a short distance they found it preserved a breadth of one hundred yards, and a depth of rather more than twelve feet, The banks were sloping and grassy, crowned with fine trees, and the men exclaimed that they had got into an English river.

To Sturt himself the moment was a supreme one; was it, or was it not that mysterious Darling, whose course through the far interior had been a subject of speculation ever since its discovery? He felt sure that it was.

"An irresistible conviction impressed me that we were now sailing on the bosom of that very stream from whose banks I had been twice forced to retire. I directed the Union jack to be hoisted, and giving way to our satisfaction we all stood up in the boat and gave three distinct cheers. It was an English feeling, an ebullition, an overflow, which I am ready to admit that our circumstances and situation will alone excuse. The eve of every native had been fixed upon that noble flag, at all times a beautiful object, and to them a novel one, as it waved over us in the heart of the desert. They had until that moment been particularly loquacious, but the sight of that flag and the sound of our voices hushed the tumult, and while they were still lost in astonishment, the boat's head was turned, the sail was sheeted home, both wind and current were in our favour, and we vanished from them with a rapidity that surprised even ourselves, and which precluded every hope of the most adventurous among them to keep up with us."

Once Pore down the now united streams of the Murray and the Darling the party made rapid progress, landing occasionally to inspect the country, but finding always a boundless flat on either side of them.

Provisions now began to get scarce with them, the barrels of salt pork that had been in the skiff when she sank in the Morumbidgee had their contents damaged by the admission of the fresh water. The fish, though abundant, were more than unattractive to their palates, and the men took no trouble to set the night lines. The strictest economy had, therefore, to become the order of the day. The skiff being only a drag to them, she was broken up, and burnt for the sake of the nails and iron-work.

On the 24th of January, the whale-boat continued its voyage alone, and the record from day to day was only broken by their intercourse with the different tribes, with whom a regular system of communication was now established. Deputies were sent ahead, from one tribe to another, to prepare them for the visit of the strangers. These deputies, by cutting off the numerous bends of the river, were enabled to travel much quicker than did Sturt, frequently doing easily in one day what it took the boat two to accomplish. Their black friends were, however, becoming rather a nuisance; little or no information could be obtained from them, and the constant handling and embracing, which they had from policy to submit to, became horribly distasteful to all of them, particularly as Sturt describes all the tribes he met with as being beyond the average filthily dirty, and eaten up with skin diseases.

On the 25th, the wanderers thought they sighted a range to the N.W., and the blacks confirmed it, pointing in that direction when Hopkinson piled up some clay in imitation of mountains.

On the 29th, the leader calculated that they were still one hundred and fifteen miles from the coast, and as they had been now twenty-two days on the river, their return began to be a matter for serious thought. From what he saw of the country, Sturt imagined that it was, for the most part, barren and sandy, and would never be utilised. But, of course, he had little or no opportunities, travelling as he did, of forming a correct judgment.

The cliffs on the river bank now showed fossilized sea shells in their strata; chains of hills, too, became visible, and one of the natives, [This old native, after the settlement of the country, was shot in cold blood by one of the South Australian police.] an old man who had taken a strange fancy to Hopkinson, described the roaring of the sea and the height of the waves, showing that he had visited the coast.

None, it may be certain, were more glad than the leader to hear of their proximity, for his thoughts were always busy with the failing condition of his men, and the accumulating difficulties of his return.

True, it had been partly arranged that a vessel should proceed to the south coast, but Sturt had little hope of meeting her, even if one had been sent. The frequent bends in the river greatly delayed their advance, but they were cheered by the flight of sea-gulls over their heads. The river, too, widened day after day, and a constant strong wind from the S.W., raised a chopping sea that almost stopped their way; the blacks they met all assured them that the ocean was at hand. On the 9th February, Sturt landing to examine the country, saw before him the lake that terminated the Murray. He had reached his goal, thirty-three days after separating from his party, at the Morumbidgee. Crossing the lake the little band landed on the southern shore, and ascertained that the communication between it and the sea was impracticable on account of its extreme shallowness; they found their position to be in Encounter Bay, east of Spencer's Gulf, and from what they saw it was evident that no ship could enter it during the prevalence of the S.W. winds. All hope of a safe return centred in themselves. The thunder of the surf, that they had so longed for, brought no message of succour, but rather warned the lonely men to hasten back, while yet some strength remained to them; and above all they were surrounded by hostile blacks. Sturt had now a terrible task before him. His men were weakened and on half rations; there was every probability that the fickle natives might be troublesome on their homeward route, and worst of all they would have to fight the steady current of the river the whole way; nor would their spirits be cheered by any hope of novelty or discovery. Under these gloomy auspices Sturt re-entered the Murray on his return on the 13th February.

The homeward journey is simply a record of unrelaxed toil day after day, Sturt and M'Leay taking their turn at the oar like the rest; added to which the blacks gave them far more trouble than before. At the fall above the junction of the Darling they once more met the friend who had saved them from coming into conflict with the natives on the 24th January; he and some of his tribe assisted them to get the boat up the rapids. On the 20th of March they reached the camp on the Morumbidgee from whence they had started, but it was now abandoned, and the hope that the relief party had pushed down there to meet them was destroyed; there was nothing for it but to pull on, but human nature was rapidly giving way; the men though falling asleep at their oars never grumbled, but worked steadily, if moodily, faithful to their duty to the last. Then the river rose, and for days they struggled vainly against it. One man went mad, and had to be relieved from the oars. At last, when ninety miles from Pontebadgery, the place where Sturt believed the relief party to be camped, he determined to dispatch two men for provisions and await their return.

After six days, when the last ounce of flour had been served out, the men came back with horses and drays, and all trouble was at an end. This was on the 18th April, eighty-eight days after their departure from the depôt, during which they had voyaged two thousand miles.

This expedition, from whatever light it is regarded, either as the most important contribution ever made to Australian geography, or as an example of most wonderful endurance, and patient heroism is equally one of the most glorious records in this history. The leader and his men were alike worthy of each other.

We have now had in review the opinion of many men on the future of the great interior, and seen how they all alike predicted for it barrenness and desolation. Even the satisfaction that Sturt felt at accomplishing the descent of the Murray was qualified by a consideration of the valueless country it flowed through. The question will naturally be asked, how could men of such ability and more than average shrewdness make such a gross mistake as the succeeding years have proved their opinion to be? The principal reason will be found in their want of experience in witnessing the development and improvement of land by stocking, and their ignorance of the value of the vegetation they condemned as worthless. Hume was the only man amongst them exceptionally fitted by training to judge of the capability of the land, and we do not often get at his direct opinion, nor is it likely that, with the memory of the green meadow lands and sparkling waters of the Morumbidgee fresh in his mind, it would be a very favourable one. Oxley and Sturt both wrote smarting under disappointment, and both had been suddenly confronted with a new and strange experience which they could associate with nothing but the idea of a desert. That all this seemingly desolate waste should one day have a distinctive value of its own was what they could hardly dream of.

Chapter IV

Settlement at King George's Sound--The free colony of Swan River founded--Governor Stirling--Captain Bannister crosses from Perth to King George's Sound--Explorations by Lieutenant Roe--Disappointing nature of the interior--Bunbury, Wilson, and Moore--Settlement on the North Coast--Melville Island and Raffles Bay--An escaped convict's story--The fabulous Kindur River--Major Mitchell starts in search of it--Discovery of the Namoi--The Nundawar Range--Failure of the boats--Reach the Gwydir River of Cunningham--The Karaula--Its identity with the Darling--Murder of the two bullock-drivers-- Mitchell's return--Murder of Captain Barker in Encounter Bay--Major Mitchell's second expedition to trace the course of the Darling--Traces the Bogan to its junction with that river--Fort Bourke--Progress down the river--Hostility of the natives--Skirmish with them--Return-- Mitchell's third expedition--The Lachlan followed--Junction of the Darling and the Murray reached--Mitchell's discovery of Australia Felix.

During the time that Oxley, Sturt, and Hume had been tracing out and painfully discovering the watershed of the Murray, a settlement had been formed at King George's Sound, in Western Australia, and some slight attempts at exploration made, but of inconsiderable extent. The settlement was entrusted to Major Lockyer, who was succeeded by Captain Barker, destined to meet a violent death at the mouth of the Murray. In 1828, Captain Stirling, in the Success, visited the coast, and made a close examination of the Swan River. He was accompanied by Frazer the botanist, who had now been present at the opening of a great deal of new country. Stirling's report was a favourable one, and the Home Government determined to form a free colony there. In 1831, we find a communication to the Colonial Government, notifying that the Isabella be dispatched to Hobart Town, to bring up a detachment of the 63rd regiment to relieve those of the 39th, at King

George's Sound. Also, directing the withdrawal from the present settlement of both prisoners and troops.

Stirling was then appointed Lieutenant-Governor, and to induce immigration and settlement, the colonists were promised land in proportion to the capital they brought into the country, and for every labourer they brought out they received two hundred acres of land additional.

At first, the prospects of this new colony seemed most hopeful, exploration was pushed out to the eastward for one hundred miles, as far as Mount Stirling, and northward for some sixty miles or so, and the country discovered gave every promise of being fitted for both pasture and agriculture.

Captain Bannister made a trip in 1831 from Perth, the new settlement, to the old one of King George's Sound; and, although he made no important discoveries, he passed through fairly available country nearly the whole of the way.

For some reason or other, however, a period of stagnation set in, and little more was done in the way of exploring until Lieutenant Grey took the field in 1837. In this new settlement, so entirely opposed to Port Jackson in situation, no difficulties of any magnitude were experienced in passing the coast range, as had been the great obstacle of the early explorers in New South Wales. Unfortunately, however, the comparatively lower altitude of the Darling Range led to there being no such flow of water inland as even those disappointing rivers the Macquarie and Lachlan had afforded. Consequently, exploration and the ensuing occupation were, as in the parent colony, strictly confined to the immediate neighbourhood of the township, to the Swan River, and its tributaries, the Avon and the Canning.

Lieutenant Roe attempted several journeys to the eastward, and discovered many salt lakes on the tableland of the interior. Messrs. Bunbury, Wilson, and Moore made other explorations, more or less succeeding in the purposes they had in view; but they all embraced so small an area, and so little details have been preserved, that they cannot take any important rank in the history of continental explorations.

During the twenties another settlement had been formed on the northern coast of Australia; but one not destined to drag out a very long existence.

Captain Gordon Bremer, in the Tamar, accompanied by two transports, sailed through Torres Straits and anchored in Port Essington, in 1824. The port was, however, at that time condemned as a site for a settlement, the supply of fresh water did not come up to expectations, and the dry months of the year had set in. Bremer sailed for Melville Island, one of twin islands lying off the coast. These islands, Melville and Bathurst, are separated from each other by a narrow strait that Captain King, the discoverer, mistook for a river. On Melville Island a favourable site with abundance of fresh water was found, and the usual routine of taking possession and forming an encampment gone through, and for a time things seemed to prosper; the soil of the island is good, and tropical fruits would flourish with little trouble; but hostilities commenced with the blacks, sickness broke out, and in 1829 it was determined to abandon the settlement, and since that date no attempt has been made to colonise this island, although it is now stocked with the increase of the buffaloes left behind by the Tamar's people.

Fort Wellington, in Raffles Bay, founded in 1826, fared no better, although controlled during its last year by the gifted and unfortunate Captain Barker. A blight of stagnation seemed in those days to hang over all attempts at settlement in the tropical regions, and in three years' time Fort Wellington was abandoned, and with it the northern coast.

Once more we must turn our attention to the southern watershed of the Darling, and the additional links of discovery in the great network of its tributaries.

Rumour, always busy with tales of the unknown interior, now spread a story of a mysterious river called the Kindur, running to the north-west. A runaway convict named Clarke, alias "the barber," brought the story up first. He said that he had long heard of the river from the natives, and at last determined to make his escape and follow it down to see if it would lead him to any other country. He, therefore, took to the bush, and started on this adventurous trip. The imaginative and highly-coloured fabrication that he related on his return, was probably invented in order to save his back, but at any rate it was plausible enough to induce the Government to dispatch an expedition to investigate the matter. This was his story. He started from Liverpool Plains, and followed a river called by the natives the Gnamoi or Nammoy, into which he said that Oxley's river Peel flowed. Crossing this he struck another river, the Kindur, and down this stream he travelled no less than four hundred miles before it was joined by the Gnamoi. Nothing daunted he stuck to the Kindur, which was broad and navigable, flowing through level country and spreading into occasional lakes, until at last he reached the sea, but he acknowledged that he had lost his reckoning, and whether it was five hundred or five thousand miles he went he could not truthfully say, but he was as quite sure upon one point, that he had never travelled south of west.

When at the mouth of the river he ascended a hill and looked out to sea where he saw an island, inhabited, the natives told him, by copper-coloured men who came in large canoes to the mainland for scented wood. In addition he introduced various details of large plains, Balyran, that he had crossed, and a burning mountain named Courada. As he saw no prospect of getting away from Australia, Clarke decided on returning.

This wild tale, and the expedition it led to, brings on the scene one of the most noted figures of the past, Oxley's successor, Surveyor-General Major Mitchell.

The Acting-Governor, Sir Patrick Lindesay, decided on sending out an expedition to find out the truth of this story, thinking that, at any rate, it would lead to the exploration of a great deal of new country. Accordingly, Major Mitchell received instructions to take charge of the party, and on the 21St of November, 1831, took his departure from Liverpool Plains. On the 15th of December, he came to the Peel, and crossing Oxley's Hardwicke Range, reached the Namoi River on the 16th. After penetrating some distance into a range, which he called the Nundawar Range, he made back for the Namoi, and proceeded to set up the canvas boats he had with him, intending to try to follow the river in them. His attempt was fruitless, one of the boats was soon snagged, and it became evident that it would be much easier to follow the Namoi on horseback. Leaving the river, after passing the range he had vainly tried to cross, Mitchell, on the 9th of January, 1832, came to the river Gwydir of Cunningham. Turning to the westward the party followed this river down for eighty miles, when he again returned to his northern course, and came to the largest river he had yet found. This was called, by the natives, the Karaula, and Mitchell descended it until convinced, by its southern course and the junction of the Gwydir, that he was on the upper part of Sturt's Darling.

As the junction of the Namoi could not be far distant, Mitchell had thus laid down the course and direction of these two large rivers, although he had as yet seen nothing of the object of his search, the Kindur.

He now prepared to move once more to the north, anxious to find a river that did not belong to the Darling system. As, however, he was on the point of starting, he was overtaken by his assistant-surveyor, Finch, who was bringing on additional supplies, with the disastrous news that the blacks had attacked his camp during a temporary absence, murdered the two men, robbed the supplies, and dispersed the cattle. This misfortune put a stop to the progress of the party. They returned, and having buried the bodies of the victims, but failed to find the murderers, made their way back to the settled districts.

This journey of Major Mitchell's helped greatly to work out the courses of the rivers crossed by Oxley, and more especially those discovered by Cunningham during his trip to the Darling Downs. Mitchell travelled, as it were, a more inland but parallel track, crossing the rivers much lower down. Thus the Field River of Oxley is the Namoi of Mitchell, Cunningham's Gwydir is recognised by the Surveyor-General, and is probably the mythical Kindur or Keinder, whilst the last found river, Mitchell's Karaula, is formed by the junction of Cunningham's Dumaresque and Condamine.

When we add to this the discovery of the Drummond Range, Mitchell's first contribution to Australian geography was sufficiently important.

This year, 1832, was marked by the murder of Captain Barker, already mentioned as in turn Commandant of Fort Wellington and King George's Sound. He was returning from the latter place, after handing over charge to Captain Stirling, and on his way home landed on the eastern shore of St. Vincent's Gulf, to see if the waters of Lake Alexandrina, the termination of the Murray, had an outlet in the Gulf. Being unsuccessful he crossed the range and paid a visit to the lake. Anxious to obtain some bearings, he swam across the channel connecting the lake with the sea in order to ascend the sandhills on the opposite side. His companions watched him take several bearings from the top of the hill, descend out of view on the other side, and he was never seen again. One of the sealers from Kangaroo Island interrogated the blacks by means of a native woman of the island, who could speak broken English, and her account was that Barker met three natives as he descended the sand dune, who attacked and speared him, unarmed and naked as he was, and then cast his body in the breakers. These natives were of the same tribes that showed such determined hostility to Sturt when he first found the lake.

Although Sturt himself felt confident that the junction of the Murray and Darling were satisfactorily proved by what he saw on his famous boat excursion, he had not convinced all of the public. Major Mitchell, for one, had an entirely different theory on the subject embracing the existence of a. dividing range between the Macquarie and Lachlan rivers which would entirely preclude the Darling and Murray from joining. Time, however, proved that Sturt's instinct had not been at fault when on reaching the junction of the two rivers in his whale-boat, he felt convinced that he there saw the outflow of his old friend, the Darling.

It must be remembered that the explorations conducted by Major Mitchell were also surveys, superintended by him as Surveyor-General, which will partly explain the presence of the large body of men and equipage which it was his custom to take with him. The roll call of the members of one of his expeditions reads like that of an invading army. [See Appendix.]

In order to get some additional information concerning the elevated country that Oxley had noticed to the westward between the Lachlan and the Macquarie (on which slight foundation Major Mitchell had built his theory of the two rivers running through distinctly different basins), Mr. Dixon was sent out in 1833. This gentleman, however, for some reason did not adhere to his instructions; he followed down the Macquarie for some distance and crossed to the Bogan (Sturt's New Year's Creek), then running strong, and having followed that river for sixty-seven miles, returned to Bathurst; nothing new nor important came of this expedition.

In March, 1833, the party formed under the superintendence of the Surveyor-General left Parramatta to travel by easy stages to Buree, where they were to be overtaken by their leader. The list of the members is a long one. We who live in the days of well-equipped small parties, composed of reliable, experienced men only, would feel considerably handicapped with such a retinue. In addition to Major Mitchell, Richard Cunningham, botanist (brother to Allan Cunningham), and Mr. Larmer, assistant surveyor, there were twenty-one men; carpenters, bullock drivers, blacksmith, shoemaker, &c.

While still on the outskirts of settlement, an unhappy fate overtook Cunningham, the botanist. Leaving the party, doubtless on some scientific quest, during the morning of the 17th of April, whilst they were pushing over a dry stage to the Bogan River, he lost his way, and was never seen again.

A long and painful search was immediately instituted for the missing man, but unfortunately, through some accident, his tracks were overlooked on the third day, and it was not until the 23rd of the month that the footsteps were found. Mr. Larmer and three men were sent with an ample supply of provisions to follow the tracks until they found Cunningham, alive or dead. Three days later they returned, having found the horse he had ridden, dead, with the saddle and bridle still on. Mitchell returned to the search once more; the lost man's trail was again picked up, and he was tracked to the Bogan River. They there met with some blacks who had seen the white man's track in the bed of the river, and made the searchers understand that he had gone to the west with the "Myall" [Wild blacks who had not visited the settlements.] blackfellows.

All hope of finding him alive was now almost abandoned, but the pursuit was continued until May 5th, when the men brought back tidings that they had followed his tracks to where it disappeared near some recent fires where many natives had been encamped. Close to one of these fires they found a portion of the skirt or selvage of Cunningham's coat, numerous small fragments of his map of the colony, and, in the hollow of a tree, some yellow printed paper in which he used to carry the map. His fate was afterwards ascertained from the blacks. [See Appendix.]

As is unfortunately so usual in these cases, Cunningham had, by wandering in eccentric and contradictory courses, accelerated his fate, by rendering the work of the tracking party so much more tedious and difficult. Had he, on finding how absolutely he was astray, remained at the first water he reached, he would have been found.

Having done all that man could do to find his lost friend, and even jeopardised the final success of his own expedition by the long delay of fourteen days, Mitchell resumed his journey by easy stages down the Bogan, and on the 25th of May reached the Darling, which was at once recognised by all the former members of the party as the "Karaula," from the peculiar attributes that characterised it. On tasting the water, they were agreeably surprised to find it fresh and sweet. The state of the country now was very different from what it was when Sturt was forced to retreat. With that explorer's graphic account of the barren solitude that he met with, fresh in the reader's memory, let him contrast it with what Mitchell writes, remembering that one was encamped beside a salt stream, and the latter writer beside a fresh water river.

"We were extremely fortunate, however, in the place to which the bounteous hand of Providence had led us. Abundance of pasture, indeed such excellent grass as we had not seen in the whole journey, covered the fine forest ground on the bank of the river. There were four kinds, but the cattle appeared to relish most a strong species of *authistiria*, or kangaroo grass."

Finding the place eligible in every respect for the formation of a depôt, a stockade of logs was erected and the encampment christened Fort Bourke.

The boats were launched, but the navigation of the river was found to be impeded by shallow rapids, so the party returned to Fort Bourke, and Mitchell with four men made an excursion down the river to the point where Sturt and Hume turned back. D'Urbans group was also 'Visited, and bearings taken to whatever elevations were in sight. On returning to the depôt the camp was broken up and the whole party started down the Darling (the Calla-watta of the natives) on the 8th June. During their progress they found the tree marked H. H. by Hume, at Sturt's limit, and they now noticed that in places the river water was salt or brackish. On the 11th of July, after following the course of the river for three hundred miles, and ascertaining beyond all doubt that it must be identical with the junction in the Murray, noticed by Captain Sturt, Mitchell determined to return; the unvarying same-ness of the country they had travelled over holding forth no hope of any important discovery being made, in the space intervening between their lowest camp and Sturt's junction. The natives, too, had been an incessant cause of annoyance to them; robbing the camp at every op-portunity, and keeping the leader in constant anxiety for the safety of any of the members of his party, whom duty compelled to leave the main body. On the very day, almost at the very hour, when Mitchell made up his mind to return, the first hostile collision between the two races occurred; a collision which had only been hitherto averted by the admirable patience of the Major and his men. On the 29th June, he wrote:--

"I never saw such unfavourable specimens of the aborigines as these children of the smoke, [Referring to their constant habit of burning the grass.] they were so barbarously and implacably hostile, and shame-lessly dishonest, and so little influenced by reason that the more they saw of our superior weapons and means of defence, the more they showed their hatred and tokens of defiance."

On the morning of this day, when he had settled in his own mind the futility of further progress, two of the men were away at the river, and five of the the bullock drivers were also at another bend, collecting their cattle. One of the blacks whom they had nick-named King Peter tried to snatch the kettle of water from the hand of the man who was carrying it; and on being resisted he struck him senseless with his nulla-nulla. The companion of the wounded man shot King Peter in the groin, and his majesty tumbled into the river and swam across. The tribe now advanced against them, and two shots were fired in self defence, one of which accidentally wounded a gin. Three men from the camp hearing the firing came up, and one more native was shot, who was preparing to spear one of the men. The natives retreating, the men went in search of the bullock-drivers, whom they found endeavouring to raise a bogged bullock: their timely arrival probably saved these men's lives, as they were unarmed and unprepared.

War being thus declared, a careful watch was kept up, but no attack was made, and the explorers departed unmolested.

In speaking of this skirmish, Mitchell, seemingly worked up to a sentimental pitch by hearing some gins crying out across the river in the night time, says:--

"It was then that I regretted most bitterly the inconsiderate conduct of some of the men. I was indeed liable to pay dear for geographical discovery, when my honour and character were delivered over to convicts, on whom, although I might confide as to courage, I could not always rely for humanity."

By his own account, as given above, the affray was provoked by the blacks, who compelled the men to use their weapons to save their own lives; the reflections then, on their humanity, and the danger in which his character stood in consequence, are slightly out of place.

The travellers now retraced their steps, and beyond the delays caused by some of the bullocks knocking up, their return journey to Fort Bourke was unmarked by anything of interest. From Fort Bourke they returned, partly along their outward track, to the head of the Bogan, and reached a newly-formed cattle station belonging to Mr. Lee, of Bathurst, on the 9th of September.

The great fact added to the geographical knowledge of Australia by the successful termination of this trip, was the identity of the Darling with the Karaula on the north, and with Sturt's Murray junction on the south. It was now satisfactorily settled that this river was the channel that received all the tributary streams flowing westward-- so far north, at any rate, as Cunningham's researches had extended, and that therefore their final outlet was in Lake Alexandrina, and the idea of a river winding through the interior to the north-west coast had to be finally relinquished.

This journey of Mitchell's was also instrumental in somewhat palliating the view held of the uninhabitable nature of the far interior; although the true character of the country had yet to be learnt and appreciated. His stay on the banks of the Darling at least lifted from those plains the stigma of a grassless, naked waste, intersected by a river of brine.

Mitchell, too, was a keen observer of the habits and customs of the blacks, he was remarkably quick at detecting tribal differences and distinctions, and his record of his intercourse with them, which occupies so large a portion of his journals, was interesting then, when so little had been written on the subject, and is interesting now as the account of the white man's first incursions into the hunting ground of a fast vanishing race.

Mitchell's next expedition took place in 1836, in the month of March. As before, it was to be more of a connecting survey, confirming and verifying previous discoveries, than a fresh departure into an utterly new region; but it turned out to be productive of the most important results.

The Surveyor-General was informed that the survey of the Darling was to be completed with the least possible delay, that having returned to the point where his last journey terminated, he was to trace the Darling into the Murray, and crossing his party over that river by means of his boats, follow it up, and regain the colony somewhere at Yass Plains. This programme was, however, departed from in many ways.

The new ground broken by Mitchell would thus be the Murray River above the junction with the Morumbidgee or Murrumbidgee, as it was now called, and it was supposed that he would be able to identify it with the Hume River of the explorer of that name.

A long continued drought was in full force when Mitchell commenced his preparations; horses and bullocks in good condition were in consequence hard to obtain; but no expense was spared by the Government in providing the animals required. On reaching Bathurst, he was informed that even the Lachlan was dry.

In spite of the state of the weather and country, Major Mitchell departed in high spirits. He writes:--

"I remembered that exactly that morning, twenty-four years before, I had marched down the glacis of Elvas to the tune of 'St. Patrick's Day in the Morning,' as the sun rose over the beleagured towers of Badajoz. Now, without any of the 'pride, pomp, and circumstances of glorious war,' I was proceeding on a service not very likely to be peaceful, for the natives here assured me that the myalls were coming up 'murry coola' [Very angry.] to meet us."

On March 17th, 1836, this start took place, but it was not until the end of the month that he reached the limit of the cattle stations, and then he was at the point where Oxley had left the river and turned south to avoid the flooded marshes. Oxley wrote of a country that no living thing would stop in if it could possibly get away; twenty years afterwards, Mitchell writes of the same place:--

"In no district have I seen cattle so numerous as all along the Lachlan, and, notwithstanding the very dry season, they are nearly all in good condition."

As might have been expected, he followed down the Lachlan riding dry-shod over the swamps and flats that had barred Oxley's progress, and finding his lakes only green and grassy plains. Such had been the effect of the exceptional season during which the late Surveyor-General had conducted his explorations, that the country, save for the few land-marks afforded by the hills here and there, could scarcely be recognised from his description. Mitchell seems to have been strongly imbued with two leading ideas, one being the existence of well-defined mountain chains in the interior, forming systematic watersheds in a country where we now know there is no system; the other that former explorers, however reliable they might have been in their main facts, were quite at sea in any deductions they had drawn from them, and that his theories would be confirmed to their discomfiture.

The Surveyor-General had with him as second on this trip, Mr. Stapylton, a surveyor, and his company consisted of Burnett, the overseer, and twenty-two men, some of whom had been with him before.

For some reason or other he seemed particularly anxious to upset Sturt's positive belief that the junction of the large river with the Murray discovered by him, was the confluence of the Darling and the Murray. During his journey down the Lachlan he returns to this idea again, and his remarks are decidedly inconsistent with his former statements. On turning back from following the Darling down, his words were:--

"The identity of this river with that which had been seen to enter the Murray, now admitted of little doubt, and the continuation of the survey to that point was scarcely an object worth the peril likely to attend it."

On the Lachlan, he writes:--

"I considered it necessary now to ascertain, if possible, and before the heavy part of our equipment moved further, whether the Lachlan actually joined the Murrumbidgee near the point where Mr. Oxley saw its waters covering the country, or whether it pursued a course so much more to the westward, as to have been taken for the

Darling by Captain Sturt. Should I succeed in reaching the Lachlan at about sixty miles west of my camp, I might be satisfied that it was this river which Captain Sturt mistook for the Darling, and then I might seek that river by crossing the range on the north. Whereas, should I find sufficient reason to believe that the Darling would join the Murray, I might continue my journey down the Lachlan until I reduced the distance across to the Darling as much as the scarcity of water might render necessary."

On the whole, then, Mitchell did not seem inclined to give Sturt any credit for his discovery, until he had actually seen the two rivers unite, and there could no longer be any room for doubt on the subject.

A long excursion to the westward for some days, resulted in nothing but thirsty nights, and having finally to turn back from country bounded only by an unbroken horizon. The descent of the Lachlan was continued, and on May 5th, they reached Oxley's lowest point on the river, where he had given up the quest as hopeless amid the shallow, stagnant lagoons that then covered the face of the country. The tree marked by Oxley himself was not found, it having been, as was ascertained, burnt down by the blacks, and the bottle buried by him, broken by a child. Two trees were seen marked respectively W.W. and I.W., 1817. This was the place where Oxley left the river the second time, after his fruitless trip to the south, and from here he struck across to the Macquarie.

Through level plains and by the beds of erstwhile lakes, the course of the river continued, and as the party proceeded they found it abundantly watered. From his intercourse with the native inhabitants, Mitchell was now convinced that the Lachlan or Kalare would soon join the Murrumbidgee, so that when on the 12th May he suddenly found himself on the banks of a river that he thought surpassed all the Australian rivers he had yet seen, he was not surprised.

Soon afterwards, as the Major was anxious not to encumber himself with all his heavy waggons to the junction of the Darling, as he would have to return again, a depôt was formed, and the men divided. Mitchell, with a lightly equipped party following down the river, leaving Stapylton in charge of the camp.

In a short time the advance party came to the Murray, and immediately found themselves amongst their former enemies of the Darling, who hearing of their approach, through the medium of other tribes, had come a distance of over two hundred miles to settle the old score between them. At first a kind of hollow truce was maintained, but this evidently could not last long; for two days the natives followed the explorers, seeking to cut off any stragglers; making the work of gathering and minding the cattle and horses one of considerable danger.

At last Mitchell was convinced that he must read them a lesson, or lose some of his men, and have to fight his way back, with the whole country roused. Half the party were then sent back, under the overseer, to conceal themselves in the scrub and allow the natives to pass on in pursuit of the tracks; this ambuscade, however, was scented out by the dogs accompanying the blacks, and the natives halted, poising their spears. One of the men hastily fired, and a retreat was made for the bank of the river by the blacks. The scrub party followed them up firing, and no sooner did those in advance hear the sound of the shots, than they rushed down to join in the fray, leaving the black boy's gin the sole protector of the drays, and equipment. On his return, the Major found her standing erect at the head of the leading horse, with a drawn sword over her shoulder.

Her appearance was, above all, both laughable and interesting. She was a tall, gaunt woman, with one disfigured eye, and her attitude, as she stood there with the naked weapon in her hand, faithful guard of all their belongings, was a picture that Mitchell did not soon forget.

The fight was soon over; in a very short space of time the over-confident warriors of the interior were driven ignominiously across the river with the loss of seven braves. This, after invading the territory of a friendly tribe in order to provoke a battle with the whites, and boasting that formerly they had driven them back from the Darling, was a blow that they could not get over, and the result was that the whites were not again molested. It turned out that this pugnacious tribe was the same that threatened Sturt at the Darling junction, when the energetic interference of one man was so effectual. This remarkable savage, it seems, was dead and his influence lost.

On the 31st May, Mitchell struck the Darling some distance above the junction, and traced its course upwards a short way, until he again felt convinced that it was the same river that he had been on before, He returned and examined the junction, which he says he recognised from the view given in Captain Sturt's work [Note, end of paragraph] and the adjacent localities described by him. Full of anxiety for the safety of his depôt, and considering that he had done enough to verify the outflow of the Darling, he at once started up the Murray, and was happily relieved by finding his camp in perfect quiet and safety.

[Note Captain Sturt, writing in 1848, and speaking of Major Mitchell's expedition, says:--"In due time he came to the disputed junction, which he tells us he recognised from its resemblance to a drawing of it in my first work. As I have since been on the spot, I am sorry to say that it is not at all like the place, because it obliges me to reject the only praise Sir Thomas Mitchell ever gave me." The original sketch of the junction having been lost, Sturt, who was nearly blind at the time of the publication of his work, got the assistance of a friend, who drew it from his verbal description.]

First fixing the junction of the Murray and Murrumbidgee, the boats were launched, and the whole of the party crossed the Murray, and the journey up the southern bank commenced. On the 20th of June, they reached Swan Hill and camped at the foot of it. The country was in every way desirable, and the progress of the party was unchecked. On the 8th of July, the Loddon was discovered and named, and on the 10th, the Avoca. Mitchell was now convinced that he had found the Eden of Australia, and his enthusiasm in describing it is unbounded. On the 18th of July, he discovered the Wimmera, and on the 31st, the Glenelg. Here he launched his boat once more, but found his way stopped at the outset by a fall, and the river had to be followed on land. On the 18th of August, after many excursions, the river being now much broader, the boats were again resorted to, and in two days they reached the coast a little to the east of Cape Northumberland.

Returning to the camp, the expedition made east, and reached Portland Bay, where they found a farm established by the Messrs. Henty, who had been there then nearly two years. Here they obtained some small supplies, and again left on their homeward journey. On the 4th September Mitchell abandoned one of his boats, in order to lighten his equipage, as the draught work was excessively heavy for his cattle, and one boat would answer the purpose of crossing rivers. On the 10th, he caught sight of a range, and named it the Australian Pyrenees, and on the 19th the party separated.

The Major and some of the men pushed on with the freshest of the animals, leaving Stapylton and the remainder of the party to spell for a while, and bring the knocked-up beasts slowly on.

On the 30th, Mitchell ascended Mount Macedon, and from the top recognised Port Phillip.

"No stockyards nor cattle were visible, nor even smoke, although at the highest northern point of the bay I saw a mass of white objects. which might have been either tents or vessels."

But Mitchell was not to arrive home without another fatality amongst his party. On October 13th, when looking for a crossing in a river, one of the men, named James Taylor, was drowned.

On the 17th, after passing through a forest, they recognised with great satisfaction, the lofty "Yarra" trees, and the low verdant alluvial flats of the Murray. Once across the river, the boat was sunk in a deep lagoon, and the boat carriage left on the bank for the use of Stapylton. Three volunteers went back to meet him, and assist in crossing the Ovens and Goulburn. The advance party were now almost within the settled districts, and with the safe arrival of Stapylton at the Murrumbidgee, on November 11th, the history of the discovery of Australia Felix ends.

Sir Thomas Mitchell had been singularly favoured during this journey, his route had led him through a country possessing every variety of feature, from snow-topped mountains to level plains, watered by permanently-flowing stream and rivers; fitted, as he says, for the immediate occupation of the grazier, and the farmer. It, therefore, was of more real benefit to the colony than the former exploratory journeys, that had met with only partial success in this respect.

He had well carried out his instructions, and obtained a full knowledge of the country south of the Murray, and of the rivers there; flowing either into that river, or into the sea; confirming the impression already entertained of the great value of the district, and the report of Hume and Hovell, who with their slender resources were unable to do much in the way of extended examination.

We have seen that the brothers Henty, of Tasmania, had formed a settlement at Portland Bay, and in 1835 the historic founding of Port Phillip settlement by Batman took place, so that the mere extension of settlement would soon have thrown open for settlement the splendid area that Mitchell was just in time to claim as his discovery. The story of Batman's compact with the blacks, by which he asserted his right to a princely territory is too well-known to require repetition; [Note, end of paragraph] it is scarcely necessary to add that such a preposterous demand was neither ratified by the government, nor recognised by the settlers.

[Note: The agreement was between Messrs. Batman, Gellibrand, Swanston, and Simpson, on the one side, and the natives were represented by Jagajaga, Cooloolook, Bungaree, Yanyan, Mowstrip, and Mommamala, the price was fixed at an annuity of two hundred a year, in return for 750,000 acres of land. Mr. Gellibrand afterwards perished in the bush with a companion, Mr. Hesse, having lost himself through persisting in keeping in the wrong direction, although warned by a guide who left them on finding Gellibrand determined to go wrong.]

It was through the energy of the Tasmanian colonists that this settlement of Port Phillip took place; as already noticed, Port Phillip was abandoned, almost without the slightest examination, by Colonel Collins in favour of Tasmania, and now, after thirty years had passed, the abundant flocks and herds of the little island forced the owners to look to the mainland for extended pastures.

One of the incidents of the early settlement was also the discovery of Buckley, a white man, who having escaped from Collins' party in 1803, had been living with the natives ever since.

In 1836 Colonel Light surveyed the shores of St. Vincent's Gulf, and selected the site of the present city of Adelaide; Governor Hindmarsh and a company of emigrants soon after arrived, and the colony of South Australia was proclaimed.

The continent was now being invaded on three sides. From Perth on the western shore, from St. Vincent's Gulf and Port Phillip on the south, and from the settled districts of New South Wales and from Moreton Bay on the east.

Henceforth, the tale of exploration embraces many simultaneous expeditions; no longer is the whole of the narrative confined to the struggle of one man, hopelessly endeavouring to surmount the coast range, or toiling across the western plains, anxiously watched by the little community at Port Jackson. Each new-formed centre had their members pushing out, month after month, and continually adding to the knowledge of Australia.

As usual, the records of most of these private expeditions have not been preserved, and the utmost the historian can do is to trace out the broad lines of discovery, leaving the reader to consider the detail filled in by the monotonous, if valuable, and untiring efforts of the pioneer squatters. Already these men and their subordinates were close on the footsteps of the explorers; should the adventurer remain some months absent from civilization, he found, on his return, settlement far across what had been the frontier line when he departed. Hundreds of lives have been laid down in this service, under as strong a sense of duty, and under circumstances as heroic as any of the deaths in the roll of martial history, and the names of the victims unknown, and their graves unhonoured. They have only been members of the great band ever forcing a way, and smoothing a road for a commercial population, to whom their deeds, their struggles, their hopes, and their fates are often but a sealed book. But the feelings of a man who knows that he has founded homes for future thousands, must be a greater recompense than any his fellowmen could give him.

Chapter V

Lieutenants Grey and Lushington on the West Coast--Narrow escape--Start with an equipment of Timor ponies--Grey wounded by the natives--Cave drawings--Return, having discovered the Glenelg--Grey's second expedition--Landed at Bernier Island, in Shark's Bay, with three whale-boats--Cross to borne Island--Violent storm--Discovery of the Gascoyne--Return to Bernier Island--Find their caché of provisions destroyed by a hurricane--Hopeless position--Attempted landing at Gautheaume Bay--Destruction of the boats--Walk to Perth--Great sufferings--Death of Smith--Eyre and the overlanders--Discovery of Lake Hindmarsh--Exploration of Gippsland--Eyre's explorations to the north--Discovery of Lake Torrens--Disappointment in the country bordering on it--Determines to go to King George's Sound--Repeated attempts to reach the head of the Great Australian Bight--Loss of horses--Barren and scrubby country--Final determination to send back most of the party-- Starts with overseer and three natives--Hardship and suffering--Murder of the overseer by two of the natives--Eyre continues his journey with the remaining boy--Relieved by the Mississippi whaler--Reaches King George's Sound.

An expedition, most unique in its composition, now made an attempt on the west coast to penetrate inland, and also verify the existence or non-existence of the large river, still currently supposed to find its way into the sea at Dampier's Archipelago. The expedition was placed under the command of Lieutenant Grey, Mr. Lushington acting as second in command. It originated in England, and its members, with one exception, were what would locally be called "new chums." The one exception was a sailor, named Ruston, who had been with Captain King on one of his surveying voyages; an experience that, under an older leader might have made him a most serviceable man, but, otherwise, scarcely deserved the stress that Grey laid upon his acquisition. Most of the equipment was procured at the Cape of Good Hope, where a small vessel--the Lynher--was chartered, and the landing-place in Australia was at Hanover Bay, on the extreme north-west coast, near the mouth of the Prince Regent's River; though, why this particular point was chosen, does not appear quite clear. Being becalmed a short distance from Hanover Bay, the foolish impetuosity of the young explorers very nearly put an abrupt ending to their journey. Grey, Lushington, and four men landed, and started to walk across to Hanover Bay, there to be picked up again by the Lynher. It was December, the middle of a tropical summer, and they took with them two pints of water. They all very soon knocked up. Grey swam across an inlet to try and signal the schooner, and nearly lost his life doing so. Fortunately, the the flashes of their guns, with which they kept firing distress signals, were noticed on board, and a boat came to their rescue. This was an inauspicious beginning.

After landing the stores, the Lynher sailed for Timor, to procure some ponies and other live stock, and on the 17th of January, 1838, she returned. At the end of January, Grey and his party started from the coast with twenty-six half-broken Timor ponies as a baggage train, and some sheep and goats. The rainy season had set in, and the stock began to die almost before they had well started, added to which, the party were entangled in steep ravines and spurs from the coast range, and their strength worn out in useless ascents and descents. On the 11th of February, they came into collision with the natives, and Grey was severely wounded.

On the leader recovering sufficiently to be lifted on one of the ponies, a fresh start was made, and on the 2nd of March they were rewarded by finding a river, which they called the Glenelg, unaware that Mitchell had already usurped the name. The adventurers followed the course of this river upward, traversing good country, well grassed and timbered, so far as their limited experience allowed them to judge. Sometimes their route was on the river's bank, and at other times by keeping to the foot of a sandstone range that ran parallel with its course, they were enabled to cut off some wearisome bends.

The party continued on the Glenelg for many days until they were checked by a large tributary coming from the north, causing them to fall back on the range, both the river and its tributary being swollen and flooded. On this range they discovered some curious paintings and drawings in the caves scattered amongst the rocks, also a head in profile cut in the face of a sandstone rock. [See Appendix.] Unable to find a pass through the mountains, which barred their western progress, and greatly weakened by his wound, Grey determined to return, but before doing so he sent Mr. Lushington some distance ahead, who, however, could find no noticeable change in the country.

The expedition, therefore retraced their footsteps, and on the 15th of April they reached Hanover Bay, and found the schooner at anchor, and H.M.S. Beagle lying in the neighbouring Port George the Fourth. Thus ended the first expedition; toil, danger, and hardships having been incurred for little or no purpose, the discovery of the Glenelg River being the only result obtained, and perhaps, some little experience. The party having embarked, they sailed for the Isle of France in the Mauritius, where they safely arrived.

In August, Grey visited the Swan River, and endeavoured to get assistance from Sir James Stirling, the Governor, to continue his explorations; no vessel being available, he had to wait some time before making a start, during which delay he made short excursions from Perth into the surrounding country.

On the 17th of February, 1839, he started once more in an American whaler, taking with him three whale-boats. The objects of this expedition are not very definite. The whaler was to land them and their boats at Shark's Bay, or on one of the islands: there they intended to form a depôt. After examining the bay, and making such incursions inland as they found possible, they were to extend their operations to the north as long as their provisions lasted, when they would return to the depôt and make their way south.

The party consisted of Grey himself, four of his former companions, a young volunteer, Mr. Frederick Smith, five other men, and a native, twelve in all. They were landed on Bernier Island, and at once their troubles commenced. The whaler sailed away taking with her, by an oversight, their whole supply of tobacco; there was no water on the island, and on the first attempt to start one of the boats was smashed up and nearly half a ton of stores lost. The next day they landed at Dorre Island, and that night both their boats were driven ashore by a violent storm.

Two or three days were occupied repairing damages, and then they made the mainland and obtained a supply of fresh water.

They landed near the mouth of a river, which, however, was dry above tidal influence, and Grey christened it the Gascoyne. After a short examination of the surrounding country, they pulled up the coast to the north, and effecting a landing one night, both boats were swamped, to the great damage of their already spoiled provisions. Here Grey ascended a hill to look upon the surrounding country, and was so deceived by the mirage, that he believed he had discovered a great lake studded with islands; in company with three of his men he started on a weary tramp after the constantly shifting vision, needless to say without reaching it. Returning to the boats they found themselves prisoners for a time, until the wind dropped and the surf abated a little, and here they had to remain for a week sick, hungry and weary, and at one time threatened and attacked by the blacks. At last a slight cessation in the gale tempted them, and they got the boats out and made for the mouth of the Gascoyne, where they refilled their water breakers. On March 20th, they made an effort to fetch their depôt on Bernier Island in the teeth of the foul weather, and reached it to find that during their absence a hurricane had swept the island, and their hoarded stores were scattered to the winds.

Their position was now nearly desperate, the southerly winds had set in, they had a surf-beaten shore to coast along, and no food of any sort worth mentioning, added to which, as may be well supposed, they were all weak and exhausted.

There was nothing for it, however, but to put out to sea again, and they managed to reach Gautheaume Bay on the 31st of March; in attempting a landing, the boat Grey was in was dashed on a rock, and the other boat too received such great damage that it was impossible to repair either of them. Nothing was now left, but to walk to Perth, and so wearied had the men become of fighting with the wind and sea, that they even welcomed this hazardous prospect as a change. They were about three hundred miles from the Swan River and had twenty pounds of damaged flour, and one pound of salt pork per man, to carry them there.

Soon after starting, a diversity of opinion sprang up about the best mode of progressing. Grey wished to get over as much ground as possible while their strength held out; most of the men, however, were in favour of proceeding slowly, taking constant rests. This feeling increased so much that, when within two hundred miles of Perth, Grey found it necessary to take with him some picked men, and push on, leaving the others to follow at their leisure. He reached Perth after terrible suffering and privation, and a relief party was at once sent out, but they only found one man, who had left the others, thinking they were travelling too slow. Meanwhile, Walker, the second in charge, had come into Perth, and related that, being the strongest, he had pushed on in order to get relief sent back to the remainder. Another party, under Surveyor-General Roe, left in search, and after some trouble in tracking the erratic wanderings of the unfortunates, came upon them hopelessly gazing at a point of rocks, that stopped their march along the beach, not having sufficient strength left to climb it. They had been then three days without any water but sea water, and a revolting substitute, which they still had in their canteens. Poor young Smith, a lad of eighteen was dead. [See Appendix.] He had lain down and died two days before they were found. He was buried in the wilderness.

During these two expeditions Grey had faced death in every shape, and shown great powers of endurance, but the results of all his toil were but meagre, and of no very great importance. He had crossed and named the rivers running into the west coast, between where he abandoned his boats and the Moore River, but in the state he was in he knew little more than the fact that they were there, having neither strength nor resources to follow them up and determine their courses. Grey claims the discovery of the Gascoyne, Murchison, Hutt, Bower, Buller, Chapman, Greenough, Irwin, Arrowsmith, and Smith Rivers. This disastrous journey may be said to have concluded his services to Australia as an explorer, although he afterwards, when Governor of South Australia, made an excursion to the south-east, but it was through comparatively stocked and well-known country in the neighbourhood of the Glenelg and Mount Gambier. Before being appointed Governor of South Australia, he was Acting Government Resident at Albany, King George's Sound.

Grey's mishaps, and the straits to which he reduced his party by his occasional want of forethought and precaution, show plainly that enthusiasm, courage, and a generous spirit of self-sacrifice are not the only requisites in an explorer, more important even, being the long training and teaching of experience.

Grey had given a very glowing description of the fertile appearance of a portion of the country he passed through, and some of the colonists were eager to make use of such a promising district. The schooner Champion was therefore directed to examine the coast and see if any of the rivers had navigable entrances. Mr. Moore, after whom the Moore River was named, was on board of the vessel, but no entrance was effected, although the party rather confirmed Grey's report. Captain Stokes, of the Beagle, however, soon after made a thorough examination of this part of the coast, and his report was so unfavourable that its immediate settlement was postponed.

It follows now, that the unexplored country west of the Darling being so much sooner reached from Adelaide than from Sydney, the former town became the point of departure from which, in future, the expeditions for the interior started.

But the rush for country, and the constant influx of stock from the mother colony, led to a series of petty explorations being continually carried on throughout the rapidly-rising district south and east of the Murray. Some of these were undertaken in quest of new runs, others in order to find the best and shortest stock routes; and the record of most of them is only preserved in the memoirs Of personal friends of the pioneers.

Edward John Eyre, who afterwards made the celebrated journey to Western Australia round the head of the Great Bight, began his bush experiences in this way. Messrs. Hawdon, Gardiner and Bonney, also about the same time, made various trips from New South Wales to Port Phillip, and from thence to Adelaide, and many minor discoveries were the result of those journeys. The he outflow and courses of rivers being determined, and the speculations of their first discoveries corrected or confirmed; as instance of this, may be mentioned the discovery of Lake Hindmarsh, which receives the Wimmera, River, the course of which had puzzled Mitchell when he discovered it in July, 1836.

Eyre left Port Phillip for Adelaide early in 1838. The usual course had been to strike to the Murray, and then to follow that river down. He intended to try a straighter route, and for a time did well; but, at last, finding himself in a tract of dry country, across which he could not take the cattle with safety, he determined to follow the Wimmera north, thinking it would take him on to the banks of the Murray, and would probably turn out to be the Lindsay junction of Sturt. From Mitchell's furthest point he traced it some considerable distance to the north-west, and at last found its termination in a large swampy lake, which he named Lake Hindmarsh, after the first Governor of South Australia. From this lake he found no outlet; so, leaving his cattle, and taking with him two men, he made an effort to reach the Murray. But the country was covered with an almost impenetrable scrub, and as there was neither grass nor water for the horses, he was forced to turn back, reaching his camp only after a weary tramp on foot, the horses having died. According to Eyre's chart, they were within five and twenty miles of the Murray when they turned back. Eyre was thus forced to retrace his steps and make for the nearest available route to the Murray, and follow that river down.

Bonney's trip from Portland Bay to Adelaide was about a year subsequently. He pursued a more southerly and westerly course, and managed to get through in safety, but experienced great hardships on the way. One of a series of lakes or marshes was found, and named Lake Hawdon.

At the end of November, 1839, Colonel Gawler, then Governor of South Australia, made an excursion to the Murray, for the purpose of examining the country around Lake Victoria, and to the westward of the great bend. He was accompanied by Captain Sturt, then Surveyor-General of the province. In the S.A. Register of that date, the following paragraph shows that by this time ladies had also taken up the task of exploration:

"His Excellency the Governor, accompanied by Miss Gawler and Captain and Mrs. Sturt, left town on Friday last week on an excursion to the Murray and the interior to the north of that river. The party is expected to be absent several weeks."

It is to be presumed that Miss Gawler and Mrs. Sturt accompanied the party but a short distance; the Murray at that date affording anything but a safe camping ground. This trip, of course, did not extend sufficiently for any important geographical discoveries to be made, but it was unfortunately marked by one of the fatalities that are bound to be a feature of exploration. Leaving the river they penetrated into waterless country, and the horses knocked up. Colonel Gawler and Mr. Bryan pushed back on the freshest animals, intending to bring back water for the others, but on the way Bryan gave in, and the Governor had to go on alone. On coming back with relief Bryan was nowhere to be found, a note was pinned to his coat, which was lying on the spot where he had been left, stating that he had gone to the south-east, much exhausted; but although all search was made he was never found.

Meantime, we have lost sight entirely of the north coast, and the attempts at settlement in that quarter. The little Beagle had been working industriously up there; but the account of her voyage belongs to the history of maritime discovery, where it will be found; however, on this occasion she visited a newly-formed, or rather twice-formed, settlement, Port Essington. This station, after the visit by Captain Bremer, was, it will be remembered, abandoned. In 1838, its former founder, now Sir Gordon Bremer, resettled it, and the nucleus of a township was formed. This time it seemed, at first, more likely to thrive; but very little was done in the way of exploration, and its existence added nothing to our knowledge of the northern interior. From a letter of one of the officers of the Beagle we learn that:--

"A good substantial mole, overlooked by a small battery, with some respectable-sized houses in the rear, gives the settlement rather an imposing appearance from the water, which I imagine is the object at present aimed at--to make an impression on the visiting Malays, the success of the colony depending so much on them."

Apparently the dependence of the colony was misplaced as it is scarcely necessary to tell the reader that it has long since passed out of existence; we shall, however, have occasion to revisit it once before its final abandonment.

The time had now come for the completion of the work commenced by Hume and Hovell sixteen years before, namely, the full exploration of the south-east corner of Australia.

In 1840, McMillan, the manager of a station near the Snowy Mountains, the property of Messrs. Buckler and M'Allister, started on a search for country in company with two companions, Messrs. Cameron and Mathew, one stockman and a blackfellow. Making their way through the Snowy Mountains to the southward, they found a river running through fine grazing country, plains and forest, until its course brought them to a large lake; here they were forced to turn westward, and although they made several attempts to reach the coast they did not succeed, having continually to turn back to the range to ford the numerous rivers they kept coming to.

Having only a fortnight's provisions with them, they were forced to return, when within about fifty miles of Wilson's Promontory. This fine addition to the already known territory was called Gippsland, after Sir George Gipps, the Governor who had the disagreeable eccentricity of insisting that all the towns laid out during his term of office should have no public squares included in their boundaries, as he was convinced that public squares encouraged the spread of democracy.

The rivers discovered by McMillan were named by him, but afterwards re-named by Count Strzelecki, whose titles were retained, whilst the rightful ones bestowed by the real discoverer are forgotten.

Doubtless Strzelecki's names, such as the La Trobe, &c., had a ring more pleasing to the official ear.

The celebrated count followed hard on McMillan's footsteps, in fact, the latter met him before reaching home and directed him to the country he had just left. McMillan, having his own interests to serve, said little or nothing about the result of his journey, not wishing to be forestalled in the occupation of the country. Strzelecki, not being interested in squatting pursuits, made public the value of the province as soon as he returned, which has led to his being often erroneously considered the discoverer of Gippsland.

Strzelecki's trip through Gippsland, in 1840, was part of the work he was undertaking to gather materials for his now well-known book, "The Physical Description of New South Wales, Victoria, and Van Die-man's Land." He mounted the Alps, and named one of the highest peaks Kosciusko, from the fancied resemblance of its outline to the patriot's tomb at Cracow. He then pushed his way through to Western Port, crossing the fine rivers and rich country just found by McMillan. They had to abandon their horses and packs during the latter part of the journey, and fight their way through a dense scrub on a scanty ration of one biscuit and a slice of bacon per day. Here the count's exceeding hardihood stood them in good stead; so weakened were his companions that it was only by constant encouragement he got them along, and when forcing their way through the matted scrub, he often threw himself bodily on it, breaking a bath through for his weakened followers by the sheer weight of his body. They reached Western Port in a most wretched condition, having subsisted latterly on nothing but native bears.

In 1841, a Mr. Orr landed at Corner Inlet and traversed part of the country surveyed by Strzelecki; he traced the La Trobe and other rivers into a large lake fifty miles from Wilson's Promontory, and confirmed the glowing reports of the former travellers.

We have now to bid a final farewell to the garden of Australia, where the explorers' steps trod the alleys of shady forests of gigantic trees, or followed the bank of some living, sparkling stream, rippling and bubbling over its pebbly bed, amid verdant meadows and fertile valleys. No more was the outlook to be over smiling downs backed up by the fleecy-topped Alps, a scene that told of nothing but peace, prosperity, and all the riches of a bountiful soil. The way of the pioneer was, in future, to lead to the north, where the earth refused to afford him pasture for his animals, the clouds to drop rain, and the very trees gave no shade to protect him from the sun in its noontide wrath. Over the lonely plains of the interior, searching for the inland sea, never to be found; for the lofty mountain chain, the backbone of Australia, that had no existence.

On the 5th of August, 1839, E. J. Eyre, and a party consisting of an overseer, three men and two natives, left Port Lincoln, on the western shore of Spencer's Gulf, on an excursion to examine the country to the westward, as far as they could penetrate. Before this he had made an expedition to the north of Adelaide terminating at Mount Arden, an elevation to the N.N.E. of the head of Spencer's Gulf. From this mountain he saw a depression which he took to be the bed of a lake, covered with mud or sand, the future Lake Torrens.

On the 25th of August, after leaving Port Lincoln, he arrived at Streaky Bay, not having crossed a single stream or river, nor even a chain of ponds, during a distance of nearly three hundred miles. Three springs only had been found, and the country was covered with the dreaded eucalyptus dumosa scrub (mallee), and the melancholy ti-tree. It must be remembered, however, that Eyre's track bordered closely on the sea coast, and the country would, as is usual in Australia, be of a barren and inhospitable character. Westward of Streaky Bay the scrub still continued, so a depôt was formed, and taking only a black boy with him, he reached within about fifty miles of the western limit of South Australia. In appearance the country was more elevated, but there was neither water nor grass, and to return was necessary; in fact, before he got back to the depôt, he nearly lost three of his horses.

From Streaky Bay he went east, to the head of Spencer's Gulf, finding the country on his route a little better, but still devoid of water, the party only getting through by means of the rain which luckily fell at the time. On the 29th of September, he reached his old camp at Mount Arden. Here he writes:--

"It was evident that what I had taken on my last journey to be the bed of a dry lake now contained water, and was of a considerable size; but as my time was very limited, and the lake at a considerable distance, I had to forego my wish to visit it. I have, however, no doubt of its being salt, from the nature of the country, and the fact of finding the water very salt in one of the creeks draining into it from the hills. Beyond this lake (which I distinguished with the name of Colonel Torrens), to the westward, was a low, flat-topped range, extending northwesterly as far as I could see."

From here Eyre pursued his old track homeward.

The objects that now excited the attention of the colonists of South Australia were, discovery to the northward, as to the extent of the newfound lake, and the nature of the interior; and the possibility of the existence of a stock route to Western Australia. Eyre, however, after his recent experience, was convinced that the transit of stock round the head of the Great Bight was impracticable, the sterile nature of the country and the absence of watercourses being against it. Such a journey it was true might be most interesting, from a geographical point of view, showing the character of the country intervening between the two settlements, and unfolding the secrets hidden behind the lofty and singular cliffs at the head of the Great Bight, but for more immediate practical results, Eyre favoured the extension of discovery to the north. This was then the course adopted; subscriptions were raised, Eyre himself finding one-third of the horses and expenses, and the Government and colonists the remainder. Meantime, it turned out that the country in the immediate neighbourhood of Port Lincoln was not altogether of of the wretched character met with by Eyre between Streaky Bay and the head of the Gulf.

A Captain Hawson, in company with Mr. William Smith and three other gentlemen, made an excursion for a short distance, and found well-grassed country and abundance of water. Where they turned back they saw a fine valley with a running stream through the centre. This valley they named Rossitur Vale, and the stream the Mississippi, after Captain Rossitur, of the French whaler Mississippi--the first foreign ship in Port Lincoln, and the man who was afterwards destined to, afford such opportune aid and succour to Eyre.

Western Australia, however, did not seem to entertain the prospect of overland communication with Adelaide with any degree of enthusiasm. The Perth Gazette of that time, indulges in a short article, which reads ludicrously like an extract from the Eatanswill Gazette:--

"Overland from King George's Sound, we have received papers from Adelaide, the mail having been obligingly conveyed by Dr. Harris. In these papers we find the proposal to open a communication between this and South Australia. The object, further than a general exploration of the country, appears undefined; therefore, to us, it seems of little interest, and the steady course of the country should not be disturbed by such wild adventurers. What is South Australia to us? They have their self-supporting system, they have revelled in moonshine long enough; and we ought not to be such fools as to be caught by a mere puffing document appointing gentlemen here to co-operate with the South Australian committee. If we wish to see them, we can soon find our way, and we require no puffing advertisements from the neighbouring colony of high-minded pretensions. We will not be licked by the dog that has bitten us; and we must say that every honest mind should receive with caution any approaches from such a quarter. We put this forward advisedly, and with a desire that such a subject may be deliberately weighed and considered. Their flummery about the existence of a jealous feeling is discreditable to the minds inventing and prompting it for their own private ends."

Evidently the editor of the Perth paper had had a bad time of it, for further on we find him still more bitter against any communication being opened up with the sister colony. It must he remembered that Western Australia was a free colony, and consequently the bug-bear of convict contamination was one that was always raised when the subject of opening up a stock route with the older colonies was on the board.

On the 18th June, 1840, Eyre's preparations were ready, and he left Adelaide after a breakfast at Government House, when Captain Sturt presented him with a flag--the Union Jack--worked for the purpose by some of the ladies of the colony.

It is unnecessary to follow him in detail to his former camp at Mount Arden. He trusted that the range of hills he had called Flinders Range, and which he had seen stretching to the north-east, would continue far enough to take him out of the depressed country around Lake Torrens, and in fact, as he says, form a stepping-stone into the interior. His party was a small one for those days, consisting of six white men and two black boys. They had with them three horse drays, and a small vessel called the Waterwitch, was sent to the head of the Gulf, with the heaviest portion of their supplies.

On the arrival of this vessel, Eyre, with one black boy, made a short trip to Lake Torrens, leaving the rest of the party to land the stores.

He started without any great hopes, and, consequently, was not much disappointed when he found this outpost of the inland sea to be:--

" . . . the dry bed of a lake coated over with a crust of salt, forming one unbroken sheet of pure white, and glittering brilliantly in the sun. On stepping upon this I found that it yielded to the foot, and that below the surface the bed of the lake consisted of a soft mud, and the further we advanced to the westward the more boggy it got, so that at last it became quite impossible to proceed, and I was obliged to return to the outer margin of the lake without ascertaining whether there was water on the surface of its bed further west or not."

At this point Lake Torrens appeared to be about fifteen or twenty miles across, having high land bounding it to the west.

The prospect, although half expected, was dismal in the extreme. There was no chance of crossing the lake, and to follow its shore to the north was impossible on account of the absence of grass and water, the very rain water turning salt after lying a short time on the saline ground. The only chance was in Flinder's Range supplying them with a little feed and rain water in its ravines, so to this range he struck.

It was a cheerless outlook. On one side was an impracticable lake of combined mud and salt; in another a desert of bare and barren plains; and on a third, a range of inhospitable rocks.

"The very stones lying upon the hills looked like the scorched and withered scoria of a volcanic region, and even the natives, judging from the specimen I had seen to-day, partook of the general misery and wretchedness of the place."

Eyre steered for the most distant point of the northern range, which on arrival he christened Mount Deception, as he had hoped from its appearance that he would find water there, but in this he was deceived. Subsisting as best they could on rain puddles on the plains, they at last found a tolerably permanent hole in a small creek, and then returned to the party at the head of the Gulf.

Arrived at the depôt, the cutter returned to Adelaide with dispatches, and the provisions having been concealed, the whole party made for the pool of water that Eyre and the boy had discovered. From here the leader and the native boy made another fruitless trip to the north-west, and although they at times discovered a few creeks with a fair amount of water in them, the 2nd of September found Eyre on the top of a small hill, that he appropriately named Mount Hopeless, gazing at the mysterious lake that, as he thought, hemmed him in on three sides, even to the east. There was no prospect visible of getting across this bed of mud and mirage, nothing to do but leave the interior unvisited by this route, and return to the Mount Arden depôt.

From the Mount Arden depôt he made his way down to Port Lincoln, having finally decided to abandon his intended trip to the interior, and go westward to King George's Sound, finding, perhaps, some outlet to the north on the road.

He divided his party at the head of the Gulf, sending the overseer with most of the stores and men straight across to Streaky Bay, where he formerly bad made a depôt. At Port Lincoln he could not obtain the supplies he wanted without sending to Adelaide; so he was, therefore, detained some time, and on the 24th of October started for Streaky Bay, the Governor having placed the Waterwitch at his disposal for use in South Australian waters. At Streaky Bay he rejoined his overseer, who had got across the desert safely, and was anxiously expecting him. Making another rendezvous with the cutter at Fowler's Bay, they separated to meet again on the 20th of November.

Leaving his party encamped at Fowler's Bay, Eyre, with one native boy, made an attempt to round the Bight, or rather to ascertain what chance he had of taking his party round. He went two days' journey, and finding neither grass nor water for his horses, had to return to his camp. On the 28th he made another attempt, taking with him a dray carrying seventy gallons of water; and on the 30th they fell in with some natives, whom they thought to induce to guide them to water; but the blacks made them understand that there was none ahead, and so Eyre found to his cost, for, still trying to discover some he reduced his horses so that it was only with the greatest difficulty, and after the loss of three of the best of them, that the party struggled back to some sandhills, where they could obtain a little brackish water by digging; and on the 16th, having had to send back for assistance, the explorers reassembled at Fowler's Bay, having done no good, and lost three valuable horses. The cutter, still in attendance, was sent back to Adelaide for a supply of oats and bran, and also to take back two of the men, for Eyre had determined to reduce the number of his people, awed by the nature of the country he had met with ahead.

Tired out with the monotony of camp life, after the departure of the cutter, he decided on another attempt, although one would have thought the suffering his horses had already gone through would have induced him to give them a longer rest.

On the 30th December he left camp, and that evening reached the sandhills where he had before obtained the brackish water. Next morning they found some natives, who told them once again that there was no water ahead. On the 2nd January he made an attempt to the north-west, undeterred by these warnings, but only got fourteen miles when he had to send the horses back, and on the 5th, making another effort from this point, only got on another seven miles. Sending the dray and horses back, Eyre, with one white man and the black boy, went on, having buried some casks of water against their return. A terribly hot day set in, which so completely exhausted the whole party, that they had to encamp on the sea shore until night fell. The next morning he sent the man back, and pushing ahead came upon some natives digging in the sand, and with their aid watered the horses. They also showed them some more water further on, and accompanied them to it. Beyond this point, they said, there was no water for a ten days' journey.

Eyre rode on some distance, and having ascertained all he could of the nature of the country at the head of the Bight, which he had by this time passed, he returned to the party, and they all shifted back to the old depôt, at Fowler's Bay, on the 20th January.

On the 25th the Hero, cutter, arrived (the Waterwitch having sprung a leak), but her charter did not extend beyond the boundary of

South Australia, so that Eyre was unable to use her to carry his heavy stores any further.

Under the circumstances he resolved to send nearly the whole of his party back by the vessel, and push his way through to King George's Sound, or perish.

In arriving at this determination, Eyre was evidently actuated by a sense of such keen disappointment, at being baffled both to the north and the west, that he could not bear the thought of returning to Adelaide a beaten man. Whilst one can give a meed of admiration to the obstinate courage that characterised this resolution, we are also astonished at his persistence in a course that, whilst inevitably entailing the greatest possible suffering on men and horses, could lead to no good nor useful result. With his small party and equipment it would at best be only a struggle for life round the coast, giving no more information than had been acquired by the marine surveys. Even the wild attempts of Grey look comparatively reasonable beside this march of Eyre's, Had he had any object in view beyond the one of being the first white man to cross the desert between the two colonies, his actions might have been excusable, but as it was, his trip was bound to be profitless and resultless.

On the 31st January the cutter departed, and Eyre, the overseer, Baxter, and three native boys, one having come by the Hero, were left alone to face the eight hundred miles of desert solitude before them.

On the 24th, after a long spell, when they were about to start, the Hero returned, bringing a request to Mr. Eyre to abandon his mad attempt and embark himself and party on board the cutter. This he refused to do, and on the 25th made another departure. After passing the water where they had met the natives, they entered upon a dry and desolate tract over which they crossed in safety, but with great suffering. Once more relieved by a native well in the sandy beach, they pushed on, only to encounter evil fortune; horse after horse knocked up, and it was after six days' travelling they managed to get water once more, by digging in the sand.

They were now about six hundred miles from King George's Sound and in a most unenviable position, with the prospect of another one hundred mile stage without water, and the full knowledge that retreat was impossible. Their horses, in consequence of the repeated sufferings from thirst that they had been forced to undergo, were so spiritless and reduced that they could travel scarcely any distance without giving in, and yet the worst was to come. For some time the black boys had been very sullen and discontented, the constant hard-ships and fatigue, added to what they well-knew lay before them, told upon their spirits. Once they ran away, but hunger forced them to re-turn; even the scanty fare at the camp was better than the slow starvation of the bush. The overseer, too, was afflicted with low spirits, and impressed by the forbidding character of their surroundings. Poor fellow, some foreboding of his fate hung over him.

The toil that had to be gone through may be conceived by the following short extract from Eyre's diary on March 11th, just after ac-complishing their first terrible stage after leaving the depôt:--

"At night the whole party were, by God's blessing, once more together and in safety, after having passed over one hundred and thirty-five miles of desert country, without a drop of water in its whole extent, and at a season of the year the most unfavourable for such an undertaking. In accomplishing this distance, the sheep had been six and the horses five days without water, and both had been almost wholly without food for the greater part of the time. The little grass we found was so dry and withered that the parched and thirsty animals could not eat it after the second day."

From this camp Eyre started in the hope of shortly coming to a second supply of water that the natives had told him of, and lured on by this idea, he got forty miles from his camp without having made the provision that he should have done before entering on a very long stage. Coming to the conclusion that he must have passed the water, he decided to send the horses back to the last camp for a fresh supply be-fore venturing further on. At midnight the overseer and the natives started back, leaving Eyre to mind the baggage with the scanty allow-ance of six pints of water to last him for six days until their return. On the 26th of March they again started, and at night reduced their bag-gage still more in the hope of getting the tired horses through; and the next day everything was abandoned, for still there was no prospect of water ahead.

On the night of the 29th the last drop of water that they had with them was consumed, and the next morning water was obtained by digging in the sand drift--their seventh day out, after travelling, by Eyre's computation, one hundred and sixty miles. It was not until the 27th of April that they left the camp, to enter on the last fearful push that was to decide their fate--and did too well decide the fate of three.

Once more the line of cliffs that had for a time been broken by the sandhills faced the ocean, and from experience Eyre knew well that he might expect no relief when travelling along their summits.

On the evening of the 29th, the third night from their last camp, Eyre took the first watch to look after the horses, as this was necessary every night to prevent them rambling too far.

The night was cold, the wind blowing hard, and across the face of the moon the scud kept rapidly driving. The horses wandered a good deal, and kept separating in the scrub, giving the lonely man much trouble to keep them together, and when his watch was nearly up he headed them for the camp, intending to call the overseer to relieve him, Suddenly the stillness of the desert was broken by the report of a gun.

Eyre was not at first alarmed, thinking it a signal of Baxter's to show him the position of the camp; he called out in reply, but no answer was returned; and, hastening in the direction, was met by one of the boys running towards him crying, "Oh massa, oh massa, come here!" but beyond that could not speak for terror.

Eyre was soon at the camp, and a glance told him that he was now indeed alone. Baxter, wounded to death, was lying on the ground in his last agony, and as Eyre raised his faithful companion, then in the convulsion of death, the frightful and appalling truth burst upon him in its full horror.

"At the dead hour of night, in the wildest and most inhospitable waste of Australia, with the fierce wind raging in unison with the scene of violence before me, I was left with a single native, whose fidelity I could not rely upon, and who, for aught I knew, might be in league with the other two, who, perhaps were, even now, lurking about to take my life, as they had done that of the overseer. Three days had passed away since we left the last water, and it was very doubtful when we might find any more. Six hundred miles of country had to be traversed before I could hope to obtain the slightest aid or assistance of any kind, whilst I knew not that a single drop of water, or an ounce of flour, had been left by these murderers, from a stock that had previously, been so small."

On examining the camp, Eyre found that the two boys had carried off both double-barrelled guns, all the baked bread, and other stores, and a keg of water. All he had left was a rifle with a ball jammed in the barrel, four gallons of water, forty pounds of flour, and a little tea and sugar.

When he had time to collect his thoughts, Eyre judged from the position of the body, that Baxter must have been disturbed by the boys plundering the camp, and getting up to stop them, had been immediately shot. His next care was to put his rifle in serviceable condition, and then as morning broke they hastened away from the fatal camp. It was impossible even to bury the body of his murdered companion; one vast unbroken surface of sheet rock extended for miles in every direction. Well might Eyre exclaim:--

"Though years have now passed away since the enactment of this tragedy, the dreadful horrors of that time and scene are recalled before me with frightful vividness, and make me shudder even now when I think of them. A lifetime was crowded into those few short hours, and death alone may blot out the impressions they produced."

That evening the two murderers re-appeared in the scrub, following the white man and boy. Eyre attempted to get close to them, but they would not come near, remaining at a distance, calling out to the remaining boy (Wylie), who, however, refused to go to them. Finding himself unable to get to close quarters with them, Eyre proceeded on his journey, and the two boys were never seen again, and, without doubt, they soon perished miserably of hunger and thirst.

At last, after being again seven days without water for the horses, they reached the end of the long line of cliffs, and amongst the sand dunes came again to a native well, and got their poor tortured horses a drink.

Moving on now in easier stages, and getting water by digging at the foot of the different sand hills he encountered, Eyre proceeded on with better hopes for the future; he felt confident that he was past the great belt of and country, and that with every day the travelling would improve.

On the 8th of May, another horse was killed, and a supply of meat dried to carry with them.

From this point water was more frequently met with, a decided change for the better took place in the face of the country, and the wretched horses they still had left began to pick up a little. At last, when their rations were quite exhausted, they sighted a ship at anchor in Thistle Cove. She turned out to be the Mississippi, whaler, Captain Rossitur, and once more Eyre had to thank fortune for relief at a critical moment.

For ten days he forgot his sufferings, and regained some of his lost strength, under the hospitable care of Captain Rossitur, who, it will be remembered, was the first foreigner to anchor in Port Lincoln.

Provided with fresh clothes and provisions, with his horses newly shod, Eyre recommenced his pilgrimage, and arrived in King George's Sound on July 8th. Having successfully crossed from Port Lincoln to King George's Sound, with incredible suffering, not alone

116

to himself, but also to his men and horses, so far as they accompanied him; added to which, his obstinate persistence, led to the death of Baxter, who, against his own convictions, went on with him, rather than leave him in his need.

It is generally said with regard to this journey of Eyre's, that it any rate established the fact that no considerable creek flowed from the interior to the south coast. But this had been pretty well-known before by the maritime surveys, for it must be borne in mind that this portion of the Australian shore in no way resembles the general coast line of Australia. Granted that numbers of the largest rivers in the continent were overlooked by the navigators, we must also remember that the conditions here were. essentially different. No fringe of low mangrove covered flats, studded with inlets and salt-water creeks, masking the entrance of a river, was here to be found. A bold outline of barren cliffs, or a clean-swept sandy shore, alone fronted the ocean, and Flinders, constantly on the alert as he always was for anything approaching an outlet or river mouth, would scarcely have missed one here. As for any knowledge of the interior that was gained, of course there was none, even the conjectures of a worn out, starving man, picking his way painfully around the sea shore, would have scarcely been of much value. Eyre has, however secured for himself a name for courage and perseverance, under the most terrible circumstances that could well beset a man, and this qualification leads us to overlook his errors of judgment. The picture of the lonely man--not separated from his fellow creatures by the sea, as has often been the case, but by countless miles of weary, untrodden waste, in his plundered camp, beside his murdered companion--is one that for peculiar horror, can never be surpassed.

Eyre was warmly welcomed on his return to Adelaide, and he was subsequently appointed police magistrate on the Murray, where his experience and knowledge of the natives was of great service. When Sturt started on his memorable trip to the central desert, he accompanied him for a long distance; but his active nature found vent in other fields than those of exploration in future.

Eyre was a man who was thoroughly distinguished by his love for the aborigines. In after life he was appointed their protector on the Murray, at the time when the continual skirmishes between the natives and the overlanders used to be a matter of almost daily occurrence.

The courage that he had exemplified, and his wonderful march round the Great Bight, was brought into force again and again, in efforts to keep peace between the rival races. The blacks of the Murray

FAVENC

Bend were always notable for their warlike character, and Eyre was
the most fitting man that could have been selected for the post.

Chapter VI

Explorations around Moreton Bay--Development of the Eastern Coast--The first pioneers of the Darling Downs--Stuart and Sydenham Russell--The Condamine River and Cecil Plains--Great interest taken in exploration at this period--Renewed explorations around Lake Torrens--Surveyor-General Frome--Death of Horrocks, the first explorer to introduce camels--Sturt's last expedition--Route by the Darling chosen--Poole fancies that he sees the inland sea--Discovery of Flood's Creek--The prison depôt--Impossible to advance or retreat--Breaking up of the drought--Death of Poole--Fresh attempts to the north--The desert--Eyre's Creek discovered--Return and fresh attempt--Discoveries of Cooper and Strzelecki Creeks--Retreat to the Depôt Glen--Final return to the Darling--Ludwig Leichhardt the lost explorer--His great trip north--Finding of the Burdekin, the Mackenzie, Isaacs and Suttor--Murder of the naturalist Gibert--Discovery of the Gulf Rivers--Arrival at Port Essington--His return and reception--Surveyor-General Mitchell's last expedition--Follows up the Balonne--Crosses to the head of the Belyando--Disappointed in that river--Returns and crosses to the head of the Victoria (Barcoo)--The beautiful Downs country--First mention of the Mitchell grass--False hopes entertained of the Victoria running into the Gulf of Carpentaria.

Disappointing as all the attempts to penetrate to the north had been, the South Australians did not by any means abandon their efforts, either public or private, to ascertain the nature and value of the interior. The supposed horseshoe formation of Lake Torrens, presenting thus an impassable barrier, was discouraging, but hopes were entertained that breaks in it would be found that would afford a passage across; and beyond, the country might prove of a less repellent character than the district immediately around the lake.

But the east coast and the country at the back of the new settlement of Moreton Bay, now commands our attention, Such an important discovery as that made by Cunningham of the Darling Downs, needless to say, attracted the attention of the graziers of the settled districts in search of fresh pastures. The country west of the Darling having received such an unfavourable name from the explorers who had made any efforts beyond it. The westward march of the overlanders was checked in that direction, and their stock spread to the north, south, and south-cast.

In March 1840, Patrick Leslie, who has always been considered the father of settlement on the Darling Downs, left an outside station in New England, and after a short inspection of the scene of Cunningham's discovery, finally, in the middle of the year, settled down on the Condamine.

In 1841 the Condamine River was followed for a hundred miles by Messrs. Stuart and Sydenham Russell, from below Jimbour, the northernmost station on a Darling Downs creek; and on the return journey some of the party made an attempt to cross the range to the Wide Bay district, but were prevented by the scrub. In the following month, November, the flow of the Condamine was again picked up in the space below Turnmervil, the lowest station on a creek above Jimbour, and the channel of the river distinguished, where it was formerly supposed to have been for awhile lost. An extensive tract of rich grazing country was found open and well-watered by anabranches, with lagoons in their beds. This district has ever since borne the well-known name of Cecil Plains, then bestowed on it.

In 1842 Stuart Russell went from Moreton Bay to Wide Bay in a boat, and made an examination of some of the streams there emptying into the sea. Amongst other adventures the party picked up with an escaped convict who had been fourteen years with the blacks. During the same year Stuart Russell explored the country from Wide Bay to the Boyne (not the river named by Oxley in Port Curtis), and subsequently followed and laid down this stream throughout, crossing from inland waters on to the head of it. Russell's work in opening up so much available country, is a fair sample of the private explorations before referred to, which fill up such a large space of the record of discovery, and yet have received so little recognition that the remembrance of most of them has been quite lost, or preserved in such a way as to be hardly looked upon as reliable history.

We are now approaching a period when the exploration of the continent was an object of absorbing interest to all the settlements fast growing into importance on the southern and eastern coasts. Three explorers, who may be classed as the greatest, the most successful, and the one whose star that rose so bright at this time was doomed to set in misfortune, were in the field at the same time. Charles Sturt, fated once more to meet and be defeated (if such a gallant struggle can be called defeat) by the inexorable desert and the stern denial of its climate. Thomas Mitchell, again the favoured of fortune, to wend his way by well-watered streams and grassy downs and plains. And Ludwig Leichhardt, to accomplish his one great journey through the country permeated by the rivers of the eastern and northern coast. But before starting in company with these deathless names, we must, for a while, return to Lake Torrens.

Eyre, it will be remembered, reached, after much labour, a hill to the north east at the termination of the range, which he named Mount Hopeless. From the view he obtained from the summit, he concluded that Lake Torrens completely enclosed the northern portion of the province of South Australia; and in fact that the province had once been an island, as the low-lying plains probably joined the flat country west of the Darling.

In 1843, the then Surveyor-General of the colony, Captain Frome, started to the north to ascertain as much of this mysterious lake as he could. He reached Mount Serle, and found the dry bed of the great lake to the eastward, as described by Eyre, but discovered an error of thirty miles in its position, Eyre having placed it too far to the eastward. Further north than this, Frome did not proceed; on his way back lie made two excursions to the eastward, but found nothing but sterile and unpromising country. He confirmed then, the existence of a lake to the eastward of the southern point of Lake Torrens, but his explorations did not go far to determine the identity of the two, nor their uninterrupted continuity. Prior to this, a series of explorations, followed by settlement, had taken place east and west of Eyre's track, between Adelaide and the head of Spencer's Gulf. One promising expedition was nipped in the bud by the accidental death of the leader, a rising young explorer, who had already won his spurs in opening up fresh country in the province. This was Mr. J. Horrocks, who formed a plan for travelling up the western side of Lake Torrens, and then, if possible, making westward and trying to reach the Swan River. This expedition is especially noteworthy as being the first one in which a camel was made use of, and to Horrocks, is due the credit of first introducing these animals as baggage carriers. When at the head of the Gulf, and about to grapple with the unknown land to the west, his gun accidentally went off, and he received the charge in his face. He lived to return to the station, but died a few days afterwards.

Amongst the other pioneers who contributed more or less to spread settlement in the province, and succeeded, may be mentioned Messrs. Hawker, Hughes, Campbell, Robinson, and Heywood.

Perhaps, of all the journeys into the interior, none have excited more sustained interest than Sturt's. It must be admitted that his account, however truthful it may have appeared to him at the time, is misleading, and overdrawn. But whilst saying this let us look at the circumstances under which he received the impressions he has put on record.

He was a thoroughly broken and disappointed man; for six months he had been shut up in his weary depôt prison, debarred from making any attempt to complete his work, watching his friend and companion die slowly before his eyes. When the kindly rains released him, he was turned back and constantly back by a strip of desert country, that seemed to dog him whichever way he turned. No wonder he fairly hated the place, and looked at all things through the heated, treacherous haze of the desert plains.

When, therefore, he speaks of the awful temperature that rendered life unbearable, and the inland slopes of Australia unfitted for human habitation, it must be recalled that the party were weak and suffering, liable to feel oppressive heat or extreme cold, more keenly than strong and healthy men. In the ranges where Sturt spent his summer months of detention, there is now one of the wonderful mining townships of Australia, where men toil as laboriously as in a temperate zone, and the fires of the battery and the smelting furnace burn steadily day and night, in sight of the spot where Poole lies buried. And at the lower levels of the shafts trickle the waters of subterranean streams that Sturt never dreamt of. But though baffled, and unable to gain the goal he strove for, never did man better deserve success. His instructions were to reach the centre of the continent, to discover whether range or sea existed there; and if the former, to note the flow of the northern waters, but on no account to follow them down to the northern sea. As usual, the Home Office, in their official wisdom, knew more than did the colonists, and instructed him to proceed by way of Mount Arden; the route already tried and abandoned by Eyre.

Sturt chose to proceed by the Darling. His plan was to follow that river up as far as the Williorara or Laidley's Ponds, a small western tributary of the Darling, opposite the point were Mitchell turned back, in 1835, after his conflict with the natives. Thence he intended to strike north-west, hoping thus to avoid the gloomy environs of Lake Torrens, and its treacherous bed.

At Moorundi, on the Murray, he was met by Eyre, then resident magistrate at that place, and here the party mustered and made their start.

Sturt was accompanied by Poole, as second in command, Browne, who was a thorough bushman and an excellent surgeon, accompanied him as a friend; with them also went McDouall Stuart, as draftsman, whose fame as an explorer afterwards equalled that of his leader, besides twelve men, eleven horses, thirty bullocks, one boat and boat carriage, one horse dray, one spring cart, three bullock drays, two hundred sheep, four kangaroo dogs, and two sheep dogs.

Eyre accompanied the expedition as far as Lake Victoria, which point they reached on the 10th of September, 1844. Here Eyre left them, and on the 11th of October the explorers arrived at Williorara, the place where they intended leaving the Darling for the interior. The appearance of this watercourse very much disappointed Sturt, he had hoped from the account of the natives to find in it a fair-sized creek, heading from a low range, distantly visible to the north-west; instead, he found it a mere channel for the flood water of the Darling, distributing it into some shallow lakes, back from the river, a distance of some eight or nine miles, Sturt, as a first step dispatched Poole and Stuart to the range, to see if they could obtain any view of the country to the north-west. They were absent four days, and returned with the rather startling intelligence, that from the top of a peak in the range, Poole had seen a large lake studded with islands.

Although in his published journal, written long afterwards, Sturt makes light of Poole's fancied lake, which, of course, was the effect of mirage, at that time his ardent fancy made him believe that he was on the eve of a great discovery. In a letter to Mr. Morphett, of Adelaide, he writes:--

"Poole has just returned from the ranges. I have not time to write over again. He says there are high ranges to the N. and N.W., and water, a sea extending along the horizon from S.W. by S., and ten E. of N., in which there are a number of islands and lofty ranges as far as the eye can reach. What is all this? Are we to be prosperous? I hope so, and I am sure you do. To-morrow we start for the ranges, and then for the waters, the strange waters, on which boat never swam, and over which flag never floated. But both shall ere long. We have the heart of the interior laid open to us, and shall be off with a flowing, sheet in a few days. Poole says the sea was a deep blue, and that in the midst of it was a conical island of great height. When will you hear from me again?"

Poor Sturt! no boat of his was ever to float on that visionary sea, nor his flag to wave over its dream waters.

The whole of the party now removed to a small shallow lake, the termination of the Williorara Channel. From here he started on an excursion to the more distant ranges reported by Poole, accompanied by Browne and two men, went ahead for the purpose of finding water of a sufficient permanency to remove the whole of the party, as at the lake where they were encamped there was always the chance of becoming embroiled with the natives. He was successful in finding what he wanted, and on the 4th of November the main body of the expedition removed there, now finally leaving the waters of the Darling.

The next day, Sturt and Browne, with three men and the cart, started on another trip in search of water ahead. This they found in small quantities, and rain coming on, Sturt returned and sent Poole out again to search, whilst the camp was moved on. On his return he reported having seen some shallow, brackish lakes, and caught sight of Eyre's Mount Serle. They were now on the western slope of the Barrier Ranges, and but for the providential discovery of a fine creek to the north, would have been unable to retain their position. To this creek (Flood's Creek) they removed the camp, and Sturt congratulated himself on the steady and satisfactory progress he was making. They now left the Barrier Range, and made for one further north, staying for some ten days at a small lagoon, during which time an examination of the country ahead was made.

On the 27th January, 1845, they removed to a creek, heading from a small range; at the head of this creek was a fine supply of permanent water, and here the explorers pitched their tents, little thinking that it would be the 17th of July following before they would be struck. Perhaps a short description from Sturt's pen will aid the reader's imagination in picturing the situation of the party.

"It was not, however, until after we had run down every creek in the neighbourhood, and had traversed the country in every direction, that the truth flashed across my mind, and it became evident to me that we were locked up in the desolate and heated region into which we had penetrated as effectually as if we had wintered at the Pole. It was long indeed ere I could bring myself to believe that so great a misfortune had overtaken us, but so it was. Providence had, in its all wise purposes, guided us to the only spot in that wide-spread desert, where our wants could have been permanently supplied, but had there stayed our further progress into a region that almost appears to be forbidden ground."

"The creek was marked by a line of gum-trees, from the mouth of the glen to its junction with the main branch, in which, excepting in isolated spots, water was no longer to be found. The Red Hill (afterwards called Mount Poole) bore N. N.W. from us, distant three and a-half miles; between us and it there were undulating plains, covered with stones or salsolaceous herbage, excepting in the hollows wherein there was a little grass. Behind us were level stony plains, with small sandy undulations bounded by brush, over which the Black Hill was visible, distant ten miles, bearing S.S.E. from the Red Hill. To the eastward, the country was as I have described it, hilly. Westward at a quarter of a mile the low range, through which Depôt Creek forces itself, shut out from our view the extensive plains on which it rises."

This then was Sturt's prison, although at first he had not realised that in spite of every precaution, his retreat was cut off until the next rainfall.

Of Sturt's existence and occupation during this dreary period little can be said. He tried in every direction, until convinced of the uselessness of so doing, sometimes encouraged and led on by shallow pools in some fragmentary creek bed, at others, seeing nothing before him but hopeless aridity. Now, too, he found himself attacked with what he then thought was rheumatism, but proved to be scurvy, and Poole and Browne too were afflicted in the same way.

We now come to one of the picturesque incidents that Sturt has introduced in his narrative, and that help to fix on our memory the strangely weird picture of the lonely band of men confronted with the unaccustomed forces of nature in this wilderness.

"As we rode across the stony plain lying between us and the hills, the heated and parching blasts that came upon us, were more than we could bear. We were in the centre of the plain, when Mr. Browne drew my attention to a number of small black specks in the upper air. These spots increasing momentarily in size, were evidently approaching us rapidly. In an incredibly short space of time, we were surrounded by hundreds of the common kite, stooping down to within a few feet of us, and then turning away after having eyed us steadily. Several approached us so closely, that they threw themselves back to avoid contact, opening their beaks and spreading out their talons. The long flight of these birds, reaching from the ground into the heavens, put me strongly in mind of one of Martin's beautiful designs, in which he produces the effect of distance by a multitude of objects vanishing from the view."

Sturt, during his detention in the depôt, made one desperate attempt to the north, when he succeeded in getting a mile above the 28th parallel, but found nothing to repay him for his trouble.

And so week after week of this fearful monotony passed on without hardly a break or change.

Once, an old native wandered to their camp. He was starving and thirsty, looking a fit being to emerge from the gaunt waste around them. The dogs attacked him when he approached, but he stood his ground and fought them valiantly until they were called off; his whole demeanour was calm and courageous, and he showed neither surprise nor timidity. He drank greedily when water was given him, and ate voraciously, but whence he came the men could not divine nor could he explain to them. He accepted what was given to him, as a right expected by one fellow-being from another, cut off in the desert from their own kin. While he stopped at their camp he showed that he knew the use of the boat, explaining that it was upside down, as of course it was, and pointing to the N.W. as the place where they would want it, raising poor Sturt's hopes once more. After a fortnight he departed as he came, saying he would come back, but he never did.

"With him," says Sturt pathetically, "all our hopes vanished, for even the presence of this savage was soothing to us, and so long as he remained we indulged in anticipations as to the future. From the time of his departure a gloomy silence pervaded the camp; we were, indeed, placed under the most trying circumstances, everything combined to depress our spirits and exhaust our patience. We had witnessed migration after migration of the feathered tribes, to that point to which we were so anxious to push our way. Flights of cockatoos, of parrots, of pigeons, and of bitterns; birds, also, whose notes had cheered us in the wilderness, all had taken the same high road to a better and more hospitable region."

And now the water began to sink with frightful rapidity, and they all thought that the end was surely coming. Hoping against hope, Sturt laid his plans to start as soon as the drought broke up, himself to proceed north and west whilst poor Poole, reduced to a frightful condition by scurvy, was to be sent carefully back as the only means of saving his life.

On the 12th and 13th of July the rain commenced, and the siege was raised, but Poole never lived to profit by it. Every arrangement for his comfort was made that the circumstances permitted, but on the first day's journey he died, and they brought his body back to the depôt and made his lonely grave there. Sturt's way was now open.

After burying his lamented friend, he again dispatched the party that was selected to return home, and, with renewed hope, made preparations for the northwest. He first, however, removed the depôt to a better grassed locality, water being now plentiful everywhere. During a short western trip, on the 4th August they found themselves on the edge of an immense shallow and sandy basin, in which were detached sheets of water, "as blue as indigo and as salt as brine." This they took to be Lake Torrens, and returned to the depôt to arrange matters for a final departure.

Stuart was left in charge of the depôt, Browne accompanying Sturt; and on the 14th a start was made. For some days, owing to the pools of surface water left by the recent rain, they had no difficulty in keeping a straightforward course. The country passed over consisted of large level plains and long sand ridges, but they crossed numerous creeks and found more or less water in all of them, and finally got into a well-grassed, pleasing looking country, which greatly cheered them with a prospect of success, when, suddenly, they were confronted by a wall of sand, and for nearly twenty miles toiled over succeeding ridges. Fortunately, they found both water and feed, but their hopes received a sudden and complete downfall. Nor did a walk to the extremity of one of the sand ridges serve to raise their spirits. Sturt saw before him an immense plain, of a dark purple hue, with its horizon like that of the sea, boundless in the direction in which he wished to proceed. This was the Stony Desert. That night they camped in it, and the next morning came to an earthy plain, with here and there a few bushes of polygonum growing beside some stray channel, in some of which they, luckily, found a little muddy rain water still left. When they camped at night they sighted, for a short time, some hills to the north, and, on examining them through the telescope, saw dark shadows on their faces as if produced by cliffs. Next day they made for these hills, in the hope of finding a change of country and feed for their horses; but they were disappointed. Sand ridges in terrible array once more rose up before them. "Even the animals," says Sturt, "appeared to regard them with dismay."

Over plains and sand dunes, the former full of yawning cracks and holes, the party pushed on, subsisting on precarious pools of muddy water and fast-sinking native wells; until, on the 3rd of September, Flood, the stockman, who was riding ahead, held up his hat and called aloud to them that a large creek was in sight.

On coming up the others saw a beautiful watercourse, the bed of which was full of grass and water. This creek Sturt called Eyre's

Creek, and it was one of the most important discoveries he made in this region. Along this watercourse they made easy stages until the 7th, when the creek was lost, and the water in the lagoons near the bank was found to be intensely salt. After repeated efforts to continue his journey, which only led him amongst the everlasting sand hills, separated by plains encrusted with salt, Sturt came to the erroneous conclusion that he was at the head of the creek, and further progress impossible. Had he but known it, he was within reach of permanently watered rivers, along which he could have travelled as far north as he wished. But there was neither sign nor clue afforded him; his men were sick, and his retreat to the depôt most precarious; there was nothing for it but to fall back again, and after a toilsome journey they reached the depôt, or Fort Grey as they had christened it, on the 2nd October.

Sturt now made up his mind for a final effort due north, and in company with Stuart and two fresh men, he started on the 9th of October; and on the second day reached Strzelecki Creek, which was the name they had given to the first creek crossed on their late expedition. On the 13th, they arrived at the banks of a magnificent channel with grassy banks, fine trees and abundant water; this was the now well-known Cooper's Creek, one of the most important rivers of the interior, its tributaries draining the southern slopes of the dividing watershed in the north.

Sturt on reaching this unexpected discovery was uncertain whether to follow its course to the eastward, or persevere in his original intention of pushing to the north. A thunder storm falling at the time made him adhere to his original course, and defer the examination of the new river until his return. In seven days after leaving Cooper's Creek, he had the negative satisfaction, as he expected, of gazing over the dreary waste of the stony desert, unchanged and forbidding as ever. They crossed it, and were again turned back by sand hill and salt plain, and forced to retrace their steps to Cooper's Creek. This creek Sturt followed upward for many days, but finding it did not take him in the direction he desired to go, and moreover, the large broad channel that they first came to, became divided into many small ones, which ran through flooded plains, making the travelling most tiring on their exhausted horses; he reluctantly turned back. They had found the creek well populated with natives, and the prospects of getting on were apparently better than they had ever met with before, but both Sturt and his men were weak and ill, and his horses thoroughly tired out, and also he was not sure of his retreat.

Following Cooper's Creek back, they found that the water had dried up so rapidly that grave fears were entertained that Strzelecki's Creek, their main reliance in going back to the depôt, would be dry. Fortunately, they were in time to find a little muddy fluid left, just enough to serve them. Here they experienced a hot wind that forced them to camp the whole day, although most anxious to get on.

"We had scarcely got there," writes Sturt, "when the wind, which had been blowing all the morning hot from the north-east, increased to a gale, and I shall never forget its withering effects. I sought shelter behind a large gum tree, but the blasts of heat were so terrific, that I wondered the very grass did not take fire. This really was nothing ideal; everything, both animate and inanimate, gave way before it; the horses stood with their backs to the wind, and their noses to the ground, without the muscular strength to raise their heads; the birds were mute, and the leaves of the tree under which we were sitting, fell like a snow shower around us. At noon, I took a thermometer, graduated to 127 degrees, out of my box, and observed that the mercury was up to 125. Thinking that it had been unduly influenced, I put it in the fork of a tree close to me, sheltered alike from the wind and the sun. In this position I went to examine it about an hour afterwards, when I found that the mercury had risen to the top of the instrument, and that its further expansion had burst the bulb, a circumstance that, I believe, no traveller has had to recount before."

Let the reader remember when reading the above description, which has been so much quoted, that the man who wrote it was in such a weakened condition, that he had no energy left to withstand the hot wind, and that the shade they were cowering under was of the scantiest description.

They had still a journey of eighty-six miles, back to Fort Grey, with little prospect of any water being found on the way. After a long and weary ride they reached it only to find that, owing to the bad state of the water, Browne had been compelled to fall back on to their old camp at the Depôt Glen.

"We reached the plain just as the sun was descending, without having dismounted from our horses for fifteen hours, and as we rode down the embankment into it, looked around for the cattle, but none were to be seen. We looked towards the little sandy mound on which the tents had stood, but no white objects there met our eye; we rode slowly up to the stockade and found it silent and deserted. I was quite sure that Mr. Browne had had urgent reasons for retiring. I had, indeed, anticipated the measure. I hardly hoped to find him at the Fort, and had given him instructions on the subject of his removal; yet, a sickening feeling came over me when I saw that he was really gone; not on my own account, for, with the bitter feelings of disappointment with which I was returning home, I could calmly have laid my head on that desert, never to raise it again."

Riding day and night, Sturt at last reached the encampment, so exhausted as to be hardly able to stand:--

"When I dismounted, I had nearly fallen forward. Thinking that one of the kangaroo dogs, in his greeting, had pushed me between the legs, I turned round to give him a slap, but no dog was there, and I soon found out that what I had felt was nothing more than strong muscular action, brought on by riding."

Now came the question of their final escape. The water in the Depôt Creek was so much reduced that they feared that there would be none left in Flood's Creek, and if so, they were once more imprisoned. Browne undertook the long ride of one hundred and eighteen miles, which was to decide the question. Preparations had to be made for his journey by filling a bullock skin with water, and sending a dray with it as far as possible; and on the eighth day he returned.

"'Well Browne,' said Sturt, who was helpless in his tent, 'what news? Is it to be good or bad?' 'there is still water in the creek,' replied Browne, 'but that is all I can say; what there is, is as black as ink, and we must make haste, for in a week it will be gone.'"

The boat that was to have floated on the inland sea, was left to rot at the Depôt Glen, all the heaviest of the stores abandoned., and the retreat of over two hundred miles to the Darling commenced.

More bullock skins were fashioned into bags, to carry water for the stock, and with their aid, and that of a kindly shower of rain, they crossed the dry stage to Flood's Creek in safety. Here they found the vegetation more advanced, and with care, and constant activity in looking out for water on ahead, they gradually left behind them the scene of their labours and approached the Darling; Sturt having to be carried on one of the drays, and lifted on and off at each stoppage.

On the 21st December, they arrived at the camp of the relief party, under Piesse, at Williorara, and Sturt's last expedition came to an end.

As he has often been termed the father of Australian exploration, it may be as well to look back on the result of his life-long labours. His burning desire to reach the heart of the continent had constantly led him into dangers and difficulties that other explorers shunned, and unfortunate as he always was in his seasons, he brought back a forbidding report of the, usefulness of the country he had dis-covered, which led to its gradual settlement, only after long years had passed, and men had grown accustomed to the desert, and laughed at its terrors; finding that experience robbed them of their first effect.

Sturt found the Darling, and traced the Murray to its mouth, thus discovering the great arteries of the water system of the most populated part of Australia, leaving the details to be filled in by others. In the interior he was the finder of Eyre's Creek and Cooper's Creek; one of the tributaries of the latter. was soon afterwards discovered by Mitchell, and named by him the Victoria, now called the Barcoo. In these two creeks, as he called them, on account of the absence of flow-ing water in their beds, Sturt unwittingly crossed the second and only other great inland river system of the continent. In the basin he trav-ersed, in which these creeks lost their character, he was riding over the united beds of the Barcoo, the Thomson, the Diamentina, and the Her-bert, west of whose waters nothing in the shape of a defined system of drainage exists, until the rivers of the western coast are reached. As a scientific explorer then, whose object was to unravel the mystery of the interior, solve, if possible, the question of its strange peculiarity, and trace out its physical formation, Sturt may well be held the first and greatest. His success, perhaps, was greater than he himself imag-ined, he came back dispirited with failure but as before he had found the broad outlines of the plan of the drainage of the great plains, to be afterwards completed by the discoveries of the tributary streams.

In addition to his longing to be the first to reach the centre of Australia, Sturt fondly hoped that once past the southern zone of the tropics, he would find himself in a country blessed with a heavier and more constant rainfall; as it was impossible for him to know at that time, that the force of the north-west monsoon was expended on the northern coast, and none of the tropical deluge found its way with any degree of regularity to the thirsty inland slope; this theory appeared on the face of it, feasible. Although an after knowledge may have now enabled us to see the mistakes he made, and to regard his descriptions of the uninhabitable nature of the interior as exaggerated, it must be admitted that others in the same place and circumstances would have made similar errors, and drawn equally false conclusions.

In taking leave of this explorer, another short extract from his journal will best show the character of the man of whom Australians should be so justly proud.

"Circumstances may yet arise to give a value to my recent labours, and my name may be remembered by after generations in Australia, as the first who tried to penetrate to its centre. If I failed in that great object, I have one consolation in the retrospect of my past services. My path amongst savage tribes has been a bloodless one, not but that I have often been placed in situations of risk and danger, when I might have been justified in shedding blood, but I trust I have ever made allowances for human timidity, and respected the customs of the rudest people."

The next prominent figure in the history of this time is Leichhardt, whose unknown fate has been the cause of so much sentiment clinging about his name.

Dr. Ludwig Leichhardt arrived in the colony in 1842, and travelled to Moreton Bay overland, where he occupied himself for two years in short excursions in the neighbourhood, pursuing his favourite study of physical science. Leichhardt was born in Beskow, near Berlin, and studied in Berlin. Through a neglect, he was excluded from the one-year military service, and thereby induced to escape from the three-yearly service. The consequence was, that he was pursued as a deserter and sentenced in contumaciam.

Afterwards, Alexander Von Humboldt succeeded, by representing his services to science on his first expedition in Australia, in obtaining a pardon from the King. By a Cabinet order Leichhardt received permission to return to Prussia unpunished. This order, whether of any value to Leichhardt or not, came too late. When it arrived in Australia he had already started on his last expedition.

When the expedition was projected from Fort Bourke, on the Darling, to the Gulf of Carpentaria or Port Essington, he was desirous of securing the position of naturalist thereon; the delay in the starting of it disappointed him, and he made up his mind to attempt one on his own account, a project in which he received little encouragement. He persevered, however, and eking out his own resources, by means of private contributions he managed to get a party together, and on the 1st of October, 1844, he left Jimbour, on the Darling Downs, with six whites and two blacks, 17 horses, 16 head of cattle, and four kangaroo dogs; his other supplies being proportionately meagre.

As Leichhardt's journal of this trip has been so widely read, and as it does not possess the same striking interest as that of Sturt's, from the more accessible nature of the country travelled through, and the absence of the constantly threatening dangers overhanging both Sturt and Eyre, a shorter account of the progress of the expedition will be found most acceptable.

His plan of starting from the Moreton Bay district, and proceeding to Port Essington, differed considerably from that proposed by Sir Thomas Mitchell. The course adopted by Leichhardt, although longer and more roundabout than that suggested from Fort Bourke, would be safer for his little band, keeping as it would, more to the well-watered coastal districts, and avoiding the constant separations entailed upon parties traversing the interior.

Leaving the head waters of the Condamine, the river which receives so many of the tributary streams of the Darling Downs, Leichhardt struck a river, which he named the Dawson, thence he passed westward, on to the fine country of the Peak Downs, whereon he named the minor waters of the Comet, Planet, and Zamia Creeks.

On the 10th of January, 1845, the Mackenzie River was discovered, and here the Doctor and the black boy, Charlie, managed to get lost for two or three days, a faculty which apparently most of the party happily possessed. Following up the Isaacs River, a tributary of the Fitzroy, they crossed the head of it on to the Suttor; the only variation in the monotonous record of the daily travel being the occasional capture of game, and the mutinous conduct of the two black boys, who at various times essayed to leave the party and shift for themselves, but were on each occasion glad to return.

Following down the Suttor, they arrived at the Burdekin, the largest river on the east coast, discovered by Leichhardt, up the valley of which they travelled, until they crossed the dividing watershed between the waters of the east coast and the Gulf of Carpentaria, on to the head of the Lynd, which river they followed to its junction with the Mitchell. Finding the course of this river leading them too high north, on the eastern shore of the Gulf, they left it, and struck to the sea coast, intending to follow round the southern coast at a reasonable distance inland. Up to this time they had been so little troubled by the natives, that they had ceased almost to think of meeting with any hostility from them.

On the night of the 28th June, 1845, they were encamped at a chain of shallow lagoons, when soon after seven o'clock, a shower of spears was thrown into the camp, wounding Messrs. Roper and Calvert, and killing Mr. Gilbert instantly. So unprepared were the party, that the guns were uncapped, and it was some time before three or four discharges made the blacks take to their heels. The body of the naturalist was buried at the camp, but his grave was unmarked, as in order to prevent the blacks from disinterring it, a large fire was lit over the grave to hide its site.

From this unfortunate camp the party proceeded slowly with the two wounded men for some days. A strange incident, scarcely credible, happened during their tramp round the Gulf. One night a blackfellow walked deliberately up to the fire round which the party were assembled, having seemingly mistaken it for his own. On discovering his mistake, he immediately climbed up a tree, and raised a horrible din, lamenting, sobbing, and crying, until they all removed to a short distance and afforded him a chance of which he eagerly availed himself, of escaping.

Leichhardt followed round the Gulf shores, naming the many rivers he crossed after friends or contributors to his expedition, or where he could identify them, retaining the names of the coast surveys. On the 6th of August, he reached a river which he mistook for the Albert, of Captain Stokes, but which now bears his name, being so christened by A. C. Gregory, who rectified his error. On this occasion, Leichhardt did not err so widely as Burke and Wills did subsequently, when they mistook the mouth of the Flinders for the Albert. With decreasing supplies and increasing fatigue, they at last reached the large river in the south-west corner of the Gulf, which he named the Roper, and here he had the misfortune to lose four horses, and had to sacrifice the whole of his botanical collection--a heavy loss. On the 17th December, when very near the last of everything, they arrived at the settlement of Victoria, at Port Essington, and their long journey of ten months was over.

This expedition, successful as it was in opening up such a large area of well watered country, attracted universal attention, and enthusiastic poets broke forth into song at Leichhardt's return, as they already had done at his reported death. He was heartily welcomed back to Sydney, and dubbed by journalists the "Prince of Explorers." But, perhaps, better still, a solid money reward was raised by both public and private subscription, and shared amongst the party, in due proportions. During his journey, Leichhardt had discovered many important rivers draining large and fertile areas. The principal being the Dawson, the Mackenzie, the Suttor, the Burdekin, and its many tributaries. The numerous streams of the Gulf of Carpentaria, and others that have since become almost household words in Australian geography. He was singularly fortunate on this occasion; although, judging by his after career, the luck which had carried him through from Moreton Bay to Port Essington deserted him suddenly and completely. His route had been through a country so easy to penetrate and well watered, that on one night only, had the party camped without water. The blacks, with the exception of the time when Mr. Gilbert was killed, were neither troublesome nor hostile, beyond occasionally threatening them. Game was fairly plentiful, and compared with the obstacles that beset Sturt, Eyre, and Mitchell, the footsteps of the explorers had been through a garden of Eden.

But what took the public fancy the most was a certain halo of romance surrounding the journey, partly from the report of the death of the traveller having been circulated, and partly from the trip having been successful in reaching the goal aimed at, and attaining the results desired, namely, an available and habitable route to the settlement at Port Essington. All these circumstances, combined with the very slender means which had enabled the young and enthusiastic explorer to succeed, threw around Leichhardt's reputation a glamour, which, fortunately for his reputation, the mystery surrounding the total and absolute disappearance of himself and party, in 1848, has deepened, and kept alive until this day.

Leichhardt added a long string of discoveries to his name during this one trip, and had his other attempts been as successful in proportion, he would have taken the first place in the history of Australian discovery, but it was not to be so, and on this undoubtedly fruitful expedition his fame now stands.

Before Leichhardt's return, Sir Thomas Mitchell had started on his long-delayed journey, which, in the main, had the same purpose in view as Leichhardt's. This expedition had been long talked of. In 1841, communications between Governor Gipps and Captain Sturt had taken place on the subject, and in December of the same year, Eyre, not long back from his journey to King George's Sound, wrote, offering his services. [See Appendix.] To this the Governor replied that he would be glad to avail himself of Mr. Eyre's services, provided that no prior claim to the post was advanced by Captain Sturt. He also desired Eyre's views as to the expense of the party.

Eyre estimated that the sum of five thousand pounds would, he thought, be sufficient to fully cover every expense, including the hire of a vessel (to meet the party on the north coast), and the payment of the wages of the men and the salaries of the surveyor and draughtsman. But the colony was not in a mood to indulge in such expense, and nothing was done just then.

In 1843, Major Mitchell submitted A plan of exploration to the Governor, who promised to consult the Legislative Council who approved, and voted a sum of one thousand pounds towards the expenses. The Governor referred the matter to Lord Stanley, who gave a favourable reply; but still the matter was delayed.

In the beginning of the following year (1844), Eyre again made an offer of his services, intimating that now the altered circumstances of the colony would allow it to be carried through at a much cheaper rate. His offer was, however, declined, on account of the Surveyor-General, to whom the honour rightfully belonged, being in the field.

In 1845, the Council increased the exploration fund to two thousand pounds, and Sir George Gipps instructed Major Mitchell to start.

The views of Sir Thomas were in favour of obtaining a road to the foot of the Gulf, instead of Port Essington, on account of reducing the land journey considerably, and also there being such a reasonable probability that a large river would be found flowing northward into it.

In a letter which the Surveyor-General received from Mr. Walter Bagot [See Appendix.] about this time, mention is made of the blacks reporting a large river west of the Darling, running to the north or north-west. As, however, the natives do not seem very clear in their knowledge of the difference between flowing from and flowing to, it was probable that Cooper's Creek, not then discovered by Sturt, was the foundation of the legend, or possibly the Paroo.

During the earlier part of the year, Commissioner Mitchell (a son of Sir Thomas) made an exploration towards the Darling, and the discoveries of the Narran, the Balonne, and the Culgoa have been attributed to him; but, as will be seen by Bagot's letter, they were known to the settlers a year before; no special interest beyond this is to be found in the narrative of the journey.

On the 15th of December, 1845, Sir Thomas Mitchell started from Buree, his old point of departure, at the head of the small army with which he was once more going to vanquish the wilderness. Mounted videttes, barometer carrier, carter, and pioneer, etc., etc., were amongst the list of his subordinates. Well might poor Leichhardt say, when thinking over his slender resources:--
"Believe me, that one experienced and courageous bushman is worth more than the eight soldiers Sir Thomas intends to take with him. They will be an immense burthen, and of no use."

But Sir Thomas thought otherwise; without soldiers he considered that certain failure awaited the rash explorer; discipline and method were the sheet anchors of his exploratory existence, every tent in his camp was pitched by line, and every dray had its station. With the fated Kennedy as second, and Mr. W. Stephenson as surgeon and collector, he had also with him twenty-eight men, eight bullock drays, three horse drays, and two boats; and thus accompanied, he marched to the north.

Sir Thomas Mitchell struck the Darling much higher than Fort Bourke, the state of the country at this time of the year rendering this change in his plan needful. It was not until he was across the Darling that he was outside the settled districts, so rapidly had the country been stocked since last he was there, and even then he was on territory that his son had lately explored.

The first river the party struck, west of the Darling, was the Narran, and this was followed up until the Balonne was reached, which Mitchell pronounced the finest river in Australia, with the exception of the Murray. Beyond this, they made the Culgoa, and, crossing it, struck the river again above the separation of the two streams, which from thence upwards preserved the name of the Balonne.

On the 12th April, they reached the natural bridge of rocks on the Balonne, where the township of St. George now stands, long known as St. George's Bridge; and from here Sir Thomas advanced with a light party, leaving Kennedy to follow on his tracks with the remainder, after a rest of three weeks.

Soon after leaving the camp, Mitchell crossed the junction of the Maranoa, but did not at that time like its appearance, and only followed it a few miles, returning and keeping the course of the Balonne until they reached the junction of the Cogoon from the westward, when they followed the course of that river, which led them into a beautiful pastoral district around a solitary hill, which the leader named Mount Abundance, and here Mitchell first noticed the bottle tree.

Passing over a low range from the Cogoon, after crossing some tributary streams, Sir Thomas found a river with a northerly and southerly course, full of fine reaches of water, which retained its native name of the Maranoa, being supposed to be the same as the junction before noticed. Here they awaited the arrival of Kennedy with the heavy waggons and main body.

On the 1st of June, the party was reunited, and the leader prepared for a fresh excursion. Before Kennedy left the first depôt, at which, it will be remembered, he was to remain six weeks, he received dispatches from Commissioner Mitchell to Sir Thomas, by which that gentleman learnt of the success of Leichhardt's expedition.

Major Mitchell has been accused of regarding Leichhardt's success with jealous eyes, but that can scarcely be the case; true, he was of a slightly imperious temper, but he must have felt far too secure of his own reputation to fear any man's rivalry. The hasty and 'impatient remarks he was occasionally betrayed into would, no doubt, be the natural result of a man of his temperament reading such paragraphs in the Sydney newspapers as those he has quoted in his journal:--
"Australia Felix and the discoveries of Sir Thomas Mitchell now dwindle into comparative insignificance."

"We understand the intrepid Dr. Leichhardt is about to start another expedition to the Gulf, keeping to the westward of the coast ranges."

The last item would be especially annoying, as it would indicate an intention of trespassing on Mitchell's then field of operation.

On the 4th, the Surveyor-General started, intending to be away from the depôt for at least four months. He followed up the Maranoa, and crossing the broken tableland at its head, reached the Warrego, afterwards explored by Kennedy. From this river Mitchell struck north, feeling inclined to think that he was at last on the long looked for dividing watershed that separated the northern from the southern flow.

On the 2nd July, they discovered a fine running stream that soon broadened into a river, and eventually into a lake, called by Mitchell Lake Salvator, the river receiving the same name. Travelling along the basin of the head-waters of the Nogoa, which, however, turned too much to the eastward for his purpose, crossing the Claude and the fine country known as Mantuan Downs, Mitchell ascended a dividing range, and struck the head of the Belyando--one of the main tributaries of the Burdekin so lately discovered by Leichhardt. Following it down through the thick brigalow scrub, which is a marked feature of this river and its companion the Suttor, of Leichhardt, the party crossed the southern tropic on the 25th July, being, as Mitchell says, the first to enter the interior beyond that line. In this he rather overlooked the fact, which he must have known, that Leichhardt's track was only a few miles to the eastward, and also what he did not then know, that he was not in the interior but still on coast waters.

On the 10th August, the camp was visited by some natives, who did not appear of the most friendly disposition. They apparently called the river Belyando, which name was adopted. On their getting noisy and troublesome, they were ignominiously put to flight by the dogs charging them. At this point Mitchell had reluctantly to alter his preconceived opinions and conjectures, and come to the conclusion that the northern fall of the waters was still to be looked for to the westward, and that a further continuance on his present course would lead him on to Leichhardt's track. Disappointed, he gave the order to turn back, and on the last days of August they were once again on the Nogoa tributaries.

At the foot of the range Mitchell established a second depôt, and on the 10th September started with the black boy and two men for a month's trip to the westward. On this trip, he must receive the credit of initiating the now commonly used water-bag for carrying water. His, it must be confessed, was a very crude one, being only a thick flour bag, covered outside with melted mutton fat.

The second day they met some natives, and from one old woman learnt the names of some of the neighbouring streams, particularly the Warrego, which river they had crossed on their outward way. The first river he encountered was the Nive, and again he, as usual, flattered himself that he was at the head of Gulf waters, little thinking that he was on the most northern tributary of the Darling. A small tributary was called the Nivelle. A short day's ride convinced him that this river ran too much to the south-east, and he turned to the north through the scrub, and on the morning of the 15th September, was rewarded with the splendid outlook that has since greeted so many wayfarers on emerging from the Nive scrub.

In his journal he says:--
"I there beheld downs and plains extending westward beyond the reach of vision, bounded on the S.W. by woods and low ranges, and on the N.E. by higher ranges, the whole of these open downs declining to the N.W., in which direction a line of trees marked the course of a river traceable to the remotest verge of the horizon. There I found then, at last, the realization of my long-cherished hopes--an interior river falling to the N.W. in the heart of an open country, extending also in that direction. . . . From the rock where I stood, the scene was so extensive, as to leave no room for doubt as to the course of the river, which thus and there revealed to me alone, seemed like a reward direct, from Heaven for perseverance, and as a compensation for the many sacrifices I had. made in order to solve the question as to the interior rivers of tropical Australia."

Once more the victim of a too sanguine belief, he followed tip his discovery by at once commencing to trace down the river that ran through this new-found paradise. He had made a great contribution to Australian geography, as great as what he hoped for; but if he had been told the truth he would scarcely have been satisfied. He had found the upper tributaries of the second great river system of the interior, as Sturt -had found its lower outflow, and he had thrown open the wonderful western prairies, but he was as far from the Gulf as ever.

Light-hearted and satisfied, the party rode on for days through the beautiful undulating downs country. On the 22nd September, we find in his journal a notice of the new kind of grass, which was in future to be so highly prized and to bear his name:

"Two kinds of grass grew on these plains, one of them, a brome grass, possessing the remarkable property of shooting up green from the old stalk."

On the 23rd, they crossed and named the Alice, and on the 26th, being fully satisfied, and their provisions running short turned back.

Mitchell for once, in honour of such a discovery, departed from his usual custom, which was the healthy plan of giving "good, sonorous native names" to the most noticeable features, and called the river the Victoria. On the 6th of October they reached the depôt camp, and found all well.

The return to the main depôt, left in charge of Kennedy, was soon accomplished, and on the 19th this was reached, and the occupants found safe and unmolested, although the absence of Mitchell had now extended over the four months. As a proof of the capabilities of the country he had travelled over, Mitchell brought back all his animals in first-rate condition, having lost only one horse, and that was through an accident.

The final return was made down the yet unexplored Maranoa, at the head of which the depôt had been fixed so long; and on the 4th November they arrived at the Balonne, having passed through splendidly-grassed and well-watered country the whole way. The party took up their old camp at St. George's Bridge, where they learnt from the natives that a party of whites had been in the neighbourhood during their absence. Kennedy was dispatched to inspect the Mooni ponds, or river, which they understood was to the eastward of them. He found them occupied by cattle stations to within a day's ride of the camp, so that the explorer's work may be considered as at an end.

This expedition, it may well be supposed, fully confirmed Mitchell's reputation. Once more he had been the means of assuring the colonists that away towards the setting sun the flocks and herds might advance unchecked, so far as he had been, and as he thought, across the great continent. Added to which, he felt convinced, and expected the public also to feel the same, that along the banks of the Victoria was the great high road to the north coast.

This was the last expedition of the Surveyor-General, and the year before concluded the active work of his old rival in the field, Charles Sturt. Both men had done wonders in the cause of exploration; but the genii of plentiful seasons and bountiful vegetation seems to have been the forerunner of Sir Thomas, whilst a demon of drought and aridity stalked in front of Sturt.

Chapter VII

*Kennedy traces the Victoria in its final course south--Re-named the
Barcoo--First notice of the pituri chewing natives--Leichhardt's second Expedition--Failure and Return--Leichhardt's last Expedition--His
absolute disappearance--Conjectures as to his fate--Kennedy starts
from Rockingham Bay to Cape York--Scrubs and swamps--Great exer-
tions--Hostile natives--Insufficiency of supplies provided--Dying
horses--Main party left in Weymouth Bay--Another separation at
Shelburne Bay--Murder of Kennedy at the Escape River--Rescue of
Jacky the black boy--His pathetic tale of suffering--Failure to find the
camp at Shelburne Bay--Rescue of but two survivors at Weymouth
Bay--The remainder starved to death--Von Mueller in the Australian
Alps--Western Australia--Landor and Lefroy, in 1843--First expedition
of the brothers Gregory, in 1846--Salt lakes and scrub--Lieutenant
Helpman sent to examine the coal seam discovered--Roe, in 1848--His
journey to the east and to the south--A. C. Gregory attempts to reach
the Gascoyne--Foiled by the nature of the country--Discovers silver
ore on the Murchison--Governor Fitzgerald visits the mine--Wounded
by the natives--Rumour of Leichhardt having been murdered by the
blacks--Hely's expedition in quest of him--Story unfounded--Austin's
explorations in Western Australia--Terrible scrubs--Poison camp--
Determined efforts to the north--Heat and thirst--Forced to return.*

The importance of deciding the final course of the Victoria
was at once recognised, and Kennedy was chosen to lead a lightly
equipped party. However convinced Sir Thomas Mitchell was of the
affluent of the Victoria being in the Gulf of Carpentaria, others did not
at once fall in with the notion. It was evident that the vast flooded
plains, and many channels of Cooper's Creek absorbed immense quantities of water from the interior, and apparently this water came from
the north-east. What more probable than that the Victoria was lost
there.

Kennedy followed the old track to the river, found by Mitchell, and reaching his lowest camp on the 13th of August, commenced to run the river down from there. On the first day's journey he met a native, from whom he learnt the aboriginal name of the Victoria, the Barcoo.

On the 15th Kennedy noticed with anxiety that the valley of the river certainly fell to the south, and that ever since it had turned from its northerly course, it was making for the point where Sturt turned back on Cooper's Creek. He consequently began to dread that he might follow the course of it, so far as not to be able to carry out the second part of his instructions, namely, to look for a road to the Gulf, not having enough means with him for both journeys. He decided to follow with two men along the Barcoo, far enough to the south to leave no doubt about its not being a north coast river. After two days' journey, the direction of the Barcoo turned west, and even north of west, and the bed contained fine reaches of water, one hundred, and one hundred and twenty yards wide. Kennedy turned back for the whole of his party, considering that his duty was to follow such a river, no matter in what direction it led him.

On the 30th August, they came upon a large tributary from the N.N.E., which was named the Thomson, and they found the country very different from the grassy plains of the upper reaches.

Finally, the river led them amongst plains gaping with fissures, grassless and waterless, where the only change in the flat character of the country was the sandhill formation, that exactly agreed with Sturt's description. In fact, it was now evident to Kennedy that the only result of his journey would be to connect with that explorer's most northerly and easterly point, and, however satisfactory or unsatisfactory this might be, it was scarcely worth risking the lives of his party, and the certain loss of his horses to attain. Grass, or feed of any sort, had now failed them for several days, and at last they could find no more water. They were confronted with the desert described by Sturt with such terrible accuracy, and there was nothing to be gained by entering into a struggle with it. Kennedy turned back quite satisfied that the end of the Victoria was in Cooper's Creek.

As the nomenclature of these watercourses is rather conflicting, and they were the field of many subsequent explorations, it may be as well to mention that the Victoria (now the Barcoo) joins Kennedy's Thomson, which still retains its name, and below the junction the united stream is always now called Cooper's Creek. Thus, as the residents out there tell you, it takes two rivers in that part of Australia to make a creek.

A noticeable incident here occurs in Kennedy's journal. Writing on the 11th September, he says:--

"A curious fact I observed here is, that the men chew tobacco; it is, of course, in a green state, but it is strong and hot."

This was almost, certainly, the pituri plant, which the natives of the interior chew, and then bury in the sand, where the heat of the sun causes it to ferment; it is then chewed as an intoxicant, the natives carrying a plug behind their car in their hair. It is offered to a stranger as an especial compliment, and great is the affront if this toothsome morsel is declined. It only grows in certain localities, far west of where Kennedy saw the natives using it, and the blacks of the locality where it is found barter it away with other tribes, by which means it is found at a considerable distance from where it grows. Amongst the natives there are pituri and non-pituri chewers.

On his downward journey Kennedy, to ease his horses as much as possible, had buried a great quantity of flour and sugar. On his return he found that the natives had discovered it, and wantonly emptied it out of the bags into the hole, reducing it to a mixture of earth and flour that was completely useless. This loss prevented Kennedy from making his intended excursion to the Gulf. The party started back, and on his way Kennedy picked up his carts, which he had also buried. He was just in time; a native, probably one of the burglars already mentioned, had been examining and sounding the ground but a short time before the party arrived.

On reaching the head of the Warrego, Kennedy determined to follow it down, and ascertain whether it was a southerly or westerly flowing river. They followed the Warrego south, through fine grazing country, the river being full of splendid reaches of water, but at last it failed them, running out in flat country in waterless channels. From here they struck across easterly to the Culgoa, which river they reached after a ride of seventy miles without water, over a barren country, timbered with pine and brigalow. Here they were delayed getting the carts across this dry track, and lost six horses from heat and thirst. Thus vanished the high hopes entertained of the Victoria River.

Meantime, Leichhardt, encouraged by his first success, had received liberal support from the public to enable him to start on a new expedition, which at once was to settle the question of the nature of the interior, the ambitious project being nothing less than to traverse the continent from the eastern to the western shore, on much the same parallel of latitude if possible.

The party travelled overland from the Hunter River to the Darling Downs, bringing with them their outfit of mules, cattle, and goats. On December 10th, 1846, the expedition left Mr. Stephens' station on the Condamine, the members then consisting of seven whites and two blacks. Of stock, they had two hundred and seventy goats, one hundred and eighty sheep, forty bullocks, fifteen horses, and thirteen mules. This stock, with their flour, tea, sugar, etc., was to last them on a two years' journey.

It is almost needless to go into particulars concerning this unfortunate trip. They never succeeded in getting away from the old Port Essington track. The rains came down on them in the sickly brigalow scrubs of the Dawson and Mackenzie. Fever was the result, and they had no medicines with them--a strange omission. Their only coverings during the wet were two miserable calico tents. Their life, as told by members of the party, consisted of semi-starvation, varied by gorging and feasting on killing days, in which the Doctor apparently set the example; in fact, his character throughout comes out in anything but an amiable light, and one is led to wonder how anyone so destitute of tact and readiness of resource ever achieved the journey to Port Essington, favoured even as he was on that occasion by circumstances and seasons. Suffice it to say, to end the miserable story, that, having first lost their sheep and goats, then their cattle and most of their horses and mules, they turned up on the 6th of July at Chauvel's station on the Condamine, having done nothing but wander about on the old track and eat their supplies.

On reaching the station, Dr. Leichhardt was put in possession of the finding of the Victoria, the Maranoa, &c., and being anxious to examine the country between Sir Thomas Mitchell's track and his own, he, in company with Mr. Isaacs and three of his late companions, left Stuart Russell's station on a short excursion, during which he crossed to the Balonne and back, making some subordinate discoveries.

Still persisting in his idea of crossing the continent, and fearful that he might be forestalled, he made great efforts to get together a small party of some sort to make another attempt. He succeeded; but this time his party was neither so well provided nor so large. In fact, very little is known of the members constituting it. The Rev. W. B. Clarke, speaking of this final trip, says:--

"The parties who accompanied Leichhardt were, perhaps, little capable of shifting for themselves in case of any accident to their leader. The second in command, a brother-in-law of Leichhardt, came from Germany to join him just before starting, and he told me, when I asked him what his qualifications for the journey were, that he had been at sea, had suffered shipwrecks, and was, therefore, well able to endure hardship. I do not know what his other qualifications were."

For some inexplicable reason, this man, whose name was Classen or Klausen, has always been selected as the hero of the many tales that have been brought in of a solitary survivor of the party living in captivity with the natives; probably, because his was the only name besides Leichhardt's generally known and remembered.

The lost expedition is supposed to have consisted of six whites and two blacks. The names known are those of the Doctor himself, Classen, Hentig, Stuart, and Kelly. He had with him fifty bullocks, thirteen mules, twelve horses, and two hundred and seventy goats, beside the utterly inadequate allowance of eight hundred pounds of flour, one hundred and twenty pounds of tea, some sugar and salt, and two hundred and fifty pounds of shot and forty of powder.

His last letter [See Appendix.] is dated the 3rd of April, 1848, from McPherson's station on the Cogoon, but in it he speaks only of the. country traversed, and says nothing of his intended route. Since the residents of this outlying station lost sight of him and his men, no clue to his fate has ever been found. The total evanishment not only of his men but of the animals (especially the goats) that accompanied him, is one of the strangest mysteries of our mysterious interior.

Leichhardt's expressed intention was to endeavour to skirt the edge of the desert--which was then supposed to exist in the centre--to the northward, seizing the first opportunity of penetrating it, and then making for Perth. From what we now know, it is quite impossible to guess how much or little of this programme was carried out, as the existence or non-existence of what he would consider a desert would entirely depend upon what the season had been like immediately before his arrival.

The perusal of his journal to Port Essington, impresses one with the opinion that, considering his scientific training, he was singularly deficient in observation. In one place he writes that horses and bullocks never showed that instinctive faculty of detecting water so often mentioned by travellers, and that they seem to be guided entirely by their sight when in search of it--an assertion which seems incredible on the part of a man with any bush training at all. If Leichhardt had ever had to steady a thirsty mob of cattle during a pitch dark night, with a strong wind blowing from water, or even across the damp bed of a lagoon or river, miles and miles away, he would soon have found out by what sense cattle are guided in their search for water.

Although one does not want to harshly criticise these obvious errors in the very rudiments of bush-craft, they serve to indicate how likely he would have been, if entrapped in dry country, to commit a mistake that would sacrifice his men. And one cannot but believe that he relied quite as much on the chapter of accidents to pull him through as upon his own helpfulness or experience. Of the causes that led to the destruction or dispersion of the whole of the party it is next to impossible to hazard a guess. The completeness of the disappearance is the most the puzzling part of the mystery. Had they been killed by the natives, relics of the explorers would long since have been recovered from them. In some shape the iron work of the implements they had with them would have survived.

Many have tried to explain it by imagining them swept away by a flood when camped on flat country, but this is scarcely likely, for even then, on the subsidence of the waters, the blacks would have found something of their belongings. Thirst was most likely the agent of their destruction, and fire completed the work.

Once across the waters that wend their sluggish way into the lake district of South Australia, Leichhardt and his followers would be in the great region of fragmentary watercourses; rivers and creeks, when met with, pursuing no definite courses--now lost in miles of level country, now reforming again for a brief existence, but always delusive and disappointing. Here they would one day find themselves in a position that left them no other chance but the slender one of still pushing forward into the unknown. Probably it was during one of the cycles of rainless years that periodically visit the continent. Led on mile after mile, following the dry bed of one creek, to lose it in some barren flat, whereon the withered stalks of blue-bush alone told of a time of past vegetation; again picking up another creek, to lose it in like manner, knowing that to retrace their steps was impossible; making at last for a hazy, blue line in the distance that turned out to be spinifex and stunted forest; trusting still that this might indicate a change that would lead them to higher country and to water, they would struggle forward, weak and disorganised.

Then would come the beginning of the end. As they pressed on, the forest became scantier, and the spinifex higher, spikier, and harder to march through. One by one their animals had fallen and died, and the desperate resort of drinking the blood had been tried by some. What little water they had in their canteens was fast evaporating. Still

147

some of them would keep heart. The ground was getting stonier, and bare patches of rock were constantly passed; surely they must be getting on higher country; they were doubtless ascending the gradual rise of one of the inland watersheds, and suddenly they hoped the ground would break away at their feet in deep gullies and ravines; below they would see the tops of green trees, shading some quiet waterhole. How anxiously they looked out for any sign of life that might be a good augury of this, but none could be seen.

Since leaving the open country, even the tireless kites had deserted them; all around was silent, still, and lifeless. It was useless to stop to rest, the ground was blistering to the touch, and there was no shade anywhere. Then came night, but no change; throughout the long watches, the radiance of the stars was never blurred by clouds. Some of the men slept and dreamt of streams of clear, cold water, awaking only to greet the dawn of another day of blinding, stifling heat, heralded by the faint sultry sigh of the hot wind. And as the day grew hotter and hotter some lost their reason, and all lost hope. Then came the end; they separated and straggled away in ones and twos and fell and died. Day after day the terrible and pitiless sun .looked down at them lying there, and watched them dry and shrivel into mummies, and still no rain fell on the earth.

By day the sky was clear and bright, and by night the stars unclouded. Years may have passed; higher and higher grew the spinifex, and its long resinous needles entangled themselves in each other, unchecked by fire for no black hunters came there in that season of drought, and the men's bodies lay there, growing more and more unlike humanity, scorched by the seven times heated earth beneath, and the glaring sun above untouched, save by the ants, those scavengers of the desert, or the tiny bright-eyed lizards. At last, the thunder clouds began to gather afar off, and when they broke, a few wandering natives ventured into the woods, living for a day or two on the uncertain rainfall. This failing, they retired again, leaving perhaps, a trail of fire behind them. Then this fire, fed by the huge banks of flammable spinifex, the growth of many years, spread into a mighty conflagration, the black smoke covering half the heavens. The hawks and the crows fled before it, swooping down on the vermin that were forced to leave the shelter of log and bush. The great silence that had reigned for so long was broken by the roar, and crash, and crackle of a sea of flames; and beneath this fiery blast every vestige of the lost explorers vanished for ever.

When, on the blackened ground, fell heavy rain once more, the spinifex sprang up, fresh and green to look at, only in spots here and there, where a human body had fertilised the soil, it was greener than elsewhere.

So Leichhardt drops out of Australian history, and with every succeeding year the chances of finding any trace grow more remote.

Expeditions have been started in search of him, but without result, and the tale of their efforts will be told in their proper order.

As if the year 1848, when Europe seemed convulsed with some strange tempest of riot and turmoil, should not be unmarked in Australia, two of the most disastrous expeditions in the annals of exploration started during its course. One, Leichhardt's, as we have just seen, vanished, and all must have perished. Of the other, under Kennedy, two ghastly famished spectres, that had once been white men, and a naked blackfellow, alone were rescued out of thirteen.

The same impulses that led to Mitchell's and Leichhardt's northern journeys, started Kennedy on his fatal venture up the eastern slope of the long peninsula that terminates in Cape York. The desire to find a road to the north coast, so that an available chain of communication should exist between the southern settlements and a northern seaport.

Kennedy started from Sydney on board the barque Tam O'Shanter, on the 29th of April, 1848. He had twelve men in his party, including Mr. Carron as botanist, one of the survivors who published the account of the trip, and Mr. Wall, naturalist. Their outfit consisted of twenty-eight horses and one hundred sheep, besides the other necessary rations, carts, &c. The instructions were to land at Rockingham Bay, and examine the eastern coast of the peninsula, to Port Albany in the extreme north, where a ship would meet and receive them. Such was the programme, alas for the performance!

On the 30th of May, they landed in Rockingham Bay, with the loss of one horse, and Kennedy made his first acquaintanceship with the tropical jungles of northern Queensland (that now is), including the terrible lawyer vine [Calamus Australis.] and the stinging tree. The first, a vine with long hooks and spurs on it, that once fast, seem determined never to let go again; the stalk being as tenacious and tough as wire, and binding the scrub trees together so as to render advance impossible without first cutting a way. The other, a tree with broad leaves, the sting produced by touching which is so painful that horses, who on first being stung have plunged about and been stung all over, have died from the fever and inflammation caused.

149

These scrubs, marshy ground, salt water creeks, and high mountain ranges, all inhabited by hostile natives, formed the pleasant prospect before Kennedy.

From the very commencement almost, the monotonous record of Carron's journal commences day after day thus--"Cutting scrub all day." Through these marshes and swamps Kennedy strove to make for the ranges, hoping at least to find clearer country to travel through. Often during this time, he must have thought of his last journey over the boundless prairies of the Barcoo, and sighed at the contrast. The natives, too, began to annoy the travellers, and at last they were fired on and four killed and wounded.

On the 18th July, the carts were abandoned, and they went on with twenty-six pack horses, their sheep being reduced to fifty, and these were rapidly falling away, as well as the horses, on the sour coast grasses. They fared no better when they reached the range, or the spurs of the Main Range, for the scrub still hemmed them in, and roads up and down the rugged hills were hard to find; then to add to all, rain set in.

On the 14th August, Carron took charge of the stores instead of Niblet, who had been very extravagant with them, and also sent in false returns; the allowance of flour was now reduced, and hopes were entertained that with care it would hold out; but at first the supply provided was insufficient. The horses too, began to knock up, and one after another they were left behind dead or dying.

Crossing the dividing watershed, the party for some time travelled along the heads of rivers running into the Gulf of Carpentaria, finding it a great improvement in every way--thence they crossed back on to the waters of the east coast once more, and their horses still giving in, one by one, they fell back on them as an article of diet.

On the 9th of November, Kennedy realised that struggling on with the whole of his party meant death by starvation to all, so he determined to push ahead with three men and the black boy to Port Albany, and send back relief by water. Port Albany, in the Pass of that name, being the rendezvous agreed upon with the relief vessel. The camp was selected on the top of a hill, fully visible from Weymouth Bay, and Mr. Carron put in charge of it.

On the 13th, Kennedy started with the best seven of the horses leaving the eight men in camp to await his return, or the relief boat. The only account ever received of his journey came from the lips of the black boy Jacky-Jacky, the sole survivor.

His story ran that three weeks after leaving Weymouth Bay they reached Shelburne Bay, after cutting through a great deal of scrub and crossing many rivers and creeks. Here Costigan accidentally shot himself, and became very weak from loss of blood, so Luff, [Luff; the man mentioned here, was with Kennedy on his Barcoo expedition, and some of the trees on the Warrego, marked "L," and ascribed to Leichhardt, were probably some of his marking.] another of the men, being ill, Kennedy left the third man, Dunn, to look after them, and one horse for food; he and the boy making a desperate effort to reach Cape York and send back succour. But it was in vain. They reached the Escape River, and were in sight of Albany Island, when they met a number of blacks who were apparently friendly, although Jacky mistrusted them. Then came the end. Jacky's story has been often told, but it will bear repetition.

"I and Mr. Kennedy watched them that night, taking it in turns every hour that night. By-and-by I saw the blackfellows. It was a moonlight night, and I walked up to Mr. Kennedy and said, 'There is plenty of blackfellows now.' This was in the middle of the night. Mr. Kennedy told rue to get my gun ready.

"The blacks did not know where we slept as we did not make a fire. We both sat up all night. After this, daylight came, and I fetched the horses and saddled them. Then we went on a good way up the river, and then we sat down a little while, and then we saw three blacks coming along our track, and then they saw us, and one ran back as hard as he could run, and fetched up plenty more, like a flock of sheep almost. I told Mr. Kennedy to put the saddles on the horses and go on; and the blacks came up and they followed us all day. All along it was raining, and I now told him to leave the horses, and come on without them, that the horses made too much track. Mr. Kennedy was too weak, and would not leave the horses. We went on this day until towards the evening; raining hard, and the blacks followed us all day, some behind, some planted before. In fact, blackfellows all around, following us. Now we went into a little bit of scrub, and I told Mr. Kennedy to look behind always. Sometimes he would do so, and sometimes he would not do so, to look out for the blacks. Then a good many blackfellows came behind in the scrub, and threw plenty of spears, and hit Mr. Kennedy in the back first. Mr. Kennedy said to me, 'Oh, Jacky Jacky shoot 'em! shoot 'em!' Then I pulled out my gun and fired, and hit one fellow all over the face with buck shot. He tumbled down, and got up again, and again, and wheeled right round, and two blacks picked him up and carried him away. They went a little way and came back again, throwing spears all round, more than they did before-very large spears.

"I pulled out the spear at once from Mr. Kennedy's back, and cut the jag with Mr. Kennedy's knife. Then Mr. Kennedy got his gun and snapped, but the gun would not go off. The blacks sneaked all along by the trees, and speared Mr. Kennedy again in the right leg, above the knee a little, and I got speared in the eye, and the blacks were now throwing always, never giving over, and shortly again speared Mr. Kennedy in the right side. There were large jags to the spears, and I cut them out and put them in my pocket. At the same time we got speared the horses got speared too, and jumped and bucked about and got into the swamps. I now told Mr. Kennedy to sit down while I looked after the saddle bags, which I did, and when I came back again I saw blacks along with Mr. Kennedy. I then asked him if he saw the blacks with him. He was stupid with the spear wounds, and said, 'No.' I then asked him where was his watch? I saw the blacks taking away watch and hat as I was returning to Mr. Kennedy. Then I carried Mr. Kennedy into the scrub. He said 'Don't carry me a good way.' Then Mr. Kennedy looked this way, very bad (Jacky rolling his eyes). Then I said to him don't look far away, as I thought he would be frightened. I asked him often, are you well now, and he said, 'I don't care for the spear wound in my leg, Jacky, but for the other two spear wounds in my side and back, and I am bad inside, Jacky.' I told him blackfellow always die when he got spear in there (the back). He said, 'I am out of wind, Jacky.' I asked him (Mr. Kennedy), are you going to leave me? And he said, 'Yes, my boy, I am going to leave you.' He said, 'I am very bad, Jacky you take the books, Jacky, to the Captain, but not the big ones, the Governor will give you anything for them.' I then tied up the papers. He then said, 'Jacky, you give me paper and I will write.' I gave him paper and pencil and he tried to write, and he then fell back and died, and I caught him as he fell back, and held him, and I then turned round myself and cried. I was crying a good while until I got well, that was about an hour, and then I buried him.

"I digged up the ground with a tomahawk, and covered him over with logs and grass and my shirt and trousers. That night I left him near dark. I would go through the scrub, and the blacks threw spears at me, a good many, and I went back again into the scrub. Then I went down the creek which runs into Escape River, and I walked along the water in the creek, very easy, with my head only above water to avoid the blacks and get out of their way. In this way I went half a mile. Then I got out of the creek and got clear of them, and walked on all night nearly, and slept in the bush without a fire."

This was the sad tale. It took poor starving Jacky thirteen days to get to Port Albany, short as the distance comparatively was. He lived on what small vermin he could catch, climbing trees every now and again to look for Port Albany and the ship. He carried the saddle bags, with Kennedy's papers, for some distance, but had to leave them hidden in a log.

Immediately that Jacky's story was told to the people of the Ariel, the schooner awaiting Kennedy's party at Port Albany, sail was made for Shelburne Bay to rescue the three men left there. A canoe was captured which contained articles that left little doubt of the fate of the unfortunates. The camp, however, was too far inland to reach without a very strong party, and as it seemed certain that help was too late, and there were eight men, whom Jacky described as being scarcely able to crawl, awaiting relief at Weymouth Bay, sail was again made there.

The wretched men at Weymouth Bay had fared but badly. Douglas died first, and he was buried; a rite which the party had afterwards to leave unperformed, through sheer weakness. Taylor died next and was buried by the side of Douglas.

Meantime, the blacks behaved in an inexplicable manner, at times they would approach and offer the whites tainted fish as if to make friends, and then come up with spears poised, and every token of hostility, compelling the weary watchers to stand on their guard, expecting an attack. Carpenter was the next to die, and he was buried with the others. On the 1st December a schooner was seen in the Bay; and joyfully the flag was hoisted and some rockets let off after dark. But she sailed away, never having seen the signals, and the agony of the disappointed men can be imagined. On the 28th December, Niblet and Wall died, and the blacks came and surrounded the camp and threatened the two helpless survivors, hardly able to stand up and hold their guns.

On the 30th, Goddard crawled out to try and shoot some pigeons, and Carron sat with a pistol in his hand, to give him warning if the blacks approached. Let him tell the end.

"About an hour after he was gone I could see some natives running over the hill towards me. I fired a pistol immediately, but before Goddard could get back they were into the camp, and handed me a piece of paper very much dirtied and torn, but I was sure by their manner that there was a vessel in the bay. It proved to be a note to me from Captain

Dobson, but I could only read part of it, it was so covered with dirt. I was for a minute or two almost senseless from the hope of being relieved from our miserable condition. I made them some presents, and wrote a note to Captain Dobson and sent them away with it. I easily made them understand what I wanted, but I soon saw that they had other intentions. I saw a great number of natives coming in all directions, well armed. I saw two from strange tribes amongst them. One man that I gave an old shirt to, and put it on him, I saw him take it off and pick up his spears. We were expecting every minute to be attacked by these treacherous villains, when, to our great joy, we saw Captain Dobson, Dr. Vallack, Jacky (the black boy), and another man who had received a spear wound in his arm (Barrett), so that he could offer no resistance to the blacks, coming across the creek. These men had risked their own lives by coming about three miles through mangroves and thick scrub (surrounded by not less than a hundred natives, well armed), with a hope of saving some of us from starving."

The camp had to be vacated in such a hurry in consequence of the threatened attack, that nothing was saved but a few instruments and botanical specimens.

This was the end of a most unfortunate expedition from the first landing. Against the impassable nature of the line of march, and the hostile inhabitants, the harassed explorers had to combat from the first. Their horses were not acclimated, so they soon wasted away, and when sickness laid its hand upon the men they were doomed. The one brightening touch in the whole gloomy picture is the simple devotion shown by poor Jacky: "He then fell back and died, and I caught him as he fell back and held him, and then I turned round myself and cried," was the funeral oration over the brave and unfortunate Kennedy.

The brig Freak was chartered by the Government to make another examination of the coast. The remains of the men at Weymouth Bay were reinterred, and search made for the missing men at Shelburne Bay, but they were never found. Some of the papers secreted by Jacky were recovered, but Kennedy's body had been taken away. This was all that was ever discovered.

In the south of Australia, in 1847, Baron von Mueller was engaged in many explorations, in some still unknown parts of the continent down there. These travels were undertaken for botanical and geographical purposes combined, partly in the province of South Australia, and latterly amongst the many unexplored recesses of the Australian Alps. The culminating points of several of the highest mountains in Australia were fixed, and their geographical positions accurately defined amongst them being Mount Hotham.

To the west coast once again. Still trusting that perseverance would be finally rewarded, the colonists on Swan River kept making vigorous attempts to penetrate what they would fain consider was only a desert belt bounding their territory.

In 1843 a small private party, consisting of Messrs. Landor and Lefroy, made a short excursion from York, being absent a fortnight. They came across several shallow lakes, both salt and fresh, but their journey was not recompensed by the discovery of any good country.

In 1846 we first come across the name of Gregory in the annals of exploration. There were three brothers of this name, led by the eldest, A. C. Gregory, who as a scientific explorer so greatly distinguished himself in after life. On the 7th August, 1846, they started from Bolgart Spring, the furthest stock station to the eastward.

Their equipment was of the slenderest, and they only took about two months supply of rations. On leaving the settled districts they at once found themselves in the barren country, that had so often stopped the outward march of the pioneers, and their first discovery was a swampy lake (fresh) on the edge of a small patch of better country, but this quickly passed, and they entered into the salt lake region, through which they pushed until they reached a range of granite hills, forming the watershed of the coast streams. Turning somewhat to the northward, they kept along these hills for the sake of the rain water to be found amongst the rocks, until, striking again to the east, they encountered an extensive salt lake or swamp; attempting to cross which their horses were bogged, and only extricated with difficulty.

This lake was found afterwards to be of great size, and to fairly hem them in to the eastward, so after several disappointments they turned to the westward to examine some of the streams crossed by Grey during his unfortunate expedition to Shark's Bay. On the head of one of these rivers (the Arrowsmith), which from the uncertainty of Grey's chart, they were unable to clearly identify; they found a seam of coal. This was the only discovery of any importance that they made, the rest of their journey was over very impoverished country, covered with scrub and sand, with here and there salt flats and lakes. They returned to Bolgart Spring on the 22nd September.

On hearing of the coal discovery the Government sent Lieutenant Helpman in the schooner Champion, to Champion Bay, which place he. reached at the end of the year, accompanied by one of the

Gregorys. They landed the cart and horses, and on the 12th December reached the scene of the coal find. They soon filled their cart with coal, and returned by a somewhat different track to the schooner. F. Gregory making a detour to the northward without any noteworthy result.

Not yet disappointed in the hope of finding country worth settling to the eastward, Surveyor-General Roe started from York on the 14th September, 1848; he had with him six men, (including H. Gregory) and twelve horses, with over three months' provisions. It will be unnecessary to follow them over the salt lake country which they inevitably met with soon after leaving civilization, or the outskirts of it Their first attempts beyond were unsuccessful; they were successively turned from their course by scrub of the densest character, and sandy plains, so they at last made for the south coast, where they rested for a while at one of the small settlements.

On the 18th, they again started, following the upward course of the Pallinup River, which was the last stream crossed by Eyre before reaching Albany, on his Great Bight expedition. They ascended a branch coming from the north-east, and for a time travelled through well grassed and promising valleys, but afterwards found themselves once more in the scrubs and sandy plains of the desert. Catching sight of a granite hill to the eastward, they proceeded there, but from its summit the outlook was as gloomy as ever. Fortunately the weather had been showery, and the want of water was not felt so much as the total absence of feed. Still, on to the eastward their difficulties increased at every step. To the impassable thickets and desolate plains was now added the absence of fresh water, and it was not until after days of privation that they reached some elevated peaks, where a little grass and water were found.

Their course was now to the south-east, towards the range sighted by Eyre, and named the Russell Range, and a desperate struggle commenced with the barren country through which they had to work their way. So weakened were the horses, and such was the nature of the belts of scrub, that it took them three days to accomplish fifty miles, and after being four days and three nights without water for the horses, they reached a rugged granite hill, called Mount Riley, where they got a scant supply. From here, their journey to the Russell Range, fifty miles away, was but a repetition of their former hardships. Nothing but continuous scrub; sometimes the thickets were too dense to attempt a passage, even with the axes, and long detours had to be made. At last, with worn-out horses, they reached the Russell Range, and every hope they had entertained of a change for the better was blasted. The range was a mass of naked rocks, and from the summit nothing but the interminable sea of scrub and the distant ocean, was visible. Fortunately, they got a little grass and water, which saved the lives of their animals.

From the Russell Range, Roe's homeward track was not far removed from Eyre's, so that no fresh geographical features could be expected, or were discovered, with the exception of another coal seam in one of the rivers running into the south coast. On the 2nd February, 1849, the Surveyor-General reached Perth.

During the time this last expedition had been endeavouring to proceed east, A. C. Gregory was put in charge of a party to make for the north, and ascertain the value of the country reported by Grey as existing on the Gascoyne. On his way, Gregory reported favourably of the country around Champion Bay, which had been extolled by Gray, and subsequently condemned by Captain Stokes. Beyond the Murchison, he did not succeed in penetrating any considerable distance; being turned back at all points, after repeated attempts, by the tract of impervious scrub that intervened between the Murchison and the Gascoyne. He therefore returned, without seeing the latter river, having attained a distance of three hundred and fifty miles north of Perth. On their return to the Murchison, a vein of galena was discovered, and the river traced upwards and downwards for a considerable distance. They reached Perth on the 17th November.

The following month Governor Fitzgerald, accompanied by A. C. Gregory, Bland, and three soldiers, went by sea to Champion Bay, and landing some horses, proceeded inland to examine the new mineral discovery. The lode was found to be more important than was at first supposed.

On their return journey to Champion Bay, an affray occurred with the natives. The blacks followed them for some time, their numbers constantly increasing, until fifty well-armed natives were present; in a thick scrub they succeeded in surrounding the whites, and commenced hostilities. The party found it necessary to resort to their firearms. and the Governor fired the first shot, bringing down the leading native, who had just thrown a spear at Gregory. A shower of spears then fell amongst the group of explorers, and the Governor was speared through the leg. The natives were, however, kept at bay, and that afternoon they reached the beach and embarked on board the schooner.

This was the second time an Australian Governor had been wounded by the natives, the first occasion being when Captain Arthur Phillip was speared.

Fears now began to be entertained in the other colonies as to the safety of Leichhardt and his party, and, in consequence of these fears being augmented by the tales and rumours that drifted in from the outside districts, gathered from the natives (referring to the murder of a party of whites to the westward), it was decided to equip an expedition to try and ascertain the truth of these reports.

The party was put in charge of Mr. Hovenden Hely, a former companion of Leichhardt on his second expedition, and in the beginning of 1852 he left Sydney on the search, his instructions being to act as circumstances should determine him.

About forty miles from Mitchell's Mount Abundance he met with the first of a series of native statements that were destined to keep luring him forward on a false scent. The story, as usual, was most circumstantial, and did credit to the imaginations of the authors; two blacks offered to conduct Hely to the scene of the massacre, and under their guidance he started, It was a very dry season, and when they reached Mitchell's old depôt camp on the Maranoa, where, it will be remembered that his party were encamped for four months, nothing of the fine sheet of water mentioned by him was seen; it had shrunk to a shallow pool in a bed of sand. Here the two guides insisted that the murder had taken place, pointing to the remains of Mitchell's encampment as a proof thereof. This naturally led Hely to disbelieve their statement, but the blacks added such details to the original story as almost again convinced him. The most minute search, however, resulted in nothing, and one of the natives managed to make his escape. The other then altered his version of the affair, and shifted the scene of the tragedy to the westward again, and the party struck northwest to the Warrego.

More blacks were met with who confirmed the tale, and one guided them to a water hole in a brigalow scrub, which she. said was the place where the tragedy was enacted. She also stated that she was present, and entered into a most minute description of the affair, describing the whole attack. Not the vestige of a trace could be found to give any colour to her story, but ten miles down the river an unmistakeable camping ground was found. There was a tree marked L, the letter being roughly cut into the bark, and inside the letter, X V A was carved; also there were indications that proved that a party of whites had been camped there during wet weather.

Still led on by the natives, Hely at last reached the Nivelle River, when his guides deserted him, and he returned.

On the Warrego he found another camp with a marked tree, exactly similar to the first one, the X V A being repeated, so that it could not have been intended to mean any distinguishing number. He also noticed amongst the natives some tomahawks formed from the battered gullet plates of saddles. His search served only to deepen the mystery around Leichhardt's fate.

The meaning of the marked tree discovered on the Warrego is perplexing, both on account of the recurring letters and its connection with an old camping ground of some white party. Mitchell's party were camped in the neighbourhood for some time; his camps were marked from XLI. to XLIll., but the weather was fine and dry during his stay. Kennedy encamped twice in the locality, and he had with him a man named Luff, whereas no name in Mitchell's camp began with L; but he, too, crossed the river when the weather was dry, and no bushman could possibly make a mistake about the state of the country during the time a large party had remained stationary in a certain position.

The most likely explanation is that these marks had nothing whatever to do with. either Mitchell, Kennedy or Leichhardt, having probably been made by some private party out run hunting.

This futile effort to track up the lost explorer has led us away from Western Australia, where again the desert country was to be encountered, and again fruitlessly.

In 1854, Mr. Robert Austin, Assistant Surveyor-General, was given charge of a party to search for available pastoral country, and also (for now the gold fever was at its height), to examine the interior for auriferous deposits.

They started from the head of the Swan River, on a northeasterly course, and on the 16th of July, reached the Cow-cowing Lake, reported by the aborigines, and hoped by the colonists, to be a sheet of fresh water in the Gascoyne valley. The take proved to be dry, and the bed covered with salt incrustation, showing its character when full. Thence Austin made directly north, and passed through the wretchedly-repellent country that seemed fated to always cross the path of the western explorer; he directed his course to a distant range of table-topped hills and peaks. Here they found feed and water, and named the highest point Mount Kenneth, after one of the party, Mr. Kenneth Brown. From thence to the north-east they traversed stony plains, broken by sandstone and ironstone ridges, and intersected by the dry beds of sandy watercourses; and in this country, one of the worst possible misfortunes happened to them. Their horses got on to a patch of poison plant, and nearly the whole of them were laid up in consequence, and unfit for work. Some few escaped, but the greater number never recovered the effects of the weed, and many died. Pushing hastily on to a safer place to recruit, Austin found himself so crippled by this accident, that he had to abandon all but his most necessary stores for no less than fourteen of the horses having succumbed.

They now turned north-west to make for Shark's Bay, where a vessel was to be sent to render them assistance or bring them away, as should be desired.

Their course to Shark's Bay led them over country that offered them no temptation to linger on the way. On the 21st September they found a cave in the face of a cliff, in which were drawings similar to those seen by Gray near the Prince Regent's River. Near this cave was a spring, and, while resting at this camp, one of the party, a young man named Charles Farmer, accidentally shot himself in the arm, and in spite of the most careful attention, the poor fellow died of lock-jaw, in terrible agony. He was buried at the cave spring camp, and the highest hill in the neighbourhood called Mount Farmer after him. Thus two lonely mountains in the desert interior watch over the graves of men who first saw them-Mount Poole and Mount Farmer.

They now got on to the head waters of the Murchison, or rather the dry channels of these tributaries, and at last reached the Murchison itself; a river with a deep-cut channel, but perfectly dry. Beyond this their efforts were in vain, they fought their way to within a hundred miles of Shark's Bay, but they had then been so long without water that it was courting certain death to proceed. Even during the retreat to the Murchison the lives of the horses were only saved by the party accidentally finding a small native well in a most unexpected situation, namely, in the middle of a bare ironstone plain.

Pushing on ahead of his party, Austin reached the Murchison twenty-five miles south-west of his former course, but the river was the same, or worse, tantalising him with pools of salt water.

A desperate search was made to the southward, during a day of fierce and terrible heat, and when in utter despair they, on the second day, made for some small hills that they sighted, providentially, they found both water and grass. The whole of the party were then moved to this spot, which out of gratitude was named Mount Welcome.

Nothing daunted by the sufferings he had undergone, Austin now made another attempt to reach Shark's Bay. On their way to the

Murchison they captured an old native, and took him with them to point out the watering places of the blacks. At first he was able to show them one or two that they would probably have missed, but after they had crossed the Murchison and got some distance to the westward, the watering places the native had relied on were found to be dry, and it was only after the most acute sufferings from thirst, and the loss of some more horses, that they managed to straggle back to Mount Welcome. Austin's conduct during these terrible marches seems to have approached the heroic. When his companions fell off one by one and laid down to die, and the native inhabitant of the wilds was cowering weeping under a bush, he managed to reach the little well that the blackfellow had formerly shown them, and without resting, tramped back with water to revive his exhausted comrades.

Arrived at Mount Welcome, they found the water there on the point of giving out, and weak as they all were, an instant start had to be made for the Geraldine mine, where a small settlement had been formed to work the galena lode discovered by Gregory. The prospect before them was most discouraging; to the mine the distance was one hundred and sixty miles, and to the highest point on the Murchison, where Gregory had found water, which would be their first stage, was ninety miles, but it had to be done. They started at midnight, and by means of forced marches, travelling day and night, reached Gregory's old camp on the river; having fortunately found a small supply of water at one place on the way. From this point they followed the river down, obtaining water from springs in the banks, and on the 20th November arrived at the mine, where they were warmly entertained. From thence they returned, some by sea and some by land, to Perth.

Austin's exploration had led to no profitable result. The large lake (Moore), that had so hampered Gregory, was found to be an arm or outlet of the still larger Cow-cowing, and that was about all. The upper Murchison had not turned out at all well, and the whole summary of the journal amounts to repetitions of daily struggles with a barren and waterless district, under the fiery sun of the southern summer.

Austin thought that eastward of his limit the country would improve, but subsequent explorations have not borne this out. He had singularly hard fortune to contend against; after the serious loss he sustained in having his horses poisoned, an accident that the greatest care will not always prevent, he was pitted against some of the worst country in Australia--dry, impenetrably scrubby, and barren; and this, too, during the hottest part of the year. That he succeeded in bringing his party safely through such difficulties, was in itself a most wonderful achievement.

Chapter VIII

A. C. Gregory's North Australian expedition in 1855-56, accompanied by Baron Von Mueller and Dr. Elsey--Disappointment in the length of 'the Victoria--Journey to the Westward--Discovery of Sturt's Creek--Its course followed south--Termination in a salt lake--Return to Victoria River --Start homeward, overland--The Albert identified--The Leichhardt christened--Return by the Burdekin and Suttor--Visit of Babbage to Lake Torrens--Expedition by Goyder--Deceived by mirage--Excitement in Adelaide--Freeling sent out--Discovers the error--Hack explores the Gawler Range--Discovers Lake Gairdner--Warburton in the same direction--Swinden and party west of Lake Torrens--Babbage in the Lake District--His long delay--Warburton sent to supersede him--Rival claims to discovery--Frank Gregory explores the Gascoyne in Western Australia --A. C. Gregory follows the Barcoo in search of Leichhardt--Discovery of a marked tree--Arrival in Adelaide--The early explorations of M'Dowall Stuart--Frank Gregory at Nickol Bay--Discovers the Ashburton--Fine pastoral country--Discovers the De Grey and Oakover Rivers--Turned back by the desert--Narrow escape.

In 1855, public interest was once more excited in the mysterious disappearance of Leichhardt; this brought forward the question of further exploration in the interior, and some generous offers were made by private individuals to provide money for the outfit of a party. The English Government, however, working through New South Wales, took the matter in hand and furnished the necessary funds.

The command was given to A. C. Gregory, who had with him the celebrated botanist, Dr. Mueller, and his brother H. C. Gregory. Mr. Elsey, surgeon and naturalist, Mr. Baines, artist, and the requisite number of men made the party up to a total of eighteen. Their live stock consisted of horses and sheep.

The plan of the expedition was to proceed north to the Victoria River, which from the report of Captain Stokes was then considered an important stream, and probably a means of easily gaining the interior.

On the 18th July, 1855, they left Sydney for Moreton Bay, in the barque Monarch, attended by the schooner Tom Tough. At Moreton Bay they took on board the remainder of the party, with fifty horses and two hundred sheep, and after some accidents caused by the Monarch running on a reef, reached Point Pearce at the mouth of the Victoria River, on the 24th September. Here the horses were landed, much weakened by their voyage, and Gregory, Dr. Mueller, and seven men proceeded to the upper part of the Victoria overland, leaving the schooner to work her way up the river with the sheep on board. The land party first made the Macadam Range, so named by Stokes, thence they went to the Fitzmaurice River, where their horses were attacked by alligators and three of them severely wounded; and on the 10th of October they reached the Victoria, and rejoined the remainder of the party. Unfortunately, troubles had now set in, the schooner was aground on a bank eight miles below the camp, and having sprung a leak a considerable quantity of stores were damaged; the sheep, too, had been foolishly kept penned up on board, and so many had died that when finally landed the number was reduced to about forty. All this considerably weakened Gregory's resources.

An attempt to ascend the river in an india-rubber boat was a failure, the craft not being adapted to surmount the obstacles encountered in the shape of rocky bars. On the 24th of November, Gregory, with his brother, Dr. Mueller, and Wilson, followed the Victoria to the south, on horseback. The party reached latitude 161 south, finding the tributary sources of the river to flow from fine open plains, and level forest country, all well grassed. From this point they returned to camp.

On the 3rd January, 1856, another start was made, with a much larger party, consisting of eight men and thirty horses. On reaching their old point below the 16th parallel, a depôt camp was formed, and accompanied by Dr. Mueller, his brother, and one man, Gregory advanced south. The head of the Victoria was found sooner than expected, and crossing the watershed, and following down some small creeks running south through the tableland, they reached a grassy plain in which these watercourses were lost; beyond, the country was sandy and barren. A westerly course was then kept, and on the 15th the head of a creek was reached, which turning at first northerly, afterwards kept a distinct S.W. course for about three hundred miles. The country passed through for a large portion of the upper part was good available pastoral land, but as the lower part of the creek was reached a more desert formation took its place, and at last the creek terminated in extensive salt lakes. Beyond this point no continuation of the channel could be found, and Gregory too easily recognised the aspect of the desert country that had baffled him before. The creek was named Sturt's Creek, and a prominent hill, parallel with the lowest salt lake was called Mount Mueller. The party then retraced their steps; the water on which they depended in Sturt's Creek drying up so rapidly as to render more extended exploration very hazardous. They rejoined their companions at the depôt camp on the Victoria, and making a detour to the eastward, followed down the Wickham, a considerable tributary of the Victoria, to its junction with that river.

Arrangements were now made for the homeward journey by way of the Gulf of Carpentaria; the Tom Tough having been repaired and caulked, started for Timor, to obtain more provisions, and then return and meet the party at a rendezvous appointed on the Albert River. The land party consisted of the leader and his brother, Dr. Mueller, Elsey, and three men. They started on the 21st June.

Following up an eastern tributary of the Victoria, they crossed on to a creek running into the Roper, which was called the Elsey, and on this creek a camp was found, which suggested the idea that it had been occupied by whites. It consisted of the framework of a substantial-looking hut, of a different shape to that usually made by the natives; but no marked trees were found, nor anything more seen to confirm the supposition. Thence the party followed down the Roper for some distance, and then crossing the head waters of the Limmen Bight River, skirted the Gulf at some considerable way south of Leichhardt's track, crossing the same rivers that he did, only higher up on their courses. They struck the Nicholson far above where it had been so named by Leichhardt, and following it down reached the rendezvous at the Albert River (which is the outlet of the Nicholson), but the schooner had not arrived.

Gregory determined not to wait, but to proceed home overland. He buried a note at the foot of a marked tree for the information of the schooner people when they should arrive, and on the 3rd of September started. Two days' journey from the true Albert, they reached a stream which Leichhardt had erroneously taken for that river, and many of the errors in his map may be traced as being due to this cause.

This also has led to a good deal of confusion about the Plains of Promise so much vaunted by Captain Stokes, Leichhardt mistaking the level country on the river that bears his name for the spot. Gregory, who rightly identified the place, professes great disappointment with them compared to what he had been led to expect. Since then many conflicting opinions have been given as to their value. Settlement, however, as it generally does, decided the question; they have been found to be very suitable for cattle, but quite unadapted for sheep breeding. Stokes gave them a taking name, which probably led to a false estimate being entertained, as the country is in no way superior to the district to the eastward.

On the morning Gregory left the Leichhardt his party was attacked by the blacks, who were, however, easily repulsed, the leading native being shot in the short struggle. The Flinders was crossed on the 9th of September, but Gregory did not think that it gave promise of draining a very large extent of country. Instead, therefore, of following it up, and thereby lessening his journey, and discovering the beautiful pastoral downs that this most important river flows through, he wandered away to the north, and followed up the Gilbert River, thus duplicating, only further to the south, the eccentric course of Leichhardt. The dividing watershed was crossed on the basaltic plateau at the head of the Burdekin, and this stream was traced to the Suttor junction, where Leichhardt first struck it. They travelled on up the Suttor, and also up the Belyando, connecting with Major Mitchell's track. Their course then lay through the country traversed by Leichhardt on both his expeditions, watered by the Mackenzie and the Comet, and on the 22nd November the party reached a station on the Dawson owned by Messrs. Fitz and Connor.

This successful conclusion to such an extensive expedition as he had undertaken, stamped Gregory as possessing the highest qualifications for an explorer. His travels embraced journeys extending over a distance of nearly five thousand miles, and he was absent in all sixteen months. His equipment certainly was of the very best, but a series of unfortunate accidents, which could not have been prevented, left him nearly as short as some of his brother explorers had been. One thing about this journey of Gregory's has always been regretted--the short and scanty record which he published, it being little more than a list of dates, and the distances daily travelled. However we may lament this reticence from a man of Gregory's ability and reputation, it is a pity that his example in this respect had not been followed by some of the explorers of the last two decades.

During Gregory's absence Australia bad lost her renowned explorer Sir Thomas Mitchell. He died on the 15th October, near Sydney. He had served on the staff of the Duke of Wellington during the Peninsular War, and in addition to his energy and activity in the field, was a well read and accomplished scholar.

The unsolved puzzle of the extent, direction, and boundaries of Lake Torrens still occupied the attention and exercised the minds of the South Australian colonists. It seemed almost like a region of enchantment, so conflicting were the accounts brought in by different parties, and so contradictory the statements made.

In 1851, two squatters in search of a run, Messrs. Oakden and Hulkes, pushed out to the western side of Lake Torrens, and according to their account found a most favourable land. They discovered a lake of fresh water, surrounded with good country; and the natives told them of other lakes to the north-west; also 'introducing descriptions of strange animals, whose appearance could have only been equalled by that of the jimbra, or apes, of Western Australia, which ruthless animals, according to blackfellows' legend, devoured the survivors of Leichhardt's party, as they straggled into the confines of that colony. Their horses giving in, Oakden and Hulkes returned; but although they applied for a squatting license for the country they had visited, it was not then settled or stocked. In 1856 Mr. Babbage made some explorations on the field to the north, traversed by Eyre and Frome. He penetrated to the plains which were supposed to occupy the central portion of the horseshoe; but, more successful than his predecessors, he found permanent water in a gum creek, and saw some fair-sized sheets of water, one of which he named Blanche Water, or Lake Blanche.

Some excursions to the south-east led to the discovery of some more fresh water and well-grassed pastoral country, and the natives directed him to a crossing-place in that portion of Lake Torrens that had been sighted in 1845, by Messrs. Poole and Browne, of Captain Sturt's party. Babbage, however, failed to find the place, and lost his horse in the attempt to cross.

In 1857, a Mr. Campbell made an excursion to the west of Lake Torrens, and discovered a creek with fresh water in it, which he called the Elizabeth. He finally came to Lake Torrens which he found in the same condition as other explorers had done--surrounded by barren country.

In April of the same year, a survey in the country where Babbage had been exploring was conducted by Deputy Surveyor-General Goyder, and he certainly got into the land of enchantment. A few miles north of Blanche Water he found many springs bubbling out of the ground, around a fine lagoon, and north was an isolated hill, which he named Weathered Hill. From the summit of this hill he had a fine specimen of the effect produced by refraction. To the north, or thereabouts, he saw a belt of gigantic gum-trees show out, beyond which appeared a sheet of water with elevated lands on the far side, while to the east was another large lake; all this, however, was but the glamourie of the desert. The gigantic gum trees dwindled down to stunted bushes, and the rising ground to broken clods of earth.

But the greatest surprise was reserved for the time Goyder actually reached Lake Torrens, for he found the water quite fresh. He described it as stretching from fifteen to twenty miles to the northwest, with a water horizon; an extensive bay forming to the southward, while to the north a bluff headland and perpendicular cliffs were clearly discerned with a telescope. From the appearance of the floodmarks, Goyder came to the conclusion that there was little or no rise and fall in the lake, inferring therefrom that its size would absorb the flood waters without showing any variation of level.

No wonder that the good people of Adelaide were overjoyed when they heard the news. The threatening desert that hemmed in their fair province on the north had been suddenly converted into the promised land. Colonel Freeling, the Surveyor-General, immediately started out, taking with him both a boat and an iron punt with which to float on these new-found waters.

What must have been the public feeling when a letter was received from the Surveyor-General, saying that the cliffs the headlands, and the grassy shores, where all built up on the basis of the mirage. The elfs and sprites of this desolate region had been playing a hoax on the former party.

It will be remembered in Sturt's expedition, how Poole came back and reported confidently having seen the inland sea, and how Gray on the west coast led his companions a tramp, after a receding lake that they never overtook, it is scarcely to be wondered at then, that Goyder was deceived, more particularly after finding the water of Lake Torrens fresh, when it had always been represented as salt.

On reaching the lake, Freeling found the water almost fresh, but one of Goyder's men who was with him said that the water had already receded half a mile. An attempt to float the punt was made, but after dragging it through mud and a few inches of water for a quarter of a mile; the idea was abandoned. Freeling, and some of the party then started to wade through the slush, but after getting three miles, found no water deeper than six inches. Some of the more adventurous went further still, but only to meet with a like result. The Surveyor-

General returned a disappointed man, and the unavailability of Lake Torrens was confirmed.

During this time--1857--Mr. Hack started with a party from Streaky Bay to examine the Gawler Ranges of Eyre, and investigate the country west of Lake Torrens. He reached the Gawler Range and examined the country very patiently, finding numerous springs, and large plains of both grass and saltbush, also sighting a large salt lake (Lake Gairdner). On the whole, his report was a very favourable one.

Simultaneously with Hack's trip, a party under Major Warburton, was out in the same direction, in fact Hack's party crossed Warburton's track on one or two occasions. Warburton's account was contradictory of Hack's; he reported the country dry and arid, and found very little to say in favour of it.

Of the two men, however, it is probable that Hack's experience enabled him to judge with most truth of the value of land seen under unfavourable conditions.

This year of 1857 was rife with explorations in South Australia. A party of settlers consisting of Messrs. Swinden, Campbell, Thompson, and Stock set out, and at about seventy miles from the head of Spencer's Gulf, found fine pastoral country, and a permanent waterhole, Pernatty. To the northward they came upon the Elizabeth, formerly discovered by Campbell, and here from want of provisions they returned. A month afterwards Swinden started again from Pernatty, and found available pastoral land north of the Gawler Ranges, which became known as Swinden's country. During this year, also, Messrs. Miller and Dutton explored the country at the back of Fowler's Bay. Forty miles to the north they saw treeless plains stretching far inland, but they found no permanent water. Warburton afterwards reported deprecatingly of this country, but Messrs. Delisser and Hardwicke in their turn stated that it was first-class pastoral land, if water could be obtained. Judging from Major Warburton's career as an explorer, he seemed quite unable to judge correctly of the value of country when seen under an adverse season, and it is only one of the many instances of the necessity of a station training to adequately fit a man to pronounce definite judgment on the availability or non-availability of country. One of Warburton's suggestions to the South Australian Government was to explore the interior-which had proved such a difficult nut to crack--by means of the police. One has to know the country well to fully appreciate the exquisite humour of this suggestion.

Before referring to two expeditions, both of great importance, one under A. C. Gregory, and the other by Frank Gregory, it may be as well to pursue the fortunes of the Lake Torrens explorers to the end.

In 1858, the South Australian Government voted a sum of money to fit out a party to continue the northern explorations. This party was put under the leadership of Mr. Babbage, and his instructions were to examine the country between Lake Torrens and the lately-discovered Lake Gairdner, and to survey and map the respective western and eastern shores of the two lakes, so as to remove for the future any doubts as to their true formation and position. This alone, apart from any more extended explorations, meant a work of considerable time; but, unfortunately for Babbage, the survey work was generally regarded as but of secondary importance, and the public looked eagerly forward to hearing of the discovery of new pasture lands, especially as the outfit had been on a most liberal scale. Considerable delay (whether avoidable or not, it is scarcely worth while to discuss) happened during the outset of this expedition; for, although the party was reported ready on the 11th February, the end of August found Babbage back in Port Augusta having passed the intervening months in surveying the shores of the two large lakes, and making short excursions to the westward, over a country that had been several times traversed by private parties looking for land. At Port Augusta he was considerably surprised to find that his second in command, Harris, had started south to Adelaide, with a great many of the horses and drays. Babbage pursued, and overtook them at Mount Remarkable, after riding one hundred and sixty miles. Here he found that fresh instructions had been issued by the Government, and forwarded by Charles Gregory, lately arrived with his brother from the north.

The explanation was, that A. C. Gregory's expedition in search of Leichhardt had arrived in Adelaide during Babbage's absence, and it having been successfully conducted with the aid of packhorses only, the South Australian Government came to the conclusion that Babbage would manage just as well without the drays, and engaged, and sent Charles Gregory to join him, and inform him that his expedition was in future to be conducted in a like manner. Not finding Babbage at his camp, Gregory had started the drays and draught horses home on his own authority. Babbage ordered his men back, but they refused to go; so after writing to the Government, complaining of the treatment he had received, he returned north with a small party and six months' provisions. He arrived at the boundary of his late surveys, and pushing on reached Chambers' Creek, so named by Stuart, who had discovered it during Babbage's absence at Lake Gairdner.

This creek, which Babbage called Stuart's Creek, he traced to a large salt lake, which he christened Lake Gregory, now known as Lake Eyre. From here he made to a range which he called Hermit Range, but from its summit could see no sign of Lake Torrens, and came to the just conclusion that it did not extend so far. West of Lake Eyre the explorers found a hot spring, and afterwards many more were discovered.

Meantime, Major Warburton had been sent to supersede Babbage, and during the time the latter gentleman was making these discoveries, Warburton was searching for him. This result had come about partly through the appearance of Babbage at Mount Remarkable, and partly through the return of Messrs. Stuart and Forster, who reported good country beyond Babbage's furthest, which naturally made the public think that that explorer should have been the first to find it.

On arriving at the camp on the Elizabeth, Warburton, who had C. Gregory with him as a second, found Babbage absent, so he sent Gregory after him to bring him back, and after waiting some time, determined to go himself, and a comical sort of hunt commenced, ending in Warburton coming up with Babbage at Lake Eyre, and there carrying out the duty imposed upon him, in a manner that says little for his generosity of spirit.

During this game of hunt-the-slipper, Warburton had made some minor discoveries on his own account. He had come upon fairly good country west of the lakes, and had found the springs which he christened Beresford Springs; he also discovered the Douglas, a creek which afterwards greatly assisted Stuart to push forward, and a range which he called the Davenport Range. He had got north-west of where Babbage was, and in fact afterwards disputed that explorer's claim to the discovery of Lake Eyre.

It seems only in keeping with the paradoxical nature of our continent that this blundering expedition should have been so conducive in establishing the great geographical fact that had so long puzzled the colonists, namely, the definite size and shape of Lake Torrens. No longer was this terror of the north to extend its encircling arms against all advancement. Henceforth, its isolated character was decided, and the supposed continuations known under independent names.

Of the whole conduct of the expedition, the less said the better; the Government instructions were vacillating and contradictory;

FAVENC

Babbage was slow and apathetic, Warburton pompous and arbitrary; and in the end the affair was further degraded by an old-womanish wrangle between the two explorers as to the priority of certain discoveries.

During this year, Surveyor Parry had advanced into what was then supposed to be the horseshoe of Lake Torrens, and found in many places both fresh water and fairly available country.

This time it is with more cheering tidings that we turn once again to the work of exploration in Western Australia.

On the 16th April, during this same year of 1858, when some exploring tarantula seemed to have bitten all the colonies, Frank Gregory left the Geraldine mine on the Murchison, where it will be remembered the gallant Austin and party arrived in such a critical state, to endeavour to reach the Gascoyne and the upper reaches of the coast rivers.

Following up the Murchison for some distance, Gregory, finding but little feed, although the country was not quite so scrubby as usual, struck north-east, and coming to a large channel with a due northern course, followed it down, and on the 3rd of May, to his great joy, reached the long-sought Gascoyne. It was flowing from the eastward and running west, but soon changed its course to the north, thence north-west, thence west and south until the junction of a large river from the north-west was reached. From this junction the Gascoyne ran due west straight for Shark's Bay, and on the 17th May, Gregory reached the mouth of the river. Returning, he explored the tributary from the north-west, which he named the Lyons, and which he followed for a considerable distance, until he came to a high mountain, three thousand five hundred feet above sea level, which he called Mount Augustus. From the summit he had a splendid view north and east, and traced the course of the river far to the eastward. Turning southeast, and crossing tributaries of the Gascoyne, and the main river itself, they reached another lofty hill-Mount Gould--from the top of which Gregory thought he could infer the course of the Murchison for nearly one hundred miles.

Following the Murchison down, they arrived at the Geraldine mine, having in the space of a little over two months completed a trip which resulted in the most favourable manner. Good pastoral country, well-watered, the great want of the settlers, had been discovered, only awaiting the finding of an available port to at once invite settlement. After so many bitter disappointments this was a much-needed encouragement to the colony.

Still in the fruitful year of 1858, we must accompany the elder brother, A. C. Gregory, on his Barcoo expedition. This expedition was organised in order to search for some traces of the course of Leichhardt's party, and although there was little hope of finding him, or any of his party, still alive, there was a great probability of at least ascertaining the route he had travelled, and possibly rescuing part of his journals.

The freshly awakened interest in the fate of the lost party may or may not have sprung from the story of a convict, in confinement in Sydney, which has since been repeated with various alterations.

This man, whose name was Garbut, started a wild and improbable legend about the existence, in the interior, of a settlement of escaped convicts, amongst whom Leichhardt and his band were held prisoners, lest they should reveal the whereabouts of the runaways. Of course such a story, which might have obtained credence in the very early days, was at once scouted; but it, at any rate, turned public attention to the strange fact that, in spite of the many explorations of the past ten years, no sign nor token of the missing men had ever been seen.

A. C. Gregory then with his brother and seven men started on the quest. They were equipped for rapid travelling, taking with them only pack horses to carry their provisions. The leader followed the now well-known track to the Warrego, and crossing the head of the Nive, reached the Barcoo waters on the 16th April. If the marked trees seen by Hely were Leichhardt's there was a great probability that they would thus be on his tracks to the west, and a sharp look-out was kept on both sides of river, which resulted in the discovery in about 241 deg. south latitude, and 145 deg. east longitude, of a tree marked L, on the eastern bank, and in the neighbourhood were stumps of trees, felled by an axe. Although Leichhardt could not have foreseen his fate, it is unfortunate that he did not mark his trees in a more unmistakeable manner, for a mysterious L without date seems to turn up in all parts of our continent.

This memorial of the visit of some white men Gregory thought might be Leichhardt's, especially as the letter was very large, after the manner of some of the trees marked on that explorer's former journeys. It may be as well to mention here that this was all that was found, and the journey henceforth was only one of pure exploration.

The travellers found the country suffering under a long-continued drought, and. feed for the horses very hard to get. Necessarily, Gregory's picture of it is very different to Sir Thomas Mitchell's;

but it would be scarcely worth while to compare the two statements now, considering that the reputation of the land as one of the best sheep-breeding districts in Australia has long since been established.

Knowing what Kennedy had encountered on the lower part of the river, and anticipating finding more traces of Leichhardt to the westward. Gregory, on reaching the Thomson, followed that river up for some distance, but turned back disheartened at the want of grass, although the river was running from recent rains. It must be remembered that he was there in the beginning of the winter, when there is little or no spring in the grass, even after heavy rain.

Returning to the junction of the two rivers, he followed down the united stream, and soon found himself involved in the same difficulties that had beset Kennedy. The river broke up into countless channels, running through barren, fissured plains. Toiling on over these, with an occasional interlude of sand hills, Gregory at last reached that portion of Cooper's Creek visited by Sturt. This he now followed down to where Strzelecki's Creek left the main stream and carried off some of the surplus flood water to the south.

Gregory followed on the many channels trending west, but finally lost them amongst sand hills and flooded plains. He turned back and once more struck Strzelecki's Creek, which he thought he traced to Lake Torrens. This lake he crossed on a firm sandy space, through which he could distinguish no connecting channel, thus helping to rob Lake Torrens of some more of its terrors. He soon arrived in the settled districts, having safely accomplished a most successful journey.

The main discovery that was the most valuable outcome of this trip was, of course, the confirmation of the supposed identity of the Barcoo and Cooper's Creek; as Gregory was otherwise on the tracks of former explorers, no fresh discoveries could well be expected on the course he followed.

Thus, after many fruitless efforts and disappointments, the second great inland river system was evolved.

We now meet with an old friend in the field, in the person of J. M'Dowall Stuart, formerly draughtsman for Captain Sturt, and one of the party who bought experience of heat, thirst, and desolation, during their long imprisonment in the depôt glen.

On the 14th May, 1858, Stuart left Oratunga for an excursion to the north-west of Swinden's country, west of Lake Torrens. He was delayed some time before he finally got away from Octaina, on the 10th June. Passing Mr. Babbage, he arrived at the Elizabeth on the 18th, but was disappointed in the expectations he had formed. Soon afterwards he found a large hole of permanent water, which he called Andamoka, and on the 23rd June caught sight of one of the arms of Lake Torrens. From here he followed a creek (Yarraout) to the north-west, in search of the country called Wingillpin that the blacks had told him of. This he was unable to find, and came to the somewhat strange conclusion that Wingillpin and Cooper's Creek were one and the same, although so widely separated, as he well knew. He also seems to have entertained broad notions of the extent of Cooper's Creek, as in one part of his journal at this period he remarks:--

"My only hope now of cutting Cooper's Creek is on the other side of the range. The plain we crossed to-day resembles those of the Cooper, also the grasses. If it is not there it must run to the north-west, and form the Glenelg of Captain Grey."

Now although we know that Grey held rather extravagant notions of the importance of the Glenelg River on the northwest coast, which time has certainly not confirmed, even he would scarcely have imagined it possible for it to be the outlet of such a mighty stream as Cooper's Creek would have become by the time it reached there.

Stuart's horses were now very lame, as the stony ground had worn out their shoes, and they had no spare sets with them. Failing, therefore, to find the promised land of Wingillpin, although he had passed over much good and well-watered country, and had also found Chambers' Creek, he turned south-west, and made some explorations in the neighbourhood and to the west of Lake Gairdner. Thence he steered for Fowler's Bay, and his' description of some of the country on his course is anything but inviting. From a spur of the high peak that he named Mount Fincke he saw--

"A prospect gloomy in the extreme; I could see a long distance but nothing met the eye save a dense scrub, as black and dismal as night."

From here they got fairly into a sandy, spinifex desert, which Stuart says was worse than Sturt's, for there, there was a little salt-bush; "here there was nothing but spinifex to be found and the horses were foodless."

Things were getting desperate with the little band, their provisions were finished, but still the leader would not desist from looking for good country; but at last he had to make back as fast as he could. Dense scrub, and the same "dreary, dreadful, dismal desert," as he calls it, accompanied them day after day. Tired out and half-starved, they reached the coast, and then they had only two meals left to take them to Streaky Bay, one hundred miles away, where they hoped to find relief, and where they safely arrived at Mr. Gibson's station. Here they were laid up with the sudden change from starvation to a full diet, and for some days Stuart was very ill. They finally reached Mr. Thompson's station of Mount Arden, which terminated Stuart's first expedition.

This severe trip only gave Stuart a fresh taste for adventure. In April, 1859, he made another start, and on the 19th, after crossing over some of the already known country, Hergott, one of his companions, discovered the well-known springs that still bear his name. Stuart crossed Chambers' Creek, and made for the Davenport Range, of Warburton, finding many of the springs resembling those mound ones crowned with reeds already mentioned. On the 6th June, he discovered a large creek, which he called the Neale. It ran through very good country, and Stuart followed it down, hoping to find its importance increase; and in this he was not disappointed, as large plains covered with grass and salt bush were crossed, and several more springs discovered. After satisfying himself of the extent and value of the country he had found, Stuart started back, his horse's shoes having again given out, and he had a lively remembrance of the misery he suffered before from want of them.

In November of the same year, he made a third expedition in the vicinity of Lake Eyre, but there is very little of interest attaching to his journal, as his course was mostly over much-trodden country. He reached the Neale again, and instituted a survey of the good country he had formerly traversed, occasionally approaching to within sight of what he calls Lake Torrens, but which was in reality Lake Eyre. All these minor expeditions of Stuart's may be considered as preparatory to his great struggle to find a passage across the continent; for which work these trips gave him a good knowledge of the country he had to face, and its difficulties. Stuart's efforts to cross Australia from south to north, and the expeditions made by others with a like object, will occupy the undivided attention of the reader so much, that in order not to lose the thread of the narrative of this peculiar and marked epoch in Australian history, it may be better to here notice an important journey undertaken in Western Australia, although slightly out of chronological order.

It was an expedition organised partly by the Imperial, and partly by the Colonial Governments, and was also aided by private subscription. Frank Gregory, the successful explorer of the Gascoyne, was put in charge of it. They left Perth in the Dolphin for Nickol Bay, on the north-west coast, where they intended to land their horses and commence operations. This was safely accomplished, and on 25th May, 1861, the party started.

Their first important discovery on a westerly course was a large river coming from the south, which they named the Fortescue. This stream they followed up until impeded by a very narrow, precipitous gorge, when they left the river, and made for a range they had sighted to the south. This range, which was called Hammersley Range, they attempted to cross, without success, so the explorers turned to the north-east, and came again on the Fortescue, above the gorge, and after some difficulty traced it to the range, through which it forced a passage. Crossing the range, partly by the aid of the river-bed, and partly by a gap, they came to fair average country stretching away to the southward. On this course the large and important river, the Ashburton, was found, which was traced upwards, flowing through a very large extent of good pastoral country. On the 25th of June, from the top of a sandstone tableland, they sighted Mount Augustus, at the head of the Lyons River. The view was most promising. Open forest and undulating country took the place of the everlasting scrubs and rocks, that had been such common objects with them, and well satisfied with what they saw the explorers turned north.

Mount Samson and Mount Bruce, two most prominent peaks of the Hammersley Range, were named by Gregory on his return; the latter being considered by him the highest point in Western Australia. From here they struck back to the coast, their horses having become terribly foot-sore, and reached the sea forty miles from Nickol Bay, and on the 19th arrived at their rendezvous in that bay, where the ship was awaiting them. After a rest of ten days, Gregory started again, and to the eastward found the Yule River; thence they crossed to the Shaw, and still pushing east they succeeded in penetrating a considerable way into the tableland, where they found good grass and springs. On the 26th of August a fine stream running to the north was discovered, and named the De Grey; and after crossing ail immense plain they came to another river, which was christened the Oakover. Up this river Gregory went, the men admiring the rich foliage of the drooping ti-trees that bordered the long reaches of water, and the horses appreciating the wide grassy flats on either bank.

Finding the course of the river trending too much westerly, they crossed to a tributary of the Oakover and thence passed easterly through a small range. Here he was confronted by a most unwelcome sight. Before him were the hills of drifted sand, the barren plains and the ominous red haze of the desert. So far he had encountered fewer obstacles and made more encouraging discoveries than had fallen to the lot of any other Western Australian explorer; and now, the desert had drawn its forbidding hand suddenly across his track, and sternly ordered him to halt.

Gregory made one effort of eighteen miles across the red sand dunes, but his 'horses were not equal to the task, and he returned to his camp at the foot of the range.

After resting for a day, he started with two companions for a final attempt, leaving the remainder camped to await his return, with instructions, if the water failed, to fall back on the Oakover. This excursion nearly proved fatal; the heat was something terrible, and when well advanced in the sand ridges, the horses gave in altogether. Afar to the east, a distant range was faintly visible, and a granite range could be seen to the south, about ten miles distant. These granite hills were their only hope, and to them they turned.

Across the sand hills now, instead of running parallel with them, the horses at once gave up, and, leaving his comrades to drive them on as best they could, Gregory pushed towards the goal on foot, but when he reached it no sign of verdure or moisture greeted him. Blasted, scorched, and barren the rocks and rugged ravines lay before him, and all his weary searching resulted only in his completely breaking down with distress and fatigue. When his companions came up with the dying horses there was nothing to do but make preparations to get back as soon as they could to the depôt, trusting that the want of water might not have compelled the main party to abandon the camp.

By dawn the wearied men commenced their retreat, but when the heat of the day set in, the poor, thirsty horses of course began to fail; and Gregory, too, was so completely exhausted with his previous day's efforts that he could not keep up with the other two. One of the party, Brown, started on ahead with the horses, the other remaining with Gregory to follow more slowly. Brown had to abandon nearly everything to get the wretched animals on, finally reaching the camp with only one; but fortunately he found the party still there. He started back at once, with fresh horses, to meet the others, and recover the equipment; but two of the horses were never found.

Gregory was now convinced that the sandy tract before him was not to be crossed with the means at his command, so that, reluctantly, he had to give way and turn to the northward, to follow down the Oakover. They found the country fertile, and the river abounding with water; and on the 18th September reached the junction of De Grey with the Oakover. Down the united streams, henceforth bearing the name of the De Grey only, the explorers travelled through fair, open land, the course of the river flowing now to the westward, until the coast was reached on the 25th.

From here the party made back to their rendezvous at Nickol Bay, crossing once more the Yule and the Sherlock, rivers named on their outward journey. On the 17th October the ship was reached, and they were taken on board.

Gregory had thus done good service to the colony during his last two expeditions. The stigma of desolation was at any rate partially removed, and it was with hopeful hearts that the colonists looked forward to the future of the valleys of the Gascoyne, the Ashburton, and the De Grey.

Another party, with less success, had been exploring to the eastward of the settled districts, in the southern part of the colony, and as it will be some time before we shall revisit Western Australia, it will be most convenient to now follow out the fortunes of the little body of colonists with the large territory.

In 1861, whilst Gregory was opening up his new country, Messrs. Dempster, Clarkson, and Harper started from Northam to make one more trial to the east to get through the dense scrubs and the salt-lake country into a more promising region. It was purely a private expedition; one of those that have done so much of the work of discovery in Australia; each member of the party found his own horses and equipment.

They left on the 3rd July, and for many days met with nothing but the usual alternations of scrub and sandy plains dotted with granite hills. On the 19th, we find in their diary the first mention of the legend amongst the blacks of white men having been murdered on a large lake to the eastward. Their informant was a native who was with them for some time as a guide, and his authority was a great traveller of the name of Boodgin, who must have revelled in the possession of a singularly fertile imagination. The account of Boodgin was to the effect that three white men with horses had many years ago come to a large lake of salt water, a long way to the eastward, and after travelling along the shore for some time, they turned back, and were either killed by the jimbras, or perished from want of water. Thus ran Mr. Boodgin's story, which we shall immediately have to refer to.

Still endeavouring to reach to the east by various detours, on the 24th they came to the largest hill they had yet seen--Mount Kennedy--and at the end of the month found themselves still in the lake district. For sixty miles they had traced the lakes, and from the hills

179

could see a continuation of the low range they were on. On one of them (Lake Grace) they had speech with a few natives, who repeated what they had formerly heard, as to the death of three white men, far away at some interior lake or inland sea. They were also acquainted with the before-mentioned Boodgin, who, unfortunately, had in some way offended them; so he was not present, the others having announced an intention of spearing him on the first opportunity. These men gave an account of the jimbra, or jingra, a strange animal, male and female, which they described as resembling a monkey, very fierce, and would attack men when it caught one singly. Thinking there might be a confusion of names, the explorers asked if the jimbra, or jingra, was the same as the ginka--the native name for devil. This, however, was not so, as the natives asserted that the devil, or ginka, was never seen, but that the jimbra was both seen and felt.

From this point the party returned homeward, having, at any rate, demonstrated the fact that the thickets to the eastward were not impenetrable, and that no insurmountable obstacles existed to further progress.

Whatever may have been the origin of the native tradition about the deaths of three white men, which Forrest afterwards investigated, it must seem strange that the natives should in the jimbra have described an animal (the ape) they could not possibly have ever seen. It may be mentioned here that reports about the bones of cattle having been found on the outskirts of Western Australia had been circulated in the Eastern colonies before Leichhardt left.

Chapter IX

We are now about to turn a page in the history of Australia which,
however marked by misfortune and disappointment, still embodies
some of the most fruitful achievements in the history of discovery. The
unfortunate result of one expedition led to so many minor ones, that an
immense area of new country was thrown open in a very short time.

An extraordinary craze had seized on the imaginations of the
southern colonies to send out expeditions to strive to be the first to
cross the continent from the southern shore to the northern one. The
South Australian Government had for a time a standing reward of
£10,000 offered for the man who should accomplish this gigantic task
with private means.

M'Dowall Stuart has been recognised as the one to whom most honour is due for successfully spanning the gap, and there are many reasons for awarding the chief praise to him. He was the first to attempt the feat, and although he was not the first to reach salt water on the north, he was the first to sight the open sea, and actually cross from sea to sea. Nor in so doing was he aided by the former successes of other explorers. He also was the one who crossed fairly in the centre of Australia, and his track extends further north, as the others made for the southern shore of the Gulf of Carpentaria, while Stuart came out at the head of Arnhem's Land.

Burke and Wills were, according to the journal of Wills, at the northern coast in February, 1861, so they could claim the honour of first crossing; next came M'Kinlay, in May, 1862. Landsborough reached the Darling from the north in June of the same year, and then Stuart on the north coast comes but a few weeks afterwards in July. On Stuart's track however, has been built the overland telegraph line, an enduring monument to his indomitable perseverance. His was but a small party when he started to reach the spot so ardently longed for by his former leader Sturt. Less than a handful of men, three in all, with thirteen horses, left on this eventful trip, a strange company to contrast with the princely cavalcade that a few months later was to leave Melbourne on a like journey.

The starting point was from Chambers' Creek, but naturally from here their course for a time was over much-trodden ground.

At Beresford Springs there were unmistakable traces of recent native warfare. Lying on his back was the corpse of a tall native, the skull broken, and both feet and hands missing. Near the place was a handful of human hair, and some emu feathers, placed between two charred pieces of wood, as a sign or token of some sort, but nothing to be interpreted by the whites as to the meaning of this strange neglect of burial rites, so unusual amongst the aborigines.

After passing the Neale, the little band commenced their march into the unknown. Their journey was, for the most part, through good pastoral country, crossing numerous well-watered creeks, which they named, respectively, the Frew, the Fincke, and the Stevenson, and on the 6th they reached a remarkable hill, which they had observed for some time. It proved to be a pillar of sandstone on a hill about one hundred feet high. The pillar itself, in addition, is one hundred and fifty feet in height, and twenty feet in width. Stuart christened it Chambers' Pillar. This freak of nature was surrounded by numerous other remarkable bills, resembling ruined castles.

Passing through a range, which was called the Waterhouse Range, and again striking a creek, christened the Hugh, they made for one of two remarkable bluffs, first sighted on the 9th of April, and reached the range of which these two bluff cliffs formed the centre on the 12th. This was the highest range Stuart had yet found, and he named it MacDonnell Range, after the then Governor of South Australia; the east bluff was called Brinkley Bluff and the west one Hanson Bluff. Crossing this range, which, although rough, was very well-grassed, the party got among spinifex and scrub, and, after being two nights without water, made for a high peak in the distance (Mount Freeling), where they found a small supply.

It was evident that they had now reached the limit of the rainfall, and were trespassing on dry country.

A search for permanent water was made before going on, and a large reservoir found in a ledge of rocks, that promised to supply their wants on their return.

On the 22nd of April, Stuart camped in the centre of Australia, and one of his hopes was accomplished; about two miles and a-half to the N.N.E. was a tolerable high mount, which he called Central Mount Stuart. The next morning, with his tried companion, Kekwick, he climbed this mount, and on the top erected a cairn of stones, and hoisted the Union Jack. What must have been his thoughts at having, with such a feeble party, so comparatively easily accomplished what others had striven in vain for? Surely he must have thought with regret that his old leader, dauntless Sturt, was not standing beside him.

The first night after leaving Mount Stuart, they camped without water, and the next day found a permanent supply under a high peak, which he called Mount Leichhardt; and while mentioning this fact, he notices that he has found no trace of that explorer having ever passed to the westward.

On the first of May they came to a small gum creek, which Stuart called the Fisher, and in which the only water they could get was in a native well. Crossing this creek they got into a dead level country, covered with spinifex and stunted gum trees. Here they came across the track of a blackfellow which differed considerably from the ordinary mark made by the foot of a native:--

"The spinifex in many places has been burnt, and the track of the native was peculiar-not broad and flat as they generally are, but long and narrow, with a deep hollow in the foot, and the large toe projecting a good deal; in some respects more like the print of a white man than a native. Had I crossed it the day before, I would have followed it. My horses are now suffering too much from the want of water to allow me to do so. If I did, and we were not to find water to-night, I should lose the whole of the horses and our lives into the bargain."

As it was, they had a hard struggle to get back to the native well at the Fisher.

After a week's interval Stuart tried again to the' east of north, but found things no better; mulga scrub and spinifex again surrounded them, and after travelling twenty-seven miles they had to camp without water. The next day was the same, Stuart getting a nasty fall, being pulled off by some scrub and dragged for a short distance. There was nothing for it but to retreat once more. Scurvy had now laid its hand upon the leader, and he began to suffer severely.

After much trouble and delay, Stuart, by working to the eastward, at last got forward again, and on the 1st of June found a large creek, the best he had yet seen, which he called the Bonney, and on the second of the month reached the range christened by him the Murchison Range. On the 6th he came to a gum creek, which he called Tennant's Creek, destined to be the site of one of the telegraph stations of the overland line. He now made an effort to the west of north to reach the head waters of the Victoria, and got into a dry strip of country that nearly put an end to the expedition. When they at last, with some losses, got the horses back to water, the animals had travelled one hundred and twelve miles, and been one hundred and one hours without a drink. Some of them had gone mad. "Thus," says Stuart, "ends my last attempt, at present, to make the Victoria River. Three times I have tried it, and been forced to retreat."

After many days' rest, he started again, this time to the eastward of north, and in ten miles came to a well-watered creek, which he named Phillips' Creek. Once more he had another two or three days of useless efforts to force his way through a dry belt, vainly flattering himself that he was approaching the watershed of the Gulf; but had to fall back on the Phillips again. Whilst camping here some natives visited them, two of them wearing a kind of helmet made of net work and feathers, tightly bound together:--

"One was an old man, and seemed to be the father of these two fine young men. He was very talkative, but I could make nothing of him. I have endeavoured, by signs, to get information from him as to where the next water is, but we cannot understand each other. After some time, and having conferred with his two sons, he turned round, and surprised me by giving me one of the Masonic signs. I looked at him steadily; he repeated it; and so did his two sons. I then returned it, which seemed to please them much, the old man patting me on the shoulder and stroking down my beard."

Whether Stuart's imagination here led him astray, it is impossible to say, but very shortly afterwards they encountered a tribe who displayed anything but the friendly feelings that should have been shown by brother masons.

On the next start they came in fourteen miles to a large gum creek, with very fair-sized sheets of water in it, and as they followed it down they passed the encampment of some natives, but did not take any notice of them, keeping steadily on their course. Finding no water lower down the creek, they had to return. When close to the place where they crossed the creek in the morning, and the evening rapidly closing in, they were suddenly surrounded by a number of well-armed natives, who started out of a scrub they were passing through. All signs of friendship, masonic or otherwise, were thrown away on them, and at last, after receiving two or three showers of boomerangs and waddies they had to turn and fire on them. So bold and determined were they in their attack upon the three men, that Stuart had to return to his camp of the night before still followed by them. Here he had to make up his mind to abandon his further progress for the present. He had too small a party to stand a pitched battle with the aboriginal proprietors; the water behind them was failing, and they had suffered considerable loss in their horses. Most wisely Stuart determined to return.

On the 27th June he commenced his retreat. On reaching the Bonney he halted for a few days, during which time the cloudy aspect of the sky made him entertain the idea of another effort to reach the Victoria River; but no rain fell, and he had to keep on his way. On the 26th of August the party arrived at Mr. Brodie's camp at Hamilton Springs, all of them very weak and reduced.

After the result of Stuart's expedition had been reported in Adelaide, and it was seen how inadequate means alone had led to the retreat of the explorer, the Government voted £2,500 to equip a larger and better-organized party, of which he was to take command. Meanwhile, such a report of the results of the journey as the Government thought might prove useful to the leaders of the Victorian expedition, then on the march, was forwarded, but, as will be seen, shared the same chapter of accidents that beset that unfortunate expedition, and never reached them.

This time Stuart's party numbered at the final start, ten men and forty-seven horses; and by the end of January, 1861, they were fairly on their way outside the settled districts, and here we must leave them to turn to that other expedition, the issue of which attracted so much attention throughout the world.

Public opinion is notably fickle, and never more so than when dealing with the memories of distinguished men. No guide, no standard is followed in the matter; the recognition of their services is made solely a matter of sentiment.

Poor Kennedy, who, confronted with almost insurmountable difficulties, harassed by hostile natives, and ill-provisioned at the start, lost his life, and the majority of his party, in a gallant effort to fulfil his task, is almost forgotten, save by the few who take an interest in the history of our country. Whilst Burke--who left the settlements, equipped with everything that a generous people could provide, and that the experience of others could suggest, to make the journey safe and ensure its success--travelled through a country that is now a vast sheep and cattle walk; and frittered away his magnificent resources, wantonly sacrificing his own life and those of his men, is elevated into a hero. It may truly be said that for the fate of the two leaders, the mistakes of others must be greatly held accountable; but at the same time it must be also kept strongly in view that, for the want of judgment that placed Burke in such a position that the mistake of a subordinate could entail such fatal results, he alone was responsible.

The action of Victoria in sending out the expedition of discovery under Burke and Wills, was, without doubt, exceptional in the annals of exploration; it was an instance of a public body emulating the generous act of a private individual. The colony itself had no territory left to explore. Her rich and compact little province was known from end to end, and it was not with her, as with others, a case of necessity to send her sons into the wilderness, to open fresh fields for emigration.

Whatever then was the upshot of the expedition, and whatever the guilty mismanagement attaching to its progress, the colony must ever look back with pride upon the noble and unselfish motives that prompted its inauguration.

Without counting the cost of the relief parties, seven lives were laid down, and over £12,000 expended, and it was all cheerfully rendered; and Victoria, in her one expedition, had the satisfaction of knowing that her representatives carried off the coveted prize, and were the first to cross the continent from south to north.

The money for the expenses was subscribed as follows:--
£6,000 voted by Government, £1,000 subscribed by Mr. Ambrose
Kyte, and the balance of the £12,000 made up by public subscription.

The outfit was on a most lavish scale; camels were imported
from Peshawar, with native drivers; provisions and stores for twelve
months provided, and no expense spared to render the whole appoint-
ments the most complete ever provided for an exploring expedition.
When the party was organised, it consisted of the leader, R. O'Hara
Burke; second in command, G. J. Landells, who had brought the camels from India; third, W. J. Wills, astronomical and meteorological
observer., Dr. Hermann Beckler, medical officer and botanist; Dr.
Ludwig Becker, artist, naturalist, and geologist; ten white men, and
three camel drivers.

It was a gala day when they left Melbourne, and their progress
through the settled districts was a triumphant march; it almost seemed
that Fate was playing with them in very mockery, smiling at the
thought of the return.

The choice of the leader has always been a puzzle to most
men, and it can only be accounted for in two ways. First, that the
committee of management did not wish (as was only natural) to go
outside of the colony for a man, and the tried and experienced explorers were all residents in other colonies; secondly, that the committee
was, with two notable exceptions, composed of men quite unable to
judge of the qualities essential in a leader; for the man of their choice,
the unfortunate Burke, was most singularly unfitted for the position.

Burke was an Irishman, from the county of Galway. He had
been in the Austrian service, and also in the Irish mounted constabu-
lary. At the time when he applied for the post, which unhappily was
awarded to him, he was an inspector of mounted police at Castle-
maine. His appointment as leader was strongly supported by the
chairman of the committee, Sir William Stawell, and it appears to have
been backed up by those kind of general testimonials as to ability
which recommend a man almost equally for any grade or position. Of
special aptitude or scientific training he possessed no pretension, and
his selection was a fatal blunder. In saying this, there is no reflection
on the private character of the mistaken leader; he paid for the wrong
estimation he held of his own fitness with his life, and the fault rests
with those who placed him in a position where he also was responsible
for the lives of others. After passing in review the different expeditions
that have added so much lustre to our history, and striving to judge
dispassionately of the characters of the men who, with good and evil

fortune, have commanded them, one cannot help being struck by the exaggerated and misplaced stress laid upon the reputation Burke possessed for personal bravery. The calm and simple courage of Sturt, the cool judgment and forethought of Mitchell, the devotion of Austin, seem all to have been lost sight of by writers, who extol Burke in a way that would lead men to believe that every other Australian leader must have been an abject craven. This mistaken laudation has done more to glaringly parade Burke's many failings than more modest and judicious praise would have done.

Of his second, W. J. Wills (who shared the fate of his leader), he appears to have been a man eminently possessed of most of the qualities that would fit him for the position he held, but apparently tempered with an amiability of disposition that led him to give way completely to the rash judgment of his superior, without striving to temper that rashness.

Before the expedition travelled outside of the settled country, trouble appeared. First, Landells resigned in consequence of a quarrel with the leader. On returning to Melbourne, he expressed publicly an opinion that, under Burke's management, the expedition would be attended by most disastrous results.

Wright was then appointed third in charge, and he apparently had not the most remote idea of any of the functions entailed on him by his position, and has since been blamed as having caused the final catastrophe. He joined the party at Menindie, which, for the purpose of explanation, may be said to occupy the same position on the Darling as Laidley's Ponds, whence Sturt started for the interior.

The foregoing estimate of the men holding the principal commands is essential to enable the reader to understand how the astonishing blunders were so constantly perpetrated, that brought the whole campaign to such utter grief.

From Menindie to Cooper's Creek was the next stage, but the country now being fairly well known, they did not follow the route of Sturt the explorer. The main body of the party was left behind. Burke took with him Wills, six men, five horses, and sixteen camels, leaving the others to follow afterwards under the guidance of Wright, who went two hundred miles with them to point out the best route. They left Menindie on the 19th of October, 1860. On the 11th of November they arrived at Cooper's Creek, and here they camped, waiting for the arrival of Wright with the main body, and making short excursions to the northward. Grass and water were both plentiful, and up to their arrival at Cooper's Creek the journey had not been so arduous as an ordinary overlanding trip with cattle.

Wright's non-arrival, and the delay caused thereby, seemed to have worked upon Burke's impatient temper, and the extraordinary notion came into his head to divide his party of eight, and with three men to start across the continent to the Gulf of Carpentaria, leaving the others in charge of Brahe, to await his return, and also Wright's long-delayed arrival. On the 16th December, 1860, Burke, having with him Wills, King, and Gray, six camels, two horses, and three months' provisions, started on this tramp, which for perverse absurdity stands unequalled. The first duty of a man entrusted with such a large party, was to have carried out its chief aim and mission of reporting on the geographical features and formation of the country he was sent to explore, and bringing back the fullest and most minute account of it, and its productions. Burke, during the most important part of his journey, left behind him his botanist, naturalist, and geologist, and started without even the means at his disposal of following up any discoveries he might make. His sole thought evidently was to cross to Carpentaria and back, and be able to say that he had done so--a most unworthy ambition on the part of the leader of such a party, containing within itself all the elements of geographical research, and one that could certainly not have been anticipated by the promoters. After all the pains and cost expended in the organisation of this expedition, we have now the spectacle of the main body, including two of the scientific members, loitering on the outskirts of the settled districts; four men killing time on the banks of Cooper's Creek, and the leader and three others racing headlong across the country ahead, all four of them being utterly inexperienced men. As might be expected, the results of the journey are most barren. Burke scarcely troubled to keep any journal at all.

Wills' diary, too, is sadly uninteresting--it is but the baldest record of the day's doings, and destitute of the sympathetic style which is so essential in an explorer's log. From it we find that their first point was to make Eyre's Creek, but, before reaching it, they discovered a fine water-course coming from the north that took them a long distance on their way, there being abundance of both water and grass along its banks. From where this creek turned to the eastward they kept steadily north, the rivers, fortunately for them, keeping mostly a north and south course. They crossed the dividing range at the head of the Cloncurry River, and by following that river down reached the

Flinders, and, finally, the mangroves and salt water in February, 1861. At the end of his scanty notes, Burke says:--

"28th March. At the conclusion of report, it would be as well to say that we reached the sea, but we could not obtain a view of the open ocean, although we made every endeavour to do so."

Wills' description of their arrival is as follows:

"Finding the ground in such a state from the heavy falls of rain that the camels could scarcely be got along, it was decided to leave them at camp 119, and for Mr. Burke and I to proceed towards the sea on foot, After breakfast, we accordingly started, taking with us the horse and three days' provisions. Our first difficulty was in crossing Billy's Creek, which we had to do where it enters the river, a few hundred yards below the camp. In getting the horse in here he got bogged in a quicksand so deeply as to be unable to stir, and we only succeeded in extricating him by undermining him on the creek side, and then lunging him into the water. Having got all the things in safety, we continued down the river bank, which bent about from east to west, but kept a general north course. A great deal of the land was so soft and rotten that the horse, with only one saddle on and twenty-five pounds on his back, could scarcely walk over it. At a distance of about five miles we again had him bogged, in crossing a small creek, after which he seemed so weak that we had some doubts about getting him on. We, however, found some better ground close to the water's edge, where the sandstone rock runs out, and we stuck to it as far as possible. Finding that the river was bending about so much that we were making very little progress in a northerly direction, we struck off due north, and soon came on some tableland, where the soil is shallow and gravelly, and clothed with box and swamp gums. Patches of the land were very boggy, but the main portion was sound enough. Beyond this we came on an open plain, covered with water up to one's ankles. The soil here was a stiff clay, and the surface very uneven, so that between the tufts of grass one was frequently knee-deep in water. The bottom, however, was sound, and no fear of bogging. After floundering through this for several miles, we came to a path formed by the blacks, and there were distinct signs of a recent migration in a southerly direction. By making use of this path we got on much better, for the ground was well-trodden and hard. At rather more than a mile the path entered a forest, through which flowed a nice watercourse, and we had not gone far before we found places where the blacks had been camping. The forest was intersected by little pebbly rises, on which they made their fires, and in the sandy ground adjoining some of the former had been digging yams, [The *dios-corea* of Carpentaria.] which seemed to be so numerous that they could afford to leave plenty of them behind, probably having selected only the very best. We were not so particular, but ate many of those that they had rejected, and found them very good. About half a mile further we came close on a blackfellow who was coiling by a camp fire, whilst his gin and piccaninny were yabbering alongside. We stopped for a short time to take out some of the pistols that were on the horse, and that they might see us before we were so near as to frighten them. just after we stopped, the black got up to stretch his limbs, and after a few seconds looked in our direction. It was very amusing to see the way in which he stared, standing for some time as if he thought he must be dreaming, and then, having signalled to the others, they dropped on their haunches and shuffled off in the quietest manner possible."

It will be, however, tedious to continue the quotation, suffice it to say that they reached a channel with tidal waters, and had to return without actually seeing the open sea. Then comes a blank in Wills' diary, and when he next writes they were on their way back.

Having accomplished their task, but with little profit, for they did not actually know their position on the Gulf, being strangely out in their reckoning; mistaking the river they were on for the Albert, over a hundred miles to the westward, the retreat commenced. Short rations and hardship now began to tell, and during the struggle back to the depôt there seems to have been an absence of that kindly spirit of self sacrifice which is so distinguishing a feature in nearly all the other expeditions whose lines have fallen disastrously. Gray fell sick, and stole some flour to make some gruel with; for this Burke beat him severely. Wills writes on one occasion that they had to wait, and send back for Gray, who was "gammoning" that he could not walk. Nine days afterwards the unfortunate man dies--an act which at any rate is not often successfully gammoned. But to bring the story to an end, they at last, on the evening of the 21St of April, reached the camp on Cooper's Creek, where they had left their four companions, and instead of finding the whole party there to greet them, found it lifeless and deserted.

Searching at the foot of a tree marked "dig" they found a small quantity of provisions concealed, and a note from Brahe stating that they had left only that morning. They sat down and ate a welcome supper of porridge, and considered their position. They could scarcely walk, and their camels were the same; they had fifty pounds of flour, twenty pounds of rice, sixty pounds of oatmeal, sixty pounds of sugar, and fifteen pounds of dried meat; a very fair stock if they only had had the means of transit; if Brahe had left three or four horses hobbled at the depôt they would have been able to follow, but as it was they could do nothing, and all the time Brahe was only separated from them by a very short distance, had they but known it,

Burke consulted his companions as to the feasibility of their being able to overtake Brahe, and they all agreed that in their tired and enfeebled condition it was hopeless to attempt it; then, according to King's narrative, Burke said that instead of returning up the creek, their old route to Menindie, they would go down to Mount Hopeless, in South Australia, following the line taken by A. C. Gregory. Wills objected and so did King, but ultimately both gave in, and this was the death warrant of two of them.

The following paper was placed in the depôt by Burke before starting:--

"Depôt No. 2, Cooper's Creek, Camp 65. The return party from Carpentaria consisting of myself, Wills and King (Gray dead), arrived here last night, and found that the depôt party had started on the same day. We proceed on to-morrow slowly down the creek to Adelaide, by Mount Hopeless, and shall endeavour to follow Gregory's track, but we are very weak. The two camels are done up and we shall not be able to travel faster than two or three miles a day. Gray died on the road from exhaustion and fatigue. We have all suffered much from hunger. The provisions left here will, I think, restore our strength. We have discovered a practicable route to Carpentaria, the chief portion of which lies on 140 deg. of east longitude. There is some good country between this and the Stony Desert. From there to the tropics the country is dry and stony. Between the tropics and Carpentaria a considerable portion is rangy, but it is well-watered and richly-grassed. We reached the shores of Carpentaria on February 11th, 1861. Greatly disappointed at finding the party here gone.

"(Signed) ROBERT O'HARA BURKE.

"April 22, 1861.

"P.S.--The camels cannot travel, and we cannot walk or we should follow the other party. We shall move very slowly down the creek."

After resting four or five days, and finding great advantage from their change of diet, the three men started, but one of the camels got bogged, and had to be shot as he lay in the creek, the explorers cutting off what meat they could from the body, and staying a couple of days to dry it in the sun. When they again started, the one camel they had left carried most of what they had, and they each took with

192

them a bundle of about twenty-five pounds; but they made no progress, all the creeks they followed to the southward ran out into earthy plains and their one solitary beast of burden being knocked up, they had to return.

Now commenced a terrible struggle for mere existence the camel being past recovery, was shot, and the meat dried, and then the men tried to live, after the fashion of the blacks, on fish and nardoo. The natives were especially kind to the unfortunate men. In Wills' diary we find frequent mention of the liberal hospitality they extended to them, but to a great extent the novelty soon died out, and the blacks began to find their white guests rather an encumbrance, and soon commenced shifting their camps to avoid the burden of their support.

On the 27th May, Wills started alone to the depôt to deposit the journals, and a note stating their condition. He reached there on the 30th, and says in his diary:--
"No traces of anyone, except blacks, have been here since we left. Deposited some journals and a notice of our present condition."

This was the notice:--
"May 30th, 1861.
"We have been unable to leave the creek. Both camels are dead. Mr. Burke and King are down on the lower part of the creek. I am about to return to them, when we shall probably all come up this way. We are trying to live the best way we can, like the blacks, but we find it hard work. Our clothes are going fast to pieces. Send provisions and clothes as soon as possible.
"(Signed) WILLIAM J. WILLS."
"The depôt party having left, contrary to instructions, has put us in this fix. I have deposited some of my journals here for fear of accidents."

Having done this, Wills returned to his companions, being fed by the friendly natives on his way back. During the intercourse that of necessity they had had with the blacks during their detention on Cooper's Creek, they had noticed the extensive use the natives made of the seeds of the nardoo [See Appendix.] plant as an article of food; but for a long time they were unable to find out this plant, nor would the blacks show it to them. At last King accidentally found it, and, by its aid, they now managed to prolong their lives. But the seeds had to be gathered, cleaned, pounded and cooked, and even after all this labour (and to men in their state it was labour) very little nourishment was derived from eating it. An occasional crow or hawk was shot, and, by chance, a little fish obtained from the natives, and as this was all they could get, they were sinking rapidly. At last they decided that Burke and King should go up the creek and endeavour to find the natives and get food from them. Wills, who was now so weak as to be unable almost to move, was left lying under some boughs, with an eight days' supply of water and nardoo, the others trusting that before that time they would have returned to him.

On the 26th June the two men started, and poor Wills was left to meet his death alone. He must have retained his consciousness almost to the last. So exhausted was he, that death must have been only like a release from the trouble of living. His last entries, though giving evidences of fading faculties, are almost cheerful. He jocularly alludes to himself as Micawber, waiting for something to turn up. It is evident that he had given up hope, and waited for death's approach in a calm and resigned frame of mind, without fear, like a good and gallant man.

King and Burke did not go far; on the second day Burke had to give in from sheer weakness, and the next morning when his companion looked at him, he saw by the breaking light that his leader was dead.

This was the sad and bitter end of the high-spirited captain of this luckless expedition; an almost solitary death on the wide western plain, after enduring weeks of hunger and starvation. What must have been King's feelings at finding himself thus left without a companion to cheer his last hours when his turn, as he then thought, must inevitably soon come?

After wandering in search of the natives, and not finding them, the solitary man returned to Wills, who was also dead, and all he could do was to cover the body up with a little sand, without any hope that the same would be done by him.

Burke's last notes in his pocket book are as follows:--
"I hope we shall be done justice to. We have fulfilled our task, but we have been aban----. We have not been followed up as we expected, and the depôt party abandoned their post."

He winds up:--
"King has behaved nobly. He has stayed with me to the last, and placed the pistol in my hand, leaving me lying on the surface as I wished."

Left to himself, King, after a few days, made another effort to find the natives, and this time succeeded, living with their assistance until rescued by Howitt's relief party on September 15th, having for nearly three months subsisted on the hospitality of the natives.

194

Meanwhile that these unfortunate men were slowly starving to death on Cooper's Creek, parties were soon to be dispatched from north, south and east in quest of them.

Left at the depôt on Cooper's Creek, Brahe remained from the 14th of December, 1860, until the 21st of April, 1861. Then he left, his instructions, according to his own account, being (verbally) to remain at the depôt three months, or longer, if provisions and other circumstances would permit. Before leaving he buried, as before stated, a small supply of provisions and a note, which in full ran:--

"Depôt, Cooper's Creek, April 21, 1861. The depôt party of V.E.E. leaves this camp to-day to return to the Darling. I intend to go S.E. from camp 60 to get on to our old track at Bulloo. Two of my companions and myself are quite well; the third--Patton-has been unable to walk for the last eighteen days, as his leg has been severely hurt when thrown by one of the horses. No person has been up here from the Darling. We have six camels and twelve horses, in good working condition.

"WILLIAM BRAHE."

Unfortunately this was worded in such a way as to leave Burke, who got it that night, under the impression that they were all, with one exception, fairly well, and would probably make long stages, whereas, on the evening of the day that Burke returned, they were camped but fourteen miles away.

Wright, meantime, with the main body of the party had been camping and wandering between the Darling and Bulloo; his men sickened and died of scurvy, and he consumed his rations, and reduced the condition of his stock to no purpose. On Brahe's return he made an extraordinary display of energy, and returned with him to the depôt on Cooper's Creek, at which place they arrived on the 8th of May, whilst Burke and Wills were making their futile attempt to reach Mount Hopeless. Wright and Brahe came to the conclusion that no one had visited the caché since Brahe's departure, although the fact seems almost incredible. Brahe states, however:--

"Mr. Burke's return being so soon after my departure caused the tracks of his camels to correspond in the character of age exactly with our own tracks. The remains of three separate fires led us to suppose that blacks had been camped there. The fires had burned to mere ashes, and left no perceptible evidence from the position of the sticks as to whether they were black men's fires or not. The ground above the caché was so perfectly restored to the appearance it presented when I left it, that in the absence of any fresh sign or mark of any description to be seen near, it was impossible to suppose that it had been disturbed."

Wright and Brahe rode away again, and when Wills afterwards visited the depôt to bury the journals, he says that he could not perceive any sign of it having been visited; a series of singular and fatal oversights that almost seem to have been pre-ordained.

On the 18th of June, Wright reached the Darling and sent in his dispatches. As may be imagined they occasioned great consternation, and no time was lost in instituting search parties to scour half the continent for the missing men. Fortunately a light party, under Mr. A. W. Howitt, had already been equipped, to follow on Burke's tracks, for the long absence and silence of Wright had already caused people to feel anxious. Howitt's party was doubled and he made all speed to Cooper's Creek. Meantime the other colonies took the matter up and three more parties were in the field. Howitt, whose fortunes we must follow, started early in July; the Victoria, steam sloop, was sent up to the mouth of the Albert River, in the Gulf of Carpentaria, from Brisbane, having Mr. W. Landsborough on board. Another Queensland expedition, under Mr. Walker, left the furthest out station, in the Rockhampton district, to proceed overland to the Gulf, and from South Australia, started M'Kinlay.

On the 8th of September Howitt, having with him Brahe, reached Cooper's Creek, and on the 13th arrived at the fatal depôt, but like all the others, he says that he could not see any sign of the caché having been touched; nor did he stop to examine it. On the 15th, while trying to follow Burke's outward track down the creek, Howitt says:--
"I crossed at a neck of sand, and again came on the track of a camel going up the creek; at the same time I found a native, who began to gesticulate in a very excited manner, and to point down the creek, bawling out, 'Gow! gow!' as loud as he could. When I went towards him he ran away, and finding it impossible to get him to come to me, I turned back to follow the camel track, and to look after my party, as I had not seen anything of them for some miles. The track was visible in sandy places, and was evidently the same I had seen for the last two days. I also found horse tracks in places, but very old. Crossing the creek I cut our track, and rode after the party. In doing so I came upon three pounds of tobacco, which had lain where I saw it for some time. This, together with the knife-handle, the fresh horse tracks, and the camel track going eastward, puzzled me extremely, and led me into a hundred conjectures. At the lower end of the large reach of water before mentioned, I met Sandy and Frank looking for me, with the

intelligence that King, the only survivor of Mr. Burke's party, had been found. [See Appendix.] A little further on I found the party halted, and immediately went across to the black's wurleys, where I found King sitting in a hut that the blacks had made for him. He presented a melancholy appearance-wasted to a shadow, and hardly to be distinguished as a civilised being, except by the remnants of clothes on him."

So soon as King had recovered sufficient strength to accompany the party they went to the place where Wills had died, and found his body in the gunyah as King had described it, there it was buried. On the 21st, Burke's body was found up the creek, he too was buried where he died.

Howitt then, after rewarding the blacks who had cared for King, started home again by easy stages taking the rescued man with him. On his return to Melbourne, Howitt was sent back to disinter the remains of the explorers, and bring them down to Melbourne, which task he safely accomplished. A public funeral then took place, and subsequently a statue was erected to their memory.

Dr. Beckler, and Messrs. Stone, Purcell, and Patton were the others whose lives were sacrificed on this unfortunate trip, the first three were members of Wright's party, the last one was with Brahe at the depôt.

Before ending the narration of this journey of Burke and Wills, it will be remembered, that an account of Stuart's expedition to Central Mount Stuart, and Attack Creek was forwarded to the leader; these papers were entrusted to Trooper Lyons to take from Swan Hill to Wright's camp. Wright ordered him on to follow the tracks of Burke, who he supposed was about two hundred miles away; he was accompanied by the saddler of the party, McPherson, and a black boy, Dick. They followed Burke's tracks for some days but never reached him, their horses gave in, and they being insufficiently provided with provisions nearly perished, finally they were picked up by a relief party under Doctor Beckler.

The nardoo which served to prolong the life of Burke and Wills for a considerable time is a small ground plant resembling clover in the shape of its leaves. These leaves are covered with silvery down, and the seeds, too, have this down on them. When fresh the seeds are flat and oval. The nardoo grows in loose soil, subject to inundation, generally on polygonum flats.

Whilst this tragedy had been enacted, Stuart was endeavouring to force his way across Australia, and at the time his fellow explorers were slowly starving to death on Cooper's Creek, he was making gallant efforts to cross the dry tableland that separated him from the heads of the coast rivers.

Stuart followed his old track by the way of the Fincke and the Hugh, and on the 12th April arrived at their former acquaintance, the Bonney, which they found running strong, with abundant green feed on its banks. They followed it down until it spread out and was lost in a large plain; so striking north, the party on the 21st April reached Tennant's Creek, and four days after, they came to the scene of their skirmish with the natives, on Attack Creek. This time, although the tracks of natives were numerous, they were permitted to pass peacefully onwards. Still pushing to the north, along the base of the line of broken range, that in that locality runs north and south, Stuart found and named many creeks, all of them heading from the range and forming for a considerable space good defined channels, but becoming lost on entering the low country. At last, on the 4th of May, he came to the end of the range, which he there called the Ashburton Range. Here he made several attempts to the north-west, but could discover neither water nor watercourses in that direction; nothing but flooded plains, beautifully grassed, but heavy and rotten to ride over; beyond this, the country changed for the worse, becoming sandy and scrubby.

On the 16th of May, he first encountered a new kind of scrub, which is now known as Stuart's hedgewood. It spreads out in many branches from the root upwards, interlacing with its neighbours on either side, forming an impervious hedge. On the 23rd, he found the magnificent sheet of water, which he called Newcastle Waters, and which at first seemed to promise him good assistance in getting to the north, but it proved delusive. Beyond the Newcastle he could not advance his party at all; north, north-cast, and north-west, it was all the same endless grassy plains, terminating in thick scrubby forest, until at last he had again to give up hope, and return to Adelaide.

Such, however, was the confidence of the authorities in him, and such his own energy, that in less than a month he was on his way to Chambers' Creek, to make preparations for a fresh start. His last journey had proved the existence of a long line of good country, fairly well-watered, and although beyond it he had not been able to proceed, still, there was no knowing what a fresh trial might bring forth. He had, at any rate, brought back his party in safety, with the loss of only a few horses; and in no way deterred by the fate of the Victorian explorers, he started once more, this time destined to meet with success.

Chapter X

On leaving the settled districts, Stuart followed his old track, now so familiar to him, until on the 14th April, 1862, we find him encamped at the upper end of Newcastle Waters, once more about to try to force a passage through the forest of scrub to the north. On the second day he was partly successful, finding an isolated waterhole, surrounded by conglomerate rock. This he called Frew's Pond, and it is now a well-known camping place on the overland telegraph line.

Past this spot he was not able to make any progress; twice he tried hard to reach some tributary of the Victoria River, but failed, and had to spend many long days in fruitlessly riding through dense mulga and hedgewood scrub. At length, after much hope deferred, and finding a few scanty waterholes that did not serve his purpose, he succeeded in striking the head of a chain of ponds running to the north.

These being followed down, led him to the head of the creek, called Daly Waters Creek, and finally to the large waterhole bearing that name, where the telegraph station now stands.

Beyond this point the creek was lost in a swamp, and Stuart was unable to find the channel where it re-formed, now known as the Birdum. Missing this watercourse, Stuart worked his way to the eastward, to a creek he called the Strangways, which led him down to the Roper River. This river he crossed, and followed up a northern tributary named by him the Chambers, a name he was so fond of conferring out of gratitude to his constant friend, John Chambers.

His troubles regarding water were now over, but his horses began to fall lame, and he had to carefully husband his stock of spare shoes to carry him back to Adelaide. From the Chambers he came to the Katherine, the lower course of the Flying Fox Creek of Leichhardt, called by Stuart as above, the name it now bears. Thence he struck across the tableland, and descended to the head waters of the river he christened the Adelaide, although at first he thought that he was on the Alligator River. Following the Adelaide, he soon found himself travelling amongst rich tropical scenery, that told him he was at last approaching the coast.

On the 24th July, he went to the north-east, intending to make the sea shore and travel along the beach to the mouth of the Adelaide River. He only told two of the party of the eventful moment awaiting them. As they rode on, Thring, who was ahead, called out, "The sea!" which so took the majority by surprise, that they were some time before they understood what was meant, and then three hearty cheers burst forth.

At this, his first point of contact, Stuart dipped his hands and feet in the sea, and the initials J.M.D.S. were cut on the largest tree they could find. He then attempted to make the mouth of the Adelaide, but found the route too boggy for the horses, and not seeing the utility of fatiguing them for nothing, had a space cleared where they were, and a tall sapling stripped of its boughs for a flagstaff; on this he hoisted the Union Jack he had carried with him. A memorial of the visit was then buried at the foot of the impromptu staff. It was an air-tight tin case containing the following paper:--

"South Australian Great Northern Exploring Expedition.--The exploring party, under the command of John M'Dowall Stuart, arrived at this spot on the 25th day of July, 1862, having crossed the entire continent of Australia, from the Southern to the Indian Ocean, passing through the centre. They left the city of Adelaide on the 26th day of October,

1861, and the most northern station of the colony on the 21st day of January, 1862. To commemorate this happy event., they have raised this flag bearing his name. All well. God save the Queen."

Stuart and the party signed their names to this document. The tree has since been found and recognised, but this memorial has not been discovered.

More fortunate than the other travellers who reached the Gulf shore, Stuart was able to survey the open sea, instead of having to be content with the sight of some mangrove trees and salt water.

Next day Stuart started on his return. His health was failing, and his horses were sadly weakened. After leaving the Newcastle, the water in the many short creeks coming from the range was found to be at the last gasp; in some there was none, in others but a scanty supply. The horses commenced to give in rapidly, and one after another they were left on successive dry stages. Stuart, too, began to think that he would never live to reach the settled districts. Scurvy had brought him down to a terrible state, and after all his success, he scarcely hoped to profit by it. His right hand was nearly useless to him, and after sunset he was blind. He could not stand the pain caused by riding, and a stretcher had to be made to carry him on. Slowly and painfully they crept along until the first station, Mount Margaret, was reached, and here the leader, who was only a skeleton, was able to get a little relief, and finally recovered sufficiently to ride to Adelaide.

This was the last exploration conducted by Stuart. He was rewarded by the Government of the colony he had served so well, and went to reside in England, where he died. He never recovered from the great suffering of his return journey.

At a re-union of returned Australians, held at Glasgow shortly before his death, he had to speak, and it was evident to all that he had quite broken down. He said that "his eyesight and his memory were so far gone that he was unable to compose a speech, or, indeed, to recollect many of the incidents that happened throughout the course of his explorations." This was the sad ending of one of our greatest explorers. Eight full years of his life had been spent in exploring Australia, and neither his means nor resources had ever been great--in fact, on some occasions they had been dangerously small--but he always brought his party back in safety, through every difficulty.

In following up Stuart's last expedition, we have lost sight for a time of the three parties sent out after Burke and Wills, which, although they were unsuccessful in their first aim, yet did sterling service in the field of discovery.

John M'Kinlay started from Adelaide-the scene of so many departures on similar errands--on October 26th, 1861. On arriving at Blanche Water, he was informed that a report was current amongst the natives that some white men and camels had been seen at a distant inland water, but knowing the little reliance to be placed on such statements, he did not at the time pay much attention to it. On the 27th of September, he crossed Lake Torrens--a feat which would have excited great interest a few years ago--and made for Lake Pando, or Lake Hope, as it is better known. From here he went north, crossing the country so often described, wherein Cooper's Creek is lost in many watercourses. He now got more definite details about the whites that he had formerly heard of, and pressed forward to the place indicated by the natives, and on the 18th October, formed a depôt camp for his main party, and started ahead in company with two white men and a native.

Passing through a country full of small shallow lakes, of all of which M'Kinlay has faithfully preserved the terrible native names, such as Lake Moolion--dhurunnie, etc., they came to a watercourse, whereon they found a grave and picked up a battered pint pot. Next morning they opened the grave, and in it was the body of a European, the skull being marked, so M'Kinlay says, with two sabre cuts. He noted down the description of the body, and, from the locality and surroundings, it has been pronounced to have been the body of Gray, who died before reaching Cooper's Creek.

If the reader will remember what was the result of the circumstantial accounts of Leichhardt's murder retailed to Hely by the natives, he will not be astonished at what follows.

The native that M'Kinlay had with him thus described the manner of the white man's death, which, of course, was all pure fiction. First, that the whites were attacked in camp by the natives, who murdered the whole party, finishing up by eating the bodies of the other men. Next, that the journals, saddles, etc., were buried at a fake a short distance away. Naturally, under the circumstances, M'Kinlay believed this story; particularly as further search revealed another grave (empty) and other small evidences of the presence of whites.

Next morning a tribe of blacks appeared, and although they immediately ran away, one was captured, who corroborated the story told by M'Kinlay's native. The prisoner had marks both of ball and shot wounds on him; he stated that there was a pistol concealed near a neighbouring lake, and he was sent to fetch it; but instead, he appeared the following morning at the head of a host of others, well armed, and bent on mischief. The leader was obliged to order his men to fire on them, and it was only after several discharges that they ran away.

M'Kinlay was now quite satisfied that he had found all that remained of the Victorian expedition; and after burying a letter for the information of any after comers, they left Lake Massacre, as he called it, and returned to his depôt camp. The letter hidden was as follows:--
"S.A.B.R. Expedition,

"October 23rd, 1861.

"To the leader of any expedition seeking tidings of Burke and party:--

"Sir,--I reached this water on the 19th instant, and by means of a native guide discovered a European camp, one mile north on west side of flat. At, or near this camp, traces of horses, camels, and whites were found. Hair, apparently belonging to Mr. Wills, Charles Gray, Yr. Burke, or King, was picked from the surface of a grave dug by a spade, and from the skull of a European buried by the natives. Other less important traces-such as a pannikin, oil can, saddle stuffing, &c., have been found. Beware of the natives, on whom we have had to fire. We do not intend to return to Adelaide, but proceed to west of north. From information, all Burke's party were killed and eaten.

"JNO. M'KINLAY.

"[P.S.--All the party in good health.]

"If you had any difficulty in reaching this spot, and wish to return to Adelaide by a more practicable route, you may do so for at least three months to come, by driving west eighteen miles, then south of west, cutting our dray track within thirty miles. Abundance of water and feed at easy stages."

M'Kinlay next sent Mr. Hodgkinson with men and packhorses to Blanche Water, to take down the news of his discovery, and to bring back rations for a prolonged exploration. Meantime he remained in camp. From one old native, with whom he had a long conversation, he obtained another version of the supposed massacre, which evidently had a certain admixture of truth.

This was to the effect that the whites repulsed an attack of the natives on their return journey; that in the affair, one white man was killed; he was buried after the fight, and the others went south. The natives then dug up the body and ate the flesh. The blackfellow then described minutely the different waters passed by Burke, and the way the men lived on the seeds of the nardoo plant, which he must have heard of from other natives.

After waiting a little over a month, Mr. Hodgkinson returned, and brought back with him the news of Howitt's success in finding King. This explained M'Kinlay's discovery as being that of Gray's body, the adjuncts of the fight turning out to be exaggerations of the natives. He made an excursion to the eastward, and visited the graves of the two men buried by Howitt, on Cooper's Creek, then he started for the north.

The perusal of his journal, containing the account of his first few weeks' travel, is hard work to accomplish. The native names of every small lake and waterhole are all given in full, and as the course of each day's travel is omitted, it becomes rather difficult to follow the track of the expedition, excepting on the map.

A fairly northerly course was, however, maintained, and M'Kinlay speaks highly of the country for pastoral purposes. As it was the dry time of the year, immediately preceding the setting in of the rains, it shows what a severe season must have been encountered by Sturt when on his last struggle north, as that explorer finally turned his-back in much the same locality.

On the 27th of February, heavy rains set in, fortunately, they were in the neighbourhood of some stony ridges and sand hills, on which they camped, and where they had plenty of space to feed their animals, although surrounded by water.

On March 10th, they started again, and steadily continued north through good travelling country, keeping back from the main creek, which was now too flooded and boggy to follow. This large creek, which was called by M'Kinlay the Mueller, is one of the main rivers of the interior, now known as the Diamantina. M'Kinlay soon kept more to the westward and crossed the stony range, which bears his name, in much the same place that Burke and Wills did. He christened many of the large tributaries of the inland watershed, but most of his names have been replaced by others, it having been difficult to determine them, as in many cases, the creeks he named were but anabranches.

The history of their progress is now monotonous in the extreme, the country through which they travelled presented no great obstacle to the travellers' advance, being well-grassed and watered; and finally on the 6th May they reached the Leichhardt River.

M'Kinlay was most anxious to get to the mouth of the Albert, it being understood that Captain Norman with the steamer Victoria, would there form a depôt for the use of the other explorers, Landsbor-

ough and Walker, and M'Kinlay's stock of rations was getting peril-
ously low.

His attempts to reach the sea were, however, fruitless. He was
continually turned back by deep and broad mangrove creeks and
boggy flats, and on the 21st May the party started for the nearest settled districts in Queensland, in the direction of Port Denison.

They were now on the country already twice described by
both Leichhardt and Gregory, and making in the same direction that
Gregory did on his return journey. Like him, too, M'Kinlay missed
following up the Flinders. He crossed on to the head of the head of the
Burdekin, which river he followed down, continually trusting to meet
the advancing flocks and herds of the settlers, then pushing forward
into the new country. On reaching Mount M'Connell, where the tracks
of the two former explorers came respectively to the river, and left it,
M'Kinlay kept down the river, crossing the formidable Leichhardt
Range, through which the Burdekin forces its way to the lower lands
of the coast. Here they came to a temporary station, just formed by Mr.
Phillip Somer, where they were received with the usual hearty hospitality. Since leaving the Gulf country the explorers had subsisted on
little else than horse and camel flesh, and were necessarily in rather a
weak condition; but whilst they were toiling down the channel of the
Upper Burdekin, suffering semi-starvation, they were actually travelling amongst the advance-guard of the pioneer squatters, and had they
but thought of resting a day and looking around, their wants would
have been relieved long before they sighted the gorge of the Burdekin,
and their toilsome journey through that gorge have been prevented.

The tracks of the camels had been seen by one squatter [Note,
below] at least within a few hours after the cavalcade had passed down
the river, and a very little trouble would have saved M'Kinlay much
suffering.

[Note: Mr. E. Cunningham, who had then just formed Burdekin Downs Station. He tells, with much amusement, how the nature of
the tracks puzzled himself and his black boy. The Burdekin pioneers
of course did not expect M'Kinlay's advent amongst them, although
they knew he was out west, and such an animal as a camel did not enter into their reckoning. Cunningham says that the only thing he could
think of was, that it was a return party who had been looking for new
country, and that, having footsore horses and no shoes left, they had
wrapped up their horses' feet with bandages.]

M'Kinlay's trip across the continent did good service at this
juncture. His track was across the country that had always been con-

sidered a terrible desert, useless for pastoral occupation. His report being of such a favourable nature, dealt a final blow to this theory, which Stuart had partly demolished. Fortunately, M'Kinlay was an experienced man, whose verdict was accepted without cavil.

The successful way in which he conducted his party across the continent, and his well-known merits, led to his afterwards being selected by the South Australian Government for a responsible post in the Northern Territory, which will be dealt with in its proper order.

On the 14th of August, 1861, the Firefly, having on board the Brisbane search party for Burke and Wills, left Brisbane. The leader of the party was Mr. William Landsborough, an experienced bushman, having already a good knowledge of new country gained in private exploration. The brig was convoyed by the Victoria, under Captain Norman, who had charge of the expedition until the party were landed. On the way up, the vessels were separated, and the Firefly suffered shipwreck on one of Sir Charles Hardy's islands; the horses being got ashore safely. On the Victoria coming up, the Firefly was repaired sufficiently to serve as a transport. hulk and the party re-embarked; she was taken in tow by the Victoria, and safely reached her destination at the mouth of the Albert River, in the Gulf of Carpentaria.

The Victoria, as arranged, remained there to render assistance to Landsborough on his return, and to the Rockhampton search party under Mr. Walker, on his arrival overland. Landsborough's track, after leaving the Albert, took him on to the banks of a new river, which had the same outlet as the Albert, but on account of the other explorers crossing below the junction, had been hitherto unnoticed. This river, which is a constantly running stream, and flows through well-grassed, level country, was named by him the Gregory. His written opinion of the much-disputed qualities of this district is most sanguine, with regard to its future as a sheep country. Experience, however, has proved otherwise, it being found to be fitted only for cattle. Higher up, Landsborough found the river drier, and presenting a far less tropical appearance than on its lower course. After continued efforts to the south, and the discovery of many tributary creeks, Landsborough, on the 21St of December, found the river which he named the Herbert, one of the most important streams running south, and joining Eyre's Creek. This river has since been re-named by the Queensland Government, in consequence of there being another Herbert River in the territory. With most questionable taste, the officials, out of a wide choice of names, could find none better than the absurd, and inappropriate one of the Georgina! by which it is now known.

The first important feature in Landsborough's Herbert, which runs through richly-grassed tableland country, was met with on the day following its discovery, when a fine sheet of water was found which they named Lake Mary; below this, some distance, was another pool-- Lake Frances. Landsborough now made an attempt to push to the westward, but failed through want of water, He then returned up the Herbert, and crossed on to the head of the O'Shanassy, a tributary of the Gregory. Down this river, and by way of Beames' Brook, they returned to the depôt on the Albert, where they arrived on the 8th February, 1862, having been absent nearly three months.

Here Landsborough learnt that during his absence Walker had arrived, and reported finding the tracks of Burke and Wills on the Flinders. He therefore determined to go home in that direction, instead of returning in the steamer, being anxious to see if he could render any assistance. The party was reduced in number to three whites and three blacks in all, namely, Messrs. Landsborough, Bourne, and Gleeson, and the three boys--Jacky, Jemmy, and Fisherman They had a decidedly insufficient stock of rations when they started the second time, being without tea and sugar, the Victoria not being able to supply them with any.

From the Albert depôt Landsborough made for the Flinders, by way of the Leichhardt, and arrived at that river on the 19th February. He followed it up, and was rewarded by being the first discoverer of the beautiful downs country through which it runs. He named the isolated and remarkable hills visible from the river Fort Bowen and Mounts Brown and Little. On the upper part of the Flinders he named Walker's Creek--a considerable tributary--and from there struck more to the south, towards Bowen Downs country discovered by himself and Buchanan two years previously. Here the leader was in hopes of finding a newly-formed station, and obtaining some more supplies; but the country was still untenanted, although in one place they observed the track of a dray, and they also saw the tracks of a party of horsemen near Aramac Creek. They now made for the Thomson, which is formed by the junction of the Landsborough and Cornish Creeks, but did not follow it down to the Barcoo, striking that river higher up. On the Barcoo they had a slight skirmish with the blacks, who nearly surprised them during the night.

Landsborough was now back in well-known country; some of it, in fact, he had been over before himself, and from the number of trees they saw marked with different initials, it was evident that before long stock would be on its way out. He crossed on to the Warrego, followed that river down, and on the 21st of May came to the station of Messrs. Neilson and Williams, where they heard of the fate of Burke and Wills, the objects of their search. From here the party proceeded to the Darling, and finally to Melbourne.

On Landsborough's arrival in Melbourne, he found that rumour had accredited him with being more interested in looking for available pastoral country than in hunting for Burke and Wills. So far as can be seen, this accusation was utterly groundless, as there was no saying to what part of the Gulf Burke and Wills would penetrate, and he was as likely to meet with traces of them on the Barcoo as well as anywhere else. With the general belief then current, of the desert nature of the interior, nobody dreamt that four inexperienced men would have been able to cross so easily in such a straight line.

The charge lay in a newspaper paragraph that went the round of the daily papers, an extract from which runs as follows:--

"Great credit must be given to Mr. Landsborough for the celerity with which he has accomplished the expedition. At the same time, its object seems to have been lost sight of at a very early stage of the journey, as there was not the remotest probability of striking Burke's track after quitting the Flinder's River, and taking a S.S.E. course for the remainder of the way. In fact, from that moment all mention [This is incorrect. Landsborough particularly mentions in his journal during his trip to the Barcoo, how anxiously he endeavoured to find out from the natives if they had seen anybody with camels.] ceases to be made of the ostensible purpose for which the party was organised, until Mr. Landsborough reached the Warrego, and received the intelligence of Burke and Wills having perished, at which great surprise was expressed. But supposing these gallant men to have been still living, and anxiously awaiting succour at some one of the ninety camping places at which they halted, on their arduous journey between the depôt and the Gulf what excuse could Mr. Landsborough have offered for giving so wide a berth to the probable route of the explorers, and for omitting to endeavour to strike their track, traces of which had been reported on the Flinders by Mr Walker? We may be reminded that 'all's well that ends well,' that the lamented explorers were beyond the reach of human assistance, and that Mr. Landsborough has achieved a most valuable result in following the course he did; but we cannot help remarking that in so doing he seems to have been more intent upon serving the cause of pastoral settlement than upon ascertaining if it were possible to afford relief to the missing men. The impression produced by a perusal of the dispatch which we published on Saturday last is that the writer was commissioned to open up a practicable route from the Warrego to the Flinders, and not that he was the leader of a party which had been organized and dispatched 'for the purpose of rendering relief, if possible, to the missing explorers under the command of Mr. Burke.' We do not wish to detract one iota from the credit due to Mr. Landsborough for what he has actually effected, but we must not lose sight of 'the mission of humanity' in which he was professedly engaged, nor the fact that this mission was replaced by one of a totally different character, strengthening, as this circumstance does, the conviction, which is gaining ground in the public mind, that we have been deluded in expending large sums of money in sending out relief expeditions which were chiefly employed in exploring available country for the benefit of the Government and people of Queensland. The cost and the empty honour has been ours, but theirs has been the substantial gain."

The reply to this is very simple. In the first place, Howitt had been sent especially to follow up Burke from the start, and would therefore be supposed to be searching the country on the direct course. Again, Walker was--as Landsborough thought--then following the homeward track of the lost party. The only chance of affording succour to the missing men, left to Landsborough, was the remote one of accidentally coming upon them. Nobody could have reasonably supposed that such a costly and elaborately got up expedition would have degenerated into a scamper across to the Gulf, and a scramble back over the same country.

Apart from all this, Landsborough did not apply for a lease of any of the country discovered by him on the search expedition, the country called Bowen Downs having been his discovery of two years previously, and considering that he closed his days in comparative poverty, after all his labour, such insinuations as the above are most unjust, and would be hardly worthy of comment save for the prominent and adverse notice taken of it by William Howitt, in general such an impartial historian.

The late William Landsborough first went north to Queensland in 1853. In 1854 Messrs. Landsborough and Ranken formed a station on the Kolan River, between Gayndah and Gladstone, where between bad seasons and blacks they had considerable trouble. In 1856 his exploring career commenced in the district of Broadsound and the Isaacs River. In 1858 he explored the Comet to the watershed, and in the following year the head-waters of the Thomson.

An old friend and comrade, writing of him, says:--

"Landsborough's enterprise was entirely founded on his own self-reliance. He had neither Government aid nor capitalists at his back when he achieved his success as an explorer. He was the very model of a pioneer--courageous, hardy, good-humoured, and kindly. He was an excellent horseman, a most entertaining and, at times, eccentric companion, and he could starve with greater cheerfulness than any man I ever saw or heard of. But excellent fellow though he was, his very independence of character and success in exploring provoked much ill-will."

It is to be hoped, therefore, that in future Landsborough's great services will be regarded in a more just light than they were by some of his contemporaries, particularly some living explorers, who resemble the one alluded to by Dr. Lang:--

"But Mr. ---- is not the only geographical explorer in Australia who, 'Turk-like, could bear no brother near the throne.' It seems to be a family failing."

Frederick Walker was the leader of the Rockhampton search expedition. He was an old bushman, had had much to do with the formation of the native police of Queensland, and took a party of native troopers with him on this occasion.

On receiving his commission he pushed rapidly out to the Barcoo, and in the neighbourhood of the tree marked L, found by Gregory, discovered another L tree. This may or may not be considered a corroboration that the first was Leichhardt's, there being arguments on both sides. From the Barcoo he struck north-west to the Alice, seeing some old horse-tracks, which he thought must be Leichhardt's, but which were probably those of Landsborough and Buchanan. From the head-waters of the Alice and Thomson, Walker struck a river he called the Barkly, in reality the head of the Flinders. Here he experienced much difficulty from the rough basaltic nature of the country which borders the upper reaches of this river. Finally getting on to the great western plains he unwittingly crossed the Flinders, and went far to the north looking for it. Bearing into the Gulf, he had several encounters with the natives, who by this time it may be supposed began to see too many exploring parties.

Walker's track down here is rather vague. He may be said to have run a parallel course to the Flinders River away to the north of it, until, on nearing the coast, the bend of the river brought it across his course again. Here he found the tracks of the camels, which assured him that Burke had at any rate reached the Gulf in safety. He therefore pushed on to the depôt at the Albert to get a supply of provisions, and return and follow the tracks up.

He reached the Victoria depôt safely, as before related, and reported his discovery, having had two more skirmishes with the natives on the way. Fresh provisioned, he made back for the Flinders, but found it impossible to follow the tracks. From what he saw, however, he formed a theory that Burke had retreated towards Queensland, and there he made up his mind to return. He regained his former course on the river he calls the Norman, but which may have been the Saxby, and up this river he toiled till he reached the network of watersheds which forms such a jumble of broken country at the heads of the Burdekin, Lynd, Gilbert and Flinders.

Here Walker's horses suffered severely from the rocks and stones, until at last, by the time they had reached the Lower Burdekin, they were well-nigh horseless, and quite starving. On the 4th of April, 1862, they reached Strathalbyn cattle station, owned by Messrs. Wood and Robison, not far from where M'Kinlay eventually arrived.

M'Kinlay's was the last party to use the roundabout and rugged road to the head of the Burdekin that seemed to have such attractions for all the explorers. Henceforth the road to the Gulf lay down the wide plains of the Flinders.

Walker was afterwards employed by the Queensland Government to explore a track for the telegraph line from Rockingham Bay to the mouth of the Norman River, in the Gulf of Carpentaria. This he carried out successfully; but when at the Gulf he was attacked by the then prevalent malarial fever, and died there.

This completes the series of expeditions undertaken for the relief of Burke and Wills. The eastern half of Australia was now nearly all known--from south to north, and from north to south, it had been crossed and re-crossed, and future enterprise was soon to expend itself upon the western half.

So far the results arrived at had been most satisfactory. Not much over forty years after Oxley's gloomy prediction of the future of the interior, country had been found surpassing in richness any that was then known. The pathways for the pioneers had been marked out, and a few more years was to see the whole of the continent up to the western boundary of Queensland the busy scene of pastoral industry.

Most noticeable in the history we have just recounted is the persistent manner in which each succeeding explorer found in all new discoveries the fulfillment of some pet theory. To the men brought up in the old school of belief in the central desert, every fresh advance into the interior was only pushing the desert back a step; it was there still, and, according to some, it is there now. Others who believed in the great river theory, imagined its source in the fresh discovery of every inland river; and those who pinned their faith on a central range, accepted the low broken ridges of the M'Donnel Ranges as the leading spurs.

But the discoveries of the luxuriant new herbage and edible shrubs of the interior were the greatest stumbling block to all. That the much-despised salsolea and other shrubs should be coveted and sought after; that the bugbear of Oxley, the acacia pendula, should now be held to indicate good country was inconceivable; and when, above everything, the most fondly cherished of all delusions, that in the torrid north the sheep's wool would turn to hair, had to be given up, it was quite evident that a new order of belief would soon be entertained.

Writers, however, were still found to argue that things must be after the old opinion. When M'Kinlay took his little flock of sheep across Australia and found them grow so fat that, when at the Gulf, he had to select the leanest one to kill from choice, they cried out triumphantly, "Ah, but the flesh was tasteless!" When he assured them that he had never enjoyed better mutton, they said that it was hunger made him think so.

Still the distinctive value of the country was not under stood. Landsborough, who ought certainly to have known better, speaks highly of the Gulf plains as a suitable sheep run; but he was not alone in this belief. The valley of the Burdekin, and many of its tributaries were stocked with sheep by men of acknowledged experience. In a few years the error was found out, and sheep pastures were sought for only in the uplands of the interior.

But the later explorations had done much good for the new colony of Queensland. Most of the work, with the exception of Stuart's, had been wrought out within her boundaries, and capital and stock flowed in from all sides. This led to many private expeditions, such as those conducted formerly by Messrs. Landsborough, Walker, and Buchanan.

Amongst these, one under the leadership of Mr. Dalrymple penetrated the coast country north of Rockhampton, and discovered the main tributaries of the Lower Burdekin, the Bowen and the Bogie rivers. They followed down the Burdekin in 1859, and discovered that its embouchere was much higher up the coast than was supposed. From this point they turned back, and ascending the coast range, reached the upper waters of the Burdekin, and discovered the Valley of Lagoons, west of Rockingham Bay. Another party, consisting of Messrs. Cunningham, Somer, Stenhouse, Allingham, and Miles explored the Upper Burdekin in the following year, and discovered tracts of good pastoral country on the many tributaries of that river. The remarkable running stream which joins the Burdekin below the township of Dalrymple, and was noticed and called by M'Kinlay the Brown River, was really first found by this party, though where it obtained its present name of Fletcher's Creek is not on record.

In the far south, the Great Bight became once more the scene of interest. In 1862, Goyder paid a visit to the much-abused region north of Fowler's Bay, but found nothing to reward him but mallee scrub and spinifex. In this year Delisser and Hardwicke went over the same country, but on a much more attractive route, as they came upon a large, limitless plain, covered with grass and saltbush. Unfortunately they could find no water, but since then this want has been supplied by sinking and boring, and pastoral settlement has extended so far.

In the year 1863, Mr. Thomas Macfarlane attempted to get inland, north of the Bight, but was forced to turn back, after suffering much hardship. He, too, found some fairly-grassed country, but quite waterless.

In Western Australia, the colonists still made efforts to find good country east of the Swan River. Lefroy and party pushed out to the eastward of York, but were not able to give a much better account of the country than their predecessors. In the north-west a party of colonists landed at the De Grey River, and settled on the country found by F. Gregory. Their account quite confirmed the one given by that explorer previously.

Once more a fresh chapter in the history of exploration has to be turned. All around the coast the fringe of settlement was rapidly creeping, the gaps of unoccupied country growing smaller and fewer every year. The adventurous traveller who now forced his way through to the late uninhabited north coast would find several infant settlements ready to receive him, and he would no longer be obliged to retrace, with weakened frame and exhausted resources, his toilsome outward track. The last stage of Australia's history was about to set in; the telegraph wire was soon to follow on Stuart's footsteps, and the ring of communication to be nearly completed around the continent.

Chapter XI

Settlement formed at Somerset, Cape York, by the Queensland Government--Expedition of the Brothers Jardine--Start from Carpentaria Downs Station--Disaster by fire--Reduced resources--Arrive at the coast of the Gulf--Hostility of the blacks--Continual attacks--Horses mad through drinking salt water--Poison country--An unfortunate camp--Still followed by the natives--Rain and bog--Dense scrub--Efforts of the two brothers to reach Somerset--Final Success--Lull in exploration--Private parties--Settlement at Escape Cliffs by South Australia--J. M'Kinlay sent up--Narrow escape from floods--Removal of the settlement to Port Darwin--M'Intyre's expedition in search of Leichhardt--His death--Hunt in Western Australia--False reports about traces of Leichhardt--Forrest's first expedition--Sent to investigate the report of the murder of white men in the interior--Convinced of its want of truth--Unpromising country--Second expedition to Eucla--The cliffs of the Great Bight--Excursion to the north--Safe arrival at Eucla.

The year 1863 was one of great activity in the northern part of Australia. At Cape York the Imperial Government had, on the recommendation of Sir George Bowen, the first Governor of Queensland, decided to form a settlement. Mr. Jardine, the police magistrate of Rockhampton was selected to take command, and a detachment of marines was sent out to be stationed there.

At the Gulf of Carpentaria the township of Burketown was springing into existence, under the care of William Landsborough, the explorer; and in the north of Arnhern's Land, M'Kinlay was looking for a suitable site to establish a port for South Australia. Somerset, the formation of which led to the expedition of the Jardine brothers, was formed on the mainland at the Albany Pass, opposite the island of that name. Mr. Jardine was to proceed by sea to his new sphere of office., but anticipating the want of fresh meat at the new settlement, he entered into an arrangement with the Government for his two sons to take a herd of cattle overland to there. Somerset was near the fatal scene of poor Kennedy's death, and knowing what tremendous difficulties that explorer had met with on the east coast, it was decided to attempt the western fall, through the unknown country fronting the Gulf.

Both the Jardines were quite young men at the time when they started, Frank, the accepted leader, being only twenty-two years old, and his brother, Alexander, twenty. Besides themselves, the party was composed of A. J. Richardson, a surveyor sent by the Government; Messrs. Scrutton, Binney and Cowderoy, and four natives. They had forty-two horses, and about two hundred and fifty head of cattle, with four months, provisions.

Before their final start from Carpentaria Downs Station, then the furthest occupied country to the north-west, and supposed to be situated on the Lynd River, of Leichhardt, Alexander Jardine made a trip of some distance ahead in order to ensure finding an available road for the cattle, and saving delay when the actual start took place.

On this preliminary journey he followed the presumed Lynd down for nearly one hundred and eighty miles, until he was convinced that there was an error, and that, whatever river it was, it certainly was not Leichhardt's, as neither in appearance, direction, nor position did it coincide with that explorer's description.

On the subsequent journey with the cattle this supposition was found to be correct, the river turning out to be a tributary of the Gilbert, now known as the Einnesleigh. On the 11th of October, after A. Jardine's return, the final start was made from Carpentaria Downs, and the whole of the party commenced a journey destined to be full of peril and adventure.

The beginning of their trip down the Einnesleigh was unavoidably rough, and on the 22nd of the month they came to a halt to spell their cattle and look for the Lynd River, to which they trusted to carry them a good distance on their way. On the 24th the two brothers started, and in about thirty miles came to another river, where they found a fine chain of lagoons, but no country at all resembling the Lynd. All search beyond being resultless, the went back to the main body; and, leaving instructions for the cattle to start by a certain date for the new-found lagoons, they made another effort to find the Lynd.

This time they were again rewarded by discovering a good-sized creek, but no sign of the Lynd was met with, nor did they ever see it, as owing to an error in the map they had with them, the location of the river had been thirty miles misplaced.

Returning to the lagoons, which the cattle had now reached, instructions were given to start forward, but the first day one of the series of heavy misfortunes befell them, that afterwards seemed to dog them so perseveringly. In the morning a large number of the horses were missing, and leaving a party behind to find them and come on with the pack-horses, the Jardines and some of the others made a start with the cattle, and on the second day reached the large creek, but, to their surprise, without being overtaken by the men with the pack-horses. After an anxious day spent in waiting, Alexander Jardine went back to see what was the matter, and on his way met the missing party charged with heavy news. Through some carelessness in allowing the grass around the camp to catch fire, half their rations, and nearly the whole of their equipment had been burnt. In addition, one of the most valuable of their horses had been poisoned. This misfortune coming at such an early stage of the journey, with all the unknown country ahead of them, was most serious, and jeopardised their prospect greatly. However, there was no help for it; so giving up all hope of the Lynd, they followed down the creek they were then camped on.

The natives soon commenced to give them a foretaste of what they kept up during nearly the whole of the journey. Once about twenty appeared at sundown, and boldly attacked the camp with a shower of spears, and two days afterwards the younger Jardine, when out alone, was suddenly surprised by them.

The creek finally led them to the Staaten River, and here the blacks succeeded in stampeding the horses, and it was days before some of them were recovered.

On the 5th December they left this ill-fated river, and steered due north, but bad luck followed them, the torment of mosquitoes and sandflies, added to bad feed, caused their horses to ramble incessantly, and whilst the brothers were away on these hunting excursions, the party at the camp allowed their solitary mule to stray away with his pack on; and despite all efforts he was never found again. Unfortunately, this animal carried a lot of their most necessary articles, and their loss reduced them almost to the same state as the blackfellows who surrounded them.

Two horses here went mad through drinking salt water, one died, and the other was too ill to travel, and had to be left.

On December the 13th they at last reached the long-desired Mitchell river, not without having another pitched battle on the way with the natives. For the blacks followed them throughout with the same relentless hostility that they formerly had shown to Kennedy, and evidently meant to mete out the same fate to them, for whilst the party were on the Mitchell they mustered in force, and fell upon the travellers with the greatest determination, and it was only after a severe contest, and heavy loss had been inflicted on the savages that they retired.

It can be imagined how these continued attacks, in addition to the harassing nature of the country, gave the party all they knew to hold their own, and but for the prompt and plucky way in which these assaults were always met, not one of the little band would have survived. From what was afterwards found out from some of the semi-civilized natives about Somerset, these tribes followed the explorers for over four hundred miles.

Leaving the Mitchell and making north, they travelled through poor country, thinly grassed, and badly watered, but the blacks were still on their heels.

On the 28th December, they commenced on the horses, driving them about, and another stand-up fight ensued. Storms of rain now set in, and they had to travel through dismal ti-tree flats, with the constant expectation of being caught by a flood on low-lying country.

On the 5th of January, they came to a well-grassed valley, with a good river running through it, which was named the Archer, and on the 9th crossed another river, which was supposed to be the Coen. On leaving this river, troubles thickened around them; the rain continued incessantly, the country was so boggy they could scarcely get their animals along at all, and to add to everything, when they reached the Batavia, two horses were drowned in crossing, and six more were poisoned [See appendix.] and died.

Fate seemed to have pretty well done her worst; they could do nothing else but face the future manfully. Burying everything they possibly could, they packed all the horses, and started resolutely on foot. On the 14th, two more horses died, and the blacks came once more to see how they were getting on. As may be imagined, the white men were in not much of a humour for patience, and the skirmish was a brief one.

On the 17th, two more horses died from the effects of the poison plant, and they were reduced to fifteen out of the forty-two with which they started. They were now approaching the narrow crest of the cape, and found themselves on a dreary waste of sandy, barren country, whereon only heath grew, intersected too with boggy creeks.

On the 10th of January, they caught a glimpse of the sea to the eastward, from the top of a tree, and on the 20th it was in plain view.

They were now amongst the same description of scrubs that had played such havoc with Kennedy, and day after day they only advanced a few miles. On the 29th, after many days of bog and scrub cutting, it was determined to halt the cattle, whilst the two Jardines made an effort to reach Somerset, and find a less difficult track, as they now believed themselves only twenty miles from that place; but in reality they were more, although, after the country they had passed through, any calculation that could be made would be only approximate.

On the 30th January, the brothers, with their most-trusted black boy, "Eulah," started to find the settlement, taking with them a small quantity of rations. For a time they were hemmed-in in a bend of what they took to be the Escape River, but on leaving it suddenly came on a large river running to the west coast, which is now known as the Jardine. This forced them to return to the main camp, and after a few days' rest, they made to the north again, swimming their horses over at the main camp, where the cattle were, and from there starting, this time down the stream.

This trip was a most fatiguing one, through dense vine scrub, through which they had to work their way tomahawk in hand. On the second day they sighted the ocean, and after travelling towards it, came to a river three-quarters of a mile wide, which they could not cross. Following it up through fearful country, as Jardine says, "too bad to describe," they had to at last camp where they were, being cut off from even approaching the river by a formidable belt of mangroves. Next day was spent in like fruitless attempts, and the next the same.

It being evident that there was no crossing-place for the cattle to be found, they turned back to the camp, having come to the conclusion that the rivers were identical, and that on their first expedition they had been deceived by a large bend.

Tired and wearied, disappointed at finding themselves so near the settlement, and yet hemmed in and embarrassed by impenetrable thickets, and impassable morasses, the brothers now made up their minds to start with the whole party, and try to get round the big bend of the Escape that they thought they must be on. After killing a bullock they started, and at their third camp, from the top of the high ridge they sighted the sea to the westward, and were able to trace the course of the river the whole way, thus convincing themselves at last that it was riot the Escape they were on.

A reference to the map will at once explain the peculiarity of the course of these two rivers that had so puzzled the explorers. The Jardine is a large river heading from the east coast, and running, with many bends, clear across the promontory to the west coast, completely heading the Escape which has been a short course. As the Jardine River was before unknown, and the Escape was well-known, it was but natural that the mistake should have occurred. Added to all this, they were in the depth of the wet season, and amidst flooded creeks whose size and importance could not be fairly gauged.

Once more the two brothers and the black boy swam the river, and made a third effort to reach Somerset. For two days they were detained on the bank of a flooded creek, crossing it on its subsidence on the third day. On the 28th February they were in better country, and a good stage was made, and the next morning they encountered a tribe of blacks who greeted them with cries of "Alico! Franco! Tobacco!" and other words. From these natives they finally selected three as guides, and at noon the following day reached the settlement.

As was but natural, their long journey had caused their father great trouble and anxiety; he had done all in his power to help them at the end, having cut a marked tree line almost across the promontory, and instructed the blacks in the few English words they could remember to greet the wanderers if they met with them, which last device succeeded admirably.

It remains but to be said that the rest of the party and the remnant of their stock were soon brought in to Somerset, where a cattle station was formed. When we look at the difficulties through which they had forced their way, and the unexpected misfortunes that beset them, one cannot help feeling the greatest admiration for the two brothers in attaining such success, not having lost a member of the party throughout the journey, in spite of the numberless treacherous attacks of the natives to which they were subjected, and the daily risks of illness, swimming flooded rivers, and other perils. Above all regret must be felt that their work was not better rewarded by the discovery of available pastoral country, but that result it was not in their power to control. They had at any rate the proud feeling of having done their duty, and that beset by the same dangers that had environed poor Kennedy, they had lived to tell the tale when he had laid down his life.

Whilst the Jardines were fighting their way through to Cape York, and rendering such good service to geographical research, a labour which the Royal Geographical Society afterwards acknowledged by electing the brothers, Fellows of the Society, and awarding the Murchison grant to each of them, the pioneer squatters were everywhere busy.

Mr. J. G. Macdonald started with a small party to visit the much lauded Plains of Promise, and discover a better route for stock than the one formerly taken by the explorers. By crossing the dividing range on to the upper part of the Flinders, and following that river down, a much shorter and more practicable route was made available for the army of cattle and sheep now marching to the western pasture land, and the magnificent country on the river named after the great navigator was brought prominently into notice.

In the far north of Australia, settlement on a fresh scale was once more undertaken; this time under purely colonial auspices. The territory beyond the northern boundary line of South Australia, extending to the shores of Arnheim's Land, and part of the Gulf of Carpentaria had long been considered No Man's Land, although the English had formerly taken possession of it. The arrival of the Astrolabe and Zelie in Raffles Bay in 1839, gave colour to the supposition that the French had a design to secure part of this territory after our first abandonment of it. Fortunately Sir Gordon Bremer was in time to make the second settlement at Port Essington a few short weeks before the appearance of M, Dumont D'Urville, even as Governor Phillip forestalled La Perouse.

The territory was provisionally annexed to the Province of South Australia by commission under the great seal, bearing date 8th July, 1863. It comprised all the country to the northward of the twenty-sixth parallel south latitude, and between the 129th and 138th degrees of east longitude.

The inland country was known only from the description of Stuart, Gregory and Leichhardt.

In 1864 an expedition left Adelaide to proceed by sea to Adam Bay, and there form a depôt, whilst search for a suitable site for a township was made. Colonel Finnis was sent in charge of the infant colony, and three vessels, the Henry Ellis, the Yatala, and the Beatrice conveyed the emigrants to their destination, where they safely arrived in August, 1864.

A discretionary power had been entrusted to the leader with regard to the choice of a suitable position; Port Essington and Raffles Bay were excepted, the former failures to establish settlements at those places being probably looked upon as ominous.

Escape Cliffs in Adam Bay, so called from the narrow escape two officers of the Beagle had from death at the hands of the natives, was chosen, but the choice was not ratified. A good deal of dissension broke out in the early days, and J. M'Kinlay, the well-known explorer, was sent north to select a more favourable position, and report generally on the capabilities of the territory. He organized an exploring party, and left the camp at Escape Cliffs with the intention of making a long excursion to the eastward; but he only reached the East Alligator River, where he was cut off and hemmed in by sudden floods, and narrowly escaped losing his whole party. Everything had to be abandoned, and the explorers escaped from their critical position by resorting to the construction of coracles of horse hide, by means of which they managed to save their lives. On his return, M'Kinlay examined the mouth of the Daly River in Anson Bay, and recommended it as a site in preference to Escape Cliffs, the suggestion was not, however, acted on.

This was M'Kinlay's last expedition. He died at Gawler, in South Australia, in December, 1874.

The affairs of the new settlement were now in such a disorganised state that a commission of enquiry was appointed, and the result was that Colonel Finnis was removed.

Mr. Goyder then selected Port Darwin as a better situation than that of Escape Cliffs, and the township was laid out and the residents removed to there. The establishment of the overland telegraph line soon caused the town of Palmerston to take permanent importance, which the discovery of gold in the Northern Territory confirmed.

Western Australia, too, had an unfortunate experience about this time, an attempt being made to establish a settlement at Camden Harbour. The country was quite unsuitable, and it was abandoned.

Some fresh interest was now aroused in the unsettled question of the fate of Leichhardt. A Mr. M'Intyre, who, in 1864, was taking stock from the Darling to the Flinders River, found himself stopped on the Queensland border by the stock regulations then in force in that colony. Whilst detained there he made several short excursions, and examined the country between the head of the Paroo and the Barcoo, discovering many well-watered creeks and a lake of considerable size. On his return, finding that there was still no chance of his being allowed to take his stock on, he determined to make a trip to the Gulf of Carpentaria and examine the country he intended taking up.

The party left the Paroo on the 21St June, 1864, and the journey led to an unexpected discovery. On the way over, M'Intyre found and buried the bodies of two unfortunate pioneers who had preceded him, Messrs. Curlewis and M'Culloch. They had. been murdered when asleep by the natives.

Twenty-two days after leaving the Paroo they reached Cooper's Creek, and then pursued much the same track to the Gulf as that formerly followed by Burke and Wills, and M'Kinlay. Three hundred miles from the sea, and to the westward of Burke's track, M'Intyre came upon two old saddle-marked horses, grazing upon what appeared to be a permanently watered creek. A short distance to the eastward he found the traces of two camps, and two trees marked L. From these circumstances M'Intyre concluded that he had come upon new and important traces of the lost explorer.

On his return to the south, public interest was at once aroused, and, aided by the championship of Baron Von Mueller, whose enthusiasm in the cause of discovery never flags, a committee was formed to organise a party to at once follow up these clues, and try to set at rest the much-vexed question.

In order to fully arouse the sympathies of the public, the matter was with much gallantry placed in the hands of the ladies of Victoria, and under their auspices a party was equipped and the command given to Mr. M'Intyre. Unfortunately for the success of the expedition, the leader died of malarial fever before the party left the settled districts of the Gulf of Carpentaria. From the course mapped out for the explorers, there is no doubt that, even if the aim of the expedition had not been reached, an earlier knowledge of much unknown country would have been obtained.

As was but natural, the construction of the overland telegraph line between Adelaide and Port Darwin led to numbers of short explorations on either side of the line, which considerably added to our knowledge of the interior, but of which no records have been kept.

The establishment of this telegraph line and its maintenance did much towards the settlement of Central Australia. It formed, as it were, a chain of outposts through the heart of the continent, and thereby greatly facilitated the success of many private expeditions undertaken in quest of country for pastoral purposes.

South Australia had served a rough apprenticeship in the cause of exploration, and the experience gained by her pioneers now stood her in good stead in the successful accomplishment of the national work she at this time undertook the establishment of telegraphic communication with England. Queensland, the youngest colony of the group, was striving very hard to secure the landing of the cable on her shores. Walker, the leader of one of the Burke and Wills search parties, was out examining the country at the back of Rockingham Bay, and marking a telegraph line from there to the mouth of the Norman River, in the Gulf of Carpentaria. South Australia, however, thanks to her energy and superior geographical position, secured the honour; and already the completion of a railway across the country which witnessed the repeated efforts of Stuart is being hastened on.

In Western Australia, in 1864, Hunt made a long excursion to the eastward of York, and travelled for 400 miles over the country lying between the 31st and 32nd parallels. He found nothing to reward him for his trouble--scrub, salt lakes and samphire flats were the same wearisome. repetition.

During the construction of the overland telegraph line it was surmised that such a close examination of the country as would necessarily ensue, might lead to the finding of traces of Leichhardt, if he ever had reached so far on his journey; but none were found. Apparently it suggested an idea to a prisoner in one of the gaols of New South Wales, for he made a statement to the effect that he had been employed as a labourer on the construction of the overland telegraph line, and whilst so engaged had been in the habit of making long excursions into the unexplored territory on either side of the line. During one of these trips he came across some blacks, who informed him that they had an old white man living with their tribe. Hume--which was the name of the hero of this story--professed to have an intimate acquaintance with the habits and customs of the natives, and willingly accompanied them to their camp. Here he found a venerable old white man, who turned out to be Classen--Leichhardt's brother-in-law--and from him Hume learnt that the death of the leader and most of his party happened through a mutiny in the camp, Leichhardt being murdered, and the party then becoming disorganised and lost. This absurd story was repeated so earnestly that inquiries were instituted, and it was found that Hume had really been employed on the telegraph line, and that whilst there he had been absent for some time on one or two occasions.

Hume was interviewed by some gentlemen who were interested in the solution of Leichhardt's fate, and he now added a little additional matter: that on a subsequent visit he found that Classen, rendered restless by the near neighbourhood of the whites, had made an effort to reach them and died in the attempt. This, with a few varia-

223

tions as to the details of the death of Leichhardt, led to Hume being released from gaol for the purpose of leading a party to the spot where Classen had pointed out that he had concealed Leichhardt's journals. But for the tragedy that ended the affair this episode would scarcely be of sufficient importance to insert in the history of explorations. Money having been furnished for the purpose, Hume and two companions started on their search. They reached Thargomindah--then the nucleus of a small township in Western Queensland--and left a station called Nockatunga to make a short cut across some dry country. One man only turned up. He said that they had lost themselves, had separated looking for water, and with much difficulty he reached the station. Search being instituted the dead bodies of Hume and the other man were found, they having perished of thirst. This story was revived many years afterwards by another man, who had lived a good deal on the frontiers of Queensland. According to him, Leichhardt and some of his party died of hunger and thirst, Classen was revived again, and the discoverer stated that he had in his possession a diary and many relics of the explorer. Although expressing his willingness to produce the relics on receiving the promise of an adequate reward, he never did so, and having attained a temporary notoriety, returned to his former obscurity. This may be said to end the rumours of the discovery of Leichhardt's memorials, They served no good end in any way.

John Forrest, of Western Australia, made his first important journey in 1869. It will be remembered that a report had been current for many years amongst the natives of Western Australia, to the effect that a party of white men coming from the east had been murdered by the natives on the shore of an interior salt lake. A Mr. Monger, when out west in search of pastoral country, came across a native who stated that he had been to the place where the murder was committed, had seen the remains, and would lead the party there.

As usual with the Australian natives, his story was most circumstantial. He described the scene of the murder as being in the neighbourhood of a large lake, so large that it looked like the sea, and that the white men were attacked and killed whilst making a damper. These artistic details with which the blacks embellish their narratives, make it very hard to refuse credence to them.

Baron Von Mueller immediately wrote to the Western Australian Government, offering to lead a party there, and ascertain the truth of the report. The Government took the matter up, and made preparations to start an expedition. Von Mueller was, however, prevented by his other engagements from taking charge, and the command was given to Mr. John Forrest, a surveyor.

On the 26th of April, 1869, Forrest and his party reached Yarraging, then the farthest station to the eastward. On the first of May, when camped at a native well, visited by Austin in 1854, Forrest says that he could still distinctly see the tracks of that explorer's horses. Past this spot he fell in with natives, who told him that a large party of men and horses died at a place in a northerly direction, and that a gun belonging to the party was still in the possession of the blacks. On closer examination this story turned out to relate to nine of Mr. Austin's horses poisoned during his expedition. Forrest continued his journey to the eastward, and on the 18th came to a large dry salt lake, which he named Lake Barlee. An attempt to cross this lake resulted in getting the horses bogged, and a good deal of hard work had to be gone through before the packs and horses were once more safe on dry land Lake Barlee was afterwards found to be of great size, extending for more than forty miles to the eastward. The native guide Forrest had with him now became rather doubtful as to the exact position of the spot where he professed to have seen the remains, and Forrest, after some searching, came across a large party of the local inhabitants. But they proved anything but friendly, threw dowaks at the blackfellow, and advised the whites to go away before they were killed. As it was getting dark they adopted this advice, and retreated some five miles and camped, Mr. Monger having unfortunately lost his revolver in the scrub. Next morning they managed to get speech with two of the blacks, who restored the revolver, which they had found, and had been warming at the fire. These men stated that the bones were two days' journey to the north, but they were the bones of horses, not of men, and offered to take the whites there, promising to come to the camp the following day, a promise which was riot kept.

No other intercourse with the blacks was obtainable, at least none that produced any good results. One old man simply howled piteously all the time they were in his company, and another one, who had two children with him, said most emphatically that he had never heard of any horses having been killed, but that the natives had just killed and eaten his brother.

After vainly searching the district for many days, Forrest determined to utilise the remainder of the time at his disposal by examining the country as far to the eastward as his resources would permit.

It was evident that the story of the white men's remains had originated from the bones of the horses that died during Austin's trip; and, as no matter how circumstantial might be the narrations of the blacks, they invariably contradicted them the next time they were interrogated, it was evident it would serve little purpose being led by them on a foolish errand from place to place.

After pushing some distance east with very little encouragement in the shape of good country, Forrest, taking with him one black boy and a seven days' supply of rations. made a final excursion ahead, and managed to reach a point one hundred miles beyond the spot where he left his companions encamped. He found nothing to reward him. It was only by means of shallow and scanty pools of water that he managed to get so far, and the country where he turned back was certainly clearer than any he had crossed but it was only open sand plains, with spinifex and large white gums. He climbed a large gum tree to have a last look to the eastward, but it was a scene of desolation. Some rough sandstone cliffs were visible, distant about six miles N.E.; more to the north, a narrow line of samphire flats appeared, with cypress and stunted gums on its edges everywhere there was spinifex, and no prospect of water. Forrest turned back, and retraced his steps to where he had left his companions.

On his homeward way he managed to cross the dry bed of Lake Barlee, which had so nearly engulfed his horses, and examined the northern side of it.

On their return track Forrest kept a more northerly and westerly course, but saw nothing to alter the unfavourable report of the country made by the former explorers. He returned to Perth on the 6th August.

Forrest was not more successful than those preceding him in finding good available country to the eastward, but he at any rate obtained a correct and reliable survey of a good deal of country hitherto unknown.

On his return to Perth, Baron Von Mueller, whose ardour in the cause was rather increased by the disappointment experienced in finding that the accounts of the natives were quite unreliable, recommended a journey from the head waters of the Murchison in the direction of the Gulf of Carpentaria. Forrest was quite willing to undertake the trip, but want of funds stood in the way just then, and the matter was not enthusiastically supported by others.

It was then proposed to make a journey to Adelaide. by way of the Great Bight, which had not been traversed since Eyre's celebrated march round it, and the leadership was offered to Forrest and accepted by him.

The party, beside the leader, consisted of his brother Alexander, two white men and two natives, one of the last having been on the former trip. A coasting schooner, the Adur, of thirty tons, was to accompany them round the coast, calling at Esperance Bay, Israelite Bay, and Eucla, there to supply the party with fresh stores. On the 30th March, they left Perth.

The first part of the journey to Esperance Bay was through comparatively settled and well-known country, so that but little interest attaches to it. At Esperance Bay, where the Messrs. Dempster had a station, they arrived a few days before the relief schooner, and on the 9th May started for Israelite Bay.

From Esperance Bay to Israelite Bay the record of the journey is equally tame, and it was not until he once more parted from his relief boat that Forrest had to encounter the serious part of his undertaking. He had now to face the line of cliffs fronting the Bight behind which he had, he knew, little or no chance of finding water for one hundred and fifty miles. Forrest says that these cliffs, which fell perpendicularly into the sea, although grand in the extreme, were terrible to gaze from.

"After looking very cautiously over the precipice, we all ran back quite terror-stricken by the dreadful view."

Having made what arrangements he could to carry water, Forrest left the last water on the 5th of April. They reached the break in the cliffs where the water was obtainable by digging amongst the sandhills, on the 13th April, without any loss, having luckily found many small rock holes filled with water, which enabled him to push steadily on.

While recruiting at the sand hills he made an excursion to the north, and after passing through a fringe of scrub twelve miles deep, came upon most beautifully grassed downs. At fifty miles from the sea there was nothing visible but gently undulating plains of grass and saltbush at far as could be seen. There being no prospect of finding water, he was forced to turn back, fortunately finding small waterholes both on his outward and homeward way.

On the 24th, they started for Eucla, the last point at which they were to meet the Adur. On this course he kept to the north of the Hampton Range, and crossed well-grassed country, but destitute of surface water, reaching Eucla on the 2nd July. The Adur was there awaiting them, and the parties were soon re-united.

On the 8th, Forrest and his brother made another excursion to the north; he penetrated some thirty miles finding, as before, beautifully-grassed, boundless plain 9, but no signs of surface water.

After leaving Eucla, the explorers had a distressing stage to the head of the Great Bight, where they obtained water by digging in the sand, the horses having been three days without a drink, suffering much more than on any previous stage. From here they soon entered the settled districts of South Australia, and the exploring came to an end.

Although this trip of Forrest's can hardly be called an exploring trip, inasmuch as he was repeating the journey made by Eyre, he embraced a great deal of new country during its performance, and, owing to the larger facilities he enjoyed, was able to pronounce a much more impartial verdict than Eyre was competent to do. Eyre, be it remembered, was struggling on for his life, Forrest travelled in comparative ease, being able to supply himself three times from the schooner during the journey; it is but natural that Eyre's report should bear a very sombre tinge.

Forrest showed that the fringe of gloomy thicket was only confined to the coast; beyond, he on every occasion found fine pastoral country. He says:--
"The country passed over between longitude 126 deg. 24 min. E. as a grazing country, far surpasses anything I have ever seen. There is nothing in the settled portions of Western Australia equal to it, either in extent or quality; but the absence of permanent water is a great drawback; . . . the country is very level, with scarcely any undulation, and becomes clearer as you proceed northward."

The rapid progress now being made in improved methods of boring for water, will soon bring this country under the sway of the pastoralists, and without doubt render it one of the most valuable provinces of Western Australia.

On his arrival in Adelaide, Forrest received a hearty welcome, and equally so on his return to Perth. In the following year Alexander Forrest took charge of a private exploring party in search of new pastoral country. He had the advantage of a good season, and reached as far as 123 deg. 37 min. E. longitude; he then struck S.S.E., towards the coast, finally returning by way of Messrs. Dempster's station in Esperance Bay.

Forrest's expedition, unfortunately, left no hope that any river existed that might possibly have been unknowingly crossed at its mouth by Eyre.

Chapter XII

The first expeditions of Ernest Giles--Lake Amadens--Determined attempts to cross the desert--Death of Gibson--Return-Warburton's expedition-- Messrs. Elder and Hughes--Outfit of camels--Departure from Alice Springs--Amongst the glens--Waterloo Well--No continuation to Sturt's Creek--Sufferings from starvation--Fortunate relief from death by thirst--Arrive at the head of the Oakover--Lewis starts to obtain succour--His return--Gosse sent out by the South Australian Government-- Exploring bullocks--Ayre's rock--Obliged to retreat--Forrest's expedition from west to east--Good pastoral country--Windich Springs--The Weld Springs--Attacked by the natives--Lake Augusta--Dry country--Relieved by a shower--Safe arrival and great success of the expedition--Ernest Giles in the field--Elder supplies camels--The longest march ever made in Australia--Wonderful endurance of the camels--The lonely desert--Strange discovery of water--Queen Victoria's Spring--The march renewed--Attacked by blacks--Approach the well-known country in Western Australia--Safe arrival--Giles returns overland, north of Forrest's track--Little or no result--Great drought--The western interior.

Before following up Forrest's career as an explorer, and tracing his most important work of crossing the centre of Australia from the sea to the telegraph line, we must see what the South Australians had been doing.

Ernest Giles, in 1872, made an excursion to the westward, starting from Chambers' Pillar. His progress was stopped by a large, dry, salt lake, to which he gave the high-sounding name of Lake Amadens, and which unhappily figures on maps of Australia in a rather misleading way, as a large, permanent, bona fide lake. Not being able with his small party to ascertain the exact limits of this obstacle, which was of the same character as those so often described as barring the way of the Western Australian explorers, Giles returned, having traversed a good deal of country, up to that time unknown and unexamined.

In the following year he again took the field, assisted by the help and sympathy of Baron Von Mueller, and a sum of money subscribed by the South Australian Government. He left the settled districts at the river now called the Alberga, which flows into Lake Eyre, and travelling north-west, made many determined attempts to cross the spinifex desert that had confronted him; but had to return beaten.

On one occasion, anxious to reach a range that he saw in the distance, and where he hoped to find a change of country, he started with one man and a supply of water on pack horses; as the horses knocked up they were left to find their way back themselves, until at last, when but two were left, Giles sent his companion, Gibson, back on one, whilst he made a final effort to reach the range.

This trip, which recalls one of the purposeless and impetuous exploits of Grey, resulted in the death of Gibson and the loss of several horses. Giles' horse soon knocked up, and he had to return on foot. Having, with really astonishing prudence, left a keg of water buried on his way out, he made for that. To his dismay, after proceeding some distance he saw Gibson's track turn off on the trail of one of the horses that had been abandoned, instead of keeping to the outward track. Hoping still that he might have found his way back, Giles hastened on to the buried keg, but it was untouched, and he knew that the unfortunate man's fate was sealed. Giles made his way back to where the rest were encamped, and they immediately went in search; but it was fruitless. Neither man nor horse were ever seen again, and the scene of his death is now marked on the maps as "Gibson's Desert." During his excursions in various directions, trying to find a westward route, Giles discovered and traversed four different ranges of mountains. The party suffered much from the hostility of the blacks, who on several occasions attacked them; and the leader, in his journal, complains, like Warburton, of the sleepless nights caused by the myriads of ants that infested the desert country. The farthest point reached was the 125th degree of east longitude. He returned to Adelaide after an absence of twelve months, during which he had gone through much hardship and danger.

The tract of country between the overland telegraph line and the western settlements now became the battlefield of the explorers; few of them, it is true, hoped to find much available country, the accounts of those who had penetrated a short distance being so depressing; but they struggled for the honour of being the first to cross the gap of unknown land, often to the neglect of careful inspection.

One of the expeditions that led to the western half of the continent being condemned as a hopeless desert was that commanded by Colonel Warburton, It was promoted by two South Australian colonists whose names have been always to the front when exploration has been concerned--Messrs. Thomas Elder and Walter Hughes. They jointly fitted out the expedition, which, it was hoped, would lead to the advancement of geographical knowledge; unfortunately, the result was not at all commensurate. The original idea was that the party should start from about the neighbourhood of Central Mount Stuart, and make for Perth, this course, however, was not adhered to. In spite of being fitted out solely with camels, Warburton suffered so much delay in getting through the sandhills that his provisions were all consumed and his camels knocked up before he got half-way through, compelling him to bear up north to the head waters of the Oakover River, discovered by F. Gregory.

The party consisted of the leader and his son Richard, Mr. Lewis (surveyor), one white man, two Afghans, and a black boy. They had seventeen camels, and six months' rations. On the 15th of April, 1873, the explorers left Alice Springs, one of the stations on the overland telegraph line, and on the 17th reached the Burt, where they left the line and struck out west. Warburton's course at first lay some seventy miles south of Central Mount Stuart; but after a vain search for the rivers Hugh and Fincke, which were supposed to flow through the M'Donnell Ranges, he altered his direction, steering to the north-west, meaning to connect with A. C. Gregory's most southerly point on Sturt's Creek. Their way for some distance was through good pastoral country, and in some of the minor ranges beautiful glens were discovered, with deep permanent pools of water in their beds. So frightened were the camels at the appearance of the rocks that surrounded these water-holes, that they would not approach them to drink, and, in fact, even refused the water when it was brought to them.

On the 22nd of May, after being some days in poor sandy country, they came to a good creek, the head of which was running, and the whole flat where the creek emerged from the hills was one spring. This spot, the best camp they had yet seen, was named Eva Springs. Leaving the main party resting at these springs, Warburton, with two companions, started on ahead, and were successful in finding some native wells, that enabled him to break up his camp and move on with the whole of the men and material.

On the 5th June they crossed the boundary line between Western Australia and South Australia; but their progress was now monotonous and most uninteresting, being through the scrubby, sandy tableland common to the interior.

At some native wells, called by them Waterloo Wells, they had an enforced spell of more than a month, and in addition lost three camels, and one of the Afghans nearly died of scurvy. Afterwards they soon got fairly into the salt-lake country, and on the 12th August, at the end of a long and exhausting march, were relieved by one of the small native wells, on which the blacks of this region exist. They were now by their reckoning within ten miles of Sturt's Creek; but although Warburton made two separate attempts to find it, he was unable to see any country that at all resembled the description given by Gregory.

He concluded there was some error in the longitude, and proceeded on his westerly course. The record of the day's journey now becomes a simple tale of traversing a barren country, and an incessant search for native wells; added to that, the excessive heat, caused by the radiation of the sandhills during the day induced the leader to spare his camels as much as possible, by travelling at night. This naturally led to a most unsatisfactory inspection being made of the country, and it is impossible to say what clues or indications to better country or more permanent waters were passed by. In fact, he more than once during this part of his journal mentions the fact of wild geese flying over the camp, although they never found any surface water to account for their presence.

Starvation was shortly looming ahead; the constant halts and delays had so protracted their journey that they were almost at the end of their resources, and still surrounded by a most inhospitable waste. Sickness, too, came on then, and the full brunt of the search work ahead fell upon Lewis and the black boy, Charley; their time was taken up in watching for the smoke of the natives' fires, or looking for their tracks. In the evening they could travel a little, and in the early morning; at night the myriads of ants proved an unbearable plague, and prevented the wearied men getting their natural rest. Their position was as well nigh hopeless as it was possible for any party to be in; if they stopped to relieve their camels they starved themselves, and without rest the camels could not carry them to look for native wells ahead. At last, on the 9th of October, they reached a small waterhole that the camels themselves had found when straying, and here perforce, they had to rest, for with the exception of Lewis and the black boy, the remainder of the party were too weak to do anything. At this camp they slaughtered another of their precious camels, and for a time satisfied their gnawing hunger with the fresh meat; they were also lucky enough to get some galar parrots and pigeons. Here they stayed for nearly three weeks, and then shifted to another well to the south.

Warburton now decided to make a desperate push to the head of the Oakover River, and effect his escape if possible from the desert; on the evening of the fourth they started, and but for the black boy would have doubtless all marched on to death. The boy had left the camp in the morning, after their first night's tramp, and coming across the tracks of some natives, ran them up, finding another well at their camp, by the time he got back, the party had been obliged to start without him; fortunately, he heard the tinkle of the camel bell as he crossed the sandhills, and by cooeeing loudly managed to attract attention. He then led the way to this new source of relief, which, but for him, the party would have missed.

Again they recommenced their journey to the Oakover, Lewis and Charley on ahead, Warburton and his son coming on as fast as their exhausted state would permit; their only hope for life now lay in the chance of the advance party finding water soon and bringing it back to them. At midday, on the 14th, Lewis appeared with a bag of water; another well had been found, but this time it nearly cost Charley's life. As he usually did, he had gone in advance when close to the native camp, in order not to alarm them. The blacks had received him kindly and given him water; but when he cooeed for his companions they took a sudden alarm, and set upon him, spearing him in the arm and back, and cutting his head open with a club. The remainder of the party were just able to rescue him. It seems quite certain that this attack was not premeditated, but the effect of timidity caused by the unexpected appearance of the white men and the camels.

At this well the party had to rest, until Lewis and one of the Afghans pushed on to the head of the Oakover, which they thought could not be so very far distant, as the nights were cool and dewy, and in the camp of the natives they found two large seashells, an old iron tomahawk, and part of the tire of a dray wheel.

On the 19th November Lewis started, and on the 25th he returned, having been successful in reaching the head waters of the Oakover, and on the 5th December the whole party arrived at the rocky creek that he had found. They now travelled very slowly down the river, but saw no signs of settlement, so the indefatigable Lewis had once more to go ahead, whilst the others waited and starved on the flesh of the last camel. He had to ride 170 miles before he arrived at the station of Messrs. Grant, Harper, and Anderson, who immediately supplied him with fresh horses and all requisites with which to return to the starving men.

It was on the 29th of December, and Warburton was lying in the shade, moodily thinking that the cattle station must be abandoned, and that Lewis had been forced to go on to Roeburne, when the black boy, who was climbing up a tree, called out, and starting to their feet the astonished men found the pack-horses of the relief party almost in their camp.

Out of the seventeen camels the two that Lewis had ridden in for help were all that survived, and for the rest of their equipment, it had been left piecemeal in the desert.

It is distressing to think that all this suffering and labour should not have been adequately rewarded. Warburton got into a strip of desert country, but apparently was too much occupied with pressing straight through to devote any time to examine any country beyond his track. Whatever may have been the aridity, the water supply must have been ample to support such large numbers of natives as he came in contact with. In one camp there were numbers of women and children and one cripple; but they quietly vacated the well when the whites came, without any apparent difficulty, showing that they had other resources within easy reach.

This trip of Warburton's, and a succeeding one by Mr. Ernest Giles, prove conclusively that the possession of camels leads men to push on, eager to be able to say that they were the first to get across, leaving the country almost as unknown as before they traversed it.

But a few days after Warburton started on his adventurous journey, Mr. W. C. Gosse, in charge of the Central and Western Exploring Expedition, left Alice Springs, a telegraph station on the overland line, with the intention of endeavouring to reach Perth.

On April 23rd, the leader reports leaving the Springs, with his party all in good spirits; beside the white men, there were three Afghan camel-drivers, and the party had a mixed equipment of camels and horses. On May 1st, they left the telegraph line, and, turning to the westward, soon found themselves in excessively dry country.

On the 14th, he had a trip lasting fifty-two hours, without water for the horses, and one of them died; this happened whilst on an excursion ahead with his brother, who was acting as collector to the party.

Having formed a depôt, and sunk a well on a creek he named the Landor, he made several short trips in different directions, and on the 21St, in a creek he called the Warburton, found a considerable pool of water, to which he shifted his main camp.

During one of his excursions from this second depôt, he had the singular experience of riding all day through the heavy rain and camping at night without water, the sandy soil having absorbed the rain as quickly as it fell. On his return he found that the creek at his camp was running, and the Afghans had made repeated attempts to cross one of the camels, but the animal obstinately refused to do so, which, probably, made the leader reflect that it was just as well they were not likely to meet with many running streams.

On June 6th, Major Warburton's tracks were seen, and a camp of his found. The next depôt formed was at the western extremity of the Macdonnell Range, at the foot of a hill named by Ernest Giles, Mount Liebig. From this depôt the party moved to the spot named by the same explorer, Glen Edith, and on their way augmented their live stock by picking up three bullocks that had been lost from Alice Springs, and apparently had started on an exploring trip by themselves. From King's Creek, their next depôt, the leader made a long excursion to the south-west, and at eighty-four miles, after passing over sandhills and spinifex country, came in sight of a hill, which, on a nearer approach, proved to be of very singular limestone formation.

"When I got clear of the sandhills, and was only two miles distant, and the hill, for the first time coming fairly in view, what was my astonishment to find it was one immense rock rising abruptly from the plain; the holes I had noticed were caused by the water in some places forming immense caves. I rode round the foot of the rock in search of a place to ascend, and found a waterhole on the south side, near which I made an attempt to reach the top, but found it hopeless. Continued along to the west, and discovered a strong spring coming from the centre of the rock, and pouring down some large deep gullies to the foot.

"This seems to be a favourite resort of the natives in the wet season, judging from the numerous camps in every cave. These caves are formed by large pieces breaking off the main rock and falling to the foot. The blacks made holes under them, and the heat of their fires causes the rock to shell off, forming large arches. They amuse themselves covering these with all sorts of devices--some of snakes very cleverly done, others of two hearts joined together; and in one I noticed a drawing of a creek, with an emu track going along the centre."

On the return journey, he crossed an arm of Lake Amadeus, and on reaching his camp, the whole party started for Ayer's Rock, which was the name Gosse gave to the singular hill he had discovered, where they arrived safely, and one of the exploring bullocks was converted into beef.

Rain having set in heavily for some days, he was enabled to penetrate some distance westward, where he came upon very good grazing country, but soon got beyond the extent of the rainfall. After many more attempts, Gosse found himself obliged to turn back, the heat of the weather and the dryness of the country--for they were now in the sandhill region-rendering it almost useless for him to think of risking his party with any hope of success.

On the 22nd September, he left his fourteenth depôt in the Cavenagh Range, and started on his return. His course home was by way of the Musgrave Ranges, where he found a greater extent of good pastoral country than he anticipated. He discovered and christened the Marryat and the Alberga, which last river they followed down almost to the telegraph line, and arrived at Charlotte Waters in December.

Mr. Gosse's exploration did not add much fresh information to what was already known of the district, but it extended the area of explored country, and he was enabled to correctly lay down many of the points discovered by Mr. Giles.

In March, 1874, Mr. Ross and his son, with a well-equipped party, consisting of another European and three Arabs, having with them sixteen camels and fourteen horses, started from the neighbourhood of the Peake Station, on the telegraph line, to endeavour to bridge the desert. He was, however, compelled to return, although he made another effort, after reducing the number of his party.

Colonel Warburton having been the first to successfully make his way from the South Australian border to the settled part of Western Australia, Forrest was the next to aim and arrive at a successful issue.

Forrest's trip was certainly the most commendable of the two, and by far the most important in its results. Warburton, with a troop of camels, reached the Oakover River naked and starving, with but two miserable animals left. Forrest, with nothing but ordinary pack-horses, crossed the middle of the continent, where the very heart of the terrible desert was supposed to exist, and took his men and most of his horses through in safety.

Forrest, having with him his brother, Alexander Forrest, two white men, and two natives, left Yuin, then the furthest outside station on the Murchison, on the 14th of April. Their course at first was along the upper part of the Murchison River, which he describes as running through fine grassy flats, good loamy soil, with white gums in bed and on flats, the water in some of the pools being rather brackish. This description of country continued for many days, some of the river water being at times quite salt. On nearing the head of the Gascoyne River, the land was found to be fine, undulating downs, admirably adapted for sheep or cattle.

On the 21st May, they ascended the watershed of the Murchison, and from the top had a fine view of their future travelling ground to the eastward. The country appeared level, with low ranges, but there was an absence of conspicuous hills--not a promising country for water, but looking as though good feed would be obtainable.

For the next few days the party were dependent on springs and small clay-pans. On the 27th when following down a creek, which was called Kennedy Creek after one of the party, they arrived at a fine permanent spring, which Forrest characterised as the best he had ever seen, the grass and herbage around being of an equally satisfactory description. The springs were named the Windich Springs after the black boy, Tommy Windich, who had been with Forrest on three expeditions. To the northwest there was a fine range of hills, which was named the Carnarvon Range.

The explorers now got into less attractive country, the spinifex sandhills began to become a familiar feature, and the water supply less to be depended on.

On the 2nd June, Forrest made his next important discovery of the Weld Springs, which he describes as unlimited in supply, clear, fresh, and running down the gully wherein it was situated for over twenty chains. Here they settled down to give their tired horses a week's rest.

On the 8th, he started with one boy, to look for water ahead, leaving instructions for the party to follow on their tracks in a day's time. He was unfortunate; the two travelled for twenty miles over undulating sandhills covered with spinifex without seeing a sign of water. At daybreak from the top of a low, stony rise the view was gloomy in the extreme. Far to the north and east it was all spinifex country with no appearance of hills or watercourse, in fact a barren worthless desert.

Turning back they met the remainder of the party about twenty miles from the spring, and the whole party retreated to their former encampment, and after a day's rest Alexander Forrest and a black boy started for a trip to the south-east in search of water.

During their absence the natives made an unexpected attack on the camp. At about one o'clock about sixty or seventy natives appeared on the brow of the hill overlooking Weld Springs, plumed and armed with spears and shields. They descended the rise and attempted to rush the camp, but were met with a volley from the whites who were prepared to receive them. They retired to the top of the hill, and after a consultation made a second attack, but were checked by a rifle shot from the leader. This put an end to the assault. That evening Alexander Forrest and the boy returned, and were much astonished to hear of the day's adventure. They had been over fifty miles from camp, had passed over some good feeding country, but had found no water.

They now set to work and built a rough hut of stone, in order to ensure safety during the night, as their stay at Weld Springs seemed likely to be indefinite, and a fresh attack might be made at any moment. When the hut was finished, Forrest, taking a boy with him, started on a flying trip due east. This time they were fortunate enough to find a small supply in some clay waterholes, and the whole party shifted camp to it.

On the 22nd, the leader made another search ahead, and in thirty miles came to a fine supply of water in a gully running through a grassy plain, whereon there was abundant feed. Eight miles to the south there was a small salt lake, which was named Lake Augusta. Another good spring in grassy country was also found, and on the 30th June, Forrest made a further exploration ahead to the eastward. This time he was unfortunate, for he soon found himself fairly in the spinifex desert, and his horses knocked up. By the aid of scanty pools of rainwater in the rocks he managed to push on some distance, walking most of the way. He reached a range, and from the top had an extensive but most discouraging view. Far to the north and east the horizon was as level and uniform as the sea; spinifex everywhere; neither hills nor ranges could be seen for a distance of quite thirty miles.

He was now perplexed as to his future movements. The main party were following up his tracks, and there seemed no prospect of getting through the country ahead of them. Fortunately they found a little water, enough to last a day or two, and there awaited the arrival of their companions.

A search amongst the low ranges was then commenced, as the only other alternative was a retreat of seventy miles. To the great relief of every one A. Forrest and the black boy found water five miles to the south-east, with some coarse rough grass around it, that would serve them for a time. The younger Forrest then went ahead, and found some springs twenty-five miles distant, which were named the Alexander Springs, after the discoverer.

Another excursion was attended with equally good results as regards water, although the country around was not at all desirable pasture land; and. this brought the explorers within one hundred miles of Gosse's furthest westerly point. To bridge this hundred miles proved a weary task. Repeated excursions only resulted in continued disappointment, and knocked up horses. At last a kindly shower of rain filled some rock holes to the north-cast of their camp, and after much labour and exertion the whole party found themselves at an old camp of Giles, which he had named Fort Mueller, and as they were also on Gosse's tracks the leader was able to congratulate himself upon the successful accomplishment of his mission.

As the course of party, from here to the telegraph line, was more or less on the track pursued by Gosse, it is unnecessary to follow their fortunes any further; some privation had to be endured and one or two more of the horses gave in; but on Sunday, the 27th September, they arrived at the telegraph line some distance north of the Peake station, thus concluding one of the most valuable journeys on record.

On their arrival at the station, Forrest learned that Giles and Ross had both been turned back by the inhospitable country that he had successfully traversed. The leader and his companions received great applause for the work they had so well performed, and it at once placed Forrest in the front rank of explorers. The fact of his having got through with but the simple and ordinary outfit showed that he possessed high qualities of foresight and judgment, and the many minor excursions he made on the way over, although, perhaps, wearisome and distressing at the time, led to his having a perfect acquaintance of the country through which he had travelled.

Ernest Giles, after being driven back twice in his attempts to reach Western Australia, was now equipped with a troop of camels by Sir Thomas Elder, and made a third and successful effort. The party started from Beltana and travelled to Youldeh, where a depôt was formed. From here they shifted north to a native well, called by the natives Oaldabinna. The water supply at this place proving but scanty, Giles started to the westward on a search for more, sending Messrs. Tietkins and Young to the north on a similar errand. The leader travelled for one hundred and fifty miles through scrub, and past dry salt lakes, until he came to a native well or dam, with a small supply of water in it. Beyond this he went another thirty miles, but found himself once more amongst saline flats and scrubs; he therefore returned to the depôt. Messrs. Tietkins and Young had not been as successful, having found no water. At their furthest point they had come upon a large number of natives, who, after decamping in a terrified manner, re-turned fully armed and painted. No attempts of the two white men to establish friendly communications and obtain information succeeded, and they were obliged to return disappointed.

A slight shower of rain having replenished the well they were camped at., Giles determined on making a bold push to the west, and trusting to the hardihood of his camels to carry him on to water.

On reaching the dam that he had formerly visited, he was agreeably surprised to find that it had been replenished by the late rains, and now contained plenty of water for their wants. There was excellent feed around this oasis, and they rested until the water gave signs of diminishing.

At the end of a week, on the 16th September, 1875, they again closed with the desert surrounding them. For the first six days of their march they passed through scrubs of oak, mulga, and sandalwood; then they entered upon vast plains, which were well-grassed, and had saltbush and other edible shrubs growing on them. After crossing these endless downs for five days, they again reentered scrub, but of a more open nature than formerly.

When two hundred and forty-two miles had been covered, Giles distributed what water he had amongst his camels, which amounted to four gallons each. The next change that occurred in the country was the reappearance of sandhills, blacks' tracks became plentiful, and smoke was occasionally seen.

On the seventeenth day, when more than three hundred miles had been travelled, Mr. Tietkins, who judged by the appearance of the sandhills that there was water in the neighbourhood, sent the black boy, Tommy, on to a ridge lying to the south of their course.. Fortunate it was that he did so, for behind it, in a hollow surrounded by sandhills, lay a tiny lake, which the cavalcade was passing by unknowingly until Tommy arrested their progress with frantic yells and shouts. Giles gave this place of succour the name of Victoria Springs, and rested there nine days.

Recruited and strengthened, a fresh start was made and they soon got amongst the peculiar features common to the southern interior of Western Australia, outcrops of granite boulders, salt lakes and swamps.

In one of these lakes they got their leading camels bogged, and it was only after hard work and much patience that they got them out again. Their next relief was at a native well two hundred miles from

Victoria Springs, and here they once more rested from their weary and long-continued march.

The monotony of their life was, however, rudely broken up at this encampment by the blacks. During their stay several natives had made their appearance, and had been kindly received and treated. No suspicions of treachery were aroused, and the explorers were just concluding their evening meal when Young caught sight of a body of armed men approaching, and gave the alarm in time for the whites to stand to their weapons. Giles says in his journal that they were a "drilled and perfectly organized force," if so, they must have been a higher class of natives than the usual type of blackfellows, whose proceedings, as a rule, have little organization about them. A discharge from the whites was in time to check them before any spears were thrown, otherwise, from the number of their assailants and the method of their attack, it was probable that the whole party would have been murdered.

On leaving this camp the caravan travelled through dense scrubs, with occasional hills and open patches; in fact, the country that has of necessity been so often described in these pages. They were fortunate enough to find some native wells on their route, and on the 4th of November arrived at an outside sheep station.

The result of this trip, satisfactory as it no doubt was to the leader, who thus saw his many gallant efforts at last crowned with success, had little or no other fruits to show, not even the negative one of proving that the desert they had passed through was an absolutely waterless waste. The very water that saved their lives they were passing by unheeded; and it was impossible for them to say whether similar formations did not exist on either hand of their line of march.

Like Warburton's, only without the suffering from starvation, it was a hasty flight on camels, through an unknown country, and, like his, barren of results beyond a thin line on the map of Australia.

Expeditions such as these must be looked at from two points of view; whilst admiring the fortitude and resolution possessed by the leader who takes his party through such a waste in safety, we must regret that fuller information and more patient deductions had not been gained. The fact of having the means, in their camels, to venture on long dry stages with impunity, led them to disdain the careful manner in which Forrest felt his way across; but in the end that explorer had certainly the best idea of the country he had travelled over.

Giles now retraced his steps from Western Australia to the overland line, following a track to the north of Forrest's route. He went by way of the Murchison, and crossed over to the Ashburton, which river he followed up to the head. Then striking to the south of east he came on to his former track of 1873, at the Alfred and Marie Range; the range he had so vainly striven to reach when the unfortunate man Gibson, met his death. He finally arrived at the Peake station, on the telegraph line.

Few watercourses were crossed, the country was suffering from extreme drought, and no discoveries of any importance were made.

The journeys of the late explorers had greatly lessened the area of the country in which fresh discoveries could be looked for; true, the results had not been encouraging. The utter and complete want of a river system, even of the rudest kind, in the western half of the interior of Australia, was plainly shown. No continuous line of country could even be traced as corresponding on the routes of the different travellers, and unfortunately, where good country was found, the want of surface water held out no encouragement for the grazier to follow up the explorers' footsteps. The reclamation of this country it was evident would have to be a work of time, and would be dependent greatly on the facility with which the underground supplies could be tapped. That these supplies exist, the pioneer work carried on, on the outskirts of the desert, has proved beyond a doubt; how far they will be carried into the interior remains to be seen.

Chapter XIII

Further explorations around Lake Eyre--Lewis equipped by Sir Thomas Elder--He traces the lower course of the Diamantina--Expedition to Charlotte Bay under W. Hann--A survivor of the wreck of the Maria--Discovery of the Palmer--Gold prospects found--Arrival on the east coast--Dense scrub--Return--The Palmer rush--Hodgkinson sent out--Follows down the Diamantina--Discovery of the Mulligan--Mistaken for the Herbert--Private expedition--The Messrs. Prout--Buchanan--F. Scarr--The Queenslander expedition--A dry belt of country--Native rites--A good game bag--Arrival at the telegraph line--Alexander Forrest--The Leopold Range--Caught between the cliffs and the sea--Fine pastoral country found--Arrival at the Katherine--The Northern Territory and its future.

But although the country to the east of the telegraph line had up to the year 1874 received such a large share of attention, in fact, the principal share, there yet remained much unknown territory to investigate, and many geographical problems to determine. Chief amongst these was the definition of the many affluents of Lake Eyre.

The western district of Queensland was drained by rivers of great magnitude, that found their way through South Australia into the lake; but their many channels, and the direction and size of them had never been fully determined. To further this end, Sir Thomas Elder equipped Mr. Lewis, who, it will be remembered, did such good service on Colonel Warburton's expedition, and under his leadership an expedition was undertaken which resulted in much valuable information being gained. Starting from the overland telegraph line, Lewis skirted Lake Eyre to the north, and penetrated to Eyre's Creek, in Queensland territory, and traced that creek and the Diamantina into Lake Eyre; also confirming the opinion so often advanced that the waters of Cooper's Creek found their way into that receptacle, as well as the more westerly streams.

In Queensland the Government had decided upon further exploration of the northern promontory ending in Cape York. More than eight years had elapsed since the Jardines had made their dashing trip, and their report taken in conjunction with Kennedy's did not offer much inducement for anyone to follow up their footsteps; but as there was yet a tract of country at the base of the promontory comparatively unknown, a party was organised and placed under the leadership of Mr. William Hann, one of the pioneer squatters of the north of Queensland.

The object of the trip was in the main an examination of the country as far north as the 14th parallel, with a special view to its mineral and other resources; the discovery of gold so far north in Queensland having caused a hope to be entertained that its existence would continue along the promontory.

Hann had with him as geologist a Mr. Taylor, and as botanist, Dr. Tate, a survivor of the melancholy New Guinea expedition that left Sydney in the brig Maria, only to suffer wreck on the Barrier Reef, where, in the sea and amongst the cannibals north of Rockingham Bay, most of the unfortunates left their bones. Apparently, his ardour for exploration had not been damped by his narrow escape.

One other member of the party, a Mr. Nation, was destined to meet a tragic death by starvation in the newly-settled district of the northern territory of South Australia. The party left Fossilbrook station, on Fossilbrook Creek, a tributary of the Lynd, which would be north of the starting point of the Jardines.

On leaving this creek they passed over much rugged and broken country, the scene of Leichhardt's first trip, and a spot which presented many indications of being auriferous. Here they devoted some days unsuccessfully to prospecting, and on resuming their northern journey came to a large river, which was named the Tate. Four days afterwards another one was struck, which received the name of the Walsh.

From the Walsh the party crossed to the upper part of the Mitchell River, and thence to a creek marked on Kennedy's map as "creek ninety yards wide," which was called the Palmer, and here Warner, the surveyor, found prospects of gold. Some further examination of the river resulted in likely-looking results being obtained, and the find is now a matter of history, verified by the discovery of one of the richest goldfields in Queensland on the waters of this river.

Above the Palmer, Hann came across a memorial of the trip of the Jardines in the tracks of some (or descendants) of the cattle, dropped by them, but he was unable to find them. This was on a creek which, he supposed, to be the one named by them the Kendall.

These animals had, no doubt, led a rather harassed life from the natives since they had last been seen by the whites.

On the 1st September, Hann reached his northern limit, the 14th parallel of latitude, and the next day commenced the ascent of the dividing range between eastern and western waters. A few days afterwards he sighted the sea, at Princess Charlotte's Bay.

From this point the party turned south, and soon came to a large river, which was named the Normanby, and here a slight skirmish occurred with the natives, with whom they had hitherto been on friendly terms. Whilst the men were collecting the horses in the morning, and not suspecting treachery, a body of blacks attempted to cut them off, each native being well armed with a bundle of spears. A few shots, however, at long distance were sufficient to disperse them, so that, fortunately, the affair ended without bloodshed.

On the 21st September, Hann came to the Endeavour, a river well-known in the history of Australia. Whilst entangled in the scrub on the upper reaches of this stream he had the misfortune to lose one of his best horses by poison, two others having also eaten of the weed.

At this point the party had terrible work to encounter; the old obstacles that had so retarded Kennedy were met with--scrub impenetrable, and steep ravines. Tracks had to be cut through the vines, and the horses led on foot down perilous descents. This went on for days, and an attempt to reach the sea coast and continue their intended route south, ended in involving them in a perfect sea of scrub, and the final conclusion that advance for white men and horses was impossible. Hann had reluctantly to make up his mind to return to the west, and abandon the fresh ground to the south of him.

After many entanglements in the ranges, and the usual confusion arising from the tortuous courses of the rivers, the watershed was at last crossed, and on the 28th October they camped once more on the Palmer River. From here they returned over the country formerly traversed on the outward course, and exploring came to an end.

The work had been very hard, especially during the time the party had been impeded in the scrubs of the east coast, which fully bore out the reports of the survivors of Kennedy's expedition as to the terribly toilsome nature of the labour to be undergone in cutting a track through them. Hann was lucky in not having his party attacked by sickness during his detention in such a dangerous locality; they all returned in safety.

The gold discoveries on the Palmer, and the rush there which occurred soon after this expedition, led to a vast deal of exploration being done under the name of prospecting. Small parties were out in all directions on the rivers named and crossed by Hann and the heads of those named by Leichhardt, the Lynd and the Gilbert, were ransacked and searched in every direction.

In 1875, the Queensland Government decided to send out an expedition to decide upon the amount of pastoral country existing to the westward of the Diamantina River, and see if it extended to the boundary of the colony. It was placed under the command of W. O. Hodgkinson, who had already seen considerable experience as an explorer, having been one of the members of the Burke and Wills party, and also a member of M'Kinlay's expedition when he traversed the continent. The second in charge was a mining surveyor and mineralogist, Mr. E. A. Kayzer.

Although the expedition was organised as early as September, it was not thought politic to start so soon before the impending wet season, so the party were directed to muster at the Etheridge (goldfield), and occupy the time between then and the end of the year, in examining and reporting on the country between there and Cloncurry gold-field, on the Cloncurry River, which was to be the final point of departure.

After some minor excursions in the neighbourhood of the Cloncurry, Hodgkinson and party left that place in May, 1876, and proceeded across the dividing watershed to the Diamantina River, and followed that river down to below the boundary of the colony of Queensland and South Australia, where it received the name of the Everett, from Lewis.

This much of the progress of the North West Expedition, as it was called, included little country not already known, and, moreover, at this time the district was being settled on in all parts by the pioneer squatters, the tracks of whose cattle were now up and down the whole length of the river.

From the lower Diamantina, Hodgkinson made west towards the boundary of the colony, and beyond Eyre's Creek found a fine watercourse running through good pastoral country, which he branded with the name of the Mulligan River. Following this river up, and finding it alternately well and poorly watered, the party crossed from the head of it on to the Herbert, unwitting that they had done so, and followed that river on until they overtook Buchanan, Landsborough's old companion, who, with a mob of cattle, was re-stocking the Herbert.

246

As this country had been at one time stocked, and stations formed and abandoned, exploration may be considered to have ceased. The surveys of Messrs. Scarr and Jopp soon explained the mistake fallen into by Hodgkinson as to the identity of Landsborough's Herbert and his own Mulligan. It will be remembered that in the central districts, the watersheds are so low and the size of the rivers so uncertain, that to find a watercourse dwindle away into nothing in one mile, and expand into a river the next is not at all surprising, so that to leave the head of a river and come on to another running in the same direction, it would appear quite feasible that it was the same river re-formed.

This was the last exploring expedition sent out by the Queensland Government; their colony being now nearly entirely known, and in fact the earlier squatters of the Herbert, before its abandonment in 1874, were settled some distance across into South Australian territory.

Unfortunately, the commercial depression of 1871 and 1872 led to the stations on the Herbert being thrown up, and the country, good as it was, lapsed into its original state of loneliness, and remained for many years quite unoccupied.

Although Queensland herself had little or no territory within her own borders left to explore, the energy and enterprise of her pioneers led to many private explorations being organized across the border into the colony of South Australia, or rather into the northern territory of that colony. Amongst those undertaken in the year 1878 may be instanced one which resulted in the loss of the entire party.

Induced by the favourable terms offered by the South Australian Government to pastoral lessees in the Northern Territory, two brothers named Prout started out with one man, looking for country across the Queensland border. They never returned, and it was not until they had been given up for months that some of their horses, and finally the bones of one of the brothers, were discovered by Mr. W. J. H. Carr Boyd.

It was evident, from the fragments of a diary recovered, that they had extended their researches far into South Australian territory, and met their death by thirst on their homeward way, probably from some of the waters they depended upon for their return having failed them.

In the same year Buchanan made an excursion to the overland line from the border of Queensland. Crossing from the Ranken--one of the main heads of the Georgina River, and so called after one of the pioneers of that district, J. C. L. Ranken--Buchanan on a westerly

247

course, came to the head of a creek, running through fine open downs; following it down for some days he eventually lost its channel in flooded country, and striking across a belt of dry country arrived at Tennant's Creek station on the overland line. This creek, which received the name of Buchanan's Creek, was a most important discovery, affording in future a highway and stock route to the great pastoral district lying between the Queensland border and the overland line.

The next to attack this unknown strip was Frank Scarr, a Queensland surveyor. He tried to cross the line, to the south of Buchanan's track, but was prevented by the waterless belt of country existing there. During one of his excursions he found the horses of the ill-fated Prout Brothers, already alluded to.

Finding he could not reach the country he desired to, from the Queensland border, Scarr made north, and by means of Buchanan's Creek arrived at Tennant's Creek station; but owing to the dry season, did not extend his researches further.

In the same year, 1878, a project for an overland railway line, between Brisbane and Port Darwin, was inaugurated in the former city. The principle of building the line by means of land grants being one of the chief features of the scheme. Mr. Gresley Lukin, the then proprietor of the leading Brisbane newspaper, organised and equipped a party to explore a line of country, the object being to find out the nature and value of the land in the neighbourhood of the proposed line, and the geographical features of the unexplored portion.

The party left Blackall, then the furthest township to the westward in Queensland, the leader being Mr. E. Favenc, accompanied by Messrs. S. G. Briggs (surveyor), G. R. Hedley, and a black boy.

From Blackall the party struck across the settled pastoral districts until they arrived at Cork station, on the Diamantina. From there they kept a north-westerly route through the then unexplored country lying between the Burke and Herbert Rivers. From the Herbert the Ranken was followed up for some distance, and the route was then to Buchanan's Creek, and down that creek to the last permanent water. From here the party struck north, and some permanent waters were discovered, amongst them being the Corella Lagoon, the finest lagoon in that district. Two lakes of large extent were also seen and named, but, although at the time of the explorer's visit they were extensive sheets of water, seven or eight miles in circumference, they were so shallow for a mile from their shores, that at that distance, they were only knee deep.

A singular feature of the lakes of this depressed region, was the fringe of dead trees that surrounded them. From the age of the trees, and even borders of all the lake beds seen, both dry and full, it was evident that this must have been the result of an excessive flood, which had inundated this district during some past year.

From the Corella Lagoon, where some two or three hundred natives were assembled to celebrate the peculiar tribal rites common to that religion, and which have never been witnessed by whites, the expedition proceeded north, and discovered a large creek running from east to west, which received the name of Cresswell Creek. This creek, which ran through fine, open downs, was followed until its course was lost in the flooded country, which is the end of most inland creeks.

The last permanent water on it was named the Adder Water-holes, on account of the number of death-adders killed there. The first excursion from there towards the telegraph line, some ninety miles away, resulted, in such days of heat, in conjunction with cracked and fissured plains, that three horses died before returning to camp. The country was soft, and full of holes and hollows, and it being the height of summer, the horses could not travel long stages without water; so there was nothing to do but await at the Adder Waterholes the falling of a kindly thunderstorm, to assist them to bridge the gap that lay between them and the telegraph line.

During their detention at this camp many excursions were made, and the country traversed found to be mostly richly grassed downs; and where flooded country was crossed numbers of the dry beds of former lakes, surrounded by the customary belt of dead forest were noticed.

The long delay exhausted the supply of rations, but by means of game, horse-flesh, and the usual bush vegetable, "bluebush and pigweed," the party fared sufficiently well.

"We made up a list of game that had already been shot for ration purposes, nearly all by Hedley, who was our chief reliance as a hunter, and the following is the account up to 11th December:--50 parrots (corellas and galars), 350 ducks (black ducks, teal, whistling ducks, wood ducks and widgeons), 150 pigeons (principally flock), 11 geese, 4 turkeys, 8 spoonbills, 7 water hens, 2 shags, 1 emu, 1 native companion, making a total of 584 birds, and in addition we had consumed 100 fish. All of them were shot for actual food, nothing. had been wantonly destroyed. We considerably added to this menu afterwards, including such choice delicacies as eagle hawk and frogs. Crows and hawks we carefully reserved to the last when all else should fail. The absence of kangaroos and other marsupials is a marked feature in this list, there being none on these wide-stretching downs."

In January, 1879, the thunderstorms set in, and enabled the explorers to reach the line safely at Powell Creek Station. From here they travelled over known country to Port Darwin.

This expedition had the effect of opening up a good deal of pastoral country, which is now nearly all stocked.

As might have been expected, the party were most hospitably received at Palmerston, where the inhabitants, in addition to its chief feature of a railway survey, saw in this expedition one of the first steps to open up to the world the vast territory they possessed; for as yet the pastoral industry had been confined to one or two spirited attempts in the immediate neighbourhood of the goldfields, the great tableland at the back whereon there was so much valuable sheep country being, untouched.

Western Australia now sent out another of the exploring parties, which form such a feature of her history. In 1879, Alexander Forrest led an expedition from De Grey River to the telegraph line. The party left Anderson's Station on the De Grey River, on the 25th February, and reached Beagle Bay on the 10th April, the country passed over being like most of the land in the immediate neighbourhood of the coast, poor and indifferent.

From Beagle Bay they followed the coast round to the Fitzroy River, which empties into King's Sound, and journeyed up that river until they reached a range which gave the explorers some trouble; in fact, they spent six weeks of constant toil and trouble endeavouring to penetrate it.

On the 2nd June, Forrest bade good-bye to the Fitzroy, which he calls "the longest and largest river in Western Australia, flowing through magnificent flats;" and which he says they had then followed for 240 miles. Leaving the river the party struck north, looking for a pass through the precipitous bluffs of King Leopold Range, as it was named. The sea was, however, reached before this range was surmounted, and following down the angle now being formed, between the sea and the range, they at last found themselves enclosed in a perfect prison; romantic and pretty according to Forrest's description, but rather militating against their success. Here too the blacks approached them in threatening numbers, but after the display of a little policy, peace was preserved. The rugged nature of the country began to tell most severely on the horses, "how on earth," says Forrest, "they are going to take us on I really cannot think." On the 22nd June, they attacked a range, and finally after a steep climb, which witnessed the death of one of the horses, they reached the height of 800 feet, and camped; here Forrest determined to rest the horses and go ahead on foot, and explore the country. The result was that they came upon endless rugged zigzags, which so involved them that they gave it up in despair and returned to camp.

Forrest had most reluctantly to abandon any idea of crossing this range and return to the Fitzroy, where they arrived on the 8th of July. Following up a tributary of this river, the Margaret, they gradually managed to work round the southern end of the range, which still frowned defiance at them, and at last reached the summit of the tableland, and saw before them good grassy hills and plains. Of this country Forrest speaks most enthusiastically, and doubtless after their late terrible struggle with the range it must have appeared a perfect picture of enchantment to them.

On the 24th, they reached a fine river, running strong, and named by Forrest the Ord, and for a time he followed its course. Leaving, he continued his way to the overland telegraph line, which they were destined not to reach without a struggle. More rivers were crossed, and the country undulated between rough ridges and well-grassed flats, and at last, on the 18th August, the Victoria River of Captain Stokes was reached.

Now commenced their first privation for want of water. Their rations were almost expended, and one of the party seriously ill. Taking with him one man (Hicks), Forrest started for the line to obtain succour, leaving his party in camp to await his return.

The first stage was for twenty-nine miles, and then they fortunately found a small pool; on the next day a stage of thirty-two miles, through the level, grassy country, timbered with box and intersected by dry swamps, which is so familiar a feature in the Northern Territory, but at the end they had to camp without water. They now had no alternative but to push on to the line at all risks, as it was the nearest point where they could obtain supplies, and it was useless to think of going back without them. Unhappily, Forrest was unprovided with a map of the line, which led to his having to strike at random; and, as it happened in the end, resulted in his turning north instead of south, which brought about needless pain and suffering. Forrest's account of their terrible trip runs as follows:--

"August 31. An hour before daylight we started, steering east for fourteen miles before we rested. The country was similar to that passed over yesterday. During the mid-day halt we walked about searching

251

for water in the dry swamps, but were unsuccessful. Here we killed a large snake, and made off it a miserable meal, thinking that it would relieve our thirst; it made us, however, a good deal worse than we were before. We had only two quarts of water with us, and we both decided not to touch this until reduced to the last extremity, as we knew not how far we might have to go before coming to water. At one o'clock we were in the saddle again, and continued on the same course until sundown, when we gave our horses a short rest. They were very tired, and did not seem able to keep up, in the state they were, for much longer. As for ourselves, we were so thirsty we could scarcely speak. We shot a hawk, and cut his throat in order to drink the blood, but it did us no good. What would we have given for water? No one can have an idea what thirst is unless he has experienced it under tropical heat. . . . After eating our hawk we saddled up, and steered east-north-east for two miles, when we reached a creek trending northwest. We thought there might be water in it lower down, so we followed it for a mile or two, when the horse I was riding knocked up, and by lying down compelled us to halt."

Forrest now decided to leave the creek, and walk all night, leading their worn out horses. Fortunately for them they had not far to go; in two miles Hicks called out that the line was in sight, and forgetting their thirst they cheered lustily. Within a short distance of where they struck the line, they came to one of the tanks stationed at intervals for the use of the repairing parties, and so their thirst was relieved; but owing to taking the wrong direction, they travelled away from the nearest station, Daly Waters, and it was four days before they overtook a repairing party, under Mr. Wood; who provided them with food and fresh horses to take back succour to their comrades.

Thus ended a most successful trip, as the country found by Forrest is amongst some of the most valuable in the northern part of Western Australia, and has since been stocked with both sheep and cattle, and large mineral wealth has been developed.

The whole of the northern part of the continent of Australia seemed for a time to suffer from a blight. The tracks of the explorers appeared to be checked by some fatal influence.

The Victoria that was thought to be such a grand discovery turned out but an ordinary coast stream, and on its further investigation to lead to nothing but disappointment. This deduction, however, under fuller knowledge is gradually departing, and there is little doubt that the time is not far away when it will attain its greatest development as a pastoral and mineral country.

There is no doubt that the east and west tracks of tile Queensland explorers, and of Alexander Forrest did more to throw open the country than did the north and south one of Stuart, although that was the most important ever made in the later days of Australia's history. Stuart showed the feasibility of crossing the continent in the centre, but even after the telegraph line was formed on his track, very little was known of the country on either side. The northern territory had, however, been the scene of many private expeditions beside those mentioned here. Some years before Alexander Forrest crossed over, two residents of the Northern Territory, Phillip Saunders and Adam Johns, accompanied by a third man, started from Roebourne in Western Australia, and crossed to the telegraph line successfully. They were prospecting for gold most of the way, but the line they took was unlucky, as although they passed through the now well-known Kimberly country, they failed to obtain anything like satisfactory prospects. They passed through much good pastoral country, but at that time stock country was of no value at such a remote distance from settlement.

There now remains but a few more explorations, and those mostly in the northern part of Australia. Whatever the yet large unknown tract of country in the interior will show in the future it is impossible now to do more than conjecture.

In 1884, Mr. Stockdale, who had had considerable experience in the other colonies, and was an old bushman, started on an expedition from Cambridge Gulf to explore the country in that neighbourhood, with a view to settlement. He proceeded there by the Whampoa, and on the 13th September he landed at the gulf, with his party of seven men and the necessary horses, this being, probably, the first landing that had taken place there since the days of Captain Stokes. Leaving the gulf, and crossing the range through a natural gap, which was named after the leader, they found themselves in well-grassed country, with a fine stream of water running through it. Their next halting-place was at a creek they called the Birdie, and they now found numerous camps of the natives, though as yet they did not come into contact with them. The next creek was named the Patrick, which was followed down for some distance through very good country. Here commenced the beginning of the trouble, which. afterwards culminated in a tragedy, one of the men (Ashton) losing himself, and delaying the party by having to be sought for. They were now on a river which was called the Forrest, after the explorer, and here they rested for the sake of their horses. On leaving it they got into rather

253

stony country until they arrived at the head of a creek called the Margaret, where they again rested.

From there they had to face great difficulties in the shape of mountainous country, the gullies and ravines reminding one of those described by Grey. On October the 14th, they came to a fine river, which they named the Lorimer, on which there was a waterfall one hundred feet high. The large creek next met with was called the Buchanan.

On the 21st of October a depôt was formed, and the leader, with three men, went south, for the purpose of making a thorough inspection of the country, leaving the other men to await his return, having first taken the precaution to bury the main portion of their stock of provisions in case of accidents.

On November 2nd they narrowly escaped an encounter with the natives. By means of a little tact bloodshed was avoided. While amongst the cliffs they came upon some of the native drawings and paintings, which have always created so much interest.

On returning to the depôt, after having passed through and discovered a fine amount of pastoral country, the leader found, much to his disgust, that the horses he had left to spell there had been used for kangaroo hunting, and were not in a fit condition to do much more work. This compelled him to shorten his trip and start towards the telegraph line.

On getting his party together again, which was a work of some difficulty, a start was effected in the direction of the Ord River, and on the road home the unfortunate occurrence happened that resulted in the death of two of the men, entirely the consequence of their own headstrong conduct. The account had better be given in the words of the leader. Speaking of one of the two men, he says:--

"He eats very heartily, and so does Ashton, and both have strong, lusty voices, but seem to have lost all heart, and the rest of the party are getting discouraged at the many and serious delays they are causing us. I have used every means to induce them to rally and pluck up heart, but it seems all to be totally lost upon them. It is a very trying situation for me, and I trust God will guide me, and help me to do what is right and just to all I have in my charge. Mulcahy acknowledged riding horses in depôt out kangarooing, also to taking apples, biscuits, jam, flour and peas, and to be unworthy of forgiveness or to remain one of the party. We all forgave him the wrong he had done us freely and truly.

"December 17 (Wednesday). Fine morning after very cool night. Thermometer at daylight, 60 deg. Mulcahy and Ashton both looking better, but both came to me, and said if I would allow them they would take three weeks' rations and camp for a spell on the river, and perhaps I would send help after them. I tried all in my power to induce them to struggle on a little further, if only as far as the Wilson River, but could not alter their determination. Called the rest of the party together, and as they one and all thought it was best under the circumstances, I had to consent, so, with Mr. Ricketson's assistance, measured out to them twenty pannikins of flour, ten of white sugar, ten of peas, fifteen of dried apples, four pounds of tea, and a tin of pre-served meat. Left them two double-barrel guns, etc., with about one hundred and fifty cartridges, fish-hooks, and lines, and camped on the Laurence River. We then packed up the remainder, and with sad hearts bade them good-bye, and firmly advised them to get either fish or game, as game is fairly plentiful around them. Ashton and Mulcahy both expressed a desire to write a few lines in my diary, and, in the presence of all hands, I allowed them. Ashton also forwarded by me a note to his aunt in England, but Mulcahy, although I earnestly desired him to, would not write to either wife or parents, all he would say be-ing, 'They will see you at no loss, old man.'

"It is a dreadful state of affairs, the two biggest and strongest of our party collapsing like this, and has had a very depressing effect on me, though I must not show it, for fear of causing a despondent feeling in the others. I do hope we shall now have fair travelling, and reach Panton and Osman's station, and send back horses and relief to those left behind. They have had any amount of provisions, meat ex-cepted sometimes five meals a day, and never less than three."

The two men were never found, although every endeavour was made to do so.

Stockdale, not finding Panton and Osman's station, had to leave some of his men in camp, and, after a hard struggle, reached the telegraph line with one companion, and sent back relief to the others, which duly reached them.

Chapter XIV

The exploration of the Continent by land almost completed--Minor expeditions--The Macarthur and other rivers running into Carpentaria traced--Good country discovered and opened up--Sir Edward Pellew Group revisited--Lindsay sent out by the S.A. Government to explore Arnheim's Land--Rough country and great loss of horses--O'Donnell makes an expedition to the Kimberley district--Sturt and Mitchell's different experiences with the blacks--Difference in the East and West Coasts--Use of camels--Opinions about them--The future of the water supply-- Adaptability of the country for irrigation--The great springs of the Continent--Some peculiarities of them--Hot springs and mound springs.

The whole of the continent being now known, and the mystery of the interior solved, there remained little more for the explorers of later years to do, but follow up the course of some tributary, stream or river, the origin of which, though, perhaps, guessed at, had never been finally settled, nor had the country drained by them been mapped or defined.

These explorations, useful though they have been in opening up fresh tracts of country for the pastoralist, have not the same amount of interest attaching to them possessed by the earlier travels. Much of the exploration of the past few years naturally centres round the northern portion of Australia; there, as the pioneer pushed out, the unknown parts had to yield up their secret, and the tracks of Macdowall Stuart were gradually elaborated. The South Australian Government had made many attempts to reach the Queensland border from their overland line, but without success. In 1778, they had dispatched two surveyors--Messrs. Barclay and Weinnecke--to proceed in that direction, starting from the neighbourhood of Alice Springs. Barclay had much dry country to contend with, and managed to reach close to Scarr's furthest point when he was making west in the same year, but failed to connect with the settlements of Queensland. He made no important discoveries, being amongst the country common to the central districts of Australia--alternate desert, and pastoral land, with few and insignificant watercourses. It being a matter of moment to settle the position of the border line between the two colonies, surveyor Weinnecke was again dispatched in 1880 to make another attempt. By following Scarr's route, via Buchanan's Creek, he succeeded in reaching the border. He travelled entirely over the country explored by Queensland parties. In 1883 Favenc traced the heads of the rivers running into the Gulf of Carpentaria, near the Queensland border, and in the following year undertook a more lengthened expedition from the tableland across the coast range to the mouth of the Macarthur River. The party left the Queensland border and crossed to the overland telegraph line, traversing mostly open downs country the whole of the way.

From the northern end of Newcastle Waters a fresh departure was as made, and the watercourse that supplies these lagoons followed up for some fifty miles. From there an easterly course was kept, and after some privation from want of water, reached a creek, which was christened Relief Creek, and which proved to be one of the head waters of the Macarthur. A large extent of valuable pastoral country was found in the basin drained by this river, and many fine permanent springs discovered. The party followed the river down to salt water, and returned by another route to Daly Waters telegraph station.

The South Australian Government soon after sent a survey steamer to the group called Sir Edward Pellew's Islands, which had not been visited since the days of Flinders. The mouth of the Macarthur was found and sounded, and shortly afterwards a township was formed at the head of navigation. The explorations conducted on this river led to a good road being formed from the interior tableland to the coast and the settlement of much new country.

The whole of the territory east of the overland line was now rapidly becoming settled, and the explorations made by Mr. Macphee east of Daly Waters may be said to have concluded the list of expeditions between the overland line and the Queensland border.

In 1883 the South Australian Government determined to complete the exploration of Arnheim's Land, and Mr. David Lindsay was dispatched on the mission. He left Palmerston on the 4th June, and proceeded, by way of the Katherine, to the country north of the Roper River. From there they proceeded to Blue Mud Bay, and, on the way, had a narrow escape from being massacred by the natives, who speared four horses, and made an attempt to surprise the camp. Lindsay got entangled in the broken tableland that caused such trouble to Leichhardt, and, with one misfortune and another, lost a great number of his horses-in fact, at one time, he anticipated having to abandon them all, and make his way into the telegraph station on foot. On the whole, the country passed over was favourable for settlement; in fact, the flats on some portions of his course were first-class sugar country.

Another journey was undertaken about this time by Messrs. O'Donnell and Carr Boyd into Western Australia, starting from the same place as Lindsay, namely, the Katherine telegraph station. The expedition succeeded in finding a large amount of pastoral country, but no new geographical discoveries of any importance were made.

Meantime, the discovery of gold in the Kimberley district of Western Australia led to that province being searched by small prospecting parties, and every creek and watercourse becoming known. This has left but little of the coastal lands still unexplored in Australia, and there is scant chance of anything noticeable being found in the interior beyond what we can fairly conjecture. The utmost an explorer can now hope to find there is some permanent lagoon or spring, affording a stand-by for the pastoralist. No such streams as the Murray or Darling will ever again gladden the eyes of the traveller in the interior,

The greater part of the territory still left to explore is situated in one colony--that of Western Australia, and, although the interior has been successively crossed by so many different men, there yet remains a large area which may be called unknown. Of what the end will be it is hard to say. Shall we find it bear out the gloomy predictions of Warburton and Giles? or the more hopeful one of Forest? One thing we do know--that, year after year, use is being found for the most repellent country. When we look back at the verdict pronounced against the interior of Australia by the early explorers, and how it has been falsified by time there is ground for hoping that even the most despised portions of our continent will yet be found available for something.

That, in spite of the monotony of the Great Plain, it is strange to note the fascination it has had for many of the most renowned explorers. Sturt, after being reduced to semi-blindness, found himself compelled to struggle with the desert once more. Eyre, left alone in the wilderness, after his awful experience at the head of the Great Bight, still longed to venture again, and accompanied his friend Sturt as far as ever his duties permitted him. Leichhardt died in harness somewhere in Australia, and Kennedy lost his life in his desire to emulate his former chief, Mitchell. Even the very sterility of the great solitude seems to have been, in its way, a lure to drag men back to encounter it once more.

Knowing now as much as we do of the interior, we can hardly help being amused at the theories propounded in the old days by some of the earlier travellers. Oxley was, we know, wedded to the idea of an inland sea. Sturt, too, when he looked on the stony desert, saw in it but the dry channel of some old ocean current; and Eyre was convinced that the interior was nothing but a parched and and desert. One after another, these fallacies were exploded, and now we find that human and animal life can as easily be adapted to the central plain as elsewhere.

But the want of knowledge displayed by the natives of anything beyond their immediate surroundings, was one great difficulty in the way of the explorers. The blackfellow of Australia seemed to partake largely of the country he lived in. His whole life was one fight for existence, and not even the sudden advent of a strange race could do more than stir him to a languid curiosity. Bounded, as he always had been, by his surroundings, and never venturing beyond tribal limits, what information he was able to impart was, as a rule, meagre and misleading, and without any good result in the way of assistance to the explorer. True, we find exceptions to this amongst them; two instances may be quoted as exemplifying two different phases of the native character. One is a picture from Sturt's journal, the other from Mitchell.

Sturt and his companions were returning to the depôt from one of their northern efforts. Suddenly they came across a party of worn and thirsty natives. What little water the whites had with them they gave them, but it was only a mouthful a-piece, and the natives indicating by signs that they were bound for some distant waterhole, disappeared at a smart trot across the sandhills. They apparently expressed no surprise at the sudden meeting in the desert, although they could not have had the slightest conception of white men before. They seem to have accepted their presence and the friendly drink of water as only a part of their strange existence.

Far different was the conduct of the Darling River blacks, who so resented Mitchell's appearance, that they travelled over some hundreds of miles to attack him on his second visit. The ingenuity with which they planned an attack on the party was a rather remarkable thing in the annals of exploration. Thinking that the clothing of the whites rendered them secure against spears, two men were told off for each member of the party, one to hold the victim whilst the other clubbed him. Fortunately the scheme was fathomed by one of the lubras with the party; but it showed very deep-seated animosity and dislike.

The intercourse, then, that the travellers could expect from the natives was either passive ignorance or violent hostility. On the few occasions when their services were made use of it amounted only to finding some scanty well. Again, the nature of the country was so persistently opposed to all the pre conceived notions that the first arrivals brought to the country. It would seem but rational to suppose that a river or creek would ultimately lead to somewhere, a larger channel, or the sea; but the rivers of the plain lived and died without any defined end, and to follow their courses only resulted in disappointment. Add to all this a dry and hot climate, and we cannot wonder at the slow progress made in the advance of the first half of the century.

There is little doubt that had fortune turned the prows of the Dutch vessels on to the north-east coast, instead of the rough and rugged shores of the west, Australia would have seen settlement long before the date of Phillip's landing. But the Dutch found no inducements whatever on the west; their ships were wrecked, their crews attacked by the natives, and they had great difficulty in finding fresh water; so that it was little wonder that even their energy and adventurous spirit recognised but nothing in Terra Australis to repay them for the trouble of taking possession. The French, too, saw little in the unclaimed portion of the country they visited to do more than threaten an occupation, which never took place, and it is doubtful if the uninviting shores of Botany Bay would have held out any hope to a body of free immigrants.

In all these halts on the way to colonization, Australia seems to have borne but the aspect of her interior plains: formidable and repellent to the intruder. Starting from the south, the first travellers had to face all the loneliness and sterility of Lake Torrens and the other salt lakes, and it was many years before it was found out that beyond existed good habitable country. Eyre and Sturt both failed in their efforts to penetrate north, and it was astonishing how easily it was afterwards accomplished by two such comparatively inexperienced men as Burke and Wills. From the west, nature was all against the explorer, and it was only after the discovery of the Ashburton that Forest managed to reach the overland line, that river having helped him well into the centre of the colony. From the north, the penetration of the Great Plain was only attempted once by A. C. Gregory, and then he was repulsed.

From the eastern shore, the steady progress, although not destined to finally succeed, gradually brought nearly half the continent under the sway of settlement, and the advance was mainly checked by the disappointment resulting from Kennedy's examination of the Barcoo, and its final course into a dreary desert. Of the many magnificent preparations made, it has not always been the lot of the best equipped parties to attain the greatest success, few men started with less outfit than did Macdowall Stuart, when he reached to and beyond central Mount Stuart; no men ever left better provided than did Burke and Wills, and their unfortunate death by starvation is too well known. The equipment of the explorer, especially as regards the use of camels, has been a matter of much dispute. M'Kinlay speaks highly in praise of them, Warburton and Giles both ascribe their safety to having them with them. But although they have been the means of achieving long stages over dry country, they are treacherous and dangerous animals to deal with. And should they make their escape, it would be impossible to recover them with only horses at command. Then, too, the possession of camels leads to hasty and hurried examination of country, and the mere fact of being in command of such means of locomotion entices a man to push on regardless of caution. M'Kinlay reports that the camels seem to thrive well on everything, but Warburton appeared to have great difficulty in obtaining feed for them in the sandhill country. Be this as it may, they have done good service in Australia, but it is not evident that they are always of equal good.

But the time will, without doubt, soon come when camels will no longer be required, and the scenes of the forced and painful marches of some of our explorers be watered by the springs now imprisoned hundreds of feet below the surface. Since these pages were commenced, one of the strongest outflows in the world has been struck near the foot of the range in Queensland, some hundreds of miles back from the central coast, in a place which witnessed the last expedition of Major Mitchell. This discovery, added to the many that have preceded it, leads to much thought as to the probability of future discoveries, and the wonderful springs that are already known to exist.

"Water! water! everywhere, and not a drop to drink." Although not absolutely true, in fact, or rather on the surface, this quotation might be uttered with a strong measure of truth by many a poor wretch perishing from thirst on a drought-blasted inland plain, whilst underneath him, at a greater or less distance, run sunless seas.

Of the magnitude of our great subterranean reservoir who shall tell? What craft will ever float on its dark surface, under domes of pendant stalactites, rippling for the first time the ice-cold waters, and disturbing the eyeless fish in their shadowy haunts? Only when here and there we tap it, and the mighty pressure sends up a thin column of water hundreds of feet in answer. Or when we notice the strong, constant springs that at intervals break through the surface crust to gladden us; or when the deeper internal fires burst forth, and hurl up its waters in scathing steam and boiling mud, can we guess of the great hidden sea beneath.

We have a problem given into our hands to solve; it is our heritage, and we have only just commenced to try and find the answer. In our fair continent there are thousands upon thousands of square miles of fertile country that Nature herself has planned and mapped out into wide fields, with gentle declivities and slopes, fit for the reception of the modest channel that shall convey the living water over the great pasture lands; and now we want the magician to come, and, with the wand of human skill, bring the interior waters to the surface, and make the desert blossom.

Of the great supply that lies awaiting us deep down in the earth's caverns we have incontestible proofs, and of the force latent in it to lift it to the surface, to be our willing slave and bondsman, we, too, have some dawning notion. Will years of study and observation give us the power to wield the wand at will? We cannot but believe it. Our vast and fertile downs were never destined to be idle and unproductive for months and months, dependent only on the niggard clouds o'erhead.

To make Australia the richest and most self-supporting country that sun ever shone upon, wherein every man could follow out the old saying of sitting under his own vine and fig tree, what is wanted? The answer to this problem is to bring to our rich alluvial surface the waters under the earth.

On the great inland plateau that occupies two-thirds of the entire continent, we find the soil teeming with elements of surpassing fertility. Even the grudging rainfall that comes so seldom has developed a wealth of indigenous herbage, grasses, and fodder plants unequalled in any other part of the globe. The earth seems to have put forth every inherent vitalising power it possesses to render its creatures independent of cruel seasons.

What traveller but has noticed the magical effect of rain upon the deep friable soil, formed by the denuded limestone rock. Almost instantaneously fresh life springs up. Within but a short time the dry and withered stalks of grass assume a deep rich green, the soft broad leaves and joints are replete with moisture. The bare ground is quickly coated with trailing vines and creepers, bearing succulent seed pods, grateful and moist. The rough-coated, staggering beast that could scarce drag its feeble legs out of the muddy waterhole, becomes in a few weeks strong and vigorous. What would not such a land be with a constant fertilizing stream of water through, and about it?

In approaching the subject of our subterranean water supply, the peculiar physical formation of Australia must be borne in mind. The great flat tableland that stretches in almost unvarying monotony from shore to shore, fringed round with its strip of coastal land, resembles--to use a homely simile--nothing so much as a narrow brimmed, flat crowned hat. The moisture-laden clouds that visit us, break on the sides of this hat, giving the brim, or coast, the full benefit of their precipitation; drifting over the plateau, or crown, with rapidly decreasing bulk. Thus, the great plain, in size the greatest, and in soil the richest part of us, is always labouring under the curse of irregular and inefficient rainfall; and whatever good we may do in the way of water storage and we may do so much-we have always the threat of many years of drought hanging over, during which our treasury of water will be drained, and not replenished.

Welling from the sides of the tableland we find large permanent springs, in many cases the sources of fine strong-flowing rivers, the component parts of whose waters now first see the light again after countless ages. Storms and floods may come and go unheeded, their steady flow is-maintained unchecked by summer or winter weather; for their birth is deep down in the earth, where meteorological disturbances are unknown. Like an old and battered tank, through whose cracked and leaky sides the water it contains is escaping, so these springs find vent through fissures in the mighty tableland, to flow down to the sea.

Up in the northern provinces where, perhaps, if anything, the contrast of these flowing streams beneath the parched surroundings is more striking than in the more temperate southern clime, there are some mighty leaks in the sides of the tableland. The Gregory River, in the Burke district of Queensland has one unvarying flow; a strong running stream, never lessened by the longest drought, but gliding beneath cool masses of tropical foliage and gurgling over rocky bars when all around is dry. What a great heritage here runs to waste unheeded.

In the northern territory, from out another vent, springs the Flora River, whose waters ripple over limestone bars in miniature cascades, from pool to pool, like pigmy reproductions of the lost terraces of New Zealand. Follow the edge of the great tableland around, and amongst the deep seams and fissures of its abrupt descent coastward, we suddenly come, midst rugged barreness and gloomy grandeur, upon these messengers from the inner earth. Some enjoying the sunlight, but for a brief span, disappearing again for ever as, suddenly as they were up-borne; others finding their way down to the habitable lowlands and to the sea. But, unfortunately, all these springs, some of great volume, find issue on the outer edge of the range; the gradual descent that marks the inner slope is not the scene of these outbursts. Here, and throughout the interior, the waters from below rise in a way that seems to best befit the weird solitude of the great plain.

At times, on a bare, baked mound elevated above the surface, there is a dwarf crater filled with water that never overflows, and when tapped and exhausted, rises once more to its former level. Again, canopied by giant ti-trees amid the shrill shrieking of thousands of noisy parrots, the traveller can pick his way along the treacherous paths that wind amongst the hot springs. Or at the foot of a low range a scanty trickle fills a rocky pool, and thence is lost.

In the bed of some far inland creek, the water rises in the sand in shallow pools, during the dark hours of night, to vanish once more beneath the sun. And in low caverns in the limestone hills, down some deep fissure, can be seen the waters of a stream, whose rise and course no man has ever traced. Again a solitary lagoon is found whereon no lily grows, and wherein no fish swims. Where the belated bushman camping for the night, finds the next morning that the water has sunk many feet, or perhaps has risen, when no rain has fallen far or near for months. All these signs and tokens from the great sea beneath us may serve as guides to the end.

When one comes to know the real value of water in a thirsty land, it almost seems like a crime on the part of Nature, that a spring should rise and flow for a comparatively short distance, to be lost in the sea. When by placing the source some fifteen or twenty miles away the course would run for hundreds of miles through a dry country. Can human ingenuity improve on nature?

In this case nature seems to have laid the ground work of a great comprehensive continental plain; to have put the lever ready for man to start it, and though the scheme is one of such magnitude that it may at first glance seem widely impossible, there is no reason, backed as it would be by natural forces, that it may not be an accomplishment of the future.

To fully understand the great problem of the water supply of Australia, it is necessary to comprehend and carry in mind the wonderfully unique river system of the continent. In an average area of 1,800 miles east and west, by 900 miles north and south, the whole drainage runs from north to south; that is to say, all that finds vent in the ocean. This, of course, is the surface formation carrying off the rainfall, and has no bearing on the outbreak of subterranean springs. But, as showing the upheaval of the land to the northward, it points out that naturally the flow of irrigation on a large scale will be from north to south.

It may be said that from the 18th parallel there is a steady slope southward, broken only by the subordinate natural features of the country, which necessarily form the irregularities of the smaller tributaries. In this great block of more than a million and a quarter of square miles there are then all. the defined channels requisite for the carriage of water throughout the heart of the continent, but with the important fact wanting that they are destitute of a constant and steady supply from the doubtful rainfall. The tilt of the northern edge of the plateau puts their sources above the level of the great springs, and causes them to be dependent on these intermittent and often scanty rains. And we know that these rains have failed in producing any comprehendable system of drainage over one third of our continent, at, least, at present with our limited knowledge, the water system appears wasteful and purposeless throughout that region.

If then the underground sea that exists beneath could be, tapped as far north as possible, the water would rise to the surface at a much higher level, than would be possible elsewhere, and much greater use could be made of it, inasmuch as a larger area would lay below it for fertilization. Now, the question of the existence of this water supply at a uniform depth beneath the earth's surface can be proved by noting the existence of the springs that we know of, that have found their way without artificial aid to the light of day. Only those can be brought in evidence that are unmistakeably outside of local influence, and are unaffected by wet weather, or dry.

In the north, on the edge of the tableland, they are most numerous. On the east coast, at the head of the Burdekin River, there are unmistakeable signs of an upward effort of the imprisoned waters to free themselves. One main tributary, a creek called Fletcher's Creek, takes its rise in a labyrinth of basaltic rocks, that for years defied the efforts of the whites to penetrate. This stream rising from its cradle in the dead lava, winds in and out of the encompassing stretches of rocks, until it emerges on the outer country, where it feeds and maintains two large lakes, ere it is lost in the sandy bed of one of the anabranches of the Burdekin. It is one of the strongest and most consistent outbreaks in the north, and its volume and continuance show the strength of the source from which it emerges.

The head of the Burdekin itself is amongst lava beds, wherein there are many similar springs; most of these take the form of permanent lagoons. To the westward we find ourselves on a more arid surface, the formation of the ranges not being so favourable to the development of springs; and where they do occur, they are evidently the product of rainfall. On the watershed we are on a corner, as it were, of the inland plain, and our ascent has put us above the spring level. Lower down, if we follow the well-known Flinders River, we find in the hot springs at Mount Brown another upshoot from below that has evidently come from the neighbourhood of the internal fires themselves. From this point right away west, skirting the edge of the tableland, great rushes of water are comparatively common. Some find their way between basaltic columns, and after feeding the flow of some large river for many miles, die suddenly, leaving the lower part of the watercourse a barren, sandy channel. The heads of the Leichhardt and Gregory Rivers are particularly prolific in springs; the latter river, as I have already noticed, being one of the steadiest flowing rivers in Australia. Westward still, the heads of all the rivers, no matter what their lower course is like, abound in springs at the break of the descent from the tableland, and, as nearly as can be computed, all these occur at nearly about an identical altitude.

To travel west, through to the western shore of Australia, only gives us the same phenomena: everywhere the belt of springs is to be found about half-way between the edge of the tableland and the coast level, just where the abrupt descent terminates and a gentler slope is entered on. It would be wearisome to enumerate them all, the fact of their existence is so well-known in these days.

To fairly see what would be the result of bringing a little of the great sea of hidden waters to the surface, let us take an instance of one of the tributaries of that great artery of Australia, the Darling. The head waters of the Warrego rise in latitude 24 deg., and at its very head, within almost a stone's throw, are large springs, that find their way down the range into the lowest river. Thence, through coastal lands, to the eastern sea board. Now had these springs broken out on the higher level of the Warrego watershed, their waters would have benefited hundreds of miles of some of the fairest country in Australia, that now suffers under constant drought.

The preserving and regulating of their waters, after guiding them into the channels prepared by Nature, would be an after-work greatly assisted by the varied formation of the country through which their courses would run.

Chapter XV

Maritime Discoveries

To exhaustively deal with the early maritime discoveries of this continent would require from the historian a vast power of research, and especially of caution, in deciding or allotting to any one country the priority of position as the "first-finders;" and while we know of few studies affording more intellectual pleasure and enjoyment, we doubt if the result would even then set at rest the mystery which still enshrouds those narratives.

Since the commencement of this work, however, the following original paper has been considered worthy of attention, as it presents the most reasonable and logical theory yet put forward for the right to consider the French as the original discoverers, and readers will have pleasure in following out the various deductions as made by one of our fellow-colonists, E. Marin La Meslée, Member of the Société de Géographie Commerciale de Paris, who has, by great research, compiled, in the following interesting article, the evidence relating to the voyage of the old Norman navigator, Paulmier de Gonneville, in 1503.

Without endorsing what is here put forward, there is much in its favour, and it shows a considerable degree of keen argument and cogent reasoning that, in any case, is a valuable contribution to this department of literature. Moreover, it may be the incentive for further exploration of the locality mentioned at some future time, with the view of solving the secrets of the strange carving and wonderful cave drawings, to which so much interest has been attracted.

Most of the modern histories of Australia contain, with regard to the voyage of De Gonneville, the same stereotyped remarks:--
"A claim has been set forth on behalf of a certain French sailor named De Gonneville, who is stated to have landed on the coast of Australia in 1503, but this claim can easily be dismissed, as there is little doubt

that the country he describes is no other than the island of Madagascar."

This opinion, so generally entertained by modern writers is probably based on the authority of Admiral Burney, and the eminent English geographer, Mr. Major, who, in referring to Burney's remarks with regard to this voyage in his paper on "Early Voyages to Terra Australis," printed in 1861, merely endorses this statement without attempting to discuss it. The voyage of Jean Binot Paulmier de Gonneville is authenticated, however, beyond the possibility of a doubt, but the mystery to be cleared up as to what part of the Austral world the old Norman navigator landed upon requires careful handling and very close discussion.

De Gonneville left Honfleur in the month of June of the year 1503, in the good ship L'Espoir, and after having rounded the Cape of Good Hope he was assailed by tempestuous weather and driven into calm latitudes. After a tedious spell of calm weather, want of water forced him to make for the first land he could sight. The flight of some birds coming from the south decided him to run a course to the southward, and after a few days' sail he landed on the coast of a large territory, at the mouth of a fine river, which he compares to the river Orne, at Caen. There he remained for six months repairing his vessel, and making exploring excursions in the neighbourhood, holding meanwhile amicable intercourse with the inhabitants. He left this great Austral Land, to which he gave the name of "Southern Indies," as being situated, in his estimation, "not far from the true course to the East Indies," on the 3rd of July of the year 1504, taking with him two of the natives, one of whom was the son of the chief of the people among whom he had resided. On the return voyage no land was seen until the day after the Feast of St. Denis, i.e., the 10th of October of the same year; but on nearing the coast of France the ship was attacked off tile islands of Guernsey and jersey by an English privateer, who robbed the navigators of all they brought from the land they had visited, the most important loss being the journal of the expedition. On his arrival at Honfleur, De Gonneville immediately entered a plaint before the Admiralty Court of Normandy, and wrote a report of his voyage, which was signed by the principal officers of his vessel.

The following is a translation of the title of this document "Judicial declaration made before the Admiralty Court of Normandy by Sieur de Gonneville, at the request of the King's procurator, respecting the voyage of the good ship *L'Espoir*, of the port of Honfleur, to the 'Southern Indies.'"

Extracts from this judicial declaration were published for the first time in 1663 by the bookseller Cramoisy, who had received them from a priest named J. B. Paulmier, then Canon of the Cathedral Church of St. Pierre de Lizieux. The document was addressed to Pope Alexander VII., and bears the title of:--
"Memorial for the establishment of a Christian mission in the third part of the world, or 'Terre Australe.' Dedicated to His Holiness Pope Alexander VII., by a priest originating from that country."

This priest was the direct descendant of one of the "Australians" (a term used for the first time by De Gonneville himself in referring to the inhabitants of "Terre Australe"), whom the Norman captain had brought to France, and to whom at his death he gave his name and fortune, in his desire to make some atonement for the wrong which the worthy sailor considered he had inflicted upon the native by taking him away from his country under a promise to return, which he was never able to redeem. De Gonneville married him to one of his relatives, and the priest in question was the grandson of the "Australian," whose native name was "Essomeric." Canon Paulmier appears to have been a man of mark in his time, since he was resident in France as representative of the King of Denmark. He was also a man of great learning, and Des Brosses informs us that he had made a particular study of geography and the history of voyages of discovery, with which he was perfectly acquainted.

The documents published by Des Brosses were translated and appeared for the first time in English in a work entitled "Terra Australis Cognita," by the Scotch geographer, Callender, who, like Des Brosses, was fully convinced that De Gonneville had landed somewhere on what is now known as the Australian Continent. This territory was named by Des Brosses Australasia as far back as 1761, and was placed to the southward of the Little Moluccas, where our maps now show the north-western portion of the Australian Continent. Some English geographers, however, such as Admiral Burney and Flinders, differ from the conclusions arrived at by both Des Brosses and Callender. Burney inclines to the belief that the land visited by De Gonneville could be no other than Madagascar. After him, Major, than whom no higher or more respected authority exists in geographical matters of this kind, seems to have too readily accepted Burney's opinion. Perhaps they each considered the claim set up on behalf of De Gonneville as based on insufficient grounds, and were disposed to doubt, in the face of later knowledge of the natives of Australia, that De Gonneville could possibly have induced one of his relatives to marry a representative of these wretched races: and it must be admitted that herein lies the great stumbling block in the way of fixing the position of the territory upon which De Gonneville actually landed. It is also probable that Burney was led to the conclusion that Madagascar was the point visited by some inaccuracies in Callender's translation with regard to the kind of head-dress described as worn by the women, which would certainly appear to refer more to the inhabitants of the great African island than to the Australians. The mystery is a difficult one to clear up, but subsequent discoveries, and a closer scrutiny of the Norman captain's narrative, prove, we think, clearly that De Gonneville's "Southern Indies" could be no other than the Australian Continent, and that he landed in reality at the mouth of some of the rivers on the north-western coast.

In the first place, the judicial declaration cited above, which had been for more than three centuries and a half mislaid among the records of the Admiralty of Normandy, was discovered in the year 1873 by the French geographer, Benoit D'Avezac, who published it in a pamphlet in which he discusses this question, and concludes that the land visited by De Gonneville must have been some part of South America. But this official document, which is similar in almost all points to the memoirs of the priest, Paulmier, and establishes at once the fidelity of his extracts and the absolute truth of the voyage of the French captain, does not contain any additional information which could lead to such conclusion, based only on his description of the natives of the "Southern Indies." D'Avezac's contention cannot be sustained, and must give way before the evidence of other facts; but as the same arguments against his theory apply also to that of Burney and Major, we need not discuss it here for the present.

It is, however, necessary, in order that the reader may form a clear idea of the subject, to quote at length the original memoirs as published by the worthy priest. As the translation of Callender is, on the whole, a fairly good one--although it may be inferred that the Scotch geographer, who wrote in 1761, was better acquainted with the pure French of the eighteenth century than with the quaint terms of the old Norman dialect, in which De Gonneville's narrative is written--we shall transcribe here that portion which bears on the subject, reserving to ourselves the duty of pointing out the few inaccuracies which may have led Burney and others to erroneous conclusions.

EXTRACT FROM THE MEMOIRS OF J. B. PAULMIER.

It were to be wished that some better hand than mine were employed to give an account of these southern regions of the world; but I cannot,

without being wanting to my character, to my birth, and to my profes-
sion, omit doing this duty to the natives of the Southern World. Soon
after the Portuguese had discovered the way to the East Indies, some
French merchants, invited by a prospect of sharing the gains of this
trade, fitted out a ship, which, in its route to the Indies, being driven
from the straight course by a tempest, was thrown upon this great
southern land. The natives of this region received the French with the
most cordial hospitality, and, during an abode of six months, did them
every good office in their power. The French, willing to bring some of
the natives home with them, prevailed upon the easy credulity of the
chief of that nation to give them one of his sons, promising that they
would return him to his country fully instructed in the European arts,
particularly that of making war, which these Australians desired above
all things. Thus was the Indian brought into France, where he lived
long enough to converse with many who are yet living, and, being
baptised, he received the name and surname of the captain who
brought him over. His godfather, in order to acquit himself in some
degree of what he owed to the Australians, procured him a small establishment in France, and married him to one of his own relations. One
of the sons of this marriage was my grandfather. The solemn promise
the French had given to the inhabitants to return him among them, and
what I owe to my original country, induces me to give the following
short account of the voyage, compiled from the memoirs of my own
family:--

"The French having formed the design of following the steps
of Vasco de Gama in the East Indies, equipped a vessel at Honfleur for
that voyage, which, being commanded by the Sieur de Gonneville,
weighed anchor in June, 1503, and, having doubled the Cape of Good
Hope, was attacked by a furious storm, which, driving them far from
their intended course, left them uncertain in what part of the world
they were. Being in want of water, and their ship having suffered
much by storm, the sight of some birds from the south induced them to
hold their course that way, where they soon discovered a large country, to which they gave the name of Southern India, according to the
usage of those days, when it was customary to give the name of India
to every new discovered country. They cast anchor in a river, which
they say was of the bigness of the Orne, near Caen. Here they spent six
months refitting their ship, but the crew, being intimidated, obliged
Gonneville to return to France. During his stay in this country he had
time to form a most curious account of the country and the manners of
its inhabitants, which he inserted in his journal; but, unfortunately,

being just off the coast of France, he was taken near the isle of Guernsey by an English privateer, who robbed him of his journal and everything he had. On his landing he complained to the Admiralty, and, having emitted the following judicial declaration, at the request of the procurator of the King, he inserted it in a short relation of the discoveries he had made. This public act, authenticated by all the proper forms, is dated 19th July, 1505, and signed by the principal officers of the ship. From this the following are extracts:--

"Item. They say that during their stay in that country they conversed in all freedom with the natives, having gained their goodwill by some trifling presents. That the said Indians were simple people, leading a careless, easy life, subsisting by hunting and fishing, and on some roots and herbs which the soil furnishes spontaneously. Some wear mantles either of skins or of woven mats, and some of them are made of feathers, like those of the gypsies in our country, only they are shorter, with a kind of apron girt above the haunches, which the men wear down to the knee, and the women to the calf of the leg. The women wear collars made of bones and small shells. The men have no ornament of this sort, but carry a bow, and arrows pointed with sharp bones. They have also a sword, made of very hard wood, burned and sharpened at the end; and these are all their weapons. The women and girls go bare-headed, with their hair neatly tied up in tresses mixed with flowers of most beautiful colours. The men let their hair hang down, but they wear crowns of feathers, richly coloured.

"They say further, that having gone two days' journey into the country and along the coasts both to right and left, they found it very fertile, and full of many birds, beasts, and fish utterly unknown in Christendom. The late Nicole Le Fevre, of Honfleur, a volunteer in this voyage, had taken exact draughts of all these things. But everything was lost, together with the journals of the voyage when the ship was taken: and this makes their account very imperfect.

"Item. They say, further, that the country is not very populous, the natives living dispersed in villages consisting of thirty, forty, or eighty huts. Those huts are made of stakes drove into the ground, the intervals being filled up with herbs and leaves, and a hole at top to let out the smoke. The doors are formed of sticks neatly tied together, and are shut with wooden keepers like those of the stables in Normandy. The beds are made of soft mats, skins, or feathers. Their household utensils are formed of wood, even the pots with which they boil water but, to preserve them from burning, they are laid over with a kind of clay an inch thick.

"Item. They say that the country is divided into many cantons, each of which has its king, or chief. These kings are highly honoured and feared by their subjects, though no better dressed or lodged than they. They have power of life and death over the subjects, of which some of the crew saw a memorable example in the person of a young man of twenty years of age, who, in a fit of passion, had struck his mother. Though no complaint was made, yet the king sent for him and ordered him to be thrown into the river with a large stone tied to his neck, having previously called together the young men of that and the neighbouring villages to witness his punishment.

"The name of this king, to whose territory the ship came, was Arosca. His canton extended a day's journey within land, having about a dozen villages in it, each of which had its particular chief, but under Arosca. The said Arosca was, to appearance, about sixty, then a widower, but had six sons--from thirty to fifteen years of age--who came often to the ship. Arosca was of middle stature, thick set, of grave but pleasant countenance. He was then at peace with the neighbouring kings, but they and he were at war with the people in the inland country, against whom he marched twice, during the ship's stay there. Each time he had a body of 500 or 600 men with him, and when he returned the last time, there were great rejoicings made on account of a victory he had gained. There was nothing but excursions for a few days, in which they begged the French to march with them, in hopes of being assisted by their firearms, but the commander excused himself.

"Item. They say that there came five of their kings to see the ship, but they wore nothing to distinguish them but their plumes of feathers, which, contrary to those of their subjects, was of one colour. The principal inhabitants wore some feathers of the colour of the king's mixed with the others. Arosca had his of green.

"Item. They say that these friendly Indians received them as angels from Heaven, and were infinitely surprised at the bulk of the ship, the artillery, mirrors, and other things they saw on board. Above all, they were astonished at our method of communicating our thoughts to each other by letters from the ship to those on shore, not being able to divine how the letter could speak. For these reasons they greatly feared the French. At the same time they were so much beloved by them, on account of some axes, mirrors and knives they gave them, that they were always ready to do anything in their power to serve the strangers, bringing them great quantities of flesh and fish, fruits, and other provisions. Besides which, they brought them large quantities of skins, feathers, and roots, of dying in different colours, in exchange for which they received different kinds of hardware of small price, and thus the French got together above one hundred quintals of their goods.

"Item. They say that, intending to leave there some memorial that this country had been visited by Christians, they erected a large wooden cross, thirty-five feet high, and painted over, placed on an eminence in view of the sea. This they did with much ceremony on the Day of Pentecost, 504, the cross being carried by the captain and his officers, all barefooted, accompanied by the King Arosca and the principal Indians, after whom followed the crew, under arms, singing the Litany. These were accompanied by a crowd of Indians, to whom they gave to understand the meaning of this ceremony as well as they could. Having set up the cross, they fired volleys of their cannon and small arms, charging the Indians to keep carefully and honour the monument they had set up, and endeavoured to gain them to this by presenting them with a number of baubles, which, though of small value, were highly prized by them. On one side of this cross were engraved the name of the Pope and that of our Sovereign, the name of the Admiral of France, and those of the captain and all his crew. On the other side appeared the Latin verses following, made by the above Nicole Le Fevre, signifying the date of this transaction--

"HIC sacra paLMarIUs, post UIt gonIVILLabInotUs,
"GreX, foCIUs parIterqUe UtraqUe progenIes.

"Item. They say that, having refitted their ship in the best way they could, they prepared to return to France, and being willing, after the manner of those who discover strange lands, to carry some of the natives with them, they persuaded the king, Arosca, to let them have one of his sons, promising to the father that they would bring him back in twenty moons at farthest, with others who should teach them the use of firearms, and how to make mirrors, axes, knives, and whatever else they admired among the Christians. These promises determined Arosca to let his son, called Essomeric, go along with them, to whom he gave for a companion an Indian of thirty-five years of age, called Namoa. He and his people convoyed them to the ship, giving them provisions, besides many beautiful feathers and other rarities, in order to present to the King of France. At parting, Arosca obliged them to swear that they would return in twenty moons, and when the ship got under way the whole people gave a great cry, and, forming the sign of the Cross with their fingers, gave them to understand that they would carefully preserve the one set up among them.

FAVENC

"Item. They say that they left this southern country July 3rd, 1504, and saw no land until the day after the Feast of St. Denis, during which time they were much distressed by a malignant fever, of which their surgeon and three more died, among whom was the Indian, Namoa. The young son of Arosca also falling sick, they baptised him by the name of Binot, after their captain, who stood godfather to him. This was done September 14th, after which the young Indian grew better and arrived in France."

Callender further remarks:--

"Thus far the judicial declaration emitted by De Gonneville before the Admiralty. The rest of the author's memoir is filled with exhortations to the French to profit by this lucky discovery, and send the writer back to the country of his ancestors; but this appears never to have been done. The author seems to have begun this extract from De Gonneville's declaration in that place where he talks of the manners of the inhabitants, omitting what went before, though it is highly probable that the navigator must have said something of the voyage outwards and the portion of the country where he landed, which would have been of great importance for us to know at this day. The French writer from whom we have translated the above account informs us that the Count de Maurepas caused search lately through all the records of the Admiralty in Normandy, in order to find the original of this declaration, but an interval of two centuries and a half, and the confusions occasioned by the civil wars, had dispersed all the old papers, and all the information that M. de Maurepas could obtain was that a tradition still subsisted there that such a piece was once among the records, but they could give no account of what was become of it. Thus the full account of an attempt which Magellan some years after finished with success is entirely lost, except the very lame extract we have been able to lay before the reader. Our French author tells us he has seen another copy of this memorial at the end of the dedication to Pope Alexander VII. The author signs his name thus, at full length, 'Paulmier, Prêtre Indien Chanoine de l'Eglise Cathédrale de Lizieux.' The proprietor of this copy has added a note, testifying that this copy was given him by the author himself in 1664. He commends him as a person of universal knowledge, and one who had travelled all over Europe. He had made the history of navigation his principal study, and was perfectly acquainted with it. In another note we are told that Essomeric, the son of Arosca, lived to the year 1583, and left posterity under the name of Binot. One of his grand-children, J. B. Binot, was President of the Treasury of Provence, and left an only daughter, who was m married to the Marquis de la Barbent, May 4th, 1725. Our readers will not be surprised that we have entered into a detail of facts in order to elucidate and confirm the truth of this first discovery of the Terra Australis, especially as this account was never seen in our language till now, and is therefore little known even to those who are otherwise well acquainted with voyages made to this part of the world."

Callender, however, has omitted to translate the remainder of Des Brosses' account, in which, among other facts, the important statement is made that the priest Paulmier had become personally known to M. Flaconet, who met him for the first time at the residence of the Lord Bishops of Heliopolis and Beryte, where he often met him in company with M. de Flacourt, who had commanded in Madagascar, and AI. Fernamel, father of the Superior of the Foreign Missions. The good abbe was doing all in his power to persuade these gentlemen to assist in sending a mission to these Australians, and it also appears that he had communicated his views on the subject to St. Vincent de Paul, who would have presented his memorial to the Pope had he not been prevented by death.

Before attempting to fix the position of the country visited by De Gonneville, it is necessary to refute here the various opinions expressed on the subject which refer to countries other than the Australian Continent. The most ancient is that brought forward by tile geographers, Duval and Nolin, and the navigator, Bouvet, who place those lands almost immediately to the south of the Cape of Good Hope. As there are no lands thereabout, this opinion is hardly worth quoting but, considering the very limited knowledge of the geography of that part of the world in those days, the error may be readily understood. Others, basing their opinion on the length of De Gonneville's voyage, have surmised that he might have landed on some part of the coast of Tasmania or of New Zealand, but this conclusion is equally untenable, as these islands are not situated within calm latitudes, and are not near or even in the direction of the "true course to the East Indies," which the French sailor was satisfied he was not far off, as, under this belief, he, on leaving the "Southern Indies" endeavoured to induce his crew to continue their voyage. Besides, the description given of the inhabitants and their manners, applies more to natives of a tropical or semi-tropical climate than to those of such cold regions as New Zealand and Tasmania.

We are, therefore, confronted with only one more opinion, which is held by most English geographers on the high authority of Admiral Burney.

"Let the whole account," says Burney, "be reconsidered without prepossession, and the idea that will immediately and most naturally occur is that Southern India, discovered by De Gonneville, was Madagascar. De Gonneville, having doubled (passed round) the Cape, was by tempests driven into calm latitudes, and so near to this land that he was directed thither by the flight of birds. The refusal of the crew to proceed to Eastern India would scarcely have happened if they had been so far advanced to the east as New Holland."

It is difficult to conceive how Burney could have expressed such an opinion, unless he was led to that conclusion by some errors in Callender's translations. There is, in fact, a passage having reference to the descriptions of the head-dress worn by the native women, in which the Scotch geographer has given the following version of Des Brosses' original:--
"The women and girls go bareheaded, with their hair neatly tied up in tresses, mixed with flowers of most beautiful colours."?

The original narrative reads thus:--
"Et vont les femmes et filles tête nue, ayant les cheveux gentiment teurchés de petits cordons d'herbes teintes de couleurs vives et luisantes."

Which means:--
"The women and girls go bare headed, having their hair ornamented with little strings of grass dyed in bright colours."

This, as will be seen, is a very different version. Callender evidently did not understand the old Norman expression--genitment teurchés, which means "nicely ornamented," and translated it by the word that appeared to him more akin in form, tresses, hence, "the hair neatly tied up in tresses", which is a characteristic custom of the native women of the island of Madagascar.

But this is a small matter. It is, however, more difficult to dispose of another fact as telling against the Madagascar theory, which apparently did not strike Burney. Gonneville states that he was driven into calm latitudes, and after tedious navigation, was directed southward by the flight of birds. It is only necessary here to compare dates in order to show how misapplied would be this description to the latitudes within which Madagascar is situated.

De Gonneville left Honfleur in June, 1503, and quilted Southern India on the 3rd of July of the following year. As he stayed six months in that country, his outward voyage had, therefore, lasted about seven months, and he must have been in the vicinity of the Cape of Good Hope about December, 1503, or January, 1504. As it is a well-known fact that tempestuous weather is generally met with from the south-west and, moreover, that the prevailing wind during that season of the year is from the north-west, De Gonneville, whose true course lay to the north-east, was probably driven much more toward the east than he expected, for he expressly states that he was convinced he was not far from the true course to the East Indies. Had the tempests blown from the south-east, there would never, in all probability, have been any need discussing his account, for he would have had none to render, as his ship would have been driven very quickly against the East African coast, or the south-east coast of Madagascar and wrecked.

It must be assumed that De Gonneville was, for his time, a man of great ability, well versed in nautical matters, and the use of the primitive instruments which were then known, and his opinion as, to the position of his ship, and his desire to proceed to the East Indies, being inwardly satisfied that he was not far from the object of his voyage, is certainly entitled to some consideration, although, unfortunately, he has not left any indication of the latitude or longitude of the country he visited. If to this be added the facts that it is precisely in the season extending from December to March, that the Madagascar latitudes are constantly visited by hurricanes, and that the cyclones which originate in the Indian Ocean burst over the islands of Mauritius and Reunion, and generally travel towards these coasts, it will be apparent that the term "calm latitudes" must necessarily apply to some other part of the Indian Ocean. It is equally well-known that the belt which extends round the globe between 10 deg. of latitude, north, and 10 deg. of latitude, south, is in all parts of the ocean, and at all times, subject to very tedious calms, though the waters may occasionally be ruffled by very heavy hurricanes and storms. These facts force us to seek for the land visited in the neighbourhood of these latitudes. The objection raised by the sailors to proceed to the East Indies means nothing, as they had no idea of their position, while as ignorant and superstitious men, tired of a long and dangerous voyage, they had little reason to share in their chief's confidence in his estimate of the locality they had reached, and had no thought but that of returning homewards without facing again the dangers of unknown seas.

Further arguments are not wanting to refute the Madagascar theory. In the first place, the Portuguese, who discovered that island in 1506, and explored its coasts in the following years, could not have lon. remained in ignorance of De Gonneville's voyage. The cross erected by his companion was, perhaps, not destroyed; but, so short a period having c-lapsed between their discoveries and the Norman captain's voyage, the natives could scarcely have forgotten so important an event. The only alternative theory would be that, in their explorations along the coast of the island, the Portuguese were so unfortunate as to land everywhere but near the spot where De Gonneville may be supposed to have resided. It is stated, moreover, that the priest Paulmier wrote his memorial to the Pope with the object of obtaining a Christian mission to the home of his ancestors; but the Portuguese missionaries were preaching the Gospel in Madagascar almost since the first visits of their countrymen to that island, and it is self-evident that the Abbe, who was often in the company of the priests who in Paris administered the foreign missions in non-Christian countries, must have been aware of this fact; while M. de Villermon positively states that he often met Paulmier in company with M. de Flacourt who had been Governor of Madagascar where France had established itself as far back as 1642. What would have been the necessity, it may be asked, of praying that a Christian mission should be sent to a country where missions had flourished for over a century, or of founding a French colony in an island which was already occupied by France, and had received resident governors ten years before the good priest wrote?

But there is one last point which is sufficient in itself to remove all doubts on the subject. Here, again, we must compare dates, and we find that:--

"They left that country on the 3rd of July, 15o4, and did not see land until the day after the Feast of St. Denis, i.e., 10th October, 1504."

De Gonneville's report to the Admiralty is dated 15th June, 1505, and admitting that there was some delay between his landing at Honfleur and the date of his report, which was signed by the principal officers of his vessel, he could hardly have reached France before March or April of that year. As he was, moreover, convinced that the country to which he had given the name of Southern India lay to the south of the East Indies, it is evident that on his return home his course must have been south-west, which, had he started from the east coast of Madagascar, or, as D'Avezac thinks, from that of South America, would have landed him on his starting point. It is evident that the land he sighted after three months' navigation could be no other than the Cape of Good Hope.

This is sufficient, we venture to think, to dispose of the Madagascar theory, as it does also of the South American one, which, it may be added, can hardly be admitted as possible, when the length of the return voyage of De Gonneville (about twelve months) is taken into consideration, together with the fact that the whole of the South American coast within the region where De Gonneville might have landed was explored and settled about the same time, and some record of his voyage would certainly have been found.

Where, then, shall we look for this Southern India, for that fine river, at the mouth of which De Gonneville remained six months, and for that fine country which his companions explored in their journeys with the natives?

A river of the size described pre-supposes a country of considerable extent, and therefore De Gonneville could not have landed on any of the islands lying between Madagascar and the Sunda Islands. It could not have been either of the latter named, as they lie to the north, and not the south of the calm latitudes referred to by De Gonneville. We are perforce obliged to admit that, as it was not and cannot have been Madagascar, it must have been Australia, and in all probability the north-west coast of the continent, about the Prince Regent and Glenelg rivers, where the explorers King and Grey found fine rivers and a rich country fairly populated with a race of warlike natives. It is certainly difficult when reading the description given of the "Australians," by De Gonneville, to imagine that they could possibly have had any resemblance to the races we are accustomed to meet with in almost all parts of Australia. Still less could they have resembled the wretched creatures which Dampier found inhabiting the west coast, between Cape Le veque and the North-west Cape, and we must, therefore, look further north for a country and a race of men answering better to the description of the Norman captain.

De Gonneville found a fine district, watered by a large river, and inhabited by men who possessed a kind of rudimentary civilization, a tribal organization, and obeyed some established individual authority. He further tells us that they lived in villages, or agglomerations of huts of the shape of the covered markets in the Normandy villages--that is to say, oval or round, made of stakes driven into the ground, and the intervals filled up with herbs and the leaves of trees; and that the speech of these people is soft and melodious. He also speaks of the birds, beasts, fishes, and other curious animals unknown in Christendom, of which Master Nicole le Fevre, of Honfleur, who was a volunteer in the voyage, had taken exact draughts. And, last of all, we are told that De Gonneville induced the chief or king of the country to allow him to take home his son and another Indian as a companion, promising to return with them in twenty "moons" at furthest, and owing to the impossibility of fulfilling that promise, he procured the young Australian an establishment in France, and married him to one of his relatives, from whom he had posterity. This last portion of the narrative would appear the most incredible of all, if we had not official and documentary evidence of its absolute truth, as it must certainly be presumed that the Australian could not possibly have belonged to the wretched races with whom we are familiar.

But, however difficult it may seem to reconcile the account of De Gonneville with our general knowledge of the natives of Australia, the task is not so hopeless as at first sight may appear; and we shall crave the attention of the reader to the following description of the country and the inhabitants of that part of North-west Australia which surrounds the Glenelg. and Prince Regent and other rivers in their neighbourhood, discovered and visited for the first time by Captain King and Lieutenant, now Sir George, Grey, the latter exploring it to some distance inland in the year 1838.

Referring to that part of the country, Lieut. Grey says in his "Expedition in North-Western and Western Australia," p. 179:--
"The peak we ascended afforded us a very beautiful view: to the north lay Prince Regent's River, and the good country we were now upon extended as far as the inlets which communicated with this great navigable stream; to the south and south-westward lay the Glenelg, meandering through as verdant and fertile a district as the eye of man ever rested on. The luxuriance of tropical vegetation was now seen to great advantage in the height of the rainy season. The smoke of native fires rose in every direction from the country which lay like a map at our feet; and when I recollected that all those natural riches of soil and climate lay between two navigable rivers, and that its sea coast frontage, not much exceeding fifty miles in latitude, contained three of the finest harbours in the world in which the tide rose thirty-seven and a half feet, I could not but feel we were in a land singularly blessed by nature."

Could any description more closely adapt itself to the fine country, fairly peopled (peuplée entre deux) of which De Gonneville speaks. Further, on page 195 g S of the same work, Grey says:--
"We at length reached a watershed connecting the country we had left with that we were entering upon. . . This watershed consisted principally of a range of elevated hills, from which streams were thrown off to the Glenelg and to Prince Regent's River. The scenery here was fine, but I have so often before described the same character of landscape that it will be sufficient to say, we again looked down from high land on a very fertile country, covered with a tropical vegetation, and

lying between two navigable rivers. *I can compare this to no other Australian scenery, for I have met with nothing in the other portions of the continent which at all resemble it.*"

Referring to the fauna, the same authority says:--

"North Western Australia seems to be peculiarly prolific in birds, reptiles, and insects, who dwell here unmolested. . . ."

After mentioning several kinds of kangaroos, opossums, native dogs, etc., the former of which animals are constantly hunted down by the natives, Grey, speaking of the birds, says:--

"To describe the birds common to these parts requires more time than to detail the names of the few quadrupeds to be found. Indeed, in no other country that I have ever visited do birds so abound. Even the virgin forests of America cannot, in my belief, boast of such numerous feathered denizens. . . . The birds of this country possess, in many instances, an excessively beautiful plumage, and he alone who has traversed these wild and romantic regions, who has beheld a flock of many-coloured parrakeets sweeping like a moving rainbow through the air, can form any adequate idea of the scenes that then burst on the eye of the wondering naturalist. As to fish, the rivers abound in many species of excellent fish."

Could there be a more fitting description of that country which De Gonneville and his companions explored along the coast and in the interior to a distance of two days' journey, which "they found very fertile and full of many birds, beasts, and fish hitherto unknown in Christendom?" To what does this latter qualification apply? Certainly not to birds, beasts, or fish of either South America or Madagascar, as the American fauna was, to a certain extent, already known in Christendom, and that of Madagascar, which resembles that of the east coast of Africa, apart from a few species not particularly remarkable or numerous, was also well-known to Europeans. These beasts, of which, to use the old Norman phrase of "Master Nicole Le Fevre, avait pourtrayé les façons," must have struck him as very peculiar indeed when he refers to them as "utterly unknown in Christendom," and we know well that no other country can boast of a fauna so essentially different to that of any other part of the world as the Australian Continent.

And now as to the natives of this part of Australia, i.e., the neighbourhood of the Glenelg and Prince Regent's River. Grey, in page 251 of the above cited work, says:--

"My knowledge of the natives is chiefly drawn from what I have observed of their haunts, their painted caves, and drawings. I have,

283

moreover, become acquainted with several of their weapons, some of their implements, and took pains to study their disposition and habits as far as I could.

"In their manner of life, their weapons, and mode of hunting, they closely resemble the other Australian tribes with which I have since become pretty intimately acquainted, whilst in their form and appearance there is a striking difference. They are, in general, very tall and robust, and exhibit in their legs and arms a fine, full development of muscle which is unknown to southern races. They wear no clothes, and their bodies are marked by scars and wales. They seem to have no regular mode of dressing their hair, this appearing to depend entirely on individual taste or caprice.

"They appear to live in tribes, subject, perhaps, to some individual authority, and each tribe has a sort of capital or head-quarters, where the women and children remain, whilst the men, divided into small parties, hunt and shoot in every direction. The largest number we saw together, including women and children, amounted to nearly two hundred.

"Their arms consist of stone-headed spears, of throwing-sticks, of boomerangs or kileys, clubs, and stone hatchets.

"These natives manufacture their water buckets and weapons very neatly, and make from the bark of a tree a light but strong cord.

"Their huts, of which I only saw those on the coast, are constructed, in an oval form, of the boughs of trees, and are roofed with dry reeds. The diameter of one which I measured was about fourteen feet at the base.

"Their language is soft and melodious, so much so as to lead to the inference that it differs very materially, if not radically, from the more southern Australian dialects, which I have since had an opportunity to inquire into. Their gesticulation is expressive, and their bearing manly and noble. They never speared a horse or sheep belonging to us, and, judging by the degree of industry shown in their paintings, the absence of anything offensive in the subjects delineated, and the careful finish of some articles of common use, I should infer that, under proper treatment, they might easily be raised very considerably in the scale of civilisation.

"A remarkable circumstance is the presence amongst them of a race, to appearance, totally different and almost white, who seem to exercise no small influence over the rest. I am forced to believe that the distrust evinced towards strangers arose from these persons, as in both instances when we were attacked, the hostile party was led by one of these light-coloured men."

We need only draw the attention of the reader to the close resemblance between the description of De Gonneville's "Australians" and that of Grey's in many particulars, especially in their tribal organization, the form of their houses, [Note, below] their language, and the fact of the existence among them, as leaders of the tribes, of that race of almost white men also observed about the same parts by Captain King, who thinks that they are of Malay origin.

[Note: Callender, in his translation omits a passage referring to the form of the huts of the Australians, which De Gonneville says were "en forme de halles," i.e., in the form of covered markets such as seen in the villages of Normandy, which are generally oval structures.]

There are certain discrepancies, however, which cannot be explained away, unless it is taken into consideration that Grey visited those coasts three hundred and thirty years after the French sailor, and that during that interval of time the customs of the inhabitants cannot fall to have undergone a change. It may be also that the light-coloured people seen amongst them are but the remnants of once numerous tribes, probably of Malay origin, as these latter have left undeniable marks of their having not intermixed with the native races throughout the whole of northern Australia. One of the points of dissemblance which might be pointed out is the fact that De Gonneville describes them as using bows and arrows, which is at variance with our knowledge of the arms of the Australians, and equally differs from Grey's description of the same; but this objection exists also as regards the inhabitants of Madagascar, who, besides, had already attained a much higher degree of civilisation than that described by De Gonneville--being acquainted with the use of iron, the manufacture of cotton and silk goods, fine mats, and many other articles of value among civilised people. The Madagascar natives never made use of the skins of animals as an article of dress, whilst this custom is common to the aborigines of all parts of Australia, where the kangaroo, opossums, native bears, and emus, furnish them with the material, with which they could manufacture these garments of skins or beds of feathers described by De Gonneville. But if the theory is accepted, which we are about to put forward regarding the inhabitants of this part of Australia--that at the time of De Gonneville's visit a people of Malay origin inhabited it in fairly large numbers, of which the light-coloured natives seen by Grey are the descendants, and that with their disappearance from that district some of their customs disappeared with

285

them, the natives of the present day retaining only those best suited to their actual mode of life--then the Norman captain's narrative will become intelligible. Besides, as regards the use of bow and arrow, certainly known to the Malays, although the intercourse of the latter with other tribes on the north Australian coast has been undoubtedly frequent, nowhere have the Australian natives adopted that kind of arm, whilst in New Guinea and all over Northern Polynesia the bow and arrow is the inevitable war accoutrement of the savage, who certainly obtained the knowledge of it from his Malay forefathers. No wonder, then, that in the district explored by Grey, these arms should have given way to the equally effective boomerang, throwing-stick, and spears, and other weapons of the North Australian savage.

The theory we have just submitted with regard to the country round the Glenelg River and that of the Prince Regent having been at one time inhabited by a different and superior race is no idle one, and is proved by the discoveries of remarkable paintings made by the same Lieutenant Grey in the caves near the mouth of the abovenamed rivers.

Again we shall have to quote this excellent author, whose clear and concise descriptions are of such value, and refer the reader to the following passages in the diary of his explorations in that part of the Australian Continent:--

"On this sloping roof the principal figure (1) which I have just alluded to was drawn. In order to produce the greater effect, the rock about it was painted black, and the figure itself coloured with the most vivid red and white. It thus appeared to stand out from the rock, and I was certainly surprised at the moment that I first saw this gigantic head and upper part of a body bending over and staring grimly down on me.

"It would be impossible to convey in words an adequate idea of this uncouth and savage figure; I shall, therefore, only give such a succinct account of this and the other paintings as will serve as a sort of description to accompany the annexed plates.

```
"Length of head and face           2 ft.  0 in.
"Width of face                     0 ft  17 in.
(sic)
"Length from bottom of face to navel  2 ft   6 in.
```

"Its head was encircled by bright red rays, something like the rays which one sees proceeding from the sun when depicted on the signboard of a public house. Inside of this came a broad stripe of very brilliant red, which was coped by lines of white; both inside and outside of this red space were narrow stripes of a still deeper red, intended probably to mark its boundaries. The face was painted vividly white and the eyes black, being, however, surrounded by red and yellow lines. The body, head, and arms were outlined red, the body being curiously painted with red stripes and bars.

"Upon the rock which formed the left hand wall of this cave, and which partly faced you on entering, was a very singular painting (2), vividly coloured, representing four heads joined together. From the mild expression of the countenances, I imagined them to represent females, and they appeared to be drawn in such a manner and in such a position as to look up at the principal figure which I have before described. Each had a very remarkable head-dress, coloured with a deep, bright blue, and one had a necklace on. Both of the lower figures had a sort of dress, painted with red, in the same manner as that of the principal figure, and one of them had a band round the waist. Each of the four faces was marked by a totally distinct expression of countenance, and although none of them had mouths, two, I thought, were otherwise rather good-looking. The whole painting was executed on a white ground, and its dimensions were:--

```
"Total length of painting            3 ft. 6¾ in.
"Breadth across two upper heads      2 ft. 6  in.
"Breadth across two lower heads      3 ft. 1½ in.
```

These remarkable paintings attracted Grey's attention, and led him wondering as to their origin. The solution to that problem he has however left to others. (Fig 1, see Appendix.)

According to him, the first two frescoes--i.e., those situated on the roof of the cave, representing the principal figure, and that representing the four persons (probably women), are one subject. A glance at their position, and the expression of their faces, leads one to accept Grey's opinion as not only admissible, but as the only accurate one. The group of women is placed in an attitude of prayer, or of submission towards the central figure, also representing a woman, as all except the head-dress, which is a little different, exactly resemble the others; it is also evident that the artist wished to represent a religious subject.

It is necessary to remark that the people among which these drawings have been found belong to an almost savage race, and in admitting that they may be the work of a superior race that once inhabited these parts (which, by the way, is the opinion of Sir George Grey), yet this superior race could hardly be any other but some Malay tribe. Among these latter, as well as among all savage, or semi-savage people, woman is considered as a being of an inferior order, more fit to become a slave than to be worshipped, and as the Malays had either

287

adopted for centuries past, either one of two creeds, that of Buddhism from the Hindoos, or that of Mahomet from the Arabs, we look in vain, save in the former, and that in only one or two well-known instances, which cannot for a moment be entertained here, for the worship of a woman. The Malay religious artistic subjects that we know of are of an order far above that of which we have a sample here, and there is no resemblance at all in their paintings with anything depicted in these caves.

There are several points of importance with regard to these pictures, to which we beg to direct the reader's attention. In the first place, the perfect oval shape of the head; secondly, the colour of the face, which is painted vividly white, evidently for some purpose; and thirdly, the fact that the kind of dress worn over the bodies exactly resembles that described by De Gonneville as worn by the women of the Southern Indies, made of some kind of matted material, sometimes also of skins, or of feathers, girt above the haunches and reaching to the knee. (Fig. 2, see Appendix.)

Compare, also, the date assigned by Grey to these pictures-two or three centuries, and this coincidence will appear still more remarkable.

But to return to the subject. It is difficult, if not impossible to credit the natives at the time of Grey's visit as being the authors of these paintings. The eminent traveller absolutely discredits such a possibility, and attributes them to a far distant epoch, and a totally different race. The perfect oval shape of the faces was not drawn so without a purpose, and neither were they painted so vividly white, if the artist had not desired to pourtray types of a race certainly not existing at present on the the Australian continent. It is difficult to admit that it might be of Malay origin, as tile head-dress, or to describe it more perfectly, the aureola surrounding the head, is met with in Buddhist paintings or sculptures only as surrounding the head of gods, who can always be recognised by their peculiar and constant characteristics, and nowhere are these aureolas surrounded with the rays in the shape of "flamèches," which confront us in the drawing of the principal figure. (Fig. 3, see Appendix.) It resembles, indeed, much better Grey's own description:--

"Its head was encircled by bright red rays, something like the rays which one sees proceeding from the sun, when depicted on the sign board of a public house."

There is evidently here some strange mixture of European and Malay art, the former exhibited in the remarkable aureolas which so commonly surround the heads of saints in the old images, in painted church windows of the middle ages, and the times of De Gonneville, and the latter in the kind of dress over the body, which appears to be meant to represent some sort of matted stuff. This painting is not the work of a native artist; it is unlikely that it could be the work of Malays, in the third place there is in its position and its peculiar appearance such a striking touch of an European conception, mingled with barbaric surroundings, that one is almost inclined to the belief that we are here in the presence of a subject of religious, nay, a Christian order.

This deduction may need additional evidence, and if the reader will kindly follow with us Lieutenant Grey's steps, he will be placed in the presence of a still more remarkable painting, which we shall presently describe.

"The cave was twenty feet deep, and at the entrance seven feet high and about forty feet wide. As before stated the floor gradually approached the roof in the direction of the bottom of the cavern, and its width also contracted so that at the extremity it was not broader than the slab of rock which formed a natural seat. The principal painting in it was the painting of a man ten feet six inches in length, clothed from the chin downwards in a red garment which reached to the wrists and ankles; beyond this red dress the feet and hands protruded, and were badly executed.

"The face and head of the figure were enveloped in a succession of circular bandages, or rollers, or what appeared to be painted to represent such. These were coloured red, yellow, and white, and the eyes were the only features represented on the face. Upon the highest bandage, or roller, a series of lines were painted in red, but although so irregularly done as to indicate that they have some meaning, it is impossible to tell whether they were intended to depict written characters or some ornament for the head. This figure was so drawn on the roof that its feet were just in front of the natural seat, whilst its head and face looked directly down on anyone who stood in the entrance of the cave, but it was totally invisible from the outside. The painting was more injured by the damp and atmosphere, and had the appearance of being much more defaced and ancient than any of the others which we have seen. There were two other paintings, one on each side of the rocks, which stood on either side of the natural seat: they were carefully executed, and yet had no apparent design in them, unless they were intended to represent some fabulous species of turtle; for the natives of Australia are generally fond of narrating tales of fabulous and extraordinary animals, such as gigantic snakes, etc." (Fig. 4, see Appendix.)

With this drawing, as well as in the others, it is evident that native talent had nothing to do. Neither had, in all probability, the Malays, as the form of the dress and its colour are incompatible with anything we know of these people. Then again the same aureola surrounds the head of the figure, and we are inclined to think that this drawing is due to the same artist who painted those already described. Although Grey believes that it is a more ancient production, the face of it having suffered more than the other is in all probability due to it being more exposed to atmospheric, or other influences, rather than to its greater antiquity. There are, however, some very interesting points to examine in this drawing, and in the first place our attention is drawn to the curious signs inscribed on the aureola surrounding the head.

At first sight, an illiterate person would at once exclaim, "these are Latin characters."

G I T I L F

Five out of six undoubtedly are such, and the sixth appears to be part of an unfinished or defaced letter, probably F or E. This is evidently very remarkable, and more so is the fact which a closer examination discloses that near the right shoulder of the figure two additional characters, c d, also undoubtedly of Latin form, are there inscribed, proving the European origin of this drawing, which resembles exactly those paintings of the middle ages, representing some holy monk or nun in their habilaments, of a coarse, brown cloth, the hands, and still more so the feet in that, position which painters of religious subjects have rendered us so familiar with on the old church windows, and other paintings of those times. The practice of printing the name of the saint on the aureola encircling the head is also a common one, and perhaps we may find there an explanation of that painting, which will also prove the others to be of like origin. These characters are, undoubtedly, Latin, whichever way one might like to turn them, and their appearance in such a spot is not due to chance alone. It would be a difficult task to attempt to explain their meaning, but, perhaps, a further exploration of these singular caves may bring to light information leading to their identification and explanation. Suffice it to say that they certainly tend to show the European and Christian character of these paintings, the first one probably representing the holy women praying before the Virgin, and the other some holy nun, as the line over the chin seems to indicate the well-known head-dress. It may be objected that the Virgin could hardly have been pourtrayed in such a

costume, to which the answer may be made, that it was a common custom at the time, among the disciples of Francis Xavier who
evangelised India, to represent the Virgin and the saints in the costume
of the country, in order to bring them in an easier way to the conception of the native mind, a practice, need it be added, which brought on
the head of the Jesuits the most severe condemnation.

If such is the case, and if these paintings are, as we believe,
the work of Europeans, we might look in their vicinity for some other
and still more convincing proof of their origin.

Such is afforded also, and the evidence is telling.

For the last time we shall quote the same eminent author, and
at page 205 of vol. 1. of his work, we read:--
"After proceeding some distance, we found a cave larger than the one
seen this morning; of its actual size, however, I have no idea, for being
pressed for time I did not attempt to explore it, having merely ascertained that it contained no paintings. I was moving on when we
observed a profile of a human face and head, cut out in a sandstone
rock which fronted the cave; this rock was so hard that to have removed such a large portion of it with no better tool than a knife and
hatchet made of stone, such as the Australian natives generally possess, would have been a work of very great labour. The head was two
feet in length, and sixteen inches in breadth in the broadest part; the
depth of the profile increased gradually from the edges where it was
nothing, to the centre where it was an inch and a half. The ear was
rather badly placed, but otherwise the whole of the work was good,
and far superior to what a savage race could be supposed capable of
executing. The only proof of antiquity that it bore about it was that all
the edges of the cutting were rounded and perfectly smooth, much
more so than they could have been from any other cause than long exposure to atmospheric influences.

"After having made a sketch of this head I returned to the
party."

Now let us examine, without prepossession or prejudice, this
remarkable sculpture, the only head sculptured in rock ever found in
Australia.

This profile is that of an European, the purity of the lines, the
perfect shape of the head, the straight and well-formed nose, the
finely-cut lips, the round chin, represent the most exact type of an
European head that it could be possible to imagine. Indeed, the fact
alone that the natives have no means of cutting out such a sculpture in
the rock, is enough to induce one to seek elsewhere for its author, and

the head is certainly not that of a Malay; the type is European, and that of the purest.

We shall go no further with this discussion, which the appearance of this sculptured profile of an European head closes on our behalf better than all volumes would do, and resume it in a few words.

De Gonneville, carried away by storms into unknown seas, lands on a coast which he estimates is situated to the south of India, and the Islands of Spices, and not far from the true course to the East Indies; at the entrance of a fine river, and in a fertile country, whose inhabitants he describes. They were in all probability of Malay stock, and there is no difficulty so far to understand his female relative having married a person of that race, the remnants of which have been met with since by other travellers.

Three hundred and thirty-five years after De Gonneville's voyage, King and Grey explore in the north-west part of Australia, a country whose description well answers to that visited by De Gonneville, and never set foot upon by Europeans in the interval. There Grey finds a river such as De Gonneville describes--a land inhabited by races that have preserved many of the customs of the "Australians" described by the Norman captain with whom, as a volunteer in the voyage, had travelled a certain Nicole Le Fevre, a man of some learning' and a kind of artist, who had pourtrayed strange beasts, etc., "utterly unknown in Christendom." In that country', at a very short distance from the coast, Grey discovers curious paintings, some strikingly resembling the pictures of saints as represented on the Church windows of the time, one of them bearing some very remarkable European letters and characters, and last of all he finds there the head of an European sculptured in the hard rock, evidently with instruments such as the natives do not possess.

What are we to conclude from these facts? That there is strong evidence that De Gonneville, who could have landed nowhere else but on Australian soil, had precisely landed on that part of the country visited by Grey, and that the paintings discovered are the work of some of his companions.

But although such evidence is strong indeed, it is not yet absolutely perfect, even for one desirous of solving the problem of fixing the exact position of the spot visited by the Norman sailor. Others, perhaps, may give a different interpretation to the figures and the characters represented above; they are, however, worthy of attracting notice, and if the result of this investigation is only to draw the attention of those who are interested in ascertaining the previous history of

the country they inhabit and love, be they members of scientific socie-
ties or of colonial governments, the task undertaken will not prove a
thankless one.

One thin. is settled, however, beyond the possibility of doubt,
and that is, that De Gonneville landed on no other soil but that of Australia, and nowhere else but at the mouth of some of the north-western
rivers.

The maps of the sixteenth century, known to have existed long
before the voyages of the Dutch and the English, bear witness to the
fact that the north-western part of the coast of Australia was sighted by
the Portuguese on their voyages to and from the East Indies and the
Spice Islands.

A critical examination of these charts, some of which have
been reproduced for the Public Libraries of the chief Australian cities
from the originals in the British Museums, tends to show--although
most of the names of features on the north-west coast are in French--
that some of them appear to have been translated from the Portuguese.
The older of these charts bears the date of the year 1542, but there are
two more maps in the "Bibliotheque Nationale de France" which are
still more ancient. One, which is the work of Guillaume Le Testu, a
pilot of Dieppe, shows a portion of the coast in a fairly correct position, indicating features which can easily be recognised, although their
longitude and latitude are not exact; the names, which are all in
French, do not exhibit any sign of having been translated from any
other language; and there is little doubt that Le Testu, who published
this chart in 1536, must have heard of the expedition of De Gonneville, which could hardly have failed to attract attention at the time
among the sailors of note in the ports of the Normandy coast. Considering the state of geographical science at that epoch, the delineation of
the north-west coast of the Australian continent is certainly as accurate
as that of the island of Java and minor islands in those regions, which
were much better known, and there is in this fact evidence enough that
the data upon which Le Testu, Jean Rotz, and other cartographers
worked, must have been fairly accurate. The Norman pilot shows on
his map the entrance of several rivers and features which closely resemble the outline of this coast as at present known, but except in the
vicinity of the rivers mentioned, the coast on the south and the north-
east is prolonged without data, and merely indicates a probable extension of land in these directions. The other maps agree fairly well in
this respect, the outlines of very small portions only of the coast being-
-susceptible of identification at present. From these facts we may infer

that Guillaume Le Testu probably obtained much of his information from the report of De Gonneville, whilst Rotz and the authors of the maps in the British Museum had theirs from Portuguese sources, and as the latters' delineation of the north-west coast is less accurate, it may be that the Portuguese sailors, from whose reports this information was obtained, merely sighted these coasts without attempting to land.

To close this discussion, it may be added, that in most instances the early voyages of the Dutch or possibly the Portuguese to Western Australia were the result of such accidents as befell De Gonneville, as they were carried by storms out of their course to India or the Sunda Islands, and thrown on the west coast of the Australian Continent.

The first claim to the discovery of the Australian Continent may be, therefore, settled in favor of De Gonneville; although, there is little doubt that the existence of a great southern land was suspected by the Chinese, and also by the ancients. This great land, situated on the opposite side of the world, was named by them Anti-chton, and its supposed inhabitants "Antichtones," and the fact of the possibility of it being inhabited at all gave rise to a good deal of discussion among ancient writers. They, however, agreed in the belief that "the fury of the sun, which burns the intermediate zone," rendered it inaccessible to the inhabitants of the world. Plinus, Pomponius Mela, Scipio, Virgilius, Cicero, and Macrobius considered this land as habitable, and the two last mentioned authors held the opinion that it was inhabited by a different race of beings.

This question was also debated by the early Christian fathers, and perhaps the most remarkable argument against the existence of the Antichtones will be found in the works of the celebrated theologian and venerated father, St. Augustine, who devotes the whole of Chapter IX., Book XVI. of his admirable work, "De Civitate Dei," to the discussion of this knotty question.

"Quod verò," writes St. Augustine, "Antipodes esse fabulantur, id est, homines a contaria parte terrae, ubi sol oritur, quando occidit nobis, adversa pedibus nostris calcare vestigia, nulla ratione credendum est. Neque hoc ulla historica cognitione didicisse se affirmant, sed quali ratiocinando conjectant, es quod intra con vexa coeli terra suspenda sit, eum demque locum mundas habeat, et infirmum, et medium: et ex hoc opinantur alteram terra pattern, quae infra est, habitatione hominum carere non posse. Nec adtendunt, etiamsi figura conglobata et rotunda mundus esse credatur, sive aliqua ratione monstretur; non tamen esse consequens, ut etiam ex illa parte ab aquarum congerie nuda sit terra devide etiamus nuda sit, neque hoc statum necesse esse, ut homines habeat, Quoniam nulla modo Scriptura ista mentitur, quae narratis praeteritis facis sidem, eo quod ejus praedicta complentur: nimisque absurdurn est, ut dicatur aliquos hornines ex hae in illam partem, oceani immensitate trajecta, navigare ac pervenive potuisse, ut etiarn illic ex uno illo primo hornine genus institueretur hurnanurn?"

The substance of which is: "That there can be nothing more absurd than the belief of some ancient writers who imagined that the land on the opposite side of the world could be inhabited by human beings. Those who made this assertion admit they have no historical fact to base it upon, and that it is merely a logical deduction of philosophy. But if we accept as true the principles upon which they base their arguments, is it to be necessarily admitted that because these countries are habitable, that they are in reality inhabited. As the Holy Scripture, which is our guide in all matters of belief, makes no mention of this, and as it is an accepted fact that the descendants of our first parents could not have sailed to and reached these countries, how is it possible that they could be inhabited."

Although the existence of a great Austral land was a subject of philosophical and theological discussion among the ancients, they, however, never attempted to sail across that ocean which was the limit of the world they knew. It is possible that the Chinese may have been more bold, but it is very doubtful whether they ever sailed so far south as to land on the coast of the Australian continent. They have left no trace of their passage, either on the land itself, or among its inhabitants. Besides, the Chinese were never very enterprising sailors, the form of their junks, their peculiar sails, and the scantiness of their nautical knowledge prevented them from extending very far the radius of their maritime explorations. Marco Polo is the authority generally quoted in this matter, as he states that the people of Cathay knew of the existence of a great land far to the southward, with the inhabitants of which they were accustomed to trade. This is rather an indefinite description, and might apply to New Guinea as well as to the Australian Continent. More so to the former and the islands surrounding it on the north and east, where evidence exists of the voyage of the Chinese traders and fishermen in search of the precious trepang. But as these holothuriae are generally found in the vicinity of the coral banks of Polynesia, to the eastward of New Guinea, and not in the direction of the Australian coast, there is much reason to think that the Chinese claim to the discovery of this continent is purely mythical, although, like the ancients, they may have believed in its existence as a logical deduction of philosophy.

Chapter XVI

Captain Cook compared to former Visitors--Point Hicks--Botany Bay-First natives seen--Indifference to Overtures--Abundant flora--Entrance to Port Jackson missed--Endeavour on a reef--Careened--Strange animals--Hostile natives--A sailor's devil--Possession Island-Territory of New South Wales--Torres Straits a passage--La Perouse--Probable fate discovered by Captain Dillon--M'Cluer touches Arnheim's Land--Bligh and Portlock--Wreck of the Pandora--Vancouver in the south--The D'Entrecasteaux quest--Recherche Archipelago--Bass and Flinders--Navigation and exploration extraordinary--The Tom Thumb--Bass explores south--Flinders in the Great Bight--Bass's Straits--Flinders in the Investigator--Special instructions--King George's Sound--Loss of boat's crew--Memory Cove--Baudin's courtesy--Port Phillip--Investigator and Lady Nelson on East Coast--The Gulf of Carpentaria and early Dutch navigators--Duyfhen Point--Cape Keer-Weer--Mythical rivers charted--Difficulty in recognising their landmarks--Flinders' great disappointment--A rotten ship--Return by way of West Coast--Cape Vanderlin--Dutch Charts--Malay proas, Pobassoo--Return to Port Jackson--Wreck of the Porpoise--Prisoner by the French--General de Caen--Private papers and journals appropriated--Prepares his charts and logs for press--Death--Sympathy by strangers--Forgotten by Australia--The fate of Bass--Mysterious disappearance--Supposed Death.

The maritime exploration of our coast may be said to have fairly commenced on the morning of the 19th of April, 1770, when Captain Cook first sighted land. True we had many visitors before, [See Introduction.] but none had given the same attention to the work, with an eye to future colonisation, nor sailed along such an extent of shore.

The present coast of Gippsland was the place that first caught the attention of Lieutenant Hicks on that eventful morning, and Point Hicks received its name in commemoration of the incident.

From this point they sailed eastward, and at the promontory, where the coast turned to the north, the name of Cape Howe was bestowed. Cook, fresh from the shores of New Zealand and its more rugged scenery, was pleasingly impressed with his distant view of Australia, but it must have been the force of contrast only, as the portion of Australia first sighted by him is devoid of interest. No available landing place was seen; the shore was too tame, and for many days they coasted along, looking for a break, or entrance, but none could he found where a safe landing could be effected.

Botany Bay was the spot where the men from the Endeavour sprang on shore for the first time, and although the flora of the surrounding country brought joy to the heart of Mr. Banks, the botanist, it could not have held out very high hopes of the future to the others.

Here they first saw the natives, "Indians," as Cook calls them, and hoped to effect a peaceable landing. He says:--
"The place where the ship had anchored was abreast of a small village, consisting of about six or eight houses; and while we were preparing to hoist out the boat, we saw an old woman followed by three children come out of the wood; she was loaded with firewood, and each of the children had also its little burden. She often looked at the ship, but expressed neither fear nor surprise. In a short time she kindled a fire, and four canoes came in from fishing. The men landed, and having hauled up their boats, began to dress their dinner, to all appearances, wholly unconcerned about us, though we were within half-a-mile of them. We thought it remarkable that of all the people we had yet seen, not one had the least appearance of clothing, the old woman herself being destitute even of a fig leaf.

"After dinner the boats were manned, and we set out from the ship. We intended to land where we saw the people, and began to hope that as they so little regarded the ship's coming into the bay, they would as little regard our coming on shore. In this, however, we were disappointed, for as soon as we approached the rocks, two men came down upon them to dispute our landing, and the rest ran away."

For some time they parleyed with the blacks, and threw them nails, beads, and other trifles, trying to make them understand that only water was wanted, and no harm would be done them; but the natives refused all offers of friendship, and three charges of small shot had to be fired at their legs before they would even allow a peaceable landing.

Many expeditions were made inland for plants, birds, and flowers, also to try if some intercourse could be established with the natives, but after the first contest they would not come near enough to speak to. Nor did they touch any of the presents--beads, ribbons, and cloth, that had been left about and in their huts.

The great quantity of plants collected here by Mr. Banks induced Cook to give it the name of Botany Bay. The King's colours were hoisted each day of the stay, and the ship's name with the date of the year was inscribed upon one of the trees near the watering place.

Having now provided a supply of fresh water, the anchor was weighed on the 6th of May, and they sailed northward. Unaware of what he had missed, Cook passed the entrance of Port Jackson, and followed up the coast for over a thousand miles to the north, without incident or adventure, beyond the routine work of the ship. But, on June 10th, this quiet was rudely broken by the Endeavour running on a coral reef when off the site of the present town of Cooktown. Fortunately a jagged point of coral stuck in the hole made, and acted as a plug, otherwise this voyage of Cook's would have proved his last, and the history of this continent been much delayed and altered.

Passing a sail under the hull, and throwing guns and other stores overboard, Cook got his ship once more afloat, and took her into the mouth of a river (now the Endeavour River) where, on a convenient beach, she was careened, and the carpenters set to work to repair her, whilst a forge was set up, and the smiths occupied making bolts and nails. Many animals strange to them were seen, and among them the first kangaroo. One of the firemen who had been rambling in the woods, told them, on his return, that he verily believed he had seen the devil.

"We naturally enquired in what form he had appeared, and his answer was in so singular a style, that I shall set it down in his own words. 'He was,' says John, 'as large as a one gallon keg, and very like it; he had horns and wings, yet he crept so slowly through the grass that if I had not been afeared, I might have touched him.' This formidable apparition we afterwards discovered to have been a bat. They have indeed no horns, but the fancy of a man who thought he saw the devil might easily supply that defect."

Many excursions Mr. Banks and the men made inland, finding one very useful plant, at the time when scurvy had appeared among them, a plant that in the West Indies is called Indian Kale, and served them for greens.

Some communication was established with the natives, but it ended as usual by their commencing to steal, and having to be chastised for it. In revenge they set fire to the grass, and the navigator very nearly lost his whole stock of gunpowder. He was astonished by the extreme inflammability of the grass and the consequent difficulty in putting it out, and vowed if ever he had to camp in such a situation again, he would first clear the grass around. Leaving the Endeavour River, Cook, after passing through the Barrier Reef and again repassing it, as he says, "After congratulating ourselves upon passing the reef we again congratulate ourselves upon repassing it," landed no more until he had left Cape York, and there on an island called "Possession Island," he formally took possession of the east coast of New Holland, under the name of New South Wales, for his Majesty King George III.

"As I was about to quit the eastern coast of New Holland, which I had coasted from latitude 38 deg. to this place, and which I am confident no European had ever seen before, I once more hoisted English colours, and though I had already taken possession of several particular parts, I now took possession of the whole eastern coast, from latitude 38 deg. to this place, latitude 10 deg. 30 min., in right of his Majesty King George the Third, by the name of New South Wales, with all the bays, harbours, rivers, and islands situated upon it. We then fired three volleys of small arms, which were answered by the same number from the ship."

This ceremony concluded, and rejoicing in the re-discovery of Torres Straits--the waters of which had borne no keel since the gallant Spaniard had passed through--he sailed to New Guinea, Cook having thus completed the survey of that portion of the South Land so long left a blank upon the map, never returned--unless his visit to Van Dieman's Land, in 1777, can be called a visit-to our shores, but the names he bestowed on the many bays, headlands, and islands of the east coast have clung to them ever since. So accurate were his surveys, even under extreme difficulties, that he left little for his successors to do but investigate those portions of the coast he had been forced to overlook.

But Cook's fame and career are such household words amongst all English-speaking races, and the results of his visit to Australia so extensive, that no space that this history could afford would be sufficiently large to appreciate the merits of his work.

When Phillip landed in Botany Bay he was followed, as is well known, by the distinguished French navigator, La Perouse, and although the name of this unfortunate man does not enter largely into the history of our colonisation, it is essential that it should come under notice. After a short stay, La Perouse sailed from Australian shores, and of him and his stately ships no tidings ever reached Europe. Years passed, and Captain Dillon, the master of an English vessel trading amongst the South Sea Islands, found a sword-belt in the possession of the natives; this led to further investigations, and the hapless story was finally elucidated.

Wrecked on the coast of one of the islands, and all attempts to save the ships having proved futile, the crews took to the boats, only to suffer death from drowning or at the hands of the savages. The guns and other heavy equipment were afterwards recovered, proving beyond doubt that that was the end of the French vessels and their unhappy commander-the Leichhardt of the sea.

In 1791, Lieutenant McCluer, of the Bombay Marine, touched upon the northern coast of Arnheim's Land, but as he did not land, no result accrued to the continent from his coming.

Before his advent, however, Captain Bligh, making his way home from the spot where the mutineers of the Bounty had set him afloat, passed through Torres Straits, and sighted the mainland of Australia. Situated as he was, he could do little more than take hasty observations.

Two years afterwards, the Pandora, under Captain Edwards, struck on a reef in Torres Straits, and sank in deep water. Thirty-nine of the crew were drowned, and the remainder, destitute of almost everything, made for the coast of Australia in four boats. Edwards landed on Prince of Wales Island, but not on the mainland. He finally reached Timor, with his shipwrecked men, amongst whom were some of the mutineers of the Bounty. Many of these men had been obliged to remain on board perforce, and in no way participated in that famous mutiny. Their treatment by the captain of the Pandora, and afterwards by the English authorities, was both harsh and unjust.

In 1792, the Providence and Assistant, Captains Bligh and Portlock, sailed through the Straits, conveying the bread-fruit plant from Tahiti to the West Indies. Serving in this expedition was Lieutenant Flinders.

In 1791, Captain George Vancouver, on his way to America, came to the southern shore, and found and named King George's Sound. He landed and examined the country, but saw nothing of any consequence, and, after a short stay, sailed away to the eastward, intending to follow the coast line, but was prevented by baffling winds.

In 1793, previously to the Investigator, and in the year following Bligh and Portlock, Messrs. William Bampton and Matthew B. Alt, commanders of the ships Hormuzeer and Chesterfeld, sailed from Norfolk Island, with the intention of passing through Torres Straits by a route which the commanders did not know had been before attempted.

The terrible dangers of the Straits encountered appear to have deterred others from following them up to the time of the Investigator.

Vancouver was quickly followed in the year 1792 by M. D'Entrecasteaux, who, having with him the ships La Recherche and L'Espérance, was in quest of the fate of La Perouse. Off Termination Island-the last land seen by Vancouver--a gale sprang up, and the French ships had to seek shelter. They remained at anchor a week, and the officers made many excursions to the islands now known as the Recherche Archipelago.

He sailed along some portions of the Great Bight, which he described as of "an aspect so uniform that the most fruitful imagination could find nothing to say of it." Water failing him, he steered for Van Dieman's Land.

We now come across one of the grandest names in the history of our colony. Bass, the surgeon of the Reliance, whose work has survived him in the name of the well-known strait.

In a tiny cockle shell, the Tom Thumb, a boat of eight feet long, he and Flinders, at first but an adventurous middy, cruised around the coast and examined every inlet and opening visible, at the very peril of their lives. It is almost equal to an imaginative story of adventures to read the tale of their various trips, suffice it they did good work, and came back safely to carry that work on with better and fuller means.

A voyage to Norfolk Island interrupted their further proceedings until the next year, 1796. Bass and Flinders then again, in the Tom Thumb, left to explore a large river, said to fall in the sea some miles to the south of Botany Bay, and of which there was no indication in Cook's chart.

In 1797, Bass obtained leave to make an expedition to the southward and was furnished with a whale boat and a crew of six men. Although he sailed with only six weeks' provisions, by birds and fish caught, and abstinence, he was enabled to prolong his voyage to eleven weeks, and his labours were crowned with a success not to be expected from such frail means. In the three hundred miles of coast examined from Port Jackson to Ram Head, a number of discoveries were made that had escaped Captain Cook.

From Ram Head--the southernmost part of the coast that had been examined by Cook-Bass began to reap a rich harvest of important discoveries, and another three hundred miles followed, the appearance of which confirmed his belief in the existence of a strait between the continent and Van Dieman's Land.

It was with great reluctance he returned before verifying this belief beyond doubt of others.

In September, 1798, we find him on board the Norfolk, associated with Flinders, seeking to prove his theory. After many and strong head winds, and much delay, the two had the supreme pleasure of greeting the westward ocean, and returning to Port Jackson with the tidings.

Flinders says:--

"To the strait which had been the great object of research, and whose discovery was now completed, Governor Hunter gave, at my recommendation, the name of 'Bass's Straits.' This was no more than a just tribute to my worthy friend and companion for the extreme dangers and fatigues he had undergone in first entering it in the whale boat, and to the correct judgment he had formed, from various indications, of the existence of a wide opening between Van Dieman's Land and New South Wales."

In 1799, Flinders, in the Norfolk, followed up Cook's discoveries in the neighbourhood of Glass House Bay, and in 1801 we must accompany him on his great voyage round Terra Australis.

The north coast of Australia, both from its more interesting formation and the lack of settlement, has received a good deal of attention from our navigators of the present century, and by far the most fascinating part of Captain Flinders' log refers to the north coast.

In 1802, we find him following the track of M. D'Entrecasteaux round the Great Bight. Flinders seems to have been as much puzzled as he was regarding the great extent of level cliffs passed. He conjectures that within this bank, as he terms it, there could be nothing but sandy plains or water, and that, in all probability, it formed a barrier between an exterior and interior sea. He little thought how, some years afterwards, a lonely white man would tramp round those barren cliffs, eagerly scanning Flinders' chart for any sign of a break in their iron uniformity.

On February 16th, 1801, Matthew Flinders was promoted to the rank of commandant, and left England with the Investigator, to prosecute his voyage to Terra Australis. His instructions were:--
"To make the best of your way to New Holland, running down the coast from 130 degrees east longitude to *Bass's* Straits, putting, if you should find it necessary, into *King George the Third's Harbour* for refreshments and water, previous to your commencing the survey, and on your arrival on the coast, use your best endeavour to discover such harbours as may be in those parts, and in case you shall discover any creek or opening likely to lead to an *inland sea or strait*, you are at liberty either to examine it or not, as you 'shall judge it most expedient, until a more favourable opportunity shall enable you so to do.

"When it shall appear to you necessary, you shall repair to Sydney Cove, for the purpose of refreshing your people, refitting the sloop under your command, and consulting the Governor of New South Wales upon the best means of carrying on the survey of the coast; and having received from him such information as he may be able to communicate, and taken under your command the Lady Nelson tender, which you may expect to find in Sydney Cove, you are to recommence your survey by first diligently examining the coast from Bass's Straits to King George the Third's Harbour."

Flinders was then instructed to repair from time to time to Sydney Cove, to be very diligent in the examination, and to take particular care to insert in his journal every circumstance that might be useful to a full and complete knowledge of the coast--the wind, weather, the productions, comparative fertility of the soil, the manners and customs of the inhabitants, and to examine the country as far inland as it was prudent to venture with so small a party as could be spared from the vessel whenever a chance of discovering anything useful to the commerce or manufactures of the United Kingdom.

From thence they were to explore the north-west coast of New Holland, where, from the extreme height of tides observed by Dampier, it was thought probable valuable harbours might be found; also the Gulf of Carpentaria and the parts to the westward. When that was completed, a careful investigation and accurate survey of Torres Straits; then an examination of the whole of the remainder of the north, the west, and the north-west coasts of New Holland.
"So soon as you shall have completed the whole of these surveys and examinations as above directed, you are to proceed to, and examine very carefully the east coast of New Holland, seen by Captain Cook, from Cape Flattery to the Bay of Inlets; and in order to refresh your

people, and give the advantages of variety to the painters, you are at liberty to touch at the Fijis, or some other islands in the South Seas."

As soon as the whole of the examinations and surveys were completed, he was to lose no time in returning with the sloop under his command to England.

The vessel was fitted with a plant cabin for the purpose of making botanical collections for the Royal Gardens at Kew, and on each return to Sydney Cove, all plants, trees, shrubs, etc., were to be transferred to the Governor's garden until the Investigator sailed for Europe.

King George's Sound being chosen as the place to prepare themselves for the examination of the south coast of Terra Australis, they anchored off Point Possession, on the south side of the entrance to Princess Royal Harbour, previous to wind and water being favourable for entering the harbour to refit and procure wood and fresh water.

Many excursions were made by the naturalist, botanist, and artist, and a new survey of King George's Sound made.
"On the east side of the entrance to Princess Royal Harbour we landed, and found a spot of ground six or eight feet square dug up and trimmed like a garden, and upon it was lying a piece of sheet copper bearing this inscription:--

"'AUGUST 27TH 1800. CHR. DIXON.'--SHIP ELLEGOOD.'"

This answered the finding of the felled trees on Point Possession, also of the disappearance of the bottle left by Captain Vancouver in 1791, containing parchment that Flinders had looked for on landing.

In Flinders' description of the country in the neighbourhood of King George's Sound he says:--
"The basis stone is granite, which frequently shows itself at the surface in the form of smooth, bare rock; but upon the sea-coast hills and the shores on the south side of the sound and Princess Royal Harbour the granite is generally covered with a crust of calcareous stone, as it is also upon Michaelmas Island. Captain Vancouver mentions having found upon the top of Bald Head branches of coral protruding through the sand, exactly like those seen in the coral beds beneath the surface of the sea--a circumstance which would seem to bespeak this country to have emerged from the ocean at no very distant period of time.

"This curious fact I was desirous to verify, and his description proved to be correct. I found, also, two broken columns of stone, three or four feet high, formed like stumps of trees, and of a thickness superior to the body of a man, but whether this was coral or wood now petrified, or whether they might not have been calcareous rocks worn into that particular form by the weather I cannot determine. Their elevation above the present level of the sea could not have been less than four hundred feet."

On January 4th, 1802, a bottle containing parchment, to inform future visitors of their arrival and departure, was left on the top of Seal Island, and on the morrow they sailed out of King George's Sound to continue the survey eastwards. They anchored on the 28th in Fowler's Bay--the extremity of the then known south coast of Terra Australis.

Off Cape Catastrophe, a cutter, with eight men, was sent on shore in search of an anchorage where water could be procured. Nothing of the boat and crew was again seen but the wreck of the boat showing that it had been stove in by the rocks. After a careful but hopeless search for the men, their pressing need for water caused them to abandon further delay, and they left to examine the opening to the northward.

"I caused an inscription to be engraven upon a sheet of copper, and set it up on a stout post at the head of the cove, which I named Memory Cove, and further to commemorate our loss, I gave each of the six islands nearest to Cape Catastrophe the name of one of the seamen."

Flinders sailed up the gulf, which he called Spencer's Gulf, and had a long look towards the interior from the summit of Mount Brown.

The Gulf of St. Vincent then fell to his share to discover, and shortly afterwards he met with the French ship Le Géographe Captain Baudin; says Flinders:--

"We veered round as *Le Géographe* was passing, so as to keep our broadside to her, lest the flag of truce should be a deception, and having come to the wind on the other tack, a boat was hoisted out, and I went on board the French ship, which had also hove to."

The two Captains exchanged passports and information, but Flinders was afterwards much annoyed to find on the publication of M. Péron's book, that all his late discoveries had been rechristened with French names, and, in fact, his work ignored completely. Parting from the French ship in Encounter Bay, as he named it, the English navigator sailed for Port Jackson.

Suddenly coming to the Harbour of Port Phillip, Flinders thinks he has entered Port Western, but finds his mistake next morning; then congratulates himself upon having made a new and most useful discovery, he says:--

"There I was again in error, this place, as I afterwards learned in Port Jackson had been discovered ten weeks before by Lieutenant John Murray, in command of the Lady Nelson. He had given to it the name of Port Phillip, and to the rocky point on the east side of the entrance Point Nepean."

On the 9th May, the Investigator anchors in Sydney Cove, and again left in company with the Lady Nelson, on the morning Of July 22nd, for the examination of the east coast, making many discoveries before reaching Torres Straits that had escaped Captain Cook, among others Port Curtis and Port Bowen.

The Lady Nelson in consequence of being disabled left the Investigator on the east coast, and returned to Port Jackson.

We will again take up Flinders' narrative during his examination of the Gulf of Carpentaria, which had not been visited since the days of the Dutch ships. The first point Flinders mentions finding corroborative of the fidelity of their charts is the entrance to the Batavia River and there is no doubt that this spot is indicated by the words "fresh water," in the map accredited to Tasman, as there is a capital boat entrance of two fathoms to this stream, and at a comparatively short distance from the mouth of the water at low tide is quite fresh. This river heads from a plateau of springs, a tableland covered with scrubby heath, and intersected by scores of running gullies, boggy and impassable; in fact, the same country as caused such trouble to the Jardine brothers when they explored this shore of the Gulf.

From this place, however, Flinders seems very doubtful as to the identity of some of the rivers laid down. One point, the most remarkable on the coast, and which Yet was not in the Dutch chart, Flinders named "Duyfhen Point," and another, he called "Pera Head," after the second yacht that entered the Gulf.

At Cape Keer-Weer he fairly gives in that he could see nothing approaching a cape, but a slight projection being visible from the mast-head, out of respect to antiquity, he puts it down on his map. The "Vereenidge River" he concludes, has no existence, and the "Nassau River" turned out to be a lagoon at the back of a beach. Still the existence of anything approaching the reality of what was indicated on the charts, proves that at any rate the ships had been there, even if they had not kept close enough to the land to be quite certain of what they saw. So shallow is the approach to this shore, that when so far from land even at the mast-head the tops of the trees could only be partially distinguished, Flinders only found from four to six fathoms of water.

Of the Staaten River he says that--"Where that river can be found I know not," and at last he begins to fancy that the formation of the mouths of the rivers must have altered since Tasman's time.

Reaching the head of the Gulf, Flinders sighted a hill, which gave him hope of a change in the flat monotony of the coast he had now followed for one hundred and seventy-five leagues. This Will, which turned out to 'be an island, Flinders judged to be a headland marked on the western side of "Maatsuyker's River." The river he failed to discover, to the island he gave the name of Sweer's Island. Here Flinders remained some time, having found fresh water. and an anchorage adapted to cleaning and caulking his ship. But a great disappointment awaited him. The report of the master and carpenter who overhauled the Investigator, was to the effect that the ship was perfectly rotten. It ends in these words:--

"From the state to which the ship seems now advanced, it is our joint opinion that in twelve months there will scarcely be a sound timber in her; but that if she remains in fine weather and happen no accident, she may run six months longer without much risk."

This was a death blow to Flinders' hope of so completing the survey of the coast, that no after work should be necessary. Under the circumstances, he determined to finish the exploration of the Gulf, and then to proceed to Port Jackson by way of the west coast, should the ship prove capable, if not to make for the nearest port in the West Indies.

Leaving Sweer's Island, Flinders next investigated Cape Van Dieman, and found it to be an island, which he called Mornington Island. Cape Vanderlin of the Dutch was the next point sighted, and it too was an island, one of the Sir Edward Pellew Group. On taking leave of this group, Flinders remarks on these discrepancies as follows:--

"In the old Dutch charts, Cape Vanderlin is represented to be a great projection from the mainland, and the outer ends of North and West Islands to be smaller points of it. There are two indents or bights marked between the points which may correspond to the opening between the islands, but I find a difficulty in pointing out which are tile four small isles laid down on the west of Cape Vanderlin; neither does the line of the coast, which is nearly W.S.W. in the old chart, correspond with that of the outer ends of the islands, and yet there is enough of similitude in the whole to show the identity. Whether any changes have taken place in these shores, and made islands of what were parts of the mainland a century and a half before--or whether the Dutch discoverer made a distant and cursory examination, and brought conjecture to aid him in the construction of a chart, as was too much the practice of that time-it is not now possible to ascertain, but I conceive that the great alteration produced in the geography of these parts by our survey, gives authority to apply a name which, without prejudice to the original one, should mark the nation by which the survey was made. I have called the cluster of islands Sir Edward Pellew Group."

As no marked change has taken place since Flinders' survey, we may conclude that his last conclusion is the right one, and that a great deal in conjecture was brought to bear on the construction of the chart.

Still following the bend of the gulf, Flinders next ascertained that Cape Maria was only an island (Maria Island) and so with many points up to the northern termination of the Gulf. Along part of the southern and most western shore of Carpentaria many indications of the Malay visits were found--scraps of bamboo, rude stone fireplaces, and stumps of mangrove trees, cut down with iron axes. When amongst the English Company's Islands, a fleet of proas was met with, fishing for trepang. A friendly interview was obtained with them, and from the chief, Pobassoo, Flinders learnt that this was the sixth or seventh voyage that he had made to the Australian coast. He had a great horror of the pigs on board the Investigator, but a decided liking for the port wine with which he was regaled.

The state of his vessel now decided Flinders to relinquish the survey, thinking himself fortunate in having escaped any heavy weather.

"We had continued the survey of the coast for more than one-half of the six months the master and carpenter had judged the ship might run without much risk, provided she remained in fine weather, and no accidents happened; and the remainder of the time being not much more than necessary for us to reach Port Jackson, I judged it imprudent to continue the investigation longer. In addition, the state of my own health, and that of the ship's company, were urgent to terminate the examination here . . . . It was, however, not without much regret that I quitted the coast . . . . The accomplishment of the survey was, in fact, an object so near my heart, that could I have foreseen the train of ills that were to follow the decay of the *Investigator*, and prevent the survey being resumed-and had my existence depended upon the expression of a wish--I do not know that it would have received utterance."

Thinking himself fortunate in escaping any heavy weather, he sailed for Coepang, and from there to Port Jackson.

In July, 1803, in the Porpoise, Captain Flinders, with the officers and men of the Investigator, left Port Jackson for England, to procure another vessel to continue the survey left incomplete on the north coast, but were wrecked on Wreck Reef, and afterwards taken prisoners by the French.

His subsequent career and early death were both unhappy, and no effort has been made by either England or Australia to do tardy justice to his name. After his shameful detention in the Isle of France, and his reluctant release, he returned to England to find his rightful promotion in the navy had been passed over during his long years of captivity, and that the licensed bravo of Napoleon, General de Caen, had retained (stolen would be the right word) his private journals; and it was only after much trouble and correspondence between the two Governments that they were restored. Flinders completed the work of his life by preparing for the press his charts and logs, and died on the 14th June, 1814, of-there is every reason to believe--a broken heart.

Captain King, when he visited the Isle of France after his Australian surveys, speaks with pride of the kindly memory entertained by the residents for the unfortunate Flinders, and the contempt bestowed upon his cowardly gaoler.

Australia at the time of the explorer's detention was not certainly in a position to demand his liberation. But what has been done since? Sir John Franklin, an official visitor to our shores, erected a memorial to him in the little township of Port Lincoln--a tribute to a brother sailor. Ask the average native-born Australian of the southern colonies about Flinders. He will tell you that it is the name of a street in Melbourne. In Queensland, the boy will say that it is the name of a river somewhere in the colony. That is the amount of honour Australia has bestowed on her greatest navigator.

What was the fate of his companion, Bass?

After the return from the investigation of Bass's Straits, the young surgeon shipped on board an armed merchant vessel on a voyage to South America. At Valparaiso the governor of the town refused to allow the vessel to trade. Bass, who was then in command, threatened to bombard the town if the refusal was not withdrawn. It was rescinded, but, watching their opportunity, the authorities seized Bass when he was off his guard, and it is supposed that he was sent to the mines in the interior, where he died. He was never heard of again, nor was any attempt made to ascertain his fate.

Not only can we admire both of these men for their dauntless courage, so often tried, but all their work on the coast of Australia was done with no hope of ulterior gain for themselves; their one thought was the extension of geographical knowledge and the benefit of their fellow men.

Chapter XVII

The French Expedition--Buonaparte's lavish outfitting--Baudin in the Géographe--Coast casualties--Sterile and barren appearance--Privations of the crew--Sails for Timor--Hamelin in the Naturaliste--Explores North-Western coast--Swan River--Isle of Rottnest--Joins her consort at Coepang--Sails for Van Dieman's Land--Examination of the South-East coast of Australia--Flinders' prior visit ignored--French names substituted--Discontent among crew--Baudin's unpopularity--Bad food--Port Jackson--Captain King's Voyages--Adventures in the Mermaid--An extensive commission--Allan Cunningham, botanist--Search at Seal Islands for memorial of Flinders' visit--Seed sowing--Jeopardy to voyage--Giant anthills--An aboriginal Stoic--Cape Arnhem and west coast exploration--Macquarie Strait--Audacity of natives--Botanical results satisfactory--Malay Fleet--Raffles Bay--Port Essington--Attack by natives--Cape Van Dieman--Malay Teachings--Timor and its Rajah--Return to Port--Second Voyage--Mermaid and Lady Nelson--East Coast--Cleveland Bay--Cocoa-nuts and pumice stones--Endeavour River--Thieving natives--Geological formation of adjacent country--Remarkable coincidences--Across Gulf of Carpentaria--Inland excursion--Cambridge Gulf--Ophthalmia amongst crew--Mermaid returns to port.

The voyage of the Géographe and Naturaliste, under Commander Baudin, was undertaken whilst the explorations of Flinders were in progress, and their meeting on the south coast, and the subsequent substitution of French for English names, led to a very sore feeling on the part of the English navigator.

The expedition was under the special sanction of Buonaparte, and there is little doubt was mainly dictated by his morbid jealously of the maritime supremacy of England.

Even at the time when the army of reserve was on the move to cross the Alps, he found leisure to attend to the details of the projected expedition and nominate twenty-three persons to accompany the ships and make scientific observations. "Astronomers, geographers, mineralogist, botanists, zoologists, draftsmen, horticulturists, all were found ready in number, double, treble, or even quintreple."

"Particular care had been taken that the stores might be abundant and of the best quality. The naval stores at Havre were entirely at the disposal of our commander. Considerable sums were granted him for the purchase of supplies of fresh provisions, such as wines, liquors, syrups, sweetmeats of different kinds, portable soups, Italian pastes, dry lemonade, extracts of beer, etc., some filtering vessels, hand mills, stoves, apparatus for distilling, etc., had been shipped on board each vessel."

Added to which a national medal was struck to preserve the memory of the undertaking, and unlimited credit opened on the principal colonies in Asia and Africa.

Think of Flinders in the crazy old Investigator, of King and Cunningham cramped up in the Mermaid, where the cabin was not big enough for their mess-table, and imagine with what scorn they would have looked on these luxurious preparations.

M. Péron writes:--

"On the shores to which we were destined were many interesting nations. It was the wish of the First Consul, that as deputies of Europe, we should conciliate these uninformed people, and appear among them as friends and benefactors. By his order the most useful animals were embarked in our vessels, a number of interesting trees and shrubs were collected in our ships, with quantities of such seeds as were most congenial to the temperature of the climate. The most useful tools, clothing, and ornaments of every sort were provided for them; even the most particular inventions in optics, chemistry, and natural philosophy were contributed for their advantage, or to promote their pleasure."

Certainly if M. Baudin failed it would not be the fault of the First Consul.

On the 27th of May, 18oi, the coast of New Holland was made--"a blackish stripe from the north to the south was the humble profile of the continent first caught sight of." Their first acquaintance with the coast was not encouraging. Landing at Géographe Bay to examine a river reported to be there, the longboat was lost, a sailor named Vasse drowned, and the Naturaliste lost two anchors. The ships now parted company, the Géographe steering north to Dirk Hartog's Road, or Shark's Bay. Here they waited some time for the appearance of the Naturaliste, but that vessel not appearing, the Géographe sailed north, and on the 27th July they were in the neighbourhood of the much visited Rosemary Island. On the 5th of August the Lacepede Islands were found and named, but no landings were effected, and the voyagers described the appearance of the islands as "hideously sterile."

"In the midst of these numerous islands there is not anything to delight the mind. The soil is naked; the ardent sky seems always clear and without clouds; the waves are scarcely agitated, except by the nocturnal tempests: man seems to fly from these ungrateful shores, not a part of which, at least as far as we could distinguish, had the smallest trace of his presence. The aspect is altogether the most whimsical and savage, at all parts raising itself into a thousand different shapes of sandy, sterile, and chalky isles, many of them resembling immense antique tombs; some of them appear united by chains of reefs, others protected by immense sand-banks, and all that one could see of the continent displayed the same sterility, and the same monotony of colour and appearance. The dismayed and astonished navigator turns away his eyes, fatigued with the contemplation of these unhappy isles and hideous solitudes, surrounded, as he views them, with continual dangers; and when he reflects that these inhospitable shores border those of the archipelago of Asia, on which nature has lavished blessings and treasures, he can scarcely conceive how so vast a sterility could be produced in the neighbourhood of such great fecundity. We continued to range the coast, which seemed to make part of the archipelago, everywhere bordered with reefs and quicksands, against which the sea struck with violence, and varied itself as it were in sheafs of foam. Never was such a spectacle before presented to our observation. 'These breakers,'" says M. Boulanger, in his journal, "'seem to form several parallel lines at the shore, and little distant one from the other, above which the waves are seen raising themselves, successively breaking with great fury, and forming a horrible cascade of about fifteen leagues in length. We navigated at this time in the midst of shallows; the lead found only at times six fathoms. Then, though more distant from the land, we were not out of sight of it. This part of New Holland is truly frightful. All the islands that we could reconnoitre presented alike hideous characters of sterility. We continued to sail in the midst of shallows and sandbanks, compelled to repeatedly tack, and avoiding one danger only to fall into another.'"

Their privations were very heavy at this time; the food to which they had been reduced since their departure from the Isle of

France had affected the health even of the strongest, and the scurvy increased its ravages. Added to that, the allowance of water beginning to fail, and their belief in the utter impossibility of taking any from these shores, the Géographe, after naming the archipelago of the north-west coast, Buonapartes, a name now obsolete, sailed for Timor, and here, after a lapse of some time, was joined by her consort. The stay at Coepang was a long one, for scurvy and sickness was rife amongst the crews and many died.

During the time Captain Hamelin of the Naturaliste was absent from his consort, he had been busy along the coast. The Swan River was explored by Bailly the naturalist, and the island of Rottnest examined.

"The River of Swans," says M. Bailly, .'was discovered in 1697 by Vlaming, and was thus named by him, from the great number of black swans he there saw. The river cannot be considered as proper to supply the water necessary for a ship; in the first place it is difficult to enter, and its course is obstructed by many shoals and sandbank; and secondly, the distance from the mouth of the river is too great before we can find any fresh water.

"In the meantime the days fixed by Captain Hamelin to wait for the Géographe had expired, and we had heard nothing of her, nor did it now appear likely that we should obtain any news of her by staying any longer on this coast, we therefore determined to sail for Endracht's Land, leaving on this island of Rottnest a flag, and a bottle with a letter for the Commander, in case he should touch there."

Leaving the Isle of Rottnest, they sailed north, intending to examine the shore, but the wind compelled them to keep off the land. After several attempts they succeeded in keeping near enough to distinguish the general constitution of the soil, and pronounced this part of Edel's Land of the same melancholy appearance as the shore of Leeuwin's Land. On the 9th of July they were in sight of the Isles of Turtel-Duyf and the Abrolhos, on which Pelsart was wrecked in the year 1629. Their first care on anchoring in the "Bay of Sea-dogs"--or Shark's Bay--so called by Dampier--was to find if the Géographe was there, or had been there, this being the second rendezvous appointed. No signs being found, they concluded to wait eight or ten days in the hope she would appear.

"Our chief coxswain, on his return from the island of Dirck Hartighs, brought us a pewter plate of about six inches in diameter, on which was roughly engraven two Dutch inscriptions, the first dated 25th of October, 1616, and the second dated 4th of February, 1697. This plate had been found on the northern point of the island, which for this reason we named Cape Inscription. When found it was half covered with sand, near the remains of a post of oak-wood, to which it seemed to have been originally nailed.

"After having carefully copied these two inscriptions, Captain Hamelin had another post made and erected on the spot, and replaced the plate in the same place where it had been found. Captain Hamelin would have thought it sacrilege to carry away this plate, which had been respected for near two centuries of time, and by all navigators who might have visited these shores. The Captain also ordered to be placed on the N.E. of the island a second plate, on which was inscribed the name of our corvette, and the date of our arrival on these shores."

Evidently M. de Freycinet had no such veneration for antiquity, for on his return from the voyage round the world he subsequently made, he is reported to have carried the relic home and deposited it in the Museum of the Institute in Paris.

Having done much to determine the size and formation of the great bight called Shark's Bay, the Naturaliste resumed her voyage, and joined her consort at Coepang, finding the Géographe had arrived there more than a month before. The Naturaliste, more fortunate than her companion, had few cases of scurvy on board, owing principally to their many and long stoppages on shore.

The ships in September took their departure from Timor for Van Dieman's Land, having on board a large proportion of sick. On drawing near the coast, the humidity of the climate and short allowance of water caused many deaths.

"On the 2nd of December, in 15 deg., we observed the first bird of paradise--the most beautiful of equatorial sea-birds. On the 22nd we saw more of them, and on this day we passed the Tropic of Capricorn. Thus these observations agree with what is so elegantly said by Buffon on the limits of the climates in which these beautiful birds are seen.

"Following the chariot of the sun in the burning zone between the tropics, ranging continually beneath that ardent sky, without ever exceeding the extreme boundaries of the route of the mighty stars of heaven, it announces to the navigator his approaching passage under the celestial signs.

"On the 29th of December, the sea appeared covered with janthines, the most beautiful of the testaceous molusques. This jellyfish, by means of a bunch of small vesicles filled with air, floats on the surface of the waters. On this shining shell I discovered a new kind of crustaceous animal, of a beautiful ultramarine blue, like the shell; I knew this to be a Pinnothera. This discovery is so much the more interesting, as it does not appear that any of these adhesive animals were ever before found in univalve shells. On this same day died my colleague, M. Levillian. During his stay in Dampier's Bay, he had made a fine collection of shells and petrifactions, which form long banks on these shores, and which are so much the more interesting, as most of them seem to have their living resemblance at the feet of the same rocks, which are composed of these petrified shells."

On their departure from Timor the ships sailed for Van Dieman's Land, having on board a large proportion of sick, and losing many lives on the way.

Through calms and wind they had much difficulty in doubling Cape Leeuwin, and on the 10th of January, 1802, they sighted the southern coast of Van Dieman's Land, and devoted some time to the examination of that island, finding many discrepancies in the chart of D'Entrecasteaux.

Sailing up the east coast, the Géographe sighted the mainland of Australia on the 28th March, near Wilson's Promontory, most carefully examining and naming all capes, bays, and harbours, little thinking that they were directly after Flinders. Whilst off this shore, the encounter with the Investigator took place, which has before been referred to. After the ships parted, Baudin continued along the south coast, already surveyed by Flinders, which he re-christened Napoleon's Land, and in Péron's narrative no reference at all is made to Flinders' prior investigation.

The French claim to the discovery and names of these shores was not received in France until after the publication of Flinders' book, which took place the day after his death.

Throughout the voyage Baudin had greatly embittered himself with his crew. He showed no sympathy nor care for the sick, and was harsh and unfeeling in his conduct to all on board; in fact, he is blamed for the constant presence of scurvy that had decimated his men. He seemed utterly to ignore all precautions for health, and refused to take the many preventatives that were accessible to prevent that dread disease. After the magnificent preparations that had been made, it is astonishing to read of the state of the ship before entering Port Jackson. M. Péron writes:--

"Several of our men had already been committed to the deep already more than the half of our seamen were incapable of service from the shocking ravages of scurvy, and only two of our helmsmen were able to get on deck. The daily increase of this epidemic was alarming to an extreme degree, and, in fact, how should it be otherwise?

"Three-quarters of a bottle of stinking water was our daily allowance; for more than a year we had not tasted wine; we had not even a single drop of brandy, instead was substituted half a bottle of a bad sort of rum, made in the Isle of France, and there only used by the black slaves. The biscuit served out was full of insects; all our salt provisions were putrid and rotten, and both the smell and taste were so offensive that the almost famished seamen sometimes preferred suffering all the extremities of want itself to eating these unwholesome provisions, and, even in the presence of their commander, often threw their allowance into the sea.

"Besides, there were no comforts of any kind for the sick. The officers and naturalists were strictly reduced to the same allowance as the seamen, and suffered with them the same afflictions of body and mind."

With unlimited credit and a princely outfit, this state of things did not speak well for the captain's management.

The sickness of his crew and want of provisions compelled the French commander to make for Port Jackson, and on arrival they heard of the safety of the Naturaliste, that vessel having parted from them off the coast of Van Dieman's Land and arrived there earlier, but left in search of them a few days before the Géographe made the port.

From Port Jackson the Naturaliste went home to France, the Géographe, in company with a small vessel purchased in Sydney, and placed in charge of Lieutenant Freycinet, pursuing her geographical labours in other parts of the world.

The many voyages of Captain P. P. King, son of the Governor of that name, are some of the most adventurous voyages ever chronicled in our history. On the 22nd December, in a tiny cutter called the Mermaid, he left Sydney for the first of his survey trips. It was the year 1817, and his mission was:--

"To examine the hitherto unexplored coasts of New South Wales from Arnhem Bay, near the western entrance of the Gulf of Carpentaria, westward and southward, as far as the North-West Cape, including the opening, or deep bay, called Van Dieman's Bay, and the cluster of islands called Rosemary Islands, also the inlets behind them, which should be most minutely examined; and, indeed, all gulfs and openings should be the objects of particular attention, as the chief motive for sour survey is to discover whether there be any river on that part of the coast likely to lead to an interior navigation into this great continent.

318

"It is for several reasons most desirable that you should arrive on this coast and commence your survey as early as possible, and you m-ill therefore, when the vessel shall be ready, lose no time in proceeding to the unexplored coasts, but you are at liberty to commence your survey at whichever side you may judge proper, giving a preference to that which you think you may be able soonest to reach, but in case you think that indifferent, my Lords would wish you to commence by the neighbourhood of the Rosemary Islands.

"Either on your way out, or on returning, you should examine the coast between Cape Leeuwin and the Cape Gosselin, in M. De Freycinet's chart, and generally you will observe that it is very desirable that you should visit those ranges of coast which the French navigators have either not seen at all, or at too great a distance to ascertain and lay down accurately."

Captain King was further instructed to take from Port Jackson seeds of all vegetables that he considered most useful to propagate on the coasts to be visited, and to plant them not only in the best situations for their preservation, but that, also, they might be in sight and reach of succeeding navigators.

All notes, surveys, and drawings were to be made in duplicate, and on every opportunity to dispatch a copy, with full report, of his progress.

The most important subjects to obtain information on were:--
"The general nature of the climate as to heat, cold, moisture, winds, rains, periodical seasons, and the temperature. The direction of the mountains, their names, general appearance as to shape, whether detached or continuous in ranges. The animals, whether birds, beasts or fishes, insects, reptiles, etc., distinguishing those that are wild from those that are domesticated. The vegetables, and particularly those that are applicable to any useful purpose, whether in medicine, dyeing carpentry, etc.; all woods adapted for furniture, shipbuilding, etc. To ascertain the quantities in which they are found, the facility, or otherwise, of floating them down to a convenient place for shipment. Minerals, any of the precious stones, how used or valued by the natives; the description and characteristic difference of the several tribes of people on the coast. Their occupation and means of subsistence. A circumstantial account of such articles growing on the sea coast, if any, as might be advantageously imported into Great Britain, and those that would be required by the natives in exchange for them. The state of the arts, or manufactures, and their comparative perfection in different tribes. A vocabulary of the language spoken by, every tribe

which you meet, using in the compilation of each word the same English words."

How much was expected to be accomplished by King with his company of seventeen, including Messrs. Bedwell and Roe as mates, and Mr. Allan Cunningham, botanical collector! he also had "Boongaree," a Port Jackson native, who had accompanied Captain Flinders in the Investigator, And promised to be of great service in any intercourse with the natives. Provisions for nine months were procured, and twelve weeks water.

The Mermaid's outfit being completed too early in the season to attempt the passage by way of Torres Straits to the north-west coast, King, rather than remain inactive, determined to sail viâ Bass' Strait and Cape Leeuwin.

At Seal Island they landed, and searched in vain for the bottle left there by Captain Flinders, containing an account of the Investigator's visit, not with any motive of removing it, but to add a memorandum. On the summit of the island or rock--for it can scarcely be called an island--the skeleton of a goat's head was found, and near it were the remains of a glass case-bottle. These, as was afterwards learned, were left by Lieutenant Forster, R.N., in 1815, on his passage from Port Jackson to Europe.

Next day they anchored off Oyster Harbour, and examined the bar, finding they could lie close to the shore. It was convenient for all purposes, the wood being abundant and close to the waterholes, which were dug in the sand; so that both wood and water could be procured without going far away from the vessel, thus preventing any possibility of a surprise from the blacks.

It was here that Captain Vancouver planted and stocked a garden with vegetables, but no signs of it now remained, also the ship Ellegood's garden, which Captain Flinders found in 1802; the lapse of sixteen years, however, would make a complete revolution in the vegetation. Cunningham made here a large collection of seeds and dried specimens from the vast variety of beautiful plants and flowers.
"A small spot of ground near our tent was dug up, and enclosed with a fence, in which Mr. Cunningham sowed many culinary seeds and peach stones; and on the stump of a tree, which had been felled by our wooding party, the name of the vessel and the date of our visit was inscribed; but when we visited Oyster Harbour three years afterwards, no signs remained of the garden, and the inscription was scarcely perceptible, from the stump having been nearly destroyed by fire."

Sickness having attacked the crew, little attempt was made to investigate the west coast, but a straight course was steered to Cape North-west, that goal of so many navigators. On the 10th of February, 1818, while at anchor off the Cape, the cable parted, and they lost one of their anchors, an accident which considerably endangered the remainder of the voyage, as on the 12th the fluke of a second anchor broke in consequence of the wind freshening during the night. Three days afterwards they reached a secure anchorage, which he named the Bay of Rest, as the crew had been long fatigued when the found it. Here a landing was effected, and Allan Cunningham took occasion to measure one of the gigantic ant-hills of that coast. He found it to be eight feet in height and twenty-six in girth, which after all is not so large as some to be seen in that region. All examinations of the country tending to give King and his companion a very poor opinion of the place; they left the inlet in which they had found shelter, and the large bay in which it was situated received the name of Exmouth Gulf.

They pursued their course to the north-east. On the 25th they arrived at Rosemary Island, so long supposed to mask the entrance to a strait, and commenced a closer examination of the coast line. Here the always active botanist planted peach stones, and the party made their first capture of an "Indian." He and some more were paddling from island to island on logs--their only means of navigation--and a regular "duck hunt" ensued before one was caught, and taken on board the cutter by a boat's crew.

"The tribe of natives collected upon the shore, consisting of about forty persons, and of whom the greater number were women and children, the whole party appeared to be overcome with grief, particularly the women, who most loudly and vehemently expressed their sorrow by cries and rolling on the ground, covering their bodies with the sand. When our captive arrived alongside the vessel, and saw Boongaree, he became somewhat pacified, and suffered himself to be lifted on board; he was then ornamented with beads and a red cap, and upon our applauding his appearance, a smile momentarily played on his countenance, but it was soon replaced by a vacant stare. He took little notice of anything until he saw the fire, and this appeared to occupy his attention very much. Biscuit was given him, which as soon, as he tasted it he spat out, but some sugared water being offered to him he drank the whole, and upon sugar being placed before him in a saucer, he was at a loss how to use it, until one of the boys fed him with his fingers, and when the saucer was emptied he showed his taste for this food by licking it with his tongue."

He was then restored to his log and around his neck a bag was suspended containing a little of everything he had appeared to fancy during his short captivity, this was to induce him to give a favourable account to his companions. He rejoined his tribe, and the amused seamen watched the interview on the beach. He was ordered to stand at a distance until he had thrown away the red cap and axe that had been given him. Each black held his spear poised, and a number of questions were seemingly put to him. Upon his answering them apparently satisfactorily he was allowed to approach, his body was carefully examined, then they seated themselves in a ring, he placed in the middle. Evidently he told them his story, which occupied about half an hour. When finished, after great shouting, the tribe departed to the other side of the island, leaving the presents on the beach, having carefully examined them first. After some days spent amongst this group of islands, endeavouring to establish friendly communication with the natives, the little vessel resumed her voyage, and on the 4th of March anchored in and christened Nickol Bay.

Steering on E.S.E. to Cape Arnheim, where the examination of the west coast was to commence, they named and passed through Macquarie Strait, and anchored off Goulburn Island, making a complete survey of the Bay in which they were anchored, and the surrounding islands, calling them Goulburn Islands. Here they found traces of the visits of the Malays on their voyages after trepang, before mentioned by Captain Flinders, and also could tell from the boldness and cunning of the natives that they were well used to visitors; they even had the audacity to swim. off after dark and cut the whale boat adrift, fortunately the theft was detected before the boat drifted out of sight.

Their hostile conduct caused much trouble whilst getting wood and water, so much so, that King determined to finish wooding on Sims Island to the northward. It was fortunate that they were not often obliged to resort to the muskets for defence, as the greater number of the twelve they had taken from Port Jackson were useless, yet they were the best they could then procure in Sydney.

Meantime Cunningham greatly added to his collection, and took advantage of a good spot of soil to sow every sort of seed he possessed, but with little hope of their surviving long; as fire no doubt would soon destroy all.

"The country, was thickly, in some parts impenetrably, clothed with eucalyptus, acacia, pandanus, fan-palms, and various other trees, whilst the beaches are in some parts studded, and in others thickly lined with mangroves. The soil is chiefly of a grey sandy earth, and in some parts might be called even rich; there was, however, very few places that could bear so favourable a character.

"The climate here seems to favour vegetation so much, that the quality of the soil appears to be of minor importance, for everything thrives and looks verdant."

Whilst on this part of the coast they encountered a fleet of Malay proas, fifteen in number, but King, with his little unarmed cutter, did not care to have any communication with such very doubtful characters.

On the 16th of April, Raffles Bay was found, and named after Sir Stamford Raffles, and the next day they entered Port Essington, which was christened after Vice-Admiral Sir William Essington.

King thought that:--

"Port Essington being so good a harbour, and from its proximity to the Moluccas and New Guinea, and its being in a direct line of communication between Port Jackson and India, as well as from the commanding situation with respect to the passage through Torres Straits, it must at no very distant period become a place of great trade, and of very considerable importance."

At Knocker's Bay, immediately to the west of this port, the natives made a very determined attack on the boat, whilst she was hemmed in amongst the mangroves, but without doing any damage. King next entered and examined Van Dieman's Gulf, so called by the three Dutch vessels that sailed from Timor in 1705. The examination of this Gulf formed a prominent feature in his instructions. Here he found part of the Malay fleet at anchor, and feeling strong enough to encounter a few of them at a time, he anchored and allowed them to come on board. He showed them his rough chart, when they instantly understood the occupation of the cutter. Like the visitors who came off to Flinders, they showed a great liking for port wine. Upon mentioning the natives of the coast, and showing a stone-headed spear, they evinced great disgust. They called them "Marega," being the Malay definition of that portion of the coast.

King, during his survey of Van Dieman's Gulf, found and named the two Alligator Rivers, afterwards traversed by Leichhardt on his trip to Port Essington. From the Gulf they sailed to Melville Island, which was named after the First Lord of the Admiralty. He says:--

"We passed round Cape Van Dieman and anchored in the mouth of a very considerable river-like opening, the size of which inspired us with the flattering hope of having made an important discovery, for as yet we had no idea of the insularity of Melville Island."

Here once more they had trouble with the natives, whose intercourse with the Malays had made them adroit and treacherous thieves.

Whilst on shore taking some bearings, the party was suddenly surprised, and, beating a hasty retreat, the theodolite stand and Cunningham's insect net were left behind, and immediately appropriated by the natives.

This stand they obstinately refused to deliver or exchange, although offered tomahawks and other tempting presents. Once, after a long discussion, they brought it down to the beach and minutely examined it, but the brass mountings took their fancy too much to allow them to part with it, and King could not take it by force without bloodshed. On the 19th May, Apsley Strait was discovered, and the second island received the name of Bathurst.

King next surveyed and named the Vernon Islands, and Clarence Strait.

"The time had now arrived for our leaving the coast; our provisions were drawing to an end, and we had only a sufficiency of bread to carry us back to Port Jackson; although we had been all the voyage upon a reduced allowance; our water had also failed, and several casks which we had calculated upon being full were found to be so bad that the water was perfectly useless; these casks were made in Sydney, and proved-like our bread casks-to have been made from the staves of salt provision casks: besides this defalcation, several puncheons were found empty, and it was, therefore, doubly necessary that we should resort to Timor without any more delay."

While at Timor, "Dramah," the principal rajah of the Malay fishing fleet, gave King the following information respecting the coast of New Holland, which he had frequently visited in command of the fleet that visits its shores yearly for trepang:--

"The coast is called by them 'Marega,' and has been known to them for many years. A fleet, to the number of two hundred proas, annually (this number seems exaggerated), leave Macassar for this fishery; it sails in January, during the westerly monsoons, and coasts from island to island until it reaches the north-east of Timor, where it steers S.E. and S.S.E., which courses carry them to the coast of New Holland; the body of the fleet then steers eastward, leaving here and there a division of fifteen or sixteen proas, under the command of an inferior rajah who leads the fleet, and is always implicitly obeyed. His proa is the only vessel provided with a compass; it also has one or two swivel or small guns, and is perhaps armed with musquets. Their provisions chiefly consist of rice and cocoa-nuts, and their water--which during the westerly monsoon is easily replenished on all parts of the coast--is carried in joints of bamboo. Besides trepang, they trade in sharks' fins and birds' nests."

Their method of curing is thus described by Flinders:--
"They get the trepang by diving in from three to eight fathoms of water, and where it is abundant a man will bring up eight or ten at a time. The mode of preserving it is thus--the animal is split down on one side, boiled and pressed with a weight of stones, then stretched open by slips of bamboo, dried in the sun and afterwards in smoke, when it is fit to put away in bags, but requires frequent exposure to the sun. There are two kinds of trepang, the black and the white or grey slug."

From Dramah's information, it would seem a perpetual warfare raged between the natives and Malays, which was unfortunate for King, as it would make it a very difficult matter to establish friendly communication with people who could not be expected to distinguish between the English and Malays. After a short stay in Timor, he sailed for Sydney by way of the west coast, and anchored in Port Jackson on the 29th of July, 1818.

The early loss of the anchors had not allowed King so much opportunity of detailed examination as would otherwise have been the case; but much of the work that he had been sent to do had been carried out; the examinations of the opening behind Rosemary Island, and of Van Dieman's Gulf, beside the survey of the numerous smaller openings and islands.
"Mr. Cunningham made a very valuable and extensive collection of dried plants and seeds; but, from the small size of our vessel and the constant occupation of myself and the two midshipmen, who accompanied me, we had neither space nor time to form any other collection of natural history than a few insects, and some specimens of the geology of those parts where we landed!"

The equipment of the vessel for the second voyage, and the construction of charts of the first, occupied Captain King until December, when he left Port Jackson to survey the entrance of Macquarie Harbour, which had lately been discovered, on the western coast of Van Dieman's Land, and in February, 18ig, he returned to Sydney.

King now started to return to the scene of his labours, this time intending to make his way along the east coast and through Torres Straits. With him went Surveyor-General Oxley, in the colonial brig,

Lady Nelson, to examine Port Macquarie, in New South Wales, where, it will be remembered, Oxley reached the coast after his descent of the Main Range. On the 8th of May, 1819, the two vessels left Port Jackson, and arrived at their destination in two days. Here, after spending a short time in the necessary examination, they parted company, the Lady Nelson returning to Sydney with the Surveyor-General, and the Mermaid continuing her voyage.

The east coast having been twice surveyed by Cook and Flinders, there was little left beyond minor details for King to complete. An opening which had escaped Captain Flinders was examined, finding good, well sheltered anchorage within. They named it Rodd's Bay. Amongst other places they landed at, was Cleveland Bay.

"Near the extremity of Cape Cleveland some bamboo was picked no, and also a fresh green cocoa-nut that appeared to have been hastily tapped for milk. Heaps of pumice stone was noticed upon this beach; not any of this production had been met with floating. Hitherto no cocoa-nuts have been found on this continent, although so great a portion of it is within the tropic, and its north-east coast, so near to islands on which this fruit is abundant. Captain Cook imagined that the husk of one, which his second Lieutenant, Mr. Gore, picked up at the Endeavour River, and which was covered with barnacles, came from the Terra del Espiritu Santo of Quiros; but from the prevailing winds it would appear more likely to have been drifted from New Caledonia, which island was at that time unknown to him; the fresh appearance of the cocoa-nut seen by us renders, however, even this conclusion doubtful; Captain Flinders also found one as far to the south as Shoal Water Bay.

"In the gullies, Mr. Cunningham reaped an excellent harvest both of seeds and plants. Here as well as at every other place that we had landed upon within the tropic, the air is crowded with a species of butterfly, a great many of which were taken. It is doubtless the same species as that which Captain Cook remarks are so plentiful in Thirsty Sound. He says, 'We found also an incredible number of butterflies, so that for the space of three or four acres the air was so crowded with them, that millions were to be seen in every direction, at the same time that every branch and twig were covered with others that were not upon the wing.' The numbers seen by us were indeed incredible; the stem of every grass tree, which plant grows abundantly upon the hills, was covered with them, and on their taking wino, the air appeared, as it were, in perfect motion."

King landed at the Endeavour River to build a boat that he had on board in frame--in all probability the very same spot that Captain Cook landed upon forty-nine years before. He took the precaution to burn the grass that the natives should not attempt the same trick upon him that they had played on Cook. During the time the boat was building the inevitable thieving of the natives took place, and the usual tactics of firing over their heads had to be resorted to.

"On the 10th of July our boat was launched and preparations were made for leaving the place which had afforded us so good an opportunity of repairing our defects.

"The basis of the country in the vicinity of this river is evidently granitic; and from the abrupt and primitive appearance of the land about Cape Tribulation, and to the north of Weary Bay, there is every reason to suppose that granite is also the principle feature of those mountains, but the rocks that lie loosely scattered about the beaches and surface of the bills on the south side of the entrance, are of quartzoze substance; and this, likewise, is the character of the hills at the east end of the northern beach. Where the rocks are coated with a quartzoze crust, that, in its crumbled state, forms a very productive soil. The hills on the south side of the port recede from the banks of the river, and form an amphitheatre of low grassy land, and some tolerable soil, upon the surface of which, in many parts, we found large blocks of granite heaped one upon another. Near the tent we found coal, but the presence of this mineral in a primitive country, at an immense distance from any part where a coal formation is known to exist, would puzzle the geologist were I not to explain all I know upon the subject.

"Upon referring to the late Sir Joseph Banks' copy of the Endeavour log, I found the following remark:--'June 21st and 22nd, 1770--Employed getting our coals on shore.' There remains no doubt that it is a relic of that navigator's voyage, which must have been lying undisturbed for nearly half a century."

Leaving the Endeavour, the next object of interest they fell in with was the wreck of a vessel, which, on examination, proved to be the Frederick, but no signs of the fate of her crew were to be seen. They next had a narrow escape of being wrecked themselves on a bank at the mouth of a river running into Newcastle Bay, which King christened Escape River, and which was afterwards destined to come into fatal prominence as the scene of Kennedy's death.

Off Good Island, in Torres Straits, the arm of their anchor broke.

327

"A remarkable coincidence of our two losses upon the two voyages has now occurred. Last year, at the North-West Cape, we lost two anchors just as we were commencing the survey; and now, on rounding the North-East Cape, to commence our examination of the north coast, we have encountered a similar loss; leaving us, in both instances, only one bower anchor to carry on the survey."

Eleven weeks now since they had left Port Jackson, during that time King had laid down the different projections of the coast, and the track within the Barrier Reefs and between the Percy Islands and Cape York; surveyed Port Macquarie, examined Rodd's Bay, and constructed the boat at the Endeavour River.

Frequent rain between Cape Grafton and Torres Straits not only increased the danger of navigation, but the continued dampness of the small cabins, and--from the small size of the vessel--no stove to dry them, caused much sickness; but on the voyage from the straits to the western head of the Gulf of Carpentaria--Cape Arnhem--they found drier air, and finer weather, which soon restored the invalids to perfect health.

King sailed across the Gulf, and sighted the land again at Cape Wessel, and on the 30th July anchored off the "Cocodriles' Eylandts" of the old charts. Here King discovered a river which he named the Liverpool, and is doubtless the Spult of the Dutch navigators. Up this river, the commander, accompanied by Bedwell and Cunningham, made a long excursion, but the country was too flat for him to gain much information.

At Goulburn Island, where they landed at their old watering place, they were again attacked by their friends, the natives, as of old. There is no doubt that the bad habits of these blacks had been induced by their long intercourse with the Malays.

Leaving Goulburn Island they passed round Cape Van Dieman, steering so as to see several parts of the coast of Melville Island, in order to check the last year's survey. After rounding the cape they kept a course down the western side of Bathurst Island. On the 27th they made land on the south side of Clarence Strait, in the vicinity of the Vernon Islands.

"This was the last land seen by us on leaving the coast in May, 1818."

Captain King's next important discovery was the now well-known Cambridge Gulf. On Adolphus Island, in the Gulf, he buried one of his seamen, named William Nicholls, and in memorial, the north-west point of the island was named after him. From this point King was very anxious to examine the coast most carefully, as the

French ships, under M. Baudin, had seen but very little of it; but he had been unable to find fresh water in Cambridge Gulf, and his stock was running low. They were very weak handed, three men, besides Mr. Bedwell, being ill.

"The greater part of the crew were affected with ophthalmia, probably caused by the excessive glare and reflection of the sun's rays from the glassy surface of the sea."

Under these unfavourable circumstances they were obliged to make for Coepang. King says:--

"In the space between Cape Bougainville and Cape Voltaire, which was named Admiralty Gulf, we have given positions to at least forty islands or islets. Having now emerged from the archipelago of islands which front this part of the north-west coast, we seized the opportunity of taking leave of it for the present, and directed our course for Timor."

Here he heard that some of the crew of the wrecked vessel, the Frederick, that they had seen on the east coast, had arrived, but the greater number of the crew in the long boat had not been heard of.

On the 12th January, 1820, the Mermaid returned to Port Jackson, having surveyed five hundred miles of coast, in addition to five hundred and forty surveyed on the previous voyage, and a running survey of the east coast from Percy Islands to Torres Straits, which had not formerly been narrowly examined.

Chapter XVIII

King's Third Voyage--Early misadventures--Examines North-West coast closely--The Mermaid careened--Unforeseen result--Return to Sydney--The Bathurst--King's Fourth Voyage--Last of the Mermaid--Love's stratagem--Remarkable cavern--Extraordinary drawings--Chasm Island--South-West explorations--Revisits his old camp--Rich vegetation--Greville Island--Skirmish at Hanover Bay--Reminiscence of Dampier--His notes on the natives and their mode of living--Cape Levêque--Buccaneers' Archipelago--Provisions run out--Sails for the Mauritius--Survey of South-West re-commenced--Cape Chatham--Oyster Harbour anchorage--A native's toilet--Seal hunt--Friendly intercourse--Cape Inscription--Vandalism--Point Cloates not an island--Vlaming Head--Rowley Shoals--Cunningham--Botanical success--Rogers Island closely examined--Mainland traced further--An amazing escape from destruction--Relinquishment of survey--Sails for Sydney--Value of King's work--Settlement on Melville Island--Port Essington--Colonisation--Fort building--A waif--Roguish visitors--Garrison life--Change of scene--Raffles Bay--Dismal reports--Failure of attempt.

King, now got ready for his third voyage, and on the 14th June, 1820, left Port Jackson to again encounter the perils of the north coast in his little cutter, with the addition to his company of Mr. James Hunter, as surgeon.

His late voyage had led him to recommend to vessels the passage of the Barrier Reef, between the reef and the shore, instead of the outside passage, that had been usually adopted by northern bound ships. His start was unfortunate; heavy weather set in, the cutter lost her bowsprit, and they had to put back. On the way up, after repairs had been effected, the little craft struck heavily on a sandbank, and damaged her hull considerably, but the voyage was continued.

On the 19th of August the voyagers were at their former anchorage at Goulburn Island, taking in fresh water, and watching narrowly for their old friends the natives, who were so long in making their appearance. They cut off Lieutenant Roe, when by himself, and nearly succeeded in spearing him; he was only rescued, when quite exhausted, by the boat's crew coming to his assistance.

King proceeded to examine that part of the north-west coast that M. Baudin had overlooked, more minutely than he had been enabled to do before. Reaching Hunter's River on September 14th, an opportunity was offered for filling the water casks. The harbour of this river is of considerable size, and in most parts offers good anchorage, with abundance of fuel and water. The harbour was called Prince Frederic's, and the sound that fronts it, York Sound.

"After passing Point Hardy we entered a fine harbour, bounded on the west by a group of islands, and on the east by the projection of land that forms the western side of Prince Frederic's Harbour. The flood tide was not sufficient to carry us to the bottom, so we anchored off the east end of the southernmost island of the group, which, on the occasion of the anniversary of the late king's coronation, was subsequently called the Coronation Islands. The harbour was called Port Nelson, and a high, rocky hill that was distinguished over the land to the southward received the name of Mount Trafalgar."

From the alarming increase of the leak which the Mermaid had sprung, it was found necessary to find a place to careen her in, in order, if possible, the damage might be repaired, that they might continue the survey, or, at least, ensure their safe return to Port Jackson. On the sandy beach of a bay, which they named Careening Bay, a place was found in every way suitable.

"These repairs were completed by the 28th, but just as we were congratulating ourselves upon having performed them, a fresh defect was discovered, which threatened more alarming consequences than the others. Upon stripping off some sheets of copper, the spike nails which fastened the planks were found to be decaying, and many were so entirely decomposed by oxidation that a straw was easily thrust through the vacant holes. As we had not enough nails to replace the copper, for that was now our only security, we could not venture to remove more than a few sheets from those parts which appeared to be the most suspicious, under all of which we found the nails so defective that we had reason to fear we might start some planks before we reached Port Jackson. . . When the repairs were completed, and the people were more at leisure, I made an excursion as far as Bat Island, off Cape

Brewster. . . . Bat Island is a mass of sandstone superincumbent upon a quartzoze basis, and intersected by nearly vertical veins of white quartz, the surface of which was in a crystallised state. The floor of the cavern was covered with heaps of water-worn fragments of quartzoze rock containing copper pyrites, in some of which the cavities were covered by a deposit of greenish calcedony. The sides of the cavern had a stalagmitical appearance, but the recess was so dark that we could not ascertain either its formation or extent. . . . On first entering it we were nearly overpowered by a strong, sulphurous smell, which was soon accounted for by the flight of an incredible number of small bats, which were roosting in the bottom of the cave, and had been disturbed at our approach. We attempted to grope our way to the bottom, but not having a light, were soon obliged to give up its further examination. . . . From the summit of this place a set of bearings were obtained, particularly of the islands to the northward and westward, and Mr. Cunningham secured here specimens of eighteen different sorts of plants."

On the 9th, leaving Careening Bay, passing between Cape Brewster and the Coronation Islands, they enter a spacious sound, which received the name of Brunswick Sound. And here they also found and named the Prince Regent's River, afterwards the scene of Grey's discomfiture. Here it was patent that, in spite of their late repairs, the cutter leaked so much that, for the safety of the crew, King had reluctantly to return to Sydney; and when off Botany Bay, narrowly escaped total wreck during a dark and stormy night.

The tiny craft that had carried King so far and so safely was now laid up for repairs, and a brig of one hundred and fifty tons was purchased and re-christened the Bathurst. On the 26th of May, 1821, King sailed from Port Jackson upon his fourth and last voyage to the north coast, accompanied by the merchant ships Dick and San Antonio, bound for Batavia, who requested permission to accompany King through Torres Straits.

Meantime, the Mermaid had been thoroughly repaired and fitted out, leaving Port Jackson to carry the first establishment to Port Macquarie, on which service she was wrecked.

Their company now numbered thirty-three, but three days after they left port, King says:--
"A discovery was made of another addition to the crew. Upon opening the hold, which had been locked ever since the day before we sailed, a young girl, not more than fourteen years of age, was found concealed among the casks, where she had secreted herself in order to accom-

332

pany the boatswain to sea. Upon being brought on deck she was in a pitiable plight . . . that her acquaintances, of which she had many on board, could scarcely recognise her. Upon being interrogated, she declared she had, unknown to all on board, concealed herself in the hold the day before the vessel sailed, and that her swain knew nothing of the step she had taken. As it was now inconvenient to return to put her on shore, and as the man consented to share his rations with her, she was allowed to remain; but in a very short time heartily repented of her imprudence, and would gladly have been re-landed, had it been possible."

Along the east coast the Bathurst was accompanied by the Dick and San Antonio, both going north, and near the wreck of the Frederick, they had a trifling brush with the natives. While here, Mr. Cunningham visited Clack's reef:

"The reef abounded with shells, of which they brought back a large collection, but not in any great variety; an indifferent *Cypraea* was the most common, but there were also some *Volutae* and other shells, besides trepang and *Asteriae* in abundance.

"Mr. Cunningham observed a singularly curious cavern upon the rock, of which he gave me a description in the following account of the island:--

"'The south and south-eastern extremes of Clack's Island presented a steep rocky bluff, thinly covered with small trees. I ascended the steep head, which rose to an elevation of a hundred and eighty feet above the sea.

"'The remarkable structure of the geological feature of this islet led me to examine the south-east part, which was the most exposed to the weather, and where the disposition of the strata was, of course, more plainly developed. The base is a coarse granular, silicious sandstone, in which large pebbles of quartz and jaspar are imbedded. This stratum continues for sixteen to twenty feet above the water; for the next ten feet there is a horizontal stratum of black schistose rock, which was of so soft a consistence, that the weather had excavated several tiers of galleries, upon the roof and sides of which some curious drawings were observed, which deserve to be particularly described. They were executed upon a ground of red ochre (rubbed on the black schistus), and were delineated by dots of white argillaceous earth, which had been worked up into a paste. They represented tolerable figures of sharks, porpoises, turtles, lizards (of which I saw several small ones among the rocks), trepang, star-fish, clubs, canoes, water-gourds, and some quadrupeds, which were probably intended to represent kangaroos and dogs. The figures, besides being outlined by the dots, were decorated all over with the same pigment in dotted transverse belts. Tracing a gallery round to windward, it brought me to a commodious cave, or recess, overhung by a portion of the schistous sufficiently large to shelter twenty natives, whose recent fire places appeared on the projecting area of the cave.

"'Many turtles' heads were placed on the shelfs or niches of the excavation, amply demonstrative of the luxurious and profuse mode of life these outcasts of society had, at a period rather recently, followed. The roof and sides of this snug retreat were also entirely covered with the uncouth figures I have already described.'

"As this is the first specimen of Australian taste in the fine arts that we have detected in these voyages, it became me to make a particular observation thereon. Captain Flinders had discovered figures on Chasm Island [Note, below] in the Gulf of Carpentaria, formed with a burnt stick, but this performance, exceeding a hundred and fifty figures, which must have occupied much time, appears at least to be one step nearer refinement than those simply executed with a piece of charred wood. Immediately above this schistose stratum is a superincumbent mass of sandstone, which appeared to form the upper stratum of the island."

[Note: "Chasm Island lies one mile and a half from a low point of Groote Eylandt, where the shore trends southward and seemed to form a bay. In the deep sides of the chasms were deep holes or caverns, undermining the cliffs; upon the walls of which I found rude drawings made with charcoal and something like red paint upon the white ground of the rock. These drawings represented porpoises, turtle, kangaroos, and a human hand; and Mr. Westall, who went afterwards to see them, found the representation of a kangaroo, with a file of thirty-two persons following after it. The third person of the band was twice the height of the others, and held in his hand something resembling the 'whaddie' or wooden sword of the native chiefs of Port Jackson, and was probably intended to represent a chief. They could not, as with us, indicate superiority by clothing or ornament, since they wear none of any kind, and, therefore, with the addition of a weapon similar to the ancients, they seem to have made superiority of person the principal emblem of superior power, of which, indeed, power is usually a consequence of the very early stages of society."]

From the wreck of the Frederick the crew had been busy during their stay here procuring all the spars and planks that would be of use to them, and on the 25th June the Bathurst got under weigh, and with her two companions resumed their course to the northward, following the same route as that traversed last year by the Mermaid--steering across the Gulf of Carpentaria to Cape Wessell, which they sighted on the 3rd June. Anchoring in South-West Bay, they landed at their former watering place on Goulburn Island, but found the stream had failed, and the parched appearance of the island showed that the season had been unusually dry. Leaving South-West Bay, they passed to the eastward of New Year's Island, and the following day sighted Cape Van Dieman. Here they parted company with their companions, the Dick and San Antonio, by an interchange of three cheers, the Dick having King's letters for conveyance to England. The course of the Bathurst was now south-west towards Cape Londonderry, sighting, during the next few days, Eclipse Hill, Sir Graham Moore's Islands, and Troughton Island. Light baffling winds detained them for two days in the vicinity of Cassini Island, and on the 23rd the Bathurst anchored about half a mile off the sandy beach of Careening Bay.

"As soon as the vessel was secured we visited the shore, and recognised the site of our last year's encampment, which had suffered no alteration except what had been occasioned by a rapid vegetation. A sterculia, the stem of which had served as one of the props of our mess tent, and to which we had nailed a sheet of copper, with an inscription, was considerably grown, and the gum had oozed out in such profusion where the nails had pierced the bark that it had forced one corner of the copper off. The large, gouty-stemmed tree on which the *Mermaid's* name had been carved in deep indented characters remained without any alteration, and seemed likely to bear the marks of our visit longer than any other memento we had left. The sensations experienced at revisiting a place which had so seasonably afforded us a friendly shelter and such unlooked-for convenience for our purposes, can only be estimated by those who have experienced them; and it is only to strangers to such feelings that it will appear ridiculous to say that even the nail to which our thermometer had been suspended was the subject of pleasurable recognition.

"No water in the gully where last year it was running, and no sign that it had contained any for some time, yet from the luxuriant vegetation and verdant appearance of the grass, it was the more astonishing. After examining the bight to the eastward, where formerly there had been a considerable stream, all hope of success in finding water here was given up, and an anchorage made in St. George's Basin, finding an abundant supply at the cascade in Prince Regent's River.

"While the boat's crew rested and filled their baricas, I ascended the rocks over which the water was falling, and was surprised to find its height had been so underrated when we passed by it last year; it was then thought to be about forty feet, but I now found it could not be less than one hundred and fifty. The rock--a fine-grained, silicious sandstone--is disposed in horizontal strata, from six to twelve feet thick, each of which projects about three feet from that above it, and forms a continuity of steps to the summit, which we found some difficulty in climbing; but where the distance between the ledges was great, we assisted our ascent by tufts of grass firmly rooted in the luxurious moss that grew abundantly about the watercourses. On reaching the summit, I found that the fall was supplied from a stream winding through rugged chasms and thickly-matted clusters of plants and trees, among which the pandanus bore a conspicuous appearance, and gave a picturesque richness to the place. While admiring the wildness of the scene, Mr. Montgomery joined me; we did not, however, succeed in following the stream for more than a hundred yards, for at that distance its windings were so confused among rocks and spinifex that we could not trace its course. Large groves of pandanus and hibiscus, and a variety of other plants, were growing in great luxuriance upon the banks of the Prince Regent's River, but, unhappily, the sterile and rocky appearance of the country was some alloy to the satisfaction we felt at the first sight of the fresh water."

Water had been obtained sufficient to last until October. Preparations were then made to leave this anchorage, when they explored Half-way Bay, finding in it a strait that communicated with Munster Water, so insulating the land that forms the northwest shore of the Bay. This island was named Greville Island.

Whilst in Hanover Bay, a skirmish with the natives enlivened proceedings. In spite of all the many warnings the party had received by this time, they would venture amongst the natives quite unarmed, and when their men came to their assistance the muskets, as a rule, would not go off. This time the surgeon, Mr. Montgomery, was speared in the back--fortunately, not fatally.

From Hanover Bay, King sailed some distance to the westward, anchoring on August 21st, near the Lacepede Islands. The next day Cape Baskerville was named, and the smoke of fires was noticed at intervals for miles along the shore; from which one might infer that this part of the coast was very populous. Captain Dampier saw forty Indians together on one of the rocky islands to the eastward of Cape Levêque, and in his quaint description of them says:--

"The inhabitants of this country are the miserablest people in the world. The Hodmadods, of Monomatapa, though a nasty people, yet for wealth are gentlemen to these, who have no houses and skin garments, sheep, poultry, and fruits of the earth, ostrich eggs, etc., as the Hodmadods have; and, setting aside their human shape, they differ but little from brutes. They are tall, straight-bodied, and thin, with small, long limbs. They have great heads, round foreheads, and great brows. Their eye-lids are always half-closed to keep the flies out of their eyes, they being so troublesome here that fanning will not keep them from coming to one's face; and without the assistance of both hands to keep them off, they will creep into one's nostrils, and mouth too, if the lips are not shut very close. So that, from infancy, being thus annoyed with those insects, they do never open their eyes as other people; and therefore they cannot see far unless they hold up their heads, as if they were looking at somewhat over them. They have great bottle noses, pretty full lips, and wide mouths. The two fore-teeth of their upper jaw are wanting in all of them, men and women, old and young. Whether they draw them out or not I know not. Neither have they any beards. They are long-visaged, and of a very unpleasant aspect, having not one graceful feature in their faces. Their hair is black, short, and curled like that of the negroes; and not long and lank like the common Indians. The colour of their skins, both of their faces and the rest of their body, is coal-black like that of the negroes of Guinea. They have no sort of clothes but a piece of the rind of a tree tied like a girdle about their waists, and a handful of long grass, or three or four small green boughs full of leaves thrust under their girdle to cover their nakedness. They. have no houses, but lie in the open air without covering, the earth being their bed and heaven their canopy.

"They live in companies-twenty or thirty men, women, and children together. Their only food is a small sort of fish, which they get by making weirs of stone across little coves or branches of the sea, every tide bringing in the small fish, and there leaving them a prey to these people, who constantly attend there to search for them at low water. This small fry I take to be the top of their fishery. They have no instruments to catch great fish should they come, and such seldom stay to be left behind at low water; nor could we catch any fish with our hooks and lines while we lay there. In other places, at low water, they seek for cockles, mussels, and periwinkles; of these shell-fish there are fewer still, so that their chief dependency is upon what the sea leaves in their weirs, which, be it much or little, they gather tip and march to the places of their abode. There is neither herb, root, pulse, nor any sort of grain for them to eat that we saw, nor any sort of bird or beast that they can catch, having no instruments. I did not perceive that they did worship anything. These poor people have a sort of weapon to defend their weirs or fight with their enemies, if they have any, that will interfere with their poor fishery. They did at first endeavour with their weapons to frighten us, who, lying ashore, deterred them from one of their fishing places. Some of them had wooden swords, others had a sort of lance. The sword is a long, straight pole, sharp at one end, and hardened afterwards by heat. I saw no iron, nor any sort of metal; therefore, it is probable they use stone hatchets. How they get their fire I know not, but, probably, as Indians do, out of wood. I have seen the Indians of Bon-Airy do it, and have myself tried the experiment. They take a flat piece of wood that is pretty soft, and make a small dent in one side of it; then they take another hard, round stick, about the bigness of one's little finger and sharpened at one end like a pencil; they put that sharp end in the hole or dent of the flat, soft piece, and then rubbing or twirling the hard piece between the palm of their hands, they drill the soft piece till it smokes and, at last, takes fire.

"These people speak somewhat through the throat, but we could not understand one word they said. . . . We went over to the islands, and there we found a great many of the natives. I do believe there were forty on one island--men, women, and children. The men, on our first coming ashore, threatened us with their lances and swords, but they were frightened by firing our gun, which we purposely fired over their heads. The island was so small that they could not hide themselves, but they were much disordered by our landing. This, their place of dwelling, was only a fire, with a few boughs before it, set up on the side the winds were off.

"After we had been here a little while, the men began to be familiar, and we clothed some of them, designing to have some service of them for it; for we found some wells of water here, and intended to carry two or three barrels of it aboard. But it being somewhat trouble some to carry to the canoes, we thought to have made these men to have carried it for us, and therefore, we gave them some old clothes; to one an old pair of breeches, to another a ragged shirt, to the third a jacket that was scarce worth owning, which yet would have been very acceptable at some places where we had been, and so we thought they might have been with these people. We put them on them, thinking that this finery would have brought them to work heartily for us; and our water being filled in small, long barrels, about six gallons in each, which were made purposely to carry water in, we brought these our new servants to the well, and put a barrel on each of their shoulders for them to carry to the canoe. But all the signs we could make were to no purpose, for they stood like statues, without motion, but grinned like so many monkeys, staring one upon another; for these poor creatures seem not accustomed to carry burthens, and I believe that one of our ship boys, of ten years old, would carry as much as one of them. So we were forced to carry our water ourselves, and they very fairly put the clothes off again, and laid them down, as if clothes were only to work in. I did not perceive that they had any great liking to them at first, neither did they seem to admire anything we had. Four men, captured while swimming, were brought aboard; two of them were middle aged, the other two young men about eighteen or twenty years old. To these we gave boiled rice, and with it turtle and manatee boiled. They did greedily devour what we gave them, but took no notice of the ship, or anything on it, and when they were set on land again, they ran away as fast as they could. At our first coming, before we were acquainted with them, or they with us, a company of them, who lived on the main, came just against our ship, and standing on a pretty high bank threatened us with their swords and lances, by shaking them at us; at last the captain ordered the drum to be beaten, which was done of a sudden with much vigour, purposely to scare the poor creatures. They, hearing the noise, ran away as fast as they could drive, and when they ran away in haste they would cry gurry-gurry, speaking deep down in the throat. Those inhabitants, also, that live on the main would always run away from us yet we took several of them. For, as I have already observed, they had such bad eyes that they could not see us till we came close to them; we did always give them victuals, and let them go again." ["Dampier." Vol. I, p464.]

August 20. King, when laying down the plan of the coast upon his chart, found Cape Levêque to be the point Dampier anchored under when on his buccaneering voyage in the Cygnet, 1688. In commemoration of his visit the name of Buccaneer's Archipelago was given to the islands that front Cygnet Bay, which bay is so named after his vessel; and on August 26, Roebuck Bay received its name after the ship Captain Dampier commanded when he visited this coast in 1699. Their water being nearly out, and the provisions generally being in a bad state, besides the want of a second anchor being very much felt, King deemed it prudent not to rely longer upon the good fortune that had attended them, but to sail for the Mauritius, entering Port Louis on September 26th.

On November 15th they were again ready for sea, and left the Mauritius to re-commence their survey on the south-west coast of New Holland. Sighting Cape Chatham, a course was directed to the eastward for King George's Sound, where they intended to get wood and water previous to commencing the examination, and anchored close to the entrance of Princess Royal Harbour. This harbour not proving suitable, their old anchorage in Oyster Harbour was taken up. The luxuriant growth of vegetation had almost entirely destroyed all traces of the visit of 1818. The garden in which Mr. Cunningham had planted seeds was covered with three or four feet of additional soil, formed of sand and decayed vegetable matter, and clothed with a thicket of plants in flower. The natives appeared to be very friendly, and some visited the vessel.

"After an absence of an hour our two friends returned, when it appeared that they had been at their toilet, for their noses and faces had evidently been fresh smeared over with red ochre, which they pointed out to us as a great ornament; affording another proof that vanity is inherent in human nature, and not merely the consequence of civilization.

"Two of them were watching a small seal that, having been left by the tide on the bank, was endeavouring to waddle towards the deep water. At last one of the natives, fixing his spear in its throwing-stick, advanced very cautiously, and when within ten or twelve yards, lanced it, and pierced the animal through the neck, when the other instantly ran up and stuck his spear into it also; and then, beating it about the head with a small hammer, very soon despatched it. This event collected the whole tribe to the spot, who assisted in landing their prize and washing the sand off the body. They then carried the animal to their fire, at the edge of the grass, and began to devour it even before it was dead. Curiosity induced Mr. Cunningham and myself to view this barbarous feast, and we landed about ten minutes after it had commenced. The moment the boat touched the sand the natives, springing up and throwing their spears away into the bushes, ran down towards us, and before we could land, had all seated themselves in the boat, ready to go on board, in as unceremonious a manner as passengers would seat themselves in a ferry-boat; but they were obliged to wait whilst we landed to witness their savage feast. On going to the place, we found an old man seated over the remains of the carcass, two-thirds of which had already disappeared. He was holding a long strip of the raw flesh in his left hand, and tearing it off the body with a sort of knife. A boy was also feasting with him, and both were too intent upon

their breakfast to notice us, or to be the least disconcerted at our looking on. We, however, were very soon satisfied, and walked away
perfectly disgusted with the sight of so horrible a repast, and the intol-
erable stench occasioned by the effluvia that arose from the dying
animal, combined with that of the bodies of the natives, who had
daubed themselves from head to foot with a pigment made of redo-
cherous earth, mixed up with seal-oil. Returning on board, the natives
were very attentive to the mixture of a pudding, and a few small
dumplings were made and given to them, which they put on the bars of
the fire-place, but, being too impatient to wait until they were baked,
ate them in a doughy state, with much relish. One of them, an old man,
was very attentive to the sail-makers cutting out a boat's sail, and, at
his request, was presented with all the strips that were of no use. When
it was completed, a small piece of canvas was missing. After a great
search, in which the old rogue assisted, it was found secreted under his
arm. The old man appeared ashamed and conscious of his guilt, and
although he was frequently afterwards with us, yet he always hung
down his head and sneaked into the background."

So with the exception of a few thefts all communication with
the natives was here carried on in a most friendly manner, and on the
1st of January the anchors were lifted, and the Bathurst left for Seal
Island, where they intended to refit the sails. Leaving King George's
Sound they sailed at a distance from the land to ensure a quicker passage to Cape Péron, Flinders and M. Baudin having minutely
examined the coast between.

Frederick Houtman's Abrolhos were sighted on January 17th,
and the passage or channel between the Abrolhos Bank and the coast
has been distinguished by the name of Vlaming's ship, the Geelvink,
since she was the first vessel that passed there, 1697. The cliffs of Red
Point named by Vlaming partake of a reddish tinge, and appear to be
of horizontal strata; behind Red Point is a bight, named by the French
Gantheaume Bay. Reaching Dirk Hartog's Island they anchored off
Cape Inscription, and searched for the historical plates, but although
the posts were standing, the plates had been removed.

King found that former navigators had taken that part of the
coast he named Point Cloates for an island, calling it Cloates Island;
the next day Vlaming Head, of the North-West Cape, came in sight,
and a north course bore him to Rowley Shoals, wishing to fix their
position with greater correctness, and to examine the extent of the
bight round Cape Levêque, which during the earlier part of their voyage they were obliged to leave unexplored. Landing next at Point

Cunningham, Mr. Cunningham botanized with great success; a fresh stream was running down the rocks into the sea, and at the back of the beach was a hollow full of sweet water; the heat was terrible, and the soil of a red coloured earth of a very sandy nature.

Another anchor lost, in a bay they afterwards called Disaster Bay. The succession of bad weather, and only one anchor left, made it desirable to go to Port George the Fourth, as they wanted both food and water; and during the delay here, a part of the crew in the boats could examine the islands in Rogers Strait, and trace the continuation of the mainland, behind the. islands, that forms the south-east coast of Camden Bay, of which nothing was known; also continuing the examination of the deep bay behind Montgomery's Islands, and connect that part with the gulf or strait behind Buccaneers' Archipelago, which King felt sure existed. Here they had a most amazing escape, that reads more like fiction than sober fact. The astonishing influx and reflux of the tides amongst these islands had been noticed by Dampier, and had led that navigator to conclude that a strait or large river must be situated near this part of the coast. Whilst among these islands, King was caught in one of these tidal draughts during a dead calm. The following is his description of the position. He was at the mast-head--his usual position for conning the ship when near the land--but seeing his vessel carried swiftly and, as he thought, inevitably on the rocks, he descended to the deck:--

"Happily, however, the stream of the tide swept us past the rocks without accident, and after carrying us about half-a-mile farther, changed its direction to south-east, and drifted us towards a narrow strait separating two rocky islands, in the centre of which was a large insulated rock, that seemed to divide the stream. The boat was now hoisted out to tow, but we could not succeed in getting the vessel's head round. As she approached the strait the channel became much narrower, and several islands were passed at not more than thirty yards from her course. The voices of natives were now heard, and soon afterwards some were seen on either side of the strait, hallooing and waving their arms. We were so near to one party that they might have thrown their spears on board. BY this time we were flying past the shore with such velocity that it made us quite giddy; and our situation was too awful to give us time to observe the motions of the Indians; for we were entering the narrowest part of the strait, and the next moment were close to the rock, which it appeared almost impossible to avoid, and it was more than probable that the stream it divided would carry us broadside upon it, when the consequences would have been dreadful. The current, or sluice, was setting past the rock at the rate of eight or nine knots, and the water being confined by its intervention, fell at least six or seven feet; at the moment, however, when we were upon the point of being dashed to pieces, a sudden breeze providentially sprang up, and filling our sails, impelled the vessel forward three or four yards. This was enough, but only just sufficient, for the rudder was not more than six yards from the rock. No sooner had we passed this frightful danger than the breeze fell again, and was succeeded by a dead calm; the tide, however, continued to carry us on with a gradually decreasing strength until one o'clock, when we felt very little effects from it."

This was the last danger that King was to escape on the northwest coast, as after a little more examination of the neighbourhood of this dangerous archipelago, the thick weather and easterly winds compelled him to relinquish his work and sail for Sydney.

King left the coast thoroughly impressed with the idea that behind Buccaneers' Archipelago there was, if anywhere, an opening into the interior of New Holland; the constant loss' of his anchors had prevented him from confirming his conjecture; but he had good reason for then thinking so. In these days of strong, well-found surveying steamers, it is wonderful to recall the work that King did in the Mermaid, amongst all the dangers of unknown seas, and constantly having to get his wood and water in the face of hostile savages.

It was not long after his return to England, and whilst engaged preparing his journal for publication, that he heard a settlement had been founded on Melville Island, one of his discoveries. As this settlement was in accordance with his recommendation, and a detailed account of its foundation has not been given in these pages, the present may be a fitting time to do so.

It must be remembered that this settlement was finally, after many removals, abandoned, and the one established at Port Essington, when Leichhardt arrived there, was a second attempt at colonisation.

The Tamar, under captain Bremer, left Sydney in August, 1824, having with her the Countess of Harcourt, and that ever useful colonial brig, the Lady Nelson.

Arrived at Port Essington, the little fleet anchored off Table Point, the marines landed, the Union Jack was hoisted, and formal possession taken of the north coast of Australia, between the meridians of 129 deg. and 136 deg. east of Greenwich. After the Tamar had fired a royal salute, and the marines three volleys, the business of finding a site commenced.

This was no such easy matter, the first object being to find fresh water; parties were despatched in all directions, but for a long time unsuccessfully; at last some was obtained at a sandy point, where there was an old Malay encampment, but it was a deficient supply, only to be got by digging holes in the sand, and the inducements for remaining were not considered sufficiently attractive. An examination of St. Asaph Bay, in Melville Island, was next made, and possession taken in like manner; but no fresh water was forthcoming there, and at last, after much searching, a small river and plenty of water were found in another part of Melville Island, opposite Harris Island. A point of the land for the town was fixed upon, and named Point Barlow, after the commandant. The cove where the ship anchored was called King's Cove, and the entrance to Apsley Strait, Port Cockburn.

A redoubt was built of logs, seventy-five feet long by fifty broad, and a ditch dug surrounding it; the quarter-deck guns were mounted, the colours hoisted, and it was formally christened Fort Dundas, under a royal salute from itself.

After all this display of enthusiasm and gunpowder, work commenced in earnest, quarters were built inside the stockade, a deep well sunk, a wharf constructed, and gardens laid out.

As might have been reasonably supposed, the evil-disposed natives of the island soon got over their first scare at this invasion of their territory. At first they came into the fort in friendly guise.

"I was greatly astonished to see amongst them," says Lieutenant Roe, "a young man of about twenty years of age, not darker in colour than a Chinese, but with perfect Malay features, and like all the rest, entirely naked; he had daubed himself all over with soot and grease to appear like the others, but the difference was plainly perceptible. On observing that he was the object of our conversation, a certain archness and lively expression came over his countenance, which a native Australian would have strained his features in vain to produce. It seems probable that he must have been kidnapped when very young, or found while astray in the woods."

All this friendliness soon disappeared, the aborigines took to robbing the working parties of their tools, and spear and musket soon came to be used on either side. Up to the time the Tamar left, however, no harm had been done. In all, the settlement consisted of one hundred and twenty-six individuals, of whom four were women, and forty-five convicts.

The fortunes of this little colony, and even its existence, being almost forgotten, it may be interesting to the reader to follow them to the end. After the Tamar left for India, and the Countess of Harcourt proceeded on her voyage, the settlement was left with the colonial brig, the Lady Nelson, as the nucleus of a fleet, but she sailed for Timor, and was never heard of again. The hostility of the natives increased, and the Malays, who were expected to visit and trade with the English, did not put in an appearance, it being out of the track of their proas; and of Fort Dundas, of which such high hopes were entertained, in a few short years not a vestige remained.

At last, what with scurvy amongst the garrison (which, considering the amount of vegetables grown, should not have been the case), the incessant feud with the natives, the most gloomy reports were sent down at every opportunity afforded by a vessel calling. Latterly, it was unsafe to venture out of the camp unarmed, and the surgeon and commissariat officer were murdered only a few yards from the stockade. The public policy pursued was not of a liberal nature, and it was decided to try the experiment of a settlement on the mainland.

As it was considered that Port Essington was deficient in fresh water, Raffles Bay was selected, and two years before Melville Island was finally abandoned, Captain Stirling, of the Success, was ordered to proceed there. The settlement was formed on the 18th June, and in honour of the date, was called Fort Wellington.

The usual scene of activity ensued, the erection of a house, the formation of a garden, and finally, the old routine of commencing intercourse with the natives; then the thieving and the usual retaliation.

Two shipwrecked men were picked up during the early days of the settlement, one a Portuguese sailor belonging to the Frederick, wrecked on the east coast, so often mentioned by King. This man, in company with two others, had escaped in a small boat, and reached Port Essington, where his two companions had died. The other was a Lascar belonging to the ship Fame, that had been wrecked in the straits. He had been with the blacks six or seven years.

On the final abandonment of Melville Island, in 1829, the live animals, stores, plants, etc., were transferred to Raffles Bay, but although such doleful accounts of the island had been sent down, Captain Lawes, who visited it only a few months before the removal, gives a favourable report of its healthiness, and of the success attending the growth of vegetables and tropical fruits. The same dismal reports concerning the unhealthiness of the climate were reported about Raffles Bay, and, much to the surprise of the commandant, Captain Barker, orders were received to abandon that place, too, in the same year.

On the 28th of August the abandonment took place. The principal natives, who had been admitted near the settlement, were taken over the stockade and garden, and an attempt made to teach them the value of the fruits.

The whites left behind them orange, lime, and lemon trees, bananas, in abundance, shaddocks, citrons, pine-apples, figs, custard apples, cocoa-nuts, sugar-cane, and many other plants. In addition, paw-paws, bananas, and cocoa-nuts were planted in many other places where it was thought they would thrive.

Poultry, pigs, a bull and three cows (buffaloes), a Timor horse, and mare in foal, were also left, in the hope of their increasing. An old Union Jack was then nailed on the deserted fort, and the garrison went on board the brig. On notice being given of the intended removal, a disposition to abscond had been evinced by many of the prisoners. Some succeeded; the idea being to hide until the departure of the commandant, and then live with the natives until the arrival of the Malay proas. All returned and gave themselves up with the exception of two, and these two were left behind. Their fate is of course unknown. This was the end of the first attempt at colonisation of the north coast.

Chapter XIX

The next voyage of importance in these waters was conducted by Captains Wickham and Stokes. Few narratives of the survey of our coasts have read with so much interest as that of the cruise of the Beagle. Partly is this owing to the intense love of exploration and discovery that seems to have animated the spirit of her commander, Captain Lort Stokes, throughout whose journal there breathes the very essence of genuine enthusiasm. In addition, the incidents and results of the survey added so much to our knowledge of Australia, that one can look upon him as a most worthy successor to Flinders and King.

The Beagle was an old surveying vessel, and Captain Stokes had served on board of her for nearly eighteen years, passing through all the grades, from midshipman upwards, in many parts of the world.

She left Plymouth on the 5th July, 1837, under the command of John Clements Wickham, who invalided in March, 1841, when John Lort Stokes, lieutenant and assistant surveyor, was appointed to the vacant command.

On board the Beagle, at her departure from Plymouth, were Lieutenants Grey and Lushington, on their way to explore the interior of Western Australia. These gentlemen parted company from the Beagle at the Cape of Good Hope, the sloop proceeding to the Swan River. In January, 1838, the Beagle left Swan River, and sailed north, where, on the 15th, they anchored in Roebuck Bay, and commenced a search for the much talked of channel supposed to exist by Captains King and Dampier--a channel that would connect Roebuck Bay with an opening behind Buccaneer's Archipelago, thus making Dampier's Land an island. As was anticipated by Stokes, this proved unsuccessful, but the stay there was terminated by an unfortunate but, luckily, not fatal accident, Lieutenant Usborne being accidentally shot.

"At the time this unlucky accident occurred, some twenty natives rushed from the concealment, whence they had been, doubtless, watching all the proceedings of the party, as though they, designed to bear a part in what probably seemed to them, as poor Usborne went down, an approaching fray; however, the sight of the two boats in the distance, which, upon deploying, they had full in view, deterred them from acting upon any hostile intentions, supposing such to have existed in their minds. The accident, however, and their sudden appearance could only serve additionally to flurry the little party, who had to convey their disabled officer to a place of safety, and Mr. Helpman, who may well be pardoned the want of his usual self-possession at such a moment, left behind a pair of loaded pistols. They would puzzle the savages greatly, of course, but I hope no ill consequences ensued; if they began pulling them about, or put them in the fire, the better to separate the wood and iron, two or three poor wretches might be killed or maimed for life, and their first recollections of the 'Quibra men,' as Miago calls us, would naturally be anything but favourable.

"Thus disastrously terminated our examination of Roebuck Bay, in which the cheering reports of former navigators had induced us to anticipate the discovery of some great water communication with the interior of this vast continent. A most thorough and careful search had clearly demonstrated that the hoped-for river must be sought elsewhere."

Touching here and there along the coast, and having occasional communication with the natives, which Stokes amusingly describes, they finally anchored in, and christened King's Sound after the narrow escape that King experienced there from the tidal race. The point had now been reached where they expected to carry on their most important operations, and the first question to settle was if they could rely on fresh water. The delightful verdure that clothed the country after the long ranges of sandhills, and shores covered with mangroves, also the fact of many natives living here, would on any other coast have been looked upon favourably, but upon the coasts, and in the heart of Australia nature seems to delight in contradiction.

Heavy rains provided them with an abundance of rain water, and they collected in the hollows of the rocks several boat loads, so preventing a more distant search.

"While waiting here a party was made up for the purpose of penetrating a little way into the interior. Everything wore a green and most delightful appearance, but the reader must bear in mind how vegetation had just been forced by heavy rains upon a light, heated soil, and also recollect that to one who has been pent up for some time on board ship a very barren prospect may seem delightful. The country was more open in character than I had before noticed it, and the numerous traces of native fires which we found in the course of the excursion seemed readily to account for this. Indeed, during dry seasons it not infrequently happens that an immense tract of land is desolated with fire, communicated either by the design or carelessness of the natives, to the dry herbage on the surface. The moment the flame has been kindled, it only waits for the first breath of air to spread it far and wide; then, on the wings of the wind, the fiery tempest streams over the hillsides and through the vast plains. Brushwood and herbage, the dry grass, the tall reed, the twining. parasite, or the giant of the forest, charred and blackened, but still proudly erect-alike attest and bewail the conquering fire's onward march; and the bleak desert, silent, waste, and lifeless, which it leaves behind, seems for ever doomed to desolation. Vain fear! The rain descends once more upon the dry and thirsty soil, and, from that very hour which seemed the date of cureless ruin, Nature puts forth her wondrous power with increased effort, and again her green and flower-embroidered mantle decks the earth with a new beauty."

Leaving this anchorage, another was found in a bay on the mainland, eleven miles N.W. from a remarkable headland, named by

Captain King Point Cunningham, and remained here a week, by which time the coast, as far as Point Cunningham, was carefully examined.

"We named this Skeleton Point, from our finding here the remains of a native, placed in a semi-recumbent position under a wide-spreading gum-tree, enveloped, or, more properly, shrouded, in the bark of the papyrus. All the bones were closely packed together, the larger being placed outside, and the general mass, surmounted by the head, resting on its base; the fleshless, eyeless skull 'grinning horribly' over the right side. The removal of the skeleton was effected, and presented by Captain Grey to the Royal College of Surgeons, in whose museum it is now to be found."

From the summit of Point Cunningham a fine view of the opposite shore of the sound was obtained. It appeared very rugged and broken, and from the geological formation of the country, and no land to the south-cast or south, Captain Stokes' hopes were again raised of finding the long and anxiously expected river. A singular cliff on the south-east side of the point is called by King, "Carlisle Head." Rounding Point Cunningham, they anchored near a red cliffy head, called by Captain King "Foul Point." It was here King was compelled to leave the coast, and Foul Point marks the limit of his survey on the northern shore.

On the 23rd February they crossed the limit of King's Sound, and entered unknown waters. Here, at Disaster Bay, Stokes was sent in command of the whaleboat and yawl, to inspect the coast ahead, whilst the survey of the bay proceeded. On the 26th, Stokes discovered a new river, which he named the Fitzroy, after his former commander. Whilst exploring this river, Stokes and his companions, Helpmann and a sailor, had a most narrow escape. They had left the boat, and were making their way through the mangrove-fringed banks on foot to a certain point where they were to meet the boat again; but rising tide proved so strong that the boat could not reach them, and although Stokes and Helpman could swim, the sailor could not, and they would not desert him. There they had to stand with the tide creeping up their bodies, and watch the desperate efforts of the crew to contend against its force. Only when the water was high enough to allow the boat to creep along the shelter of the mangroves, and they were shoulder deep, were they rescued.

On the return to the ship, a fresh expedition was immediately despatched, Captain Wickharn himself taking command, and they pulled up the Fitzroy a distance of twenty-two miles in a straight direction, and ninety miles following the bend of the river. Returning,

Stokes had the satisfaction of seeing a monster alligator reposing on the mud-bank, where he had such a near escape from drowning.

After a lengthened survey of the sound, the Beagle returned to Port George the Fourth, where she arrived on the 7th of April, from whence they made a boat excursion to Collier Bay. Many natives were seen on the shore, evidently wanting to be friendly. On board the Beagle, the party had a native of Swan River--Miago. He turned out an excellent gun room waiter, and they hoped that in any communication with the natives he might prove useful. When off Point Swan, Stokes says:--

"They closely examined the heroic Miago, who submitted to be handled by these much-dreaded 'northern men' with a very rueful countenance, and afterwards construed the way in which one of them had gently stroked his beard, into an attempt to take him by the throat and strangle him--an injury and indignity which, when safe on board, he resented by repeated threats, uttered in a sort of wild chant, of spearing. their thighs, back, loins, and, indeed, every individual portion of the frame.

"When Captain Wickharn and myself left the ship at Point Cunningham, in the hope of inducing the natives to return with us, Miago, hearing of the expected visit, immediately went below and dressed himself to the best possible advantage. No sooner did the boat come alongside, than he appeared at the gangway, inquiring, with the utmost possible dignity, 'Where blackfellas?' and was evidently deeply mortified that he had no opportunity of 'astonishing the natives.'"

On their return to the ship, from the examination of Collier Bay, they found the exploring party, under Grey and Lushington, had arrived on the coast at Hanover Bay, twelve miles away.

"From Lieutenant Grey's description of the tribes his party had encountered, he must have been among a people more advanced in civilization than any me had hitherto seen upon this coast. He found several curious figures, images, and drawings, generally in colours, upon the sides of caves in the sandstone rock, which, notwithstanding their rude style, yet evince a greater degree of advancement and intelligence than we have been able to find any traces of; at the same time, it must be remembered that no certain date absolutely connects these works with the present generation; the dryness of the natural walls upon which they are executed, and the absence of any atmospheric moisture may have, and may yet preserve them for an indefinite period, and their history, read aright, may testify-not the present condition of the Australian School of Design, but the perfection which

FAVENC

it had formerly attained. Lieutenant Grey, too, like ourselves, had seen certain individuals, in company with the natives, much lighter in colour, and widely differing in figure and physiognomy from the savages by whom they were surrounded, and was inclined to believe that they are descended from Dutch sailors who, at different times suffering shipwreck upon the coast, have intermarried with its native inhabitants; but as no authentic records can be produced to prove that this portion of the coast was ever visited by Dutch navigators at all, I am still more disposed to believe that these lighter coloured people are Malays captured from the trepang fishers, or, perhaps, voluntarily associating with the Australians, as we know that the Australian not unfrequently abandons his country and his mode of life to visit the Indian Archipelago with them."

From Port George the Fourth the Beagle sailed for Swan River, where she arrived on the 25th of May. Her most important discovery during this cruise was King's Sound and the Fitzroy River. As they neared Miago's birthplace, Stokes says he questioned him upon the account he intended giving his friends of the scenes he had witnessed.

"I was quite astonished at the accuracy with which he remembered the various places we had visited during the voyage. He seemed to carry the ship's track in his memory with the most careful accuracy. His description of the ship's sailing and anchoring was most amusing. He used to say: 'Ship walk--walk--all night--hard walk--then, by-and-by, anchor tumble down.' His manner of describing, his interviews with the wicked 'northern men' was most graphic. His countenance and figure became at once instinct with animation and energy, and no doubt he was then influenced by feelings of baffled hatred and revenge, from having failed in his much-vaunted determination to carry off in triumph one of their gins. I would sometimes amuse myself by asking him how he was to excuse himself to his friends for having failed in the promised exploit, but the subject was evidently a very unpleasant one, and he was always anxious to escape it.

"We were considerably amused with the consequential air Miago assumed towards his countrymen on our arrival, which afforded us a not uninstructive instance of the prevalence of the ordinary infirmities of our common human nature, whether of pride or vanity, universally to be met with, both in the civilised man and the uncultivated savage. He declared that he would not land until they first came off to wait on him. Decorated with an old full-dress lieutenant's coat, white trousers, and a cap with a tall feather, he looked upon himself as

352

a most exalted personage, and for the whole of the first day remained on board, impatiently, but in vain, prying into each boat that left the shore for the dusky forms of some of his quondam friends. His pride, however, could not long withstand the desire of display. Yielding to the impulse of vanity he, early the following morning, took his departure from the ship. Those who witnessed the meeting described it as cool on both sides, arising on the part of his friends from jealousy; they, perhaps, judging from his costume that he had abandoned his bush life."

The Beagle had arrived at Fremantle just in time to allow her company to share in the annual festivities with which the inhabitants celebrate the formation of the colony. It may give some idea of the neglected state of this then infant colony to mention that during the six months' absence of the Beagle, only one boat had arrived there, and that, H.M.S. Pelorus from the Indian station. Communication with the home country was sadly needed, apart from the wish for news. Necessary articles of home manufacture or importation were becoming unattainable.

From the Swan River settlement, the Beagle proceeded to Sydney, passing Cape Leeuwin on the 23rd June, the south-western extremity of the continent named by the first discoverer in 1622, "Landt van de Lewin," or the Land of Lions. It was their intention to pass through Bass's Strait, but the weather had been extreme on rounding Cape Leeuwin, making that impossible.

On the morning of the 8th, the south-western extremity of Van Dieman's Land was seen. Van Dieman's Land, as before noted, was discovered in 1633 by Abel Janz Tasman, the Dutch navigator, and so named by him after the Governor of Batavia, under whose authority his voyage had been performed, but the insularity of the island was not fully proved until Bass passed through the Strait in 1798.

The bad state of weather detained the Beagle in Hobart Town for some time, reaching Port Jackson on July 24th.

It was not until the 11th of November that the Beagle left Port Jackson, and anchored close to the southern shore of Port Phillip. Surveying operations were set to work in good earnest, chiefly in determining the position of the mouths of the various channels intersecting the bank that extended across the entire bay, three miles from the entrance, then continuing the examination to the westward. Passing the mouth of the Barwon, the nature of the country begins to change, and high grassy downs, with rare patches of woodland, present themselves; then, as they near Cape Otway, a steep rocky coast, with dense woodland rising abruptly over it. Cape Otway, being the northern point of the western extremity of Bass's Strait, is swept by all the winds that blow into that end of the funnel, and this is the cause of the stunted appearance of the trees in that neighbourhood.

Having coasted the northern side of the strait, they cross to Tasmania to examine the south side.

Again, in May 1840, the Beagle left Sydney to cruise on the north coast, and explore the north-western part of the continent, this time taking the inside passage between the east coast and the Barrier Reef to reach her destination, and after discovering the mouth of a river near Cape Upstart (the present Burdekin), and making other minor corrections and additions in King's chart, the vessel anchored at the new settlement of Port Essington. In 1829, it will be remembered that Fort Dundas and Fort Wellington had been abandoned, and it was not until the year 1829 that any fresh attempt was made. The ships Alligator and Britomart, under Sir Gordon Bremer and Lieutenant Owen Stanley, were then despatched to Port Essington; but the new settlement to be formed was intended to be a purely military one, and although many intending settlers volunteered and sought permission to try their fortunes, no inducement was held out to them.

The township (destined to follow the date of its predecessors) received the imposing name of Victoria. Not long after the arrival of M. D'Urville with the Astrolabe and Zelie in Raffles Bay, Lieutenant Stewart, when visiting that bay to invite the French officers to the new settlement, found nothing remaining of the old one, but the graves of those buried there; the garden and stockade had totally disappeared.

Leaving Port Essington, the Beagle discovered a river at the head of Adam Bay, which was explored for eighty miles, and called the Adelaide. Here occurred the trago-comic episode that gave the name of Escape Cliffs to the neighbourhood.

"Messrs. Fitzmaurice and Keys went ashore to compare the compasses. From the quantity of iron contained in the rocks it was necessary to select a spot free from their influence. A sandy beach at the foot of Escape Cliffs was accordingly chosen. The observations had been commenced and were about half completed, when on the summit of the cliffs, which rose about twenty feet above their heads, suddenly appeared a large party of natives with poised and quivering spears, as if about immediately to deliver them. Stamping on the ground and shaking their heads too and fro, they threw out their long shaggy locks in a circle, whilst their glaring eyes flashed with fury as they champed and spit out the ends of their long beards (a custom with

Australian natives when in a state of violent excitement). They were evidently in earnest, and bent on mischief. It was therefore not a little surprising to behold this paroxysm of rage evaporate before the happy presence of mind displayed by Mr. Fitzmaurice, in immediately beginning to dance and shout, though in momentary expectation of being pierced by a dozen spears. In this he was imitated by Mr. Keys, and they succeeded in diverting them from their bad designs until a boat landing in a bay drew off their attention.

"Messrs. Fitzmaurice and Keys had fire-arms lying on the ground within reach of their hands, the instant, however, they ceased dancing, and attempted to touch them, a dozen spears were pointed at their breasts. Their lives hung upon a thread, and their escape must be regarded as truly wonderful, and only to be attributed to the happy readiness with which they adapted themselves to the perils of their situation. This was the last we saw of the natives in Adam Bay, and the meeting is likely to be long remembered by some and not without pleasant recollections, for although at the time it was justly looked upon as a serious affair, it afterwards proved a great source of mirth. No one could recall to mind, without laughing, the ludicrous figure necessarily cut by our shipmates, when to amuse the natives they figured on the light fantastic toe; they literally danced for their lives."

The Beagle now returned to Port Essington, first examining the southern shore of Melville Island. It was a visit not soon to be forgotten. Here they encountered their first experience of the green ants. Standing under a tree, whilst taking some observations, they found themselves covered, and nothing but undressing, at least tearing off their clothes, relieved them of the torture. The name of Ant Cliffs records this visit on the south shore of Melville Island.

Leaving Port Essington for the second time on September 4th, 1839, the Beagle threaded her way through Clarence Straits, to examine the western entrance, and on the 7th came in sight of the mouth of an opening not examined by Captain King. The next morning, with the boat provisioned for four days, they started on their exploring trip, and named the opening Hope Inlet, to commemorate the feelings it excited on its first discovery, and the bay in which it lies, Shoal Bay, it being very shallow at the head. Another wide opening, some fifteen miles ahead, having a more favourable appearance, they pulled for it, and reached the entrance at dark. In the morning, they found themselves at the entrance of a large and promising harbour, which they at once proceeded to investigate, and Stokes gave it the name of Port Darwin. Stokes seems to have been far more anxious to discover a river than a harbour; the discovery of the Adelaide elated him far more than did the finding of Port Darwin, and he does not seem to have at all antici-pated finding the site of the future capital of the north, that was to take the place of all the former settlements. Stokes returned to the ship, and the Beagle entered the new found port, and a thorough survey was made. Resuming her voyage, the Beagle, after examining Port Patter-son and Bynoe Harbour, sailed for a large opening one hundred and forty miles to the westward.

"Captain King's visit to this part of the coast was in 1819, and under very adverse circumstances; his vessel had but one anchor left, and the strong easterly winds then prevailing, with thick hazy weather, ren-dered his progress into the opening both difficult and hazardous. After a trial of two days, and having several narrow escapes from getting on shore, he bore away to examine the coast to the south-west, where he was repaid for his disappointment by the discovery of Cambridge Gulf. Thus did the exploration of this wide and interesting opening fall to our good fortune."

The explorers had great hopes of finding the mouth of an im-portant river. These hopes were rewarded by the discovery of the Victoria, which Stokes, in his extravagant joy, deemed equal in impor-tance to the Murray. Captain Wickharn bestowed the present name on it, and the delighted explorers proceeded to trace their new found stream, and pulled up it thirty miles. After their return, Lieutenant Fitzmaurice returned, having also discovered a river more to the east-ward, which received the name of Fitzmaurice, after its discoverer. A long and interesting task now commenced--the examination of the new river, and the process of taking the vessel up as far as possible. After this had been successfully accomplished, Captain Wickharn being un-well, Stokes was put in charge of a boat party to follow the river up as far as possible. Taking the boats as far as practicable, and then forming a land party, they managed to reach a distance of one hundred and forty miles from the sea, and finding the river still of considerable size, and full of large freshwater reaches, Stokes hugged the belief that at last the highway to the interior was discovered.

His raptures on this point led to a much higher estimate of the value of this river being entertained than it deserved; and until its ex-ploration by Gregory, many shared Stokes' opinion as to its future importance. The party returned in safety, and on going to weigh the anchors found them so firmly embedded in the bottom, which must have been a quicksand, that they had to slip both.

While anchored at the mouth of this river, Stokes went on shore to take observations, and, when ahead of his companions, was suddenly surprised and speared by the natives; the wound narrowly escaped being a fatal one. By December 12th he was sufficiently recovered to bear the motion of the ship, and sail was made for Swan River, where they arrived safely, having made some most important discoveries. A cruise on the west coast, and to Coepang, followed, and thence they returned by way of the west coast and Cape Leeuwin to Adelaide.

In the beginning of June, 1841, the Beagle, now in charge of Captain Stokes, Captain Wickharn having gone home on sick leave, left Sydney for another northern cruise. On the way up the ship fell in with four merchant vessels, which she convoyed as far as Booby Island, she herself pursuing her way down the Gulf of Carpentaria. Their first stay of any length was at Sweer's Island, and all the coastal inlets in the neighbourhood were well examined, resulting in the discovery of the Flinders River, on the 20th July, and of the Albert on the 1st of August. On the merits of this river Stokes waxes nearly as eloquent as he did over the Victoria, and once more indulges in excited hopes of reaching the centre of the continent. At fifty miles from the mouth the fallen logs stayed the progress of the boats, and the party landed and made an excursion on foot. Stokes now saw the plains to which he gave the name of the Plains of Promise, the position of which gave rise to so much discussion amongst the land explorers in after years. As may be imagined, the extent of level country, and its apparent richness, gave rise to much enthusiastic speculation on his part, and he returned to his ship well satisfied with his work.

During the discovery and examination of the Albert, Mr. Fitzmaurice had been engaged to the eastward, where he found the other mouth of the Flinders River, known as Bynoe Inlet. Unfortunately, another gun accident resulted in his being lamed for life, a charge of shot having entered his foot. This was the second accident while in the Gulf, a gun having burst with Lieutenant Gore, and badly lacerated his hand.

On the banks of the Flinders a native burial tree was found:--
"On the eastern bank rose a tree, the branches of which were laden with a most singular looking bundle or roll of pieces of wood. Struck with its appearance, we rested our oars to observe it. Landing, I advanced for nearer inspection towards the huge bundle of sticks before mentioned. It seemed almost like the nest of some new bird, and greatly excited my curiosity. As I approached a most unpleasant smell

assailed me, and on climbing up to examine it narrowly I found that it contained the decaying body of a native.

"Within the outer covering of sticks was one of net, with an inner one of the bark of the papyrus tree enveloping the corpse. According to the singular practice of uncivilised peoples of providing for the wants of those who have nothing more to do with earthly things, some weapons were deposited with the deceased in this novel kind of mortuary habitation, and a little beyond was a rill of water."

The Beagle then sailed to Booby Island, and from there to Victoria--the settlement at Port Essington--which they found in a comparatively flourishing state. Strange to say, Stokes, the discoverer of Port Darwin, says of Port Essington:

"As steam communication, moreover, must soon be established between Singapore and our colonies on the south-eastern shores of Australia, this port, the only real good one on the north coast, will be of vast importance as a coal depôt."

Another of the many instances of the hasty and fallacious deductions of first discovery, a second proof of which was afforded on the arrival of the Beagle at Swan River, whither, after calling at Coepang, they directed her course. Here they found the colonists in a state of doubt as to the existence of an inlet called Port Grey. A large number of immigrants had arrived from England, with the intention of settling there, but owing to the rumours of its non-existence, the name was changed to Leschenault Inlet. Captain Stokes was asked to settle the question, which he did by confirming the rumour that there was no Port Grey, and that the fertile country at the back of the spot indicated had likewise no existence. Grey, it will be remembered, reported seeing this available country when on his return from the hair-brained expedition to Sharks' Bay, and called it the Province of Victoria, but no subsequent exploration ever confirmed its existence.

The work of exploration by the Beagle now came to an end. Her remaining cruises in Australian waters were in the neighbourhood of the south coast and Tasmania. The work performed by her was more intimately connected with land exploration than that done by any other survey ship, and her close examination of the north coast resulted in the discovery of many important rivers. The Flinders, the Albert, the Adelaide, Victoria, and Fitzroy, all owe their names to the commander of the Beagle, and with her last cruise the maritime explorations of Australia may be said to close.

Chapter XX

Nationality of the first finders of Australia--Knowledge of the Malays--The bamboo introduced--Traces of smallpox amongst the natives in the north-west--Tribal rites--Antipathy to pork--Evidence of admixture in origin--Influence of Asiatic civilisation partly visible--Coast appearance repelling--Want of indigenous food plants--Lack of intercourse with other nations--Little now left of unexplored country--Conclusions respecting various geological formations--Extent of continental divisions--Development of coastal towns--Inducements for population--Necessity of the first explorings--Pioneer squatters' efforts--First Australian-born explorer--Desert theory exploded--Fertile downs everywhere--Want of water apparently insurmountable--Heroism of explorers--Inexperience of the early settlers--Grazing possible--Rapid stocking of country--The barrenness of the "Great Bight"--Sturt, the Penn of Australia--Results--Mitchell's work--Baron von Mueller's researches--A salt lake--Stuart first man across the continent--Burke and Wills' heroism--Services of McKinlay and Landsborough--John Forrest's journeys--Camel expedition by Giles--The Brisbane Courier expedition--Further explorations--Stockdale at Cambridge Gulf--Carr-Boyd and O'Donnell open good country in Western Australia--Work done by explorers--Their characteristics--Conclusion.

By common consent the nationality of the first navigators who landed on our shores is awarded to the Spanish. Following them came the Dutch, and, finally, the French and English. And, although the record of the Spanish visit to our northern coast is but vague, the fact of their being the first to acquaint the Western nations with the undoubted existence of a far southern land is generally allowed. Amongst the people inhabiting the many islands of the Malay Archipelago and portions of the mainland of Asia, there can be little doubt that our continent was known, and intercourse of an occasional kind carried on with its natives. That no permanent settlement was ever formed, or probably attempted, we may ascribe to the unpromising nature of the soil, compared to the fertile islands left by the visitors, and the fact that the products of which they came in search were mostly found in the sea itself, the shore only being at times visited for obtaining fresh water or seeking shelter.

During these visits no inducements would be forthcoming for undertaking an excursion inland. The monotonous character of the country would not excite curiosity, and the absence of all temptation in the way of articles of barter and traffic likely to be found, would confine their investigations chiefly to the sea shore. A temporary camp for drying the sea-slugs of commerce, a refuge for their crafts when the sudden storms of the tropics broke loose, met all their requirements. It is to the Malay ancestors of the men whose proas are still to be found fishing among the outlying reefs of the north, that we must look for the first discoverers of our island continent, and failing all written record or existing monument of their doings, search amongst the natives themselves for confirmation of the fact.

The presence of the bamboo in Arnheim's Land only, and its indigenous nature, is strong evidence of its Malay origin. It is found in abundance over this large promontory, and on the banks of the different rivers and creeks. Its extensive spread and thick growth point to many centuries of introduction, and that the Australians first obtained it from their northern visitors is almost certain. In abandoned camps pieces of bamboo would be left sticking in the ground, and formed, as most of their camps are, on the sandy banks of a creek, their growth would be under favourable circumstances, and their spread down the watercourses rapid.

Amongst all the tribes whose hunting grounds are between Cape Arnheim, and Cambridge Gulf, the traces of small-pox can be seen unmistakeably on many of the old men. Some are blind, and deeply pitted, others but lightly marked. Apparently the disease has worn itself out, for only the oldest members of the tribes have suffered. None seem to have it now, nor are the marks of the disease to be seen on the middle-aged men. The ravages of this scourge must have been confined to the coast tribes, as no evidence of its having been amongst the natives of the interior is to be found. The belt of dry country separating the aborigines of the plain from those of the sea may have saved the former, as this belt is often left uncrossed for years. This disease must have been brought from the north, and the date of its introduction would probably lie many centuries back.

Many of their customs and tribal rites bear a close resemblance to some that may be found in the New Testament, and are foreign to the usual habits of the Australian blackfellow. Add to this an innate antipathy to the flesh of swine when tasted for the first time, and it seems evident that some of the laws and traditions of more civilised nations have drifted down and been partly appropriated by the Australians.

In many of the sea-coast blacks of the north, sleepy eyes and straight-cut noses are often prominent, and render some of them especially remarkable; these features giving their faces an entirely different aspect to the common blackfellow type adjoining them inland. That, in the event of the wreck of a proa on the coast, some intermixture of the races would take place, and the survivors, perhaps, pass the remainder of their lives amongst the blacks, is quite possible, seeing that to many of our countrymen it has happened.

The close acquaintanceship shown by the Malay bêche-de-mer fishers with the nooks and inlets that are so thickly strewn along the coast, west of Cape Wessell, appears to be the result of much old-world seafaring lore, handed down from father to son. Whether the Chinese ever ventured so far south as Australia cannot be affirmed with certainty. Accident may have led them to our shores, but it is scarcely probable that the love of adventure would have tempted them so far.

Taking, then, the exceptional customs common to the natives of that portion 'of Australia still visited by the Malays, and seeing that these customs would only be the outcome of some centuries of intercourse, it is reasonable to suppose that from these outposts of Asiatic civilisation came the first adventurous traders to the lone land of the south. The distinct type of the Australian, while showing in exceptional cases the signs of foreign blood, precludes the idea that the continent was peopled from the north; but, at the same time, it is evident that some rudimentary forms of a higher development drifted down in after ages from that source.

The effect that the repellant nature of the Australian coast has had upon the southern progress of semi-civilisation is remarkably distinct. Each successive wave of improvement from the Asiatic continent seems to grow weaker and weaker as it travels south, until it breaks hopelessly on Australia. Nor is it hard to find the reason. The savage, coming from islands where a rude cultivation of indigenous fruits, valuable in their nature, had induced primitive land laws, and consequently settled habitations and a defined code of laws concerning

361

tribal rights and boundaries, found himself amongst a nomadic race, trusting to hunting and fishing solely for the means of existence. The soil, formed of the denudation of the sandstone rocks, scantily fertilised here and there by the decaying jungle, presented no field for rude agriculture, even had the dry seasons permitted; and gave forth no native fruits, save tasteless berries and half-poisonous roots. No knowledge of minerals would tempt him into the semi-scorched ranges inland; he would simply see that life after the old fashion of village existence was no longer for him, and would become a hunter and fisher like his fellows.

It would have been of inestimable benefit to the Australians, had tribes from the northern countries, only slightly higher than themselves in the scale, established a permanent footing on the mainland, and gradually worked their way throughout the land, carrying their superior knowledge with them, and having in the extended area before them a wide field for future development. Intermixing socially with the aborigines, they would have in a few generations made an indelible mark upon their mental capacity, which, after all, is only dormant; and the march of improvement once set in motion, centuries of confirmed intercourse with races of greater culture, and the consequent spread of new ideas would have peopled our continent with a different race to the improvident native of the present.

But the force of nature was against it; the new land of the south held forth no inducements even for the pirate or marauder. In the hand to mouth struggle for existence, not even a supply of food would be found in a ransacked camp; no land seen tempting settlement by its luxuriant vegetation and produce. The visitors of the straits scorned the inhospitable coast, and returned north. Only those whom ill-fate had deprived of the means of return stayed perforce, and lost their identity amongst the aborigines.

The white man, when he came, looked upon the country as he would upon an uninhabited land; the native was too far beneath him to profit by his coming, no inter-mixture of races could take place, the difference was too widely marked; and the aborigines of Australia were from the first numbered amongst the doomed tribes of the earth. An earlier introduction of the spirit of progress, however meagre in form, might have saved them. Had our northern coasts but possessed some lure for Asiatic nations, the story would have travelled and brought their overflowing population down to settle the continent long before the advent of our countrymen.

It is an accepted fact that on the continent of Australia proper there is very little unexplored territory left, and that we pretty well know what resources, in the way of land, we have still to fall back upon. This acceptance of our knowledge of the unsettled regions of our country is both right and wrong. Right, inasmuch that in a general sense, arguing from our knowledge of climatic influences in different latitudes, we can infer the particular nature of a particular district, although untrodden as yet by any one capable of giving us information. Wrong, in that the geographical formations of Australia are so persistently antagonistic that no true nor reliable deduction can always be arrived at. When I say persistently antagonistic, I mean that the two formations common to the interior, namely, sandstone and limestone, produce either a desert or a rich prairie. As a rule, in the vast interior, still unvisited and unsettled, the conditions are that the soil either grows grasses and herbs of the most nutritive character, or such as are totally unfitted to support graminivorous animal life. And these two conditions we may call antagonistic, as far as our efforts at practical settlement are concerned. When the outcrop is limestone, we may reckon on good pastoral country, and a fair water supply. When the outcrop is the pure red sandstone, we can hope for little else but the desert spinifex.

The distinction between these two formations is so strongly marked that it almost seems that a hard and fast line had, in places, been drawn between the productive and unproductive portions of Australia. That these strange and sudden alterations occur right through the continent, we have the evidence in the diaries of Giles and Forrest; and although we cannot doubt that a great portion of unexplored Australia consists of country that will never support population, we have as yet no valid reason for condemning the whole.

The continent of Australia contains, roughly speaking, three millions of square miles less about thirty-five thousand square miles. It may be summarised as follows: that New South Wales contains no unexplored country; Victoria, none; Queensland, a small portion of Cape York Peninsula; South Australia, a considerable area; and Western Australia, a very great deal. All the important explorations of late years have been in the last two mentioned colonies, for the very reason that in these colonies only the unknown exists. South Australia has at least 300,000 square miles of unexplored and partly explored country, and Western Australia can claim more than half a million of miles just touched here and there by the tracks of Eyre, Gregory, Giles, Forrest, and Warburton.

In speculating upon the future capabilities of this great expanse, we must fairly weigh the testimony of these men, and, by comparison, see what chance we have in the future of finding fresh pasture lands for the next generation. On the whole the testimony is unfavourable, but, on close inspection, there are strange coincidences in their diaries which would lead one to think that, perhaps, after all the "hopeless desert" that witnessed both their struggles and successes may yet hold secrets worth knowing and worth seeking for. In our time we have seen how the desert theory has been exploded in New South Wales--forced, as it were, outside our boundaries by the mere expansion of settlement. It is but a question of time for the mysteries of the yet unknown interior to share the same fate, and in the solution of the unknown great possibilities exist.

The development of the towns along the northern sea-board must necessarily be rapid. From the sheep-growing downs of the inland plateau, to the sugar and coffee-growing flats of the coast, the exports will be ever on the increase, and the wants of a growing people will necessitate ports in places that are now uninhabited. That the north will become one of the richest portions of our continent there is no doubt; its immense mineral wealth stands but partially revealed, while its adaptability for settlement is practically unbounded. The progress and utilisation of the waste lands of the north will be an interesting experiment to watch. Nature has, to a great extent, indicated the laws of settlement that will dominate the territory. To the capitalist she has given the rich wool-growing slopes of the inland country, where the expenditure of money is necessary, in order that the full value may be reaped from the land leased; money expended in water-storage, that repays the owner in a hundred ways. To the man of humbler means the well-watered coast districts offer facilities for small cattle stations and selections, and on the banks of some of the rivers the planter will soon be making a home, whilst for the miners are the broken ranges and gullies of the Dividing Range.

A settled Australia--that is, comparatively settled-this century may not witness, but that it will be a fact of the future, few, who have lived in the colonies during the last two decades, can doubt.

We may look forward to the crowning work of the future, when we shall no longer be altogether dependent upon the caprices of climate; nor sit idly by whilst our heritage of rainfall rushes past us into the ocean.

From the arrival of Governor Phillip with the first fleet, 1789, to the year 1813, when Wentworth, Lawson, and Blaxland succeeded in crossing the main range--the Blue Mountains--all attempts at exploration into the interior had been limited, the main range proving an impenetrable barrier. For the wants of the colony, the country up to that time found had proved sufficient. In the neighbourhood of Sydney, the Nepean, Grose, and Hawkesbury; to the north, the River Hunter; and to the south, the district known now as the Illawarra. But combined with the severe drought of 18 13, and the increase of stock, it was necessary to seek pastures new.

Their hopes of finding a navigable river flowing west into the sea were never realised, although for years it was each explorer's dream. On following a stream, they invariably found it run out into a shallow swamp, and then thought the continent possessed an inland sea or lake. Oxley pronounced this portion desert, and to them it then was; no thought could enter their minds of how after years of stocking, the entire country would change; how time and labour alone could make that vast waste profitable.

Directly the pass of the Blue Mountains had been won, and a public road made across the range, settlers with their stock steadily flowed west; the township of Bathurst sprang up, and settlement was made south towards the Shoalhaven River. The first large expedition into the interior was undertaken by Oxley, and he again comes to the conclusion that "the interior westward of a certain meridian is uninhabitable, deprived, as it is, of wood, water, and grass . . . that the interior of this vast country is a marsh, and uninhabitable." Only the edge of the interior crossed, it was early to come to this conclusion. But we must remember that the party were weary and disgusted with their want of success-the barren country, with no variety of trees, or soil; everything always the same. Eventually they reached good, well-watered country, and turning back from the Macquarie, delighted with the river, believed that the high road to the interior had been found.

This trip successful, he again left to follow the Macquarie, and although the inland sea remained undiscovered, large tracts of fertile country were opened for settlement; moreover, he had crossed the coast range to the north, and discovered that Port Macquarie (which, on following down the River Hastings, he had found and named) proved a practicable route to the interior.

About this time the pioneer squatter took share with the explorer, and settlement quickly advanced. Lawson and Scott were disappointed in their attempt to reach Oxley's discovery of Liverpool Plains; unable to penetrate the southern boundary of the plains, they discovered the Goulburn River. The year 1823 found Oxley, Cunningham, and Currie, all out in different directions; Currie to the south of Lake George, Cunningham engaged north of Bathurst, first in his capacity of botanist, and the discovery of a pass through the northern range on Liverpool Plains, which Lawson and Scott had sought in vain. He found and named the Pandora Pass, it proving practicable as a stock route.

Oxley then left Sydney in the Mermaid, to examine the inlets of Port Curtis, Moreton Bay, and Port Bowen, with a view to forming a penal settlement there. It was on this trip, while at Moreton Bay, that they rescued from the blacks the two men Pamphlet and Finnigan, who had been wrecked at Moreton Island seven months before. Oxley named the Brisbane River. This was his last work, and he died near Sydney in 1828. His career as an explorer was very successful. He had done much to aid the new colony, but was ever disappointed in his hopes of reaching the inland sea or lake, and of proving, except to his own satisfaction, whether any large rivers entered the sea between Cape Otway and Spencer's Gulf. Then Sir Thomas Brisbane thought of landing a party of prisoners near Wilson's Promontory, and by offer of a free pardon and a land grant, to find their way back to Sydney.

Mr. Hume, the first Australian-born explorer, and Mr. Hovell, took a party from Lake George, at that time the most outside station, to Western Port, and they were the first to see the Australian Alps. This trip helped to prove the hasty condemnation of Oxley's "desert" theory, and besides giving to the colony millions of acres of well-watered fertile country, and adding another large and important river--the Murray--it also held out far higher hopes for the future of the interior. During this time a settlement was formed at Moreton Bay, and subsequently removed to a better site on the Brisbane River. Cunningham, in 1827, left on a trip destined materially to effect the immediate progress of this new colony. Crossing Oxley's track, and entering the unexplored region, after naming the Gwydir and Dumaresque Rivers, he finally emerged on the Darling Downs. He was in raptures at the inexhaustible range of cattle pasture, the permanent water, and the grass and herbage generally. Then a passage across the range to Moreton Bay was found by way of Cunningham's Gap, but it was not used until the next year, when, accompanied by Mr. Frazer, colonial botanist, they proceeded by sea to Moreton Bay, and connected the settlement with the Darling Downs. How easy was the main range crossed here, and the fertile downs laid open, compared to the years of labour spent on the pass of the Blue Mountains. In the year following Cunningham made his last expedition, closing ten years of unceasing work in the cause of exploration.

Sturt followed Oxley's tracks. He exposed some of Oxley's mistakes, but only to make others as great; for the land was smitten with drought, and the rivers that Oxley had followed were now mere creeks, and in passing judgment no allowance was made for the seasons, and the country was valued according to the standard of other countries. His descriptions of the interior are wonderful pictures of the desolate, waterless, abandoned desert, "I scorched beneath a lurid sun of burning fire." His mission was to ascertain what lay beyond the shallow bed of reeds to the westward, in which Oxley lost the Macquarie; but as suddenly and as mysteriously the river ran out, and they were as completely baffled as Oxley had been. Dry on all sides, nothing was found but stony ridges or open forest, the country was monotonously level, and no sign of a river. Creek after creek they followed, only to lose it in a marsh. Suddenly they found themselves on the banks of a noble river, and from its size and saltness, Sturt conjectured he was near its confluence with an inland sea; but to be convinced in a few more days that the saltness was of local origin, fed by saline springs. This river Sturt called the Darling. The homeward march began, and the same harassing hunt for water; no break in the country, or change in the vegetation; all brown, blank, and desolate; not even inhabited by a bird-the drought had so long continued. Sturt had found the Darling, and he it was who eventually traced its course and outlet. Starting for that purpose the next year, they sailed down the Murray, proving its confluence with the Darling, and on down the united streams of the Murray and Darling with boundless flats on each side. The river widened day by day; the flight of sea-gulls, and the chopping sea caused by the wind, surely showed they were near the ocean. Still, Sturt had reached his goal--the Murray ended in a lake. They had hoped that succour would have waited them, had the ocean been reached. Now they must re-enter the Murray while the weary party had still strength to face each day's never-ending toil, and return to the camp on the Murrumbidgee. The great satisfaction of having successfully followed the course of the Murray was damped by the apparently valueless nature of the country passed through. And this trip, while adding greatly to Australian geography, gave a proof of the most patient endurance and courage--even to heroism--not excelled in the many records of bravery and dangers undergone by other explorers.

We have now looked through the reports of the country given by many men, and become familiar with their opinions of the future of the interior; they are almost unanimous in pronouncing it barren and uninhabitable. We must remember it was not their want of ability, but their inexperience of the value of the native grasses and herbs. In comparison with other countries, they appeared worthless. They did not realize that stocking would force the waters into natural channels, and that the stock would bring fresh grasses in their train, getting accustomed to and, after a while, fattening on the despised bushes and herbs. To them it was the embodiment of a desert--irreclaimable.

During the time these explorations were in progress, a settlement had been formed in Western Australia, and some attempt at exploration made, but for a few years not to any great distance. No difficulties here presented themselves to a passage through the coast range, and the country discovered seemed fitted both for pasture and agriculture.

For many years little was done in the way of fresh expeditions, until the year 1831. Major Mitchell in charge of a party traced the rivers, discovered by Oxley and Cunningham; his explorations were also surveys and the river system of the continent was partially worked out, but the hope of a river running through the interior to the north-west coast bad to be finally abandoned. His report of the country was also more favourable, and his after expeditions, merely connecting surveys, confirming and verifying previous discoveries, rather than an exploration into the unknown. His reports were glowing of the country passed through generally; from snow-topped mountains to level plains, watered with permanent streams and rivers, fitted for immediate occupation of the grazier or farmer.

Now it may be said the difficulties were overcome of entering the interior, for it was assailed from three points; Perth on the west, Port Phillip and St. Vincent's Gulf on the south, and from the settled parts of New South Wales and Moreton Bay on the east. Henceforth the settler so promptly followed the explorer, that the country became settled and stocked almost as quickly as known, and, foot by foot, the desert driven back.

Grey and Lushington wishing to verify the existence or not of a large river supposed to empty itself into the sea, at Dampier's Archipelago, endured great hardships. They were without experience of the colonies, or of the capabilities of the country; but as far as they could judge, pronounced the country well grassed and timbered. Their second trip resulted in the discovery of the Gascoigne, but little else; no great results to compensate for their terrible suffering and privation.

Small explorations were rapidly carried on to provide for the number of stock imported and the best stock routes; and now it was time to turn north, to look for the inland sea and the chain of mountains--Australia's backbone--that was supposed to exist. E. J. Eyre's discovery of Lake Torrens turned the colonists' attention north as a practicable stock route to Western Australia. From the sterile nature of the coast of the bight, and the absence of any rivers emptying into the sea, it was useless to seek in that direction. His march round the Great Bight was a journey of terrible suffering; it certainly proved that no water flowed into the south coast, and gave us our knowledge of the barren country shut in by the impenetrable, monotonous cliff line that closed its secrets against our mariners, but it gave no knowledge of the interior. After some of his men had deserted, and the one that remained murdered, Eyre, alone, on foot, with his stubborn courage, wearied out and starving, followed the coast line for numberless miles. Any errors of judgment leading to the tragic end of his expedition must needs be overlooked in the face of the great dangers and the perseverance that carried him through.

Sturt has been called the father of Australian exploration, and may well be held as one of our greatest scientific explorers--his object always to solve the mystery of the great interior; its strange peculiarity and physical formation. He returned disappointed, baffled. But was he in reality beaten? He was exceptionally unlucky in his seasons, and the report of the land he brought back caused settlement to progress slowly; only after years, when men had grown accustomed to the terrors of the desert, and knew that experience robbed them of their effect, Sturt found, but unwittingly, the outflow of the second river system. He longed to be the first to reach the centre of Australia, and hoped that once past the southern zone of the tropics he would reach a country blessed with a heavy and constant rainfall. Always he looked back with pleasure upon his travels, and said: "My path amongst savage tribes has been a bloodless one."

Next among our explorers comes Dr. Ludwig Leichhardt, and his trip from Fort Burke, on the Darling, to the Gulf of Carpentaria, which opened up so much well-watered country and attracted universal attention; but, unlike Sturt, he had exceptional good fortune, travelling always through country easy to penetrate and well watered-- not one night had the party to camp without water.

During this expedition, Sir Thomas Mitchell started with one having almost the same end in view as Dr. Leichhardt's. He did not reach the Gulf, but threw open our wonderful western prairies, and found the upper tributaries of the second great river system. This was his last expedition, and it fully confirmed his reputation. More fortunate than Sturt, he had been favoured in having plentiful and bountiful seasons of water and vegetation; but both men had done wonders in the cause of exploration. Mitchell's discovery of the Victoria, along the banks of which river he felt the high road to the north coast was found, was continued by Kennedy, who had been second in command during the first expedition of Sir Thomas Mitchell.

With a lightly equipped party Kennedy started to follow the course of the Victoria. Finally the river led them into the desert described by Sturt: "Plains gaping with fissures, grassless and waterless," and he turned back satisfied that the Victoria had not its outflow in the Gulf of Carpentaria, as hoped for by Sir Thomas Mitchell, but lost itself in Cooper's Creek. The loss of flour, through the natives, prevented Kennedy from extending his explorations towards the Gulf.

Kennedy's second trip, to examine Cape York Peninsula, ended most disastrously. Out of his party of thirteen only two men and a black boy were rescued. Through marshes and scrubs--seemingly the one monotonous entry in their journal being, "Cutting scrub all day"-- they endeavoured to push their way to Port Albany, the extreme north of the Peninsula, where a ship would meet them. Saltwater creeks and marshy ground, with the ranges inhabited by hostile natives, was their prospect, while their horses were rapidly failing on the sour coast grasses. From first to last this was a most unfortunate expedition-the awful and impassable nature of the country travelled through, the hostile blacks and loss of the horses, and then, when sickness came upon the little band, it was doomed.

In the south, Baron von Mueller was busy exploring some of the unknown portion of South Australia and the Australian Alps-botanical and geographical researches combined. The heights of several of the highest mountains in Australia were fixed, and geographical positions accurately placed.

Leichhardt, encouraged by his successes, makes his final venture, but what befel his party--shall we ever know? It is so late now that we can entertain little hope of ever elucidating his fate.

In 1846, the Gregory brothers are in the west, led by A. C. Gregory, who so distinguished himself afterwards as a scientific explorer, and in 1855 he was in command of the North Australian

Expedition; with him his brother and the celebrated botanist Baron Von Mueller. Captain Stokes reported the Victoria as an important stream, and the probable means of gaining access to the interior, upon which Gregory traced its course. He professed great disappointment at the reality of Captain Stokes' "Plains of Promise," compared to what he had been led to expect. The successful conclusion of this expedition, which had covered nearly five thousand miles, proves Gregory an explorer of undoubted qualifications, and it is to he regretted that so scanty a record of his travels has been published.

Lake Torrens still occupied the attention of the South Australian colonists, its probable extent and direction, and several expeditions were undertaken to solve the question. To the south-east fresh water and well grassed pastoral country, but Lake Torrens still remained as on its first discovery by Eyre--a dry bed covered with a thick incrustation of salt, and far away surrounded on all sides by barren country. Goyder found fresh water in the lake, but its unavailability was confirmed.

M'Dowall Stuart has been recognised as the man who first crossed from sea to sea, from the south to the north coast, and now on Stuart's track is built the overland telegraph line, a lasting witness of his indomitable perseverance. In his subsequent expeditions following his old tracks, he was destined to meet success, and come to the sea near the mouth of the Adelaide River. Stuart dipped his hands and feet in the sea, and his initials were cut on the largest tree they could find. This was his last trip, and he never recovered from the great suffering of his return journey.

The expedition under Burke and Wills left amid great celebration; in fact, it was a gala day in Melbourne, and their journey through the settled districts one triumphant march. Their purpose was to cross to Carpentaria. Fate seemed so propitious that one would think in irony she laughed, as she thought of their return.

They accomplished their task; they reached the Gulf; but did not know their exact position; and when they turned back it became a terrible struggle for existence. In spite of the princely outfit with which they started, short rations and great hardships was their lot, and the men tried to live like the blacks, on fish and nardoo, and an occasional crow or hawk which they shot. Wills met his death alone, while Burke and King were searching for food, and to him, suffering from such extreme exhaustion, death must have come as the "comforter." He met it as a gallant man would, without fear. From his last entries he had given up hope and waited calmly. Burke died the second day; when

371

King looked at him in the dawning light, he saw that he was really, alone. Meantime, the rest of the party were left on Cooper's Creek, and were slowly starving to death. Parties from all sides were now being equipped to go in search of them.

M'Kinlay's trip across the continent did great service. It verified Stuart's report that the country always considered as a terrible desert was not unfit for all pastoral occupation, and, being an experienced man, his report carried conviction.

One of the search parties for Burke and Wills was under William Landsborough, having, through previous explorations, good knowledge of the country; and another, in charge of Frederick Walker, composed of native troopers. Now the eastern half of Australia was nearly all known; it had been crossed and re-crossed from south to north; still, the distinctive value of the country had yet to be learned, and the delusion that the sheeps' wool would turn to hair in the torrid north to be given up. All around the coast settlement was surely and steadily creeping, and unoccupied country going further back every day.

On the north coast, Burketown, under the care of William Landsbrough, was growing up, and in the north of Arnheim's Land, M'Kinlay was looking for a suitable site to establish a port for the South Australian Government. Somerset was formed on the mainland of Cape York Peninsula, and the formation of this led to the expedition of the Jardine brothers. The successful termination of their journey, when we look at the difficulties through which they passed, and the misfortunes they had to encounter, merits our greatest admiration; and although it did not result in the discovery of good pastoral country, still they accomplished their object.

The overland telegraph line, and the small explorations made on either side of it, led greatly to our knowledge of the interior.

John Forrest made his first important journey in 1869, but found no great results in good country to the eastward of Perth. Then a journey was made from Perth to Adelaide by way of the Great Bight-- never traversed since Eyre's journey. Owing to a better equipment, he was able to give a more impartial report of the country passed through; for Eyre was struggling for life, and it was natural that nature to him would then look at her blackest.

Warburton and Giles now occupied attention, and their great hope, the country between the overland telegraph line and the western settlements.

Warburton's expedition led to the western half of the continent being condemned as a hopeless desert. He no doubt got into a strip of barren country, and being so occupied in pressing straight through, devoted no time to the examination of country on either side.

Giles was twice driven back in his attempts to reach Western Australia. Then, with an equipment of camels, made a third, and successful, attempt. No discoveries of any importance were made; the country was suffering from severe drought.

William Hann, one of the pioneer squatters of the North of Queensland, took charge of a party sent by the Queensland Government to investigate the tract of country at the base of Cape York Peninsula, both for its mineral and other resources. Naming the Palmer, and finding here prospects of gold, the further examination of the river resulted in the discovery of what turned out to be one of the richest goldfields in Queensland.

Again the Queensland Government sent out an expedition, under charge of W. 0. Hodgkinson, to determine the amount of pastoral country to the west of the Diamantina River.

Buchanan and F. Scarr next attacked the country between the overland telegraph line and the Queensland border, and in 1878, Mr Lukin, proprietor of the Courier, in Brisbane, organised an expedition for the purpose of exploring the country in the neighbourhood of a proposed railway line, which had been inaugurated in Port Darwin, and to find the nature, value, and geographical features of the unexplored portions. Under the leadership of Ernest Favenc, the party started from Blackall. This expedition had the effect of opening up a great area of good pastoral country, nearly all of which is now stocked.

In 1883, Favenc traced the heads of the rivers running into the Gulf of Carpentaria, near the Queensland border, and in the year following, crossed from the Queensland border to the telegraph line, and across the coast range to the mouth of the Macarthur River. Soon after, the South Australian Government surveyed this river, and opened it as a port; a good road was formed from the interior to the coast, and the settlement of the country followed.

In Western Australia, Alexander Forrest led an expedition from the De Grey River to the telegraph line, which they reached after a great struggle. It was a most successful trip, and the district found contains some of the best country in Western Australia, both for pastoral and mineral purposes.

Stockdale, with a view to settlement, explored the country in the neighbourhood of Cambridge Gulf. Landing there by steamer, he began the journey, which ended in a tragedy. After a hard struggle, he reached the telegraph line.

McPhee's exploration east of Daly Waters may be said to conclude the expeditions between the Queensland border and the overland line.

To complete the exploration of Arnheim's Land, the South Australian Government fitted out an expedition under the guidance of Mr. David Lindsay, but the country passed over was not available for pastoral settlement, some of it being good sugar country. Messrs. Carr Boyd and O'Donnell, undertaking another trip from the Katherine River to Western Australia, were more fortunate in finding good country, but no geographical discovery resulted.

Thus our island continent has been opened to us by the indomitable courage and endurance of navigators and explorers. Can we look for instances of greater bravery in the exploration of any other portion of the globe? Our old navigators, with their meagre equipment, searched minutely every portion of the coast, until the termination of the survey of the Beagle, for the mouth of some river that would communicate with the interior, as our earlier explorers hoped to find a waterway in the wilderness through which they travelled.

The idea of the work they did, being verified as it now is, could never have been dreamt of. Think of Flinders, in the old Investigator, as he. sailed from group to group of islands, and from point to point of reefs; when he got at last through Torres Straits, and stood down the Gulf, looking up the old land marks of the early Dutch visitors to our shores--Duyfhen Point, the Van Alphen River, Groote Eylandt, and the rest--names still preserved, that bear witness to the brave old navigator who visited these shores before we did. Many an anxious day and night, doubtless, he had. Now, with steam at our command, the straits have become the safe highway of traffic to all the leading marts of the world.

It is well for us to bear in mind that, as a rule, experienced bushmen do find the best points of new country, and not the worst. The after result generally is that the discoveries of the first explorers are extended, but not improved on. Therefore, in comparing the different routes that traverse the western half of our continent, we can safely allow that each man found, and noted, the most promising features on his line of travel.

By close comparison of the work done by the men who have laid bare so many of the secrets of the interior, and by deductions to be drawn from the physical conformation and climatic peculiarities already revealed, we may, to some extent, conjecture the possibilities of the future. With every variety of climate between temperate and tropical, with enormous mineral treasures--the extent of which, even at the present time, can only be conjectured--boundless areas of virgin soils, and a coastline dotted with good harbours and navigable rivers, we have all the elements of a nation yet to take rank among the recognised powers of the world. But in the interim there is much to be done. The flat and monotonous nature of most of the continent, which is at present to a certain extent our bane, will, when the principles of water storage, and its distributation are fully understood, be of wonderful assistance. The physical formation of the interior lends itself to the creation of artificial channels, and the work of leading waterways through the great areas of unwatered country, that for months lie useless and unproductive, will be comparatively easy. We have always, or nearly always, our annual floods to depend upon, and the supply furnished by them should be amply sufficient for use. Flood water is surplus water, and its conservation should be the thing aimed at. Many a dry watercourse, that is now but a slight depression, could be utilised as a channel for conducting the flood waters to the back country. What would be impossible in an island of bold mountain ranges, becomes easy in the flats of our dry interior.

In the dry inland plains, a water supply that will relieve the frontage from overstocking during the droughty months, means the preservation of some of our most valuable indigenous fodder plants. The overcrowding of stock on the natural permanent waters during dry periods, has often been the cause of a depreciation in the natural grasses on some of our principal rivers. And whilst this has been going on, sun-cracked lagoons and lakes, surrounded by good, if dry, feed have been lying unnoticed and useless, waiting for the time to come when they would be turned to account.

Back from the main watercourses are countless natural reservoirs, that lie for years dry, and drought-smitten, save in an exceptional flood. They are never filled, and the fact of supplying them with water is practicably feasible.

In many districts of the inland slope, the rivers have sandy beds, incapable of retaining the water for more than a few months; whilst running parallel with them on either side, are chains of lagoons that often run dry through the floods not being excessive enough to overflow the banks. These lagoons are, as a rule, well calculated to hold water, and could be brought under the influence of ordinary floods, instead of being, as now, dependent upon extraordinary ones; thus atoning for the insufficient retaining power of the river bed.

The present great need of Australia is the conservation of water, and the irrigation works which have been already commenced on the banks of the Murray River, coupled with the recent discoveries of an apparently unlimited artesian supply on the and plains of Western Queensland, testify alike to the recognition of the want, and to the ease with which it may be met. One inevitable rule of settlement is that population follows water; present prospects therefore amply justify the hope that at no very distant date the one-time "central desert" of the first explorers will be the centre of attraction for the fast-growing population of the coast line; and that in the merging together of the peoples of the colonies, now separated by merely imaginary boundary lines, will be found the one great help to the fulfilment of the desire of every true Australiana Federated Australia--a grand result of the indomitable courage, heroic self-sacrifice, and dogged perseverance of the men of all nationalities, who have established a claim to the proud title of "Australian Explorer."

APPENDICES

APPENDIX - The Pandora Pass.

The following memorandum, written on parchment, was enclosed in a bottle, and buried under a marked tree in the Pandora Pass:
"MEMORANDUM.

"After a very laborious and harassing journey from Bathurst, since April last, a party, consisting of five persons, under the direction of Allan Cunningham, H.M. Botanist (making the sixth individual), having failed of finding a route to Liverpool Plains, whilst tracing the south base of the Barrier Mountains (before us north), so far as fifty miles to the eastward of this spot, at length upon prosecuting their research under this great mountain belt, in a westerly direction, reached this valley, and discovered a practicable and easy passage through a low part of the mountain belt, north by west from this tree, to the very extensive levels connected with the abovementioned plains, of which the southernmost of the chain is distant about eleven or twelve miles (by estimation), N.N.W. from this valley, and to which a line of trees has been carefully marked, thus opening an unlimited, unbounded, seemingly well-watered country, N.N.W., to call forth the exertions of the industrious agriculturist and grazier, for whose benefit the present labours of the party have been extended. This valley, which extends to the S.W. and W.S.W., has been named 'Hawkesbury Vale,' and the highest point of the range, bearing N.W. by W. from this tree, was called 'Mount Jenkinson,' the one a former title, and the other the family name of the noble earl whose present title the plains bear, and which, from the southern country, this gap affords the only passage likely to be discovered. The party in the earlier and middle stages of their expedition encountered many privations and local difficulties of travelling to, and in their return from the eastward; in spite, however, of these little evils, 'a hope at the bottom,' or, at this almost close of their journey, an encouragement induced them to persevere westerly a limited distance, and thus it was this passage was discovered. It has therefore been named 'Pandora's Pass.' Due east and west by compass from this tree, in a direct line (by odometrical admeasurement) were planted the fresh stones of peaches, brought from the colony in April last, with every good hope that their produce will one day or other afford some refreshment to the weary farmer, whilst on his route beyond the bourne of the desirable country north of Pandora's Pass. A like planting took place on the plains, twelve miles distance north at the last marked trees, with similar good wishes for their growth. A remarkably high mount above the pass east, being a guide to the traveller advancing south from the plains, has been named 'Direction Head.' The situation of this tree is as follows:--Latitude, observed on the 7th and 8th of June, 1832, 32 deg. 15 min. 19 sec. S; its longitude being presumed about 149 deg. 30 min. E. The party now proceed with the utmost despatch south for Bathurst.

"ALLAN CUNNINGHAM.

"June 9th, 1823.

"Buried for the information of the first farmer who may venture to advance so far to the northwards as this vale, of whom it is requested this document may not be destroyed, but carried to the settlement of Bathurst, after opening the bottle."

(See Chapter II.)

APPENDIX - Death of Surveyor-General Oxley.

ABSTRACT FROM THE "GOVERNMENT GAZETTE" OF MAY 27TH, 1828.

"It would be impossible for his Excellency, consistently with his feelings, to announce the decease of the late Surveyor-General without endeavouring to express the sense he entertains of Mr. Oxley's services, though he cannot do justice to them.

"From the nature of this colony, the office of Surveyor-General is amongst the most important under Government, and to perform its duties in a manner Mr. Oxley has done for a long series of years is as honourable to his zeal and abilities as it is painful for the Government to be deprived of them.

"Mr. Oxley entered the public service at an early period of his life and has filled the important situation of Surveyor-General for the last sixteen years.

"His exertions in the public service have been unwearied, as has been proved by his several expeditions to explore the interior. The public have reaped the benefit, while it is to be apprehended that the event, which they cannot fail to lament, has been accelerated by the privations and fatigue he endured during the performance of these arduous services. Mr. Oxley eminently assisted in unfolding the advantages of this highly-favoured colony from an early stage of its existence, and his name will ever be associated with the dawn of its advancement. It is always gratifying to the Government to record its approbation of the services of meritorious public officers, and in assigning to Mr. Oxley's name a distinguished place in that class to which his devotion to the interests of the colony has so justly entitled him, the Government would do honour to his memory in the same degree as it feels the loss it has sustained in his death."

(See Chapter II.)

APPENDIX - List of the Men Comprising Sir Thomas Mitchell's Party on his Expedition to the Victoria (Barcoo), 1846.

Sir T. L. Mitchell, Kt., Surveyor-General--Chief of the Expedition. Edmund B. Kennedy, Esq., Assistant Surveyor--Second in Command. W. Stephenson, M.R.C.S.L--Surgeon and collector of objects of natural history. Peter M'Avoy, Charles Niblett, William Graham--Mounted videttes. Anthony Brown--Tent-keeper. William Baldock--In charge of the horses. John Waugh Drysdale--Store-keeeeper. Allan Bond, Edward Taylor, William Bond, William Mortimer, George Allcot, John Slater, Richard Horton, Felix Maguire--Bullock-drivers. James Stephens, Job Stanley--Carpenters. Edward Wilson--Blacksmith. George Fowkes--Shoemaker. John Douglas--Barometer-carrier. Isaac Reid--Sailor and chainman. Andrew Higgs--Chainman. William Hunter, Thomas Smith--With the horses. Patrick Travers--Carter and pioneer, Douglas Arnott--Shepherd and butcher. Arthur Bristol--Sailmaker and Sailor.

Eight drays, drawn by eighty bullocks, two boats, thirteen horses, four private horses, and three light carts, comprised the means of conveyance, and the party was provided with provisions for a year; two hundred and fifty sheep (to travel with the party) constituting the chief part of the animal food. The rest consisted of gelatine, and a small quantity of pork.

(See Chapter IV.)

APPENDIX -
Richard Cunningham's Fate.

REPORT OF LIEUTENANT ZOUCH, OF THE MOUNTED
POLICE, REGARDING THE DEATH OF RICHARD
CUNNINGHAM.

"SIR, "Bathurst, December 7th, 1835.

"I have the honour to state that, in conforming with the instructions contained in the Colonial Secretary's letter of the 16th October, together with your orders, directing me to proceed to the interior for the purpose of ascertaining the fate of Mr. Cunningham, I proceeded with the party on the 24th of October for Buree, which place I left on the 29th, accompanied by Sandy (the native black mentioned in my instructions). On the 2nd of November I fortunately met with two blacks who knew the particulars of a white man having been murdered on the Bogan, also the names and persons of the perpetrators of the deed. They likewise offered to accompany the police to where the tribe to which the murderers belonged were encamped. I accordingly took them as guides, and on the evening of the 6th they informed me they could see the smoke from the fires of the Myall blacks, on the borders of a lake called Budda.

"On arriving at the banks of the lake, we found a tribe encamped consisting of upwards of forty men, women, and children, all of whom we succeeded in making prisoners, without any resistance on their part. Having questioned them as to the murder of a white man, they acknowledge to one having been killed on the Bogan by four of their tribe, three of whom they delivered up; the fourth, they stated, was absent on the Big River. On searching the bags of the tribe, we found a knife, a glove, and part of a cigar case, which the three blacks acknowledged they had taken from the white man, and which Muirhead said he was sure belonged to Mr. Cunningham.

"The three murderers, whose names are Wongadgery, Boree-boomalie, and Bureemal, stated that they and another black, about six moons ago, met a white man on the Bogan, who came up and made signs that he was hungry; that they gave him food, and that he encamped with them that night. The white man repeatedly getting up during the night excited suspicion, and they determined to destroy him the following morning, which they did by Wongadgery going unperceived behind him and striking him on the back of the head with a nulla-nulla. The other three men then rushing upon him with their weapons, speedily effected their purpose.

"I then determined to proceed to the spot where the murder was committed, which I was informed by the blacks was distant three days' journey, but, learning from them that there was a great scarcity of water, Muirhead, and one of the prisoners (Burreemal) as a guide across to the Bogan, leaving the other two prisoners in charge, under the command of Corporal Moore, to proceed to a station about thirty miles distant from Wellington, there to await my return.

"On Tuesday, the 10th, I arrived at a place called Currindine, where the black showed me some bones, which he said were those of a white man they had killed, and pointed out a small portion of a coat, and also of a Manilla hat. Being thus convinced of the truth of their statement, and also of the spot where the melancholy event had occurred, I collected all the remains I could discover, and having deposited them in the ground, raised a small mound over them, and barked some of the nearest trees, as the only means in my power of marking the spot.

"Having thus accomplished the object of my expedition, I proceeded on my return, and on rejoining the party under Corporal Moore, I learned the escape of the two prisoners, which took place on the night of the 11th November, when trooper Lard was on sentry, against whom I have forwarded a charge for neglect of duty. The fulfilment of my instructions being thus partially defeated, I considered it my duty to proceed in search of the runaways, and continued the pursuit, I regret to say, without success, until I was obliged to return, our stock of provisions being consumed. I arrived here with the party yesterday, and shall forward the prisoner, 'Bureemal,' to Sydney, together with the articles I was enabled to collect, supposed to have belonged to the late Mr. Cunningham.

"I have the honor to be, etc., "W. ZOUCH, "Lieut. Mounted Police."

FAVENC

     "To CAPTAIN WILLIAMS, "Commandant of Mounted Po-
lice."

     (See Chapter IV)

APPENDIX - Cave Drawings.

The singular cave paintings found by Lieutenant George Grey near the Glenelg River, in Western Australia, during the expedition of 1838.

"The cave was twenty feet deep, and at the entrance seven feet high, and about forty feet wide. As before stated, the floor gradually approached the roof in the direction of the bottom of the cavern, and its width also contracted, so that at the extremity it was not broader than the slab of rock, which formed a natural seat. The principal painting in it was the figure of a man ten feet six inches in length, clothed from the chin downwards in a red garment, which reached to the wrists and ankles; beyond this red dress the feet and hands protruded and were badly executed.

"The face and head of the figure were enveloped in a succession of circular bandages or rollers, or what appeared to be painted to represent such. These were coloured red, yellow, and white, and the eyes were the only features represented on the face. Upon the highest bandage or roller, a series of lines were painted in red, but although so regularly done as to indicate they have some meaning, it was impossible to tell whether they were intended to depict written characters, or some ornament for the head. This figure was so drawn on the roof that its feet were just in front of the natural seat, whilst its head and face looked directly down on any one who stood in the entrance of the cave, but it was totally invisible from the outside.

"It would be impossible to convey in words an adequate idea of this uncouth and savage figure; I shall, therefore, only give such a succint account of this and the other paintings as will serve as a sort of description. Its head was encircled by bright red rays, something like the rays which one sees proceeding from the sun, when depleted on the signboard of a public house; inside of this came a broad stripe of very brilliant red, which was coped by lines of white, but both inside and outside of this red space were narrow stripes of a still deeper red, intended probably to mark its boundaries. The face was painted vividly white and the eyes black; being, however, surrounded by red and yellow lines, the body, hands and arms were outlined in red, the body being curiously painted with red stripes and bars.

"Upon the rock which formed the left hand wall of this cave, and which partly faced you on entering, was a very singular painting, vividly coloured, representing four heads joined together. From the mild expression of the countenances, I imagined them to represent females, and they appeared to be drawn in such a manner, and in such a position, as to look up at the principal figure which I have before described; each had a very remarkable head dress coloured with a deep bright-blue, and one had a necklace on. Both of the lower figures had a sort of dress, painted with red in the same manner as that of the principal figure, and one of them had a band round her waist. Each of the four faces was marked by a totally distinct expression of countenance, and although none of them had mouths, two, I thought, were otherwise rather good looking.

"The whole painting was executed on a white ground. The next most remarkable drawing in the cave was an ellipse, three feet in length, and one foot ten inches in breadth. The outside line of this painting was of a deep-blue colour, the body of the ellipse being of a bright yellow, dotted over with red lines and spots, whilst across it ran two transverse lines of blue. The portion of the painting above described formed the ground, or main part of the picture, and upon this ground was painted a kangaroo in the act of feeding, two stone spearheads, and two black balls. One of the spear-heads was flying to the kangaroo, and one away from it, so that the whole subject probably constituted a sort of charm, by which the luck of an enquirer in killing game could be ascertained.

"There was another rather humorous sketch, which represented a native in the act of carrying a kangaroo, the height of the man being three feet. The number of drawings in the cave could not altogether have been less than from fifty to sixty, but the majority of them consisted of men, kangaroos, etc., the figures being carelessly and badly executed, and being evidently a very different origin to those which I have first described.

"Another very striking piece of art was exhibited in the little gloomy cavities, situated at the back of the main cavern. In these instances some rock at the sides of the cavity had been selected, and the stamp of a hand and arm by some means transferred to it. This outline

of the hand and arm was then painted black, and the rock about it white, so that on entering that part of the cave it appeared as if a human hand and arm were projecting through a crevice, admitting light."
(See Chapter V.)

Appendix - SMITH, A LAD OF EIGHTEEN, FOUND DEAD, MAY 8TH, 1839.

The following is Warrup's account of the finding of Smith's body, the young volunteer of Grey's party who died. Warrup was a Western Australian native who accompanied the search party under Mr. Roe:--

"7th Day. The next day away, away, away, away, returning, on our tracks returning, on our tracks returning. At Barramba we sit down; we eat bread and meat; they eat fresh-water mussels; the natives eat not fresh-water mussels.

"Away, away, away, away; we reach the water of Djunjup; we shoot game. Away, away, away, through a forest away, through a forest away; we see no water. Through a forest away, along our tracks away. We sleep at Ka-jil-up; rain falls; the water here is good, the horses feed, well do the horses feed.

"Away, away; along our tracks away; hills ascending; then pleasantly away, away, through a forest away, through a forest away; we see a water-the water of Goonmarrup. Along the river away, along the river away, a short distance we go, then away, away, away, through a forest away.

"Then along another river away, across the river away. At Meergamuny we sleep, raising huts.

"Still we go onwards along the sea away, through the bush away, then along the sea away, along the sea away. We see three white men, three of them we see; they cry out, 'Where is water?' water we give them-brandy and water we give them. We sleep near the sea.

"Away, away we go (I, Mr. Roe, and Kinchela), along the shore away, along the shore away, along the shore away. We see a paper--the paper of Mortimer and Spofforth. I see Mr. Smith's footsteps ascending a sand-hill; onwards I go, regarding his footsteps. I see Mr.

Smith dead. We commence digging the earth. Two sleeps had he been dead; greatly did I weep, and much I grieved. In his blanket folding him, we scraped away the earth.

"We scrape earth into the grave, we scrape the earth into the grave, a little wood we place in it. Much earth we heap upon it-much earth we throw up. No dogs can dig there, so much earth we throw up. The sun had inclined to the westward as we laid him in the ground."

(See Chapter V.)

Appendix - EYRE'S LETTERS.

Adelaide, 4th January, 1844.

"Having observed that during the past year the subject of an overland journey from Moreton Bay to Port Essington has again been mooted by the Legislative Council of New South Wales, I do myself the honour of applying to you for information as to whether the Executive Government have any such expedition in contemplation during the present year.

"In the event of such being the case, I beg leave respectfully to offer my services to conduct the explorations, and should his Excellency the Governor do me the honour to confide in me so honourable and important an employment, his Excellency may confidently rely that no effort or exertions should be wanting on my part to ensure all practicable success. In a former communication on the subject, I had the honour of giving a rough estimate of the probable expense of the undertaking, if carried out in accordance to a plan of operations and a scale of party then proposed. The altered circumstances of the colonies would now probably enable an equipment to be prepared at much lower prices than were then estimated for, and I may remark that, although in my former letter to his Excellency, Sir G. Gipps, I specified, in accordance with his Excellency's request, the nature of the party I thought it advisable to have, and the general line of route I deemed most likely to be practicable, I shall be most happy to endeavour to carry out any views his Excellency may entertain upon the subject, with any party or any direction his Excellency may think desirable. The only point to which I would call the attention of his Excellency the Governor, in the event of an expedition being now in contemplation, is the great necessity there would be for the party to take the field early in the season, so as to have the whole winter before them for active operations; and, even then, I feel very doubtful whether it would be possible for a party to accomplish the whole distance to Port Essington in less than two winters, being, as I am, strongly of opinion that it will be found quite impracticable to travel in a tropical climate during the summer months.

"I have the honor to be,

"Yours obediently,

"E. J. EYRE."

"Adelaide, 23rd December, 1841.

"Sir,--Having understood from Captain Sturt that your Excellency is desirous of sending an expedition into the interior from the northeast coast towards Port Essington, I do myself the honour of. addressing your Excellency upon the subject, as I feel a very great interest in the investigation of the interior of this singular continent, and shall be most ready to give my services to conduct an expedition should your Excellency decide upon fitting one out, and confide to me that responsible and honourable duty. In September last I met with a printed copy of a letter addressed by your Excellency to Lord John Russell, in which some allusion was made to your wish to send an expedition to explore the interior, and I at once wrote to the Colonial Secretary of Sydney to volunteer my services, but, from various causes, I am induced to believe that my communication must have miscarried, and I now therefore beg leave to renew that offer.

"As I am not in possession of your Excellency's views as to the nature of the expedition it might be in contemplation to send out, or the direction it might be considered desirable to take, I cannot do more at present than express my willingness to engage in the undertaking generally, and should your Excellency do me the honour of entertaining the offer I have made, I shall be most happy, when put in possession of your Excellency's wishes on the subject, to enter more fully into the necessary detail.

"Being now engaged in the public service at some distance inland, I should be most anxious to have as early notice as possible of your Excellency's reply to my proposal, so that, by giving timely notice to the colonial Government here, no obstruction of the public service might take place. It would also be necessary for me to be in Sydney as early as may be practicable to prepare the equipment of the expedition in time to take the field at the close of the summer.

"E. J. EYRE."

NOTE BY SIR GEORGE Gipps.

"Acknowledge receipt, and say I shall be happy to avail myself of the offer of Mr. Eyre's services in the proposed expedition, provided no prior claim be preferred by Captain Sturt, with whom I have had some communication on the subject. The whole expense of the expedition would be defrayed by the Government; but before I can enter into any engagement with Mr. Eyre it will be necessary that I should be furnished with some account of the equipment, etc., which would be considered necessary, in order that some estimate of the expense of the expedition may be formed.

"G. G.

"November 12."

(See Chapter VI.)

Appendix - EXTRACT OF LETTER FROM MAJOR MITCHELL.

"5th September, 1845.

"In attention to your letter of yesterday, I have now the honour to submit the outlines of my plan for the exploration of the northern interior.

"I would therefore first beg leave to observe that my proposed line of route is founded on views which I have always entertained respecting the interior, but not more so than on the expediency of ascertaining the character of that portion of the colony to the northwest of the River Darling. To avoid unnecessary repetition, I shall annex a quotation here from my despatch, dated Peel's River, 29th February, 1832, in which my reasons for believing that there is a dividing range beyond the Darling, and that a great river may be looked for beyond it, are stated at length. I have had no occasion to alter my plans or views respecting the interior since that time; on the contrary, subsequent experience has rather tended to support these views. The course of the Condamine, now better known, affords now a better indication that the high ground is in the situation I supposed. And I annex also a communication from Walter Bagot respecting that portion of the country beyond the Darling which is nearly opposite to Fort Bourke, affording additional evidence of the existence of a lofty range to the north-west, and a great river beyond it. The overflowing of the 'Waramble' agreed so well with what I observed at the upper part of the Darling in 1831, and near Fort Bourke in 1836, and the situation of the range and river beyond accord so well with all that can reasonably be assumed, as to leave no doubt in my mind as to the accuracy of Mr. Bagot's statement, even where it is founded on that of the natives."

MINUTE BY SIR G. Gipps.

"Acknowledge receipt, and inform Sir Thos. Mitchell, that desiring to leave him as far as possible free to act upon his own judgment in the arduous undertaking in which he is about to embark, I do not consider it necessary to do more than communicate to him my approval of the course which he has proposed. Mr. Townsend will be authorised to accompany him, and act as his next in command, and Mr. Stephenson may, should Sir Thomas himself approve of it, be engaged at a salary of 7s. 6d. per diem from the day of his leaving Sydney; he must, however, find his own horse.

"Mr. Townsend will, during his absence, as well as Sir Thomas Mitchell himself, continue to receive his usual salary from the land fund, but every other expense will be charged against the sum voted for the purpose by the Legislative Council, which is now increased to £2,000."

(See Chapter VI.)

Appendix - EXTRACT OF A LETTER OF MR. WALTER BAGOT.

"20th January, 1844.

"The country beyond the Darling for the first few miles from the river exhibits the same features as on its southern bank, the soil blackish, soft, and yielding; the trees principally myall, and a species of myall, called by the squatters rosewood, interspersed with the small and gnarled forest oak. About ten miles from the river, and nearly parallel to it, is the Waramble, a sort of swamp, boggy, and difficult to cross after wet weather, directly after which water remains in the holes along its course. From thirty to forty miles beyond this is the Nareen Creek. Here, except in very dry seasons, water stands. This I know from the Nareen blacks coming into the Barwin only at those times when they are in much danger from the Barwin blacks, who are extremely hostile to them. I cannot tell where the Nareen joins the Barwin; as far as I am acquainted with it, it is nearly parallel to it, slightly converging to the river westward. Between the Waramble and Nareen there is no perceptible rising ground; from the harder nature of the soil, the plain becoming more open, and the timber straighter and larger. I have no doubt that there is a gradual ascent. The grass is extremely luxuriant, like all the unstocked portions of rich ground in this country, the long kangaroo grass rising to the saddle skirts. The brigalow, which I have never seen in any but high ground, is here too.

"I now come to the reports of the blacks, which are: That about three days' journey of theirs (ninety miles) beyond the Barwin is a lofty range of mountains (I have beard of these mountains also from a gentleman who got a distant view of them from a plain near the Nareen); that a river, called the Culgoa, runs at the foot of these mountains, which river, from the similarity of the name, I am inclined to think, is one which empties itself into the Barwin, about one hundred miles lower down than the junction of the Castlereagh. I have re-marked that the word Culgoa in the Wilem dialect signifies 'waterfall,' which adds to the likelihood of its being a mountain stream; that after crossing the mountains, which occupies one day (thirty miles), and travelling for two days (sixty miles), still north-west, they reach a large river, broader and deeper than the Barwin, the waters of which river never fail. Their name for this river I cannot now recollect. The old black, who gave the clearest account of this river, and who was the only one I have seen who admitted having been actually at this river, distinctly described its course to be different from that of the Barwin, and, perhaps, north or south-west. Might not this river be a tributary to one of the large rivers which flow into the Gulph of Carpentaria? and if so, how well adapted for a line of road traversing its valley to the Gulph? I have often wished, while residing on the Barwin, to make up a party to explore the size and course of this river, but the dangerous character of the black tribes in its direction, with the late long-continued drought, were enough to prevent it."

(See Chapter VI.)

Appendix - THE LAST LETTER RECEIVED FROM DR. LEICHHARDT.

"M'Pherson's Station, Cogoon,

"April 3, 1848.

"I Take the last opportunity of giving you an account of my progress. In eleven days we travelled from Mr. Burell's station, on the Condamine, to Mr. M'Pherson's, on the Fitzroy Downs. Though the country was occasionally very difficult, yet everything went on very well. My mules are in excellent order-my companions in excellent spirits. Three of my cattle are footsore, but I shall kill one of them to-night, to lay in our necessary stock of dried beef. The Fitzroy Downs, over which we travelled for about twenty-two miles from east to west, is indeed a splendid region, and Sir Thomas has not exaggerated their beauty in his account. The soil is pebbly and sound, richly grassed, and, to judge from the Myalls, of the most fattening quality. I came right on Mount Abundance, and passed over a gap in it with my whole train. My latitude agreed well with Mitchell's. I fear that the absence of water on Fitzroy Downs will render this fine country to a great extent unavailable. I observe the thermometer daily at 6 a.m. and 8 p.m., which are the only convenient hours. I have tried the wet thermometer, but am afraid my observations will be very deficient. I shall, however, improve on them as I proceed.

"The only serious accident that has happened was the loss of a spade, but we are fortunate enough to make it up on this station. Though the days are still very hot, the beautiful clear nights are cool, and benumb the mosquitoes, which have ceased to trouble us. Myriads of flies are the only annoyance we have.

"Seeing how much I have been favoured in my present progress, I am full of hopes that our Almighty Protector will allow me to bring my darling scheme to a successful termination.

"Your most sincere friend,
"LUDWIG LEICHHARDT."
(See -Chapter VII.)

398

Appendix - THE NARDOO PLANT.

The Nardoo appears generally to be considered the seed of the lentil, or some other plant of the bean tribe, whereas it belongs to one of those cryptogamic or flowerless plants, which, like ferns and mosses, do not produce perfect seeds, but are increased by cellular bodies named spores. It belongs to the genus Marsillea, order Marsilleaceae, and that class of sexual or flowerless plants called Acrogens, which have distinguishable stems and leaves, in contra-distinction to Thallogens, in which stems and leaves are indistinguishable, as seaweeds, fungi, and lichens. The part used for food is the Involucen Sporangium, or spore case, with its contained spores, which is of an oval shape, flattened, and about one-eighth of an inch in its longest diameter; hard and horny in texture, requiring considerable force to crush or pound it when dry, but becoming soft and mucila ginous when exposed to moisture. The natives pound it between two stones, and make it into cakes like flour. The spores vegetate in water, and root in soil at the bottom, where the plant grows to maturity. After the water dries up, the plants die, and leave the spore cases on, in many instances quite covering the surface of the dried mud. It is then that they are gathered for food. On the return of moisture, the spore cases softened, become mucilaginous, and discharge their contents to form a fresh crop of plants. The foliage is green, and resembles clover somewhat, being composed of three fleshy leaflets on the top of a stalk a few inches in length.
(See Chapter IX.)

Appendix - THE FINDING OF JOHN KING.

The details connected with the rescue of John King, the sole survivor of the Burke and Wills Expedition, have, strangely enough, never yet found their way into print, owing to a series of minor accidents, into the particulars of which it is not necessary to enter here.

The relief party, under the leadership of Mr. A. W. Howitt, fully equipped and provisioned to follow the supposed track of the expedition to the Gulf of Carpentaria, if necessary, knew nothing up to the time of the actual finding of King of the miserable fate which had overtaken the lost explorers; nor had they the faintest reason for supposing that they were actually on the verge of the discovery which was to so completely elucidate the mystery of their disappearance.

Early in September, 1861, Howitt's party reached Cooper's Creek, accompanied by W. Brahe, a member of Burke's expedition, who had been left in charge of the depôt at Fort Wills by Burke. He had remained there a month over the time mentioned in his instructions; his men were attacked by scurvy; the blacks in the neighbourhood were getting troublesome, and his provisions getting low. He therefore planted all the stores he could spare under a tree, marked "dig," and with them an explanatory letter to his leader, in the event of the return of the absent men, and retired to the depôt at Bulloo. He then started for Melbourne to report himself, but was intercepted by Howitt and taken back to Cooper's Creek as a guide.

King was found by Mr. Edwin J. Welch, the surveyor, and second in command of Howitt's party, a gentleman who afterwards identified himself with journalism, and who has been for many years favourably known in connection with the country press as a proprietor of newspapers, both in Northern and Western Queensland and Victoria. The following interesting account of his first meeting with King is taken from Mr. Welch's diary:--

"13th September, 1861. Shortly after leaving camp this morning, Howitt and I, accompanied by Brahe, rode on down the creek, ahead of the party, to the depôt at Fort Wills, hoping against hope that we should find Brahe's plant empty and some record of the missing men. We were doomed to disappointment. After a careful examination of the spot, Brahe declared that everything was as he had left it six weeks before. The *caché* had not been disturbed, and nothing but a few blacks' tracks in the loose soil existed to show that any human life had broken the solitude. We, therefore, continued our way, wondering what could have become of them, and discussing with keen interest the suggestions offered by each to guide us in our future movements. . . Camped the horses and camels about 3 p.m., on the bank of a large waterhole in the creek, covered with wild-fowl and partially surrounded by a dense growth of dead mallows of great size and height.

"14th September. Proceeded slowly westward, along the north bank of the creek, carefully searching for tracks. . . . Country opening out and improving in character. Magnificent reaches of water in the creek; some of the water quite salt, other holes containing water of a milky tint, sweet and pleasant to the taste, while in others again, it was brackish, and the edges were lined with petrified boughs, leaves, and some few fish. . . . Several times during the day we noticed blacks stealthily watching our movements from a distance, and travelling through the long grass in the direction we ourselves were going. . . . In the afternoon, Howitt, who had been riding well out from the creek, returned with the news that he had struck fresh camel tracks trending northwards, apparently those of a lost camel. . . . Another comfortable camp on the creek, with plenty of feed.

"15th September (Sunday). Left camp at 8 a.m. Howitt, with one of the black boys, started to run the camel track seen yesterday. I gave Sampson (the leading man of the file) a compass bearing to follow, with instructions to keep as closely to it as the windings of the creek would permit, and rode on ahead, actuated by curiosity as to the movements of our black friends of yesterday. After travelling about three miles, my attention was attracted by a number of niggers on the opposite bank of the creek, who shouted loudly as soon as they saw me, and vigorously waved and pointed down the creek. A feeling of something about to happen excited me somewhat, but I little expected what the sequel was to be. Moving cautiously on through the undergrowth which covered the banks of the creek, the blacks kept pace with me on the opposite side, their cries increasing in volume and intensity; when suddenly rounding a bend, I was startled at seeing a large body of them gathered on a sandy neck in the bed of the creek, between two large waterholes. Immediately they saw me, they too commenced to howl, throw their arms about, and wave their weapons in the air. I at once pulled up, and considered the propriety of waiting the arrival of the party, for I felt far from satisfied with regard to their intentions. But here, for the first time, my favourite horse--a black cob, known in the camp as 'Piggy,' a Murray Downs bred stock horse, of good local repute, both for foot and temper--appeared to think that his work was cut out for him, and the time arrived in which to do it. Pawing and snorting at the noise, he suddenly slewed round, and headed down the steep bank, through the undergrowth, straight for the crowd, as he had been wont to do after many a mob of weaners on his native plains. The blacks drew hurriedly back to the top of the opposite bank, shouting and gesticulating violently, and leaving one solitary figure, apparently covered with some scarecrow rags, and part of a hat, prominently alone in the sand. Before I could pull up, I had passed it, and as I passed it tottered, threw up its hands in the attitude of prayer, and fell on the ground. The heavy sand helped me to conquer Piggy on the level, and when I turned back, the figure had partially risen. Hastily dismounting, I was soon beside it, excitedly asking, 'Who, in the name of wonder, are you?' He answered, 'I am King, sir.' For a moment I did not grasp the thought that the object of our search was attained, for King being only one of the undistinguished members of the party, his name was unfamiliar to me. 'King?' I repeated. 'Yes,' he said; 'the last man of the exploring expedition.' 'What, Burke's?' 'Yes.' 'Where is he--and Wills?' 'Dead--both dead, long ago;' and again he fell to the ground. Then I knew who stood before me. Jumping into the saddle, I rode up the bank, fired two or three revolver shots to attract the attention of the party, and, on their coming up, sent the other black boy to cut Howitt's track and bring him back to camp. We then put up a tent to shelter the rescued man, and by degrees, as he recovered from the excitement of the meeting, we got from him the, sad story of the fate of his leader. We got it at intervals only, between the long rests which his exhausted condition compelled him to take, and the main facts are, as summarised, given below:--

"'Burke, Wills, Gray, and I, left the depôt in charge of Brahe, at Fort Wills, on the 16th December, 1860, with six camels, one horse, and provisions for three months. The stock was in splendid condition, and we were in high spirits. Keeping a steady course northwards, we reached salt water and mangrove swamps on--but I can't tell you the date; you will find it in Wills' field-books. He said it was the Gulf of

Carpentaria, and we were satisfied; we could not get through the mangroves, and never saw the open water, but we had accomplished the object of the expedition. One of the camels had knocked up some distance back, and we had to plant his load, so that we were afraid to stay too long, for fear of getting short of rations. We did not follow our own tracks all the way back, but hurried as much as possible to reach the depôt in time. On the way back we killed the horse and one camel for meat, and one of the camels got away from us, so that we had only two left to finish the journey. We all walked, and threw away everything except the rations, a gun, and the clothes we had on. At one of the camps we buried all Mr. Wills' instruments, but I don't remember which one it was. Gray was getting knocked up worse and worse every day, and then he got to taking more than his share of the flour and sugar when he got a chance. Mr. Burke threatened him and boxed his ears for this, and when he turned in one night, about two days before we expected to reach the depôt, he said he felt he would not live till morning, and, sure enough, he didn't. When we turned out at daylight, Gray was dead; so we stopped there that day, and scooped a hole in the sand about three feet deep with our hands, and buried him in it. The next morning we pushed on for the depôt, and when we got there, two days after, it was deserted. The fire was still alight, and the tracks of Brahe's party were all fresh. There was a tree marked 'DIG,' and when we were able to get at the plant we found Brahe's note, which said they had left that morning; but we did not mind it very much, as there was plenty to eat. Of course, we were disappointed, but Mr. Burke said we could get back by Strzelecki's Creek to Mount Hopeless, and so to Adelaide. We stopped at the depôt five days, which was a good spell for ourselves and the two camels, and we felt much better. When we were ready to start, we buried all the field-books and some letters, to let anybody who came by know where we were going, and then covered up the plant carefully, so that the blacks should not find it out. We went westerly down the creek, and saw lots of blackfellows, but Mr. Burke did not care to try and make friends with them; he said there were too many of them, and it was no good wasting time. After we got some distance down the creek, it was decided to cross and strike to the southward, but we must have picked a bad place, for one of the camels got stuck in a quicksand at the end of a waterhole, and we could not get him out, although we worked hard for nearly twenty-four hours; so, as there was nothing else left for it, we shot him, cut off as much meat as we could carry, and, after drying it, started on again; but our load was so much heavier now that we had to travel very slowly, and the other camel was beginning to knock up. After two days more, he got so weak that he couldn't get up off the ground, so we had to shoot him too, pack some more of the meat, and then go on. We got on to a branch creek, which ran in the direction we wanted to go, but after a few more miles it ran out, and lost itself in channels in an earthy plain: so we had to go back to the last water. We were all three beginning to feel bad now, so it was decided to take a good spell before making another attempt. While we were doing this the rations were getting very short, and we began to cat nardoo the same as the blacks. Sometimes the blacks would come by and give us a few fish, which we could not catch ourselves, and sometimes we managed to shoot a crow or a hawk, but we had no strength to go and look for anything. Mr. Wills, however, determined to go back to the depôt, and see if anybody had been there, and he was away some days by himself. When he came back, he told us that he had seen nobody, but that he had opened the plant in the night, to bury another letter to the committee, and carefully covered it up again. A good thing for us, it happened that the weather was very fine, although cold at night, and we felt the cold badly, having very few clothes. Then we shifted camp a little higher up the creek, where there were two or three blacks' gunyahs, and Mr. Wills got so weak that he could not move out of his at all. Mr. Burke and I were getting very weak, too, but I was not so bad as they were, and managed to collect and pound enough nardoo to keep us all from starving outright. In a few days things were so bad that Wills, who was getting worse all the time and suffering great pain, persuaded Mr. Burke and I to go up the creek, while we had strength, and look for the blacks, as our only chance of life. We didn't like the idea of separating, but it seemed to be our only chance, so we made him some nardoo bread, and left it, with a billy of water, beside him, and went away. Together, Mr. Burke and I wandered slowly up the creek, but could not see a sign of any blacks, and after we had gone fourteen or fifteen miles, Mr. Burke said he could not go any farther, and lay down under a tree. I found some nardoo close by, and had the good luck to shoot a crow. The night was very cold, and we felt it dreadfully, and before daylight Mr. Burke said he was dying, and told me not to try and bury him or cover up his body in any way, but just put his pistol in his right hand. I did this, and then he wrote something in his pocket-book, and died about two hours after sunrise. When I was able to move, I went on again, to try and find help for Wills, but the blacks had all disappeared. I found some nardoo in one of their camps, though, and with this and another crow I shot, I started back to Wills. It took me four days to get back, and when I got there I found he was dead, too. I covered up his body with boughs and sand as well as I could, and then rested for two days, and started off again to look for blacks. I don't know how many days it was before I found them, but I think a good many. At first they were very kind to me, and gave me plenty to eat; after that they tried to drive me away, but I stuck to them, and the women gave me some nardoo every day, and sometimes one of the men would give me some fish. I don't know how long I have been with them, but I think it must be about three months. I knew you were coming before I saw you, for some strange blacks came down the creek and brought the news to the others, and somehow I got to understand that they had seen some white men on horses, who I knew would look for me. I could not learn to talk to them, but I began slowly to understand what they were saying. I think I could have lived for a long time with them, for I was all the while getting a little bit stronger.'"

From the foregoing narrative it will be at once seen that the unfortunate collapse of Gray, when within only two days' journey of the depôt, was the direct cause of the death of Burke and Wills. King was a young man, of good physique, and of a nature in which the disposition to mental worry or anxiety had no part. The leaders had to endure this in addition to their physical sufferings, and the bitterness of dying within the reach of help, after having successfully accomplished the most dashing feat ever recorded in the annals of Australian exploration. They had performed their allotted task, and they perished miserably in the hour of their success.

The criticisms of Australians generally, and of bushmen in particular, were for a long time afterwards directed to the apparently unaccountable circumstance that neither Howitt, Welch, nor Brahe detected at their first visit to the depôt that the caché had been opened. King's narrative showed that it had actually been twice opened, but it must be borne in mind that on each occasion the best precautions were adopted to conceal the fact, and thereby avoid attracting the attention of the blacks. The unfortunate men, who were slowly starving to death on the banks of the creek, had left no visible sign of their visit to the spot. Brahe, who made the plant, positively asserted that it had not been interfered with, and Howitt, therefore, wisely declined to burden himself with an additional weight of stores for which he had no present use. Even had it been opened on that 13th of September, the knowledge which it would have revealed was too late to be of service, and could not have expedited the rescue of King by more than a few hours, if at all. (See Chapter IX.)

Appendix - POISON PLANTS.

The properties of the Australian plants are only imperfectly known, very few species having been chemically examined; numbers are suspected, but have not been positively proved. The poison plant that caused such havoc amongst the horses of both Jardine and Austin mostly affects the spinifex country. It is a ground plant, and liable to be cropped by a horse amongst the grass, when the animal would probably refuse to touch a bush.

Amongst the most poisonous plants known in Australia may be mentioned the "thorny apple," Datura Stramonium, and Datura tatula; also the Excaecaria agallocha, and Lolium termulentum.

The indigo plant, Swainsona galegifolia, is a glabrous perennial, or undershrub, with erect flexuose branches, sometimes under one foot, sometimes ascending, or even climbing, to the height of several feet. The flowers are rather large, and deep-red in the original variety; pod much inflated, membranous one to two inches long, on a stipe varying from two to six lines. The species varies, with light, purplish-pink flowers, S. coronillaefolia; and white flowers, S. albiflora. The difference in the length of the stipes of the pod does not, as had been supposed, coincide with the difference in the colour of the flower. This plant acts in a peculiar way upon sheep, driving them insane until death ensues. The sheep, however, select it as an especial tit-bit, it, apparently, possessing an irresistible fascination for them.

The "Darling pea" Swainsona procumbens. Glabrous; or the young shoots and foliage slightly silky; or sometimes pubescent, or hirsute, with procumbent ascending, or erect stems of one to three feet. Leaflets varying from oblong or almost linear, and one-quarter inch to half-inch long, to lanceolate, or linear-acute, and above one inch long. Flowers: large, fragrant, violet, or blue; pod sessile, above one inch long.

The "Pitchuri plant," Anthocercis Hopwoodii. A glabrous tree, or shrub. Leaves: narrow-linear, acutely acuminate, with the point often recurved, entire, rather thick, narrowed into a short petiole, two to four inches long; fruit unknown.

"Australian Tobacco," Nicotian suaveolens. An erect annual, or biennial, of one to two feet. Flowers: white, or greenish on side; sweet-scented, especially at night.

Amongst those that are but slightly poisonous are: Typhonium Brownii, and Colocasia Macrorrhiza; the Crinum flaccidum and C. pendunculatum, both bulbous herbs; Carcumbum populifolium and C. Stillingiaefolium, tall shrubs; Duboisea myoporoides and D. Leichhardtii, shrubs; Aristolochia praevenos, a tall, climbing shrub; A. pubera, a small, prostrate, or trailing herb; Chamae fistula laevigata and C. Sophera, erect, glabrous shrubs.

The "Nightshade," Solanum Nigrum. An erect annual, or biennial, with very spreading branches, one to nearly two feet high. Leaves: petiolate, ovate, with coarse, irregular, angular teeth, or nearly entire, one to two inches long. Flowers; small and white, in little cymes, usually contracted into umbels on a common peduncle, from very short, to nearly one inch long. Berry: small, globular, usually nearly black, but sometimes green-yellow, or dingy-red.

The "Bean tree," Castanospermum Australe. A tall, glabrous tree; pods eight or nine inches long, about two inches broad; the valves hard and thick, the spongy substance inside dividing it into three to five cells each, containing a large, chestnut-like seed.

(See Chapter XI.)

Appendix - INDEX OF NAMES, DATES, AND INCIDENTS

"Adventure" (The)--
> Under Captain Tobias Furneaux, in search of the South Continent, touched on the coast of Tasmania. 1772.

Alouarn, M. de St.--
> Anchored near Cape Leeuwin, but no record of his visit has been preserved. 1777.

Alt, Matthew B--
> With the ships Hormuzeer and Chesterfield, through Torres Straits. 1793.

"Amsterdam," (The) "Klyn," and "Wezel"--
> From Banda. commanded by Gerrit Tomaz Poole; revisited Arn-heim's Land. Captain Poole was killed on the New Guinea coast. 1636.

"Arnheim" (The) and "Pera"--
> On the coast of New Guinea. Captain Jan Carstens, with eight of his crew murdered; but the vessels proceeded to, and touched on the north coast of New Holland, west of the Gulf of Carpentaria, still known as "Arnheim's Land." 1623.

"Assistant" (The) and "Providence"--
> Under command of Captains Bligh and Portlock, through Torres Straits. 1792.

"Astrolabe" (The) and "Boussole"--
> French discovery ships, under La Perouse. Anchored in Botany Bay. 1778.

"Atrevide" (The) and "Descobierte"--
> Spanish Discovery ships, under command of Don Alexandra Malaspina, at Sydney. 1793.

"Astrolabe" (The)--
> Under command of Captain Dumont D'Urville, touched at Bass's Strait. 1826.

Austin, Robert—
Assistant Surveyor-General, Western Australia; in search of pastoral country, and to examine the interior for auriferous deposits. Their horses got on a patch of poison plant, and, in consequence, nearly the whole of them were laid up, unfit for work; some escaped, but the greater number died. On the return of the party to Shark's Bay, where a vessel awaited them, they found a cave in the face of a cliff, in which were drawings, similar to those reported by Grey near the Prince Regent's River. One of the party (Charles Farmer) accidentally shot himself, and died of lockjaw; he was buried at the cave spring. The exploration led to no profitable result. 1854.

Babbage, Surveyor--
Conducted a party to explore the country between Lake Torrens and Lake Gairdner. 1856.

Bampton, William--
With Matthew B. Alt, in the ships Hormuzeer and Chesterfield, through Torres Straits. 1793.

Banks, Joseph (afterwards Sir)--
Accompanied Captain James Cook on his voyage of discovery to Australia, as botanist. 1770.

Bannister, Major--
Crosses from Perth to King George's Sound. 1831.

Barker, Captain--
Murdered at Lake Alexandrina, the mouth of the Murray. 1832.

Barker, Dr.--
Albert Brodribb and Edward Hobson were the first to walk from Melbourne to Gippsland. The present road follows their tracks. 1841.

Barrailher, Ensign--
Attempted exploration of the Blue Mountains. 1802.

Bass, Dr. George--
With Matthew Flinders, in the Tom Thumb, along the coast. 1795. And again to Port Hacking. 1796.
    Attempted exploration of the Blue Mountains. 1796-97.
    In a whale-boat, with a crew of eight, round Wilson's Promontory, and explore Western Port. Examined six hundred miles of coastline. 1797.

Bass, Dr. George, and Matthew Flinders--
In the Norfolk; discover Bass's Straits. 1798.

"Batavia" (The)--
Commanded by Francis Pelsart, and wrecked on Houtman's Abrolhos. 1629.

Batman, John--
Founded Port Phillip. 1836.

"Bathurst" (The)--
In which Captain King completed his fourth and last voyage round the Australian coast. 1820.

Baudin, Captain Nicholas--
In command of the French ships Géographe and Naturaliste. 1801-2.

Beresford, W., and J. W. Lewis--
Sent by the South Australian Government to survey the country about Lake Eyre. 1875.

Blackwood, Captain--
In the Fly, continued the survey of Captains Wickham and Stokes. Made a minute examination of the Great Barrier Reef. 1842-45.

Blaxland, Gregory--
With Lieutenant William Lawson and William Charles Wentworth; succeed in their attempt to cross the Blue Mountains. 1813.

Bligh, Captain William--
Passed Cape York, on his way to Coepang, in the Bounty's launch. (Afterwards Governor of New South Wales.) 1791.

Bligh, Captain William, and Captain Nathan Portlook--
In the ships Providence and Assistant. Explore Torres Straits. 1792.

Bougainville, De--
Discovered the Louisade Archipelago. 1768.

"Boussole" (The) and "Astrolabe"--
French discovery ships; La Perouse in command; at Botany Bay. 1778.

Bowen, Lieutenant--
Visited Jervis Bay. 1796.

Bremer, Sir Gordon--
In the Tamar to Port Essington. 1824.

Re-settles Port Essington. 1838.

Briggs, S. G.—
Second in command, and surveyor of Queenslander Trans-Continental Expedition; leader, Ernest Favenc, from Blackall to Powell's Creek, overland telegraph line. 1878-79.

Buchanan, N.—

Made an excursion from the overland line to the Queensland border; crossed the Ranken, so called after one of the pioneers of that
district, J. C. L. Ranken. Buchanan's Creek was a most important
discovery of this trip, affording a highway and stock route to the
great pastoral district lying between the Queensland border and the
overland telegraph line. 1878.

Burke, Robert O'Hara (Leader), and William John Wills (Surveyor and
Astronomer)—

Left Melbourne on August 20th, 1860, accompanied by Charles
Gray and John King, etc.; successfully cross the continent, reaching the Gulf of Carpentaria, and then return towards the depôt
formed by others of the party on Cooper's Creek. Gray died;
Burke, Wills, and King stop to bury him by scraping a hole in the
sand, and reached the depôt only to find that Brahe and the other
three men had left that morning. Stopping to bury Gray cost Burke
and his companions their lives. They could scarcely walk, and
their camels were in the same state. Gray died of exhaustion and
fatigue. Wills, who was so weak, was left lying under some
boughs, with a supply of water and nardoo, to meet his death
alone. Two days after, Burke gave in, and King found himself
alone. The remains of the explorers were eventually disinterred,
and brought to Melbourne, where they were given a public funeral.
1860-61.

Campbell, Murdock--

West of Lake Torrens. 1857. And again with party west of Lake
Eyre, looking for pastoral country. 1857.

Carpenter, Captain Pieter--

Discovered the Gulf of Carpentaria. 1628.

Carr-Boyd, W. J. H.--

With O'Donnell, from the Katherine Station, overland telegraph
line, to Western Australia. Found good country, but no new geographical discovery. 1882.

Carstens, Captain Jan—

With the yachts Pera and Arnheim, landed on the coast of New
Guinea, and was murdered with eight of his crew. The vessels
proceeded on their voyage, and touched on the north coast of New
Holland, still known as Arnheim's Land. 1623.

Cayley, George--

A botanist, sent out by Sir Joseph Banks, from Kew Gardens; attempted exploration over the Blue Mountains. 1803.

"Champion" (The)--
> Schooner, examined the west coast for any rivers with navigable entrances, in view of settlement. Captain Stokes, of the Beagle, gave so unfavourable a report of that part of the coast that its immediate settlement was postponed. 1839.

"Chatham" (The) and "Discovery"--
> Vessels under command of Captain George Vancouver when he explored the south-west coast and discovered King George's Sound. 1791.

"Chesterfield" (The) and "Hormuzeer"--
> Under command of Matthew B. Alt and William Bampton, through Torres Straits. 1793.

Clarkson, B.--
> With Messrs. Dempster and Harper, make a trial to the eastward. 1861.

Collins, Lieutenant-Governor Daniel—
> From England with H.M.S. Calcutta and Ocean to form a penal settlement at Port Phillip. Deciding that the place was unfit for settlement they proceeded to Tasmania, where all were killed at Hobart Town. 1803-4.

Colonists--
> Landed at the De Grey River, and settled on country found by F. Gregory. 1863.

Cook, Captain James—
> In the Endeavour, landed at Botany Bay; carefully surveyed the east coast to Cape York, naming nearly all the principal capes and bays. At Possession Island he formally took possession of the continent, in the name of King George the Third, under the name of New South Wales. 1770.

Cox--
> Completed road over Blue Mountains to Bathurst. 1815.

Crozet, Captain--
> With Captain Marion du Fresne, in the ships Mascarin and Castres to Tasmania, the first visitors after Tasman. Thence to New Zealand, where they were murdered by the Maories. 1772.

Curry, Captain--
> With Major Ovens, to Lake George; discovered Monaroo Plains and the Morumbidgee. 1823.

Cunningham, Allan--
> Found "Pandora's Pass"--a practical stock route to Liverpool Plains. 1823.

412

Journeying by way of Pandora's Pass, which he had before discovered, examined the tableland to the north of Bathurst. 1825.

To Darling Downs--one of his most, eventful trips. Discovers the Darling Downs, the Dumaresque, Gwydir, and Condamine Rivers, &c. 1827.

Accompanied by Charles Fraser, proceeded by sea to Moreton Bay, and connected the settlement with the Darling Downs by way of Cunningham's Gap. 1828.

His last expedition. Explores the source of the Brisbane River. 1829.

Died in Sydney. 1839. [See Appendix.]

Cunningham, E.--

And Messrs. Somer, Stenhouse, Allingharn and Miles explore the Upper Burdekin, and discover good pastoral country on the many tributaries of that river. 1860.

Cunningham, Richard—

Botanist (brother to Allan Cunningham), accompanied Sir Thomas Mitchell's second expedition. While still on the outskirts of settlement, leaving the party on some scientific quest, he lost his way, and was never again seen. A long search was made for him, and eventually his fate was ascertained from the blacks. [See Appendix.] 1833.

"Cygnet" (The)--

With Dampier and crew of buccaneers, visited the northwest coast of New Holland. 1688.

Dale--

From the Upper Swan River, Western Australia. Followed up the Avon. 1830.

Dalrymple, G. E.—

Penetrated the coast country north of Rockhampton, and discovered the main tributaries of the Lower Burdekin, the Bowen, and Bogie Rivers. 1859.

Ascending the coast range, reached the upper waters of the Burdekin, and discovered the Valley of Lagoons, west of Rockingham Bay. 1862.

Daly--

A convict afterwards hanged for burglary; instigated the first gold prospecting party in Australia. Having broken up a pair of brass buckles, he mixed the fragments with sand and stones, and presented it as specimens of ore he had found. 1789.

Dampier, Captain William—

The first Englishman to land in New Holland. He visited the north-west coast in the Cygnet, with a crew of buccaneers. 1688.

In charge of the Roebuck, sent by the English Government to explore the northwest coast; visited the archipelago that now bears his name. 1699.

Dawes, Lieutenant--

With Tench and Morgan explore south and west of Rose Hill. 1790.

Crossed the Nepean. 1789.

"De Brak," "Zeemeuw," and "Limmen"--

Commanded by Abel Janz Tasman, surveyed a great portion of the north and north-west coasts of New Holland. 1644.

De Lissa and Hardwicke--

Explore from Fowler's Bay to the edge of the Great Victorian Desert. 1862.

Delft, Martin Van--

With the ships Vossenbach, Wayer, and Nova Hollandia, to investigate the west coast. This was the last voyage of exploration undertaken by the Dutch, and closes the early discovery of New Holland. 1705.

D'Entrecasteaux, Admiral Bruni--

With the ships Recherché and L'Esperance, left Brest to seek La Perouse, anchored on the south coast of Australia. 1792.

"Descobierta" (The), and "Etrevida"--

Spanish discovery ships, under Don Alexander Malaspina, at Sydney. 1793.

Dillon, Captain--

In the Research, on the south coast. 1826.

Dirk Hartog, Captain—

In command of the ship Endracht, from Amsterdam, discovered the west coast of New Holland. He left a tin plate, with an inscription, on an island in Dirk Hartog's Roads, which was afterwards found by Vlaming, in 1697, who added another inscription. In 1801, the boatswain of the Naturaliste found the plate, and Captain Hamelin had it replaced on another post; but in 18ig Al. L. de Freycinet, while on his voyage round the world, took it home with him, and placed it in the Museum of the Institute, Paris. 1616.

"Discovery" (The) and "Chatham"--

Under Captain George Vancouver, on the south-west coast and King George's Sound. 1791.

Dixon, Christopher--
In the ship Ellegood, visited King George's Sound, leaving on a sheet of copper the name of his vessel and date of visit, which was found in 1801 by Flinders. 1800.

Dixon, Surveyor--
On the Bogan. 1833.

"Duke and Duchess" (The)--
Under Captain John Hayes, visited Tasmania, and renamed the discoveries of D'Entrecasteaux. 1794.

Duperry, Captain--
In La Coquille, voyaged amongst the Line Islands. 1822-24.

D'Urville, Captain Dumont--
With the Astrolabe, from Toulon, touched at Bass's Straits. 1826.

Dutton, C. W.--
With Miller; explored country back of Fowler's Bay 1857.

"Duyfhen" (The)—
Yacht from Bantam. Her commander (name unknown) unwittingly crossed tile entrance of Torres Straits, sailed across the Gulf of Carpentaria, and turned back from Cape Keer-Weer (Turn Again), being in want of provisions. 1606.

Eredia, Manoel Godinho--
A Spaniard, claims an early discovery of New Holland, but it is doubtful. 1601.

Edels, John Van--
On the west coast. 1619.

Edwards, Captain Edward--
In search of the mutineers of the Bounty. Lost on the reefs, and reached Timor in boats. 1791.

"Ellegood" (The)
Commanded by Christopher Dixon, visited King George's Sound. 1800.

"Endeavour" (The)--
Captain Cook's vessel when on his voyage of discovery to Australia. 1770.

Evans, Deputy-Surveyor--
Discovered the first Australian inland river. 1815.

Eyre, E. J.—
Port Phillip to Adelaide; discovered Lake Hindmarsh. 1838.
Left Port Lincoln on the western shore of Spencer's Gulf, to examine the country to the westward. Discovered Streaky Bay and Lake Torrens. 1839.

March round the Great Bight. 1840-41.

Favenc, Ernest—

In charge of the Queenslander Transcontinental Expedition, organised to discover the nature and value of the country in the neighbourhood of a then proposed line to Port Darwin, and the geographical features of the unknown portion. Leaving Blackall, the then most western settlement in Queensland, the party made Powell's Creek on the Overland Telegraph Line. Discovering the Corella Lagoon, Cresswell Creek, Sylvester, and De Burgh Creeks, etc. This expedition had the effect of opening up a great area of good pastoral country which is now stocked. 1878-1879.

Traced the heads of the rivers running into the Gulf of Carpentaria near the Queensland border, and in the f ollowing year took a more lengthened expedition across the coast range to the mouth of the Macarthur River. A large extent of valuable country was found in the basin drained by this river, and a fine permanent spring discovered. Followed this river down to salt water, then returned by another route to Daly Waters Telegraph Station. 1882-83.

Finnis, Colonel--

Formed settlement at Escape Cliffs. 1864.

Fitzgerald, Governor--

Western Australia. Accompanied by A. C. Gregory and party, proceeded to Champion Bay by sea, and thence inland to examine the new mineral discovery. On their return they had an affray with the natives, the Governor being speared in the leg. 1848.

Fitzroy, Captain R.--

In the Beagle, visited King George's Sound. 1829.

Flinders, Matthew—

With Bass in the Tom Thumb traced the coast from Sydney in 1795. And the following year in the same boat reached Port Hacking. 1796.

With Bass in the Norfolk, discovered Bass's Straits. 1799.

In the Norfolk, dispatched by Governor Hunter to explore the coast to the northward; reached Hervey Bay. 1799.

In command of the Investigator and Lady Nelson, left England to examine the coasts of Terra A ustralis. First sighted Australia at Cape Leeuwin. Examined the south and east coasts of Australia, and explored the Gulf of Carpentaria and the coast of Arnheim's Land. The Investigator being then found unseaworthy, he returned to Port Jackson, after a visit to, Timor. For the purpose of procuring another vessel to continue the survey, he took passage for

England with his officers and crew in the Porpoise. Seven days after leaving Sydney, the vessel was wrecked on the Barrier Reef, and Flinders in an open boat made his way back to Sydney, a distance of seven hundred miles. Governor King gave him the Cumberland, in which vessel he proceeded homeward, and on putting in to the Mauritius, he was there made prisoner by General de Caen, the French Governor, and detained in the Isle of France nearly seven years. Flinders' journal of his discoveries was published the day after his death. It was Flinders who suggested the name of Australia. 1801-1803.

"Fly" (The)--

Under command of Captain Blackwood, made a minute survey of the Great Barrier, and continued the survey of Captains Wickharn and Stokes. 1842-45.

Forrest, Alexander--

Took charge of a private expedition, in search of new pastoral country. 1871.

Led an expedition from De Grey River to the telegraph line, striking Daly Waters. A most successful trip; finding some of the most valuable country in the northern part of Western Australia; which has since been stocked with both cattle and sheep, and large mineral wealth has been developed. 1879.

Forrest, John--

First expedition, Lake Barlee. Not Successful in finding good available country, but obtained a reliable survey of a great deal of country hitherto unknown. 1869.

Accompanied by his brother, made a journey from Perth to Adelaide by way of the Great Bight, not traversed since Eyre's celebrated march; and was able to give a more impartial verdict of the country, travelling, as he did, with larger facilities. His report showed that the fringe of gloomy thicket was only confined to the coast. Beyond, he found fine pastoral country. 1870.

With his brother, Alexander Forrest, started from the furthest outside station on the Murchison, and made a successful trip to Peak Station, on the overland telegraph line. With nothing but pack-horses, crossed the middle of the continent, where the very heart of the terrible desert is supposed to exist, taking his men, and most of his horses, in safety; concluding one of the most valuable journeys on record. 1874.

Fort Wellington--

At Raffles Bay. Founded 1826; abandoned 1829.

Frazer, Charles--
The botanist who accompanied Captain Stirling in H.M.S. Success during survey of coast from King George's Sound to the Swan River. 1828.
Freeling, Colonel--
Surveyor-General of South Australia. Sent to verify Goyder's reports on Blanche Water and Lake Torrens, and found that the principal features of Goyder's reports were the results of mirage. 1857.
Fremantle, Captain--
Hoisted the British Flag at Fremantle. 1829.
Fresne, Captain Marion du--
With Captain Crozet in the Mascarin and Castres, from Nance to Tasmania--the first visitors after Tasman. Thence to New Zealand, where they were murdered by the Maories. 1772.
Freycinet, L. de--
In L'Uranie, saw Edels' Land, Shark's Bay, and landed at Sydney. 1817.
Frome, Captain--
Surveyor-General of South Australia. Made some explorations in the neighbourhood of Lake Torrens. 1843.
Furneaux, Captain Tobias—
With the Adventure, accompanied Cook on his second voyage in search of the Southern Continent. Separated from Cook, and afterwards, when they met, gave his opinion that Tasmania and New South Wales were joined with a deep bay intervening. This opinion Cook thought sufficient to prevent a further examination by himself being necessary. 1772.
Gawler, Colonel--
Governor of South Australia. Made an excursion to the Murray. He was accompanied by Captain Sturt (Surveyor-General), Miss Gawler, and Mrs. Sturt, but it is to be presumed Miss Gawler and Mrs, Sturt accompanied the party but a short distance. 1839.
"Geelvink" (The)--
(See Vlaming.)
Gibson--
Died when out with Ernest Giles' second expedition. Scene of his death named "Gibson's Desert." 1873.
Gilbert--
The naturalist accompanying Leichhardt's first expedition. Killed by the blacks at the head of the Gulf of Carpentaria. 1845.

Giles, Ernest—

Starting from Chamber's Pillar, South Australia, made a journey to the westward, but was stopped by a large dry salt lake. He named it Lake Amadens. He returned, having traversed a great deal of country before unknown. 1872.

Left on his second trip, starting from the Alberga, that flows into Lake Eyre, travelling north-west. Made many determined attempts to cross the spinifex desert, but returned unsuccessful. One of the party, Gibson, died, and several horses. The scene of Gibson's death is now marked as Gibson's Desert. 1873.

With an equipment of camels, made his third and successful attempt to reach Western Australia, but, from want of water, no knowledge of the country was obtained beyond their immediate track. Giles then retraced his steps to the overland line, following a track to the north of Forrests route, by way of the Murchison, and crossed over to the Ashburton. Then striking south of east he came to his former track of 1873, at the Alfred and Marie Range--the range he had so vainly tried to reach when the man Gibson met his death. Finally arrived at Peak Station. 1875-76.

Gonneville, Paulmier De--

Visited the south seas, and is claimed by the French to have landed on New Holland. 1503.

Gosse, W. C.—

In charge of the Central and Western Exploring Expedition. Left Alice Springs, on the overland telegraph line, with the intention of reaching Perth, having a mixed equipment of camels and horses. After many attempts to penetrate westward, Gosse was obliged to return, the heat of the weather and the dryness of the country rendering it useless to think of risking his party with any hope of success. 1873.

Gould, Captain--

On the south coast, near Port Lincoln, 1827-28.

Goyder, G. W.--

Deputy Surveyor-General of South Australia. Gave a most glowing account of Blanche Water, and the country around Lake Torrens. Subsequently Colonel Freeling discovered that Goyder had been misled by a mirage. 1857.

In the Great Bight, to the north of Fowler's Bay. Found nothing but mallee scrub and spinifex. 1862.

Selected Port Darwin as a suitable site for a township, and removed to that place the settlement from Escape Cliffs. 1865.

419

Grant, James--
   In Lady Nelson, the first vessel to pass through Bass's Straits, and verified Bass's examination. 1801.
Gray, Charles--
   One of the members of Burke and Wills' expedition. (See Burke.) 1860-61.
Gregory, Frank—
   Reached the long-sought Gascoyne, and followed it to Shark's Bay. Followed the Murchison down to the Geraldine mine, finding good pastoral country, and well watered. This was a much needed encouragement to the colony. 1858.

   In charge of party, left Perth in the Dolphin for Nickol Bay, on the north-west coast, to land their horses and commence the trip. Discover the Fortescue, the Hammersley Range, and the Ashburton, which was traced upwards through a large extent of good pastoral country. Named the De Grey and Oakover rivers. The stigma of desolation was now partially removed by the discoveries of this expedition. 1861.
Gregory, A. C.—
   Accompanied by his two brothers. Their first expedition in Western Australia; travelled through a large extent of salt swampy country, entering the salt lake region, until they reached a range of granite hills forming the watershed of the coast streams. After several disappointments, turned to the westward to examine rivers discovered by Grey. On the head of one of these (the Arrowsmith) they found a seam of coal; and returned to Bolgart Springs. 1846.

   With party to explore the Gascoyne. Found a galena lode on the Murchison. 1848.

   With Baron Von Mueller, the celebrated botanist, and his brother, H. C. Gregory. North Australian expedition in search of Leichhardt. Proceed north to follow the Victoria. Reached the head of that stream, and discovered Sturt's Creek and the Elsey. Crossing the head waters of the Limmen Bight River, skirted the Gulf for some distance south of Leichhardt's track, crossing the rivers that he did, only higher up on their courses. Greatly disappointed with the Plains of Promise--so named by Captain Stokes. 1855.

   Barcoo expedition to trace the course of Leichhardt's party. Confirmation of the supposed identity of the Barcoo and Cooper's Creek. No fresh discoveries were made, but the second great inland river system was evolved. 1858.

Grey, Lieutenant--
Explorations on the west coast. 1837.

Grey, Lieutenant, and Lushington (Second in Command)—
Expedition to verify the existence or not of the large river supposed to find its way into the sea at Dampier's Archipelago. This expedition originated in England. Found the Glenelg, and discovered cave drawings. 1838.

(Afterwards Governor of South Australia), Started on his second expedition from the west coast. Encountering great troubles Grey had to push on to Perth and send back a relief party. A party under Lieutenant Roe, after some trouble in tracking the erratic wanderings of the unfortunates, came upon them hopelessly gazing at a point of rocks that stopped their march along the beach, too weak to climb it. They had been three days without fresh water, and Smith, a lad of eighteen, was dead. [See Appendix.] Grey claims the discovery of the Gascoyne, Murchison, Hutt, Bower, Buller, Chapman, Greenough, Irwin, Arrowsmith, and Smith Rivers. 1839.

Grimes, Surveyor-General--
Accompanied Lieutenant Murray when Port Phillip was discovered, and surveyed it. 1802.

"Gulde Zeepard"--
Under command of Captain Pieter Nuyts, touched on the south coast. 1627.

Hack, Stephen--
With Miller examined Gawler Range, and sighted Lake Gairdner. 1857.

Hacking, Quarter-master--
Attempted to cross the Blue Mountains. Reached the foot of the range. 1794 and 1798.

Hamelin, Captain--
With commander Baudin, in the French ships Naturaliste and Géographe, exploring the coasts of Australia. 1801-2.

Hann, William—
A pioneer squatter of Queensland, led an expedition, equipped by the Queensland Government, to make an examination as 'far north as the fourteenth parallel, with a special view to its mineral and other resources. Naming the Walsh, the party crossed the upper part of the Mitchell River, and thence to the river they named the Palmer. Here Warner, the surveyor, found prospects of gold,

which resulted in the discovery of one of the richest goldfields in Australia. 1872.

Harper--

With Messrs. Dempster and Clarkson in Western Australia, explored from the settled districts as far as Mount Kennedy. 1861.

Hartog, Captain Dirk--

In the Endracht, from Amsterdam. Discovered the west coast of New Holland. (See Dirk Hartog, 1616.)

Harvey and Ross--

Explorations around Charlotte Waters, South Australia. 1877.

Hawkesbury River--

Discovered. 1789.

Hawson, Captain--

In company with some other gentlemen, made a short excursion from Port Lincoln, finding good, well-grassed country, and an abundance of water. They named Rossitur Vale and the Mississippi. 1840.

Hay--

Discovered the Denmark River, and explored the country back of Parry's Inlet. 1829.

Hayes, Captain John--

With the Duke and Duchess, visited Tasmania, renaming the discoveries of D'Entrecasteaux. 1794.

Hedley, G.--

Accompanied the Queenslander Transcontinental Expedition, led by Ernest Favenc, from Blackall to Powell's Creek, overland telegraph line. 1878-79.

"Heemskirk" (The)--

Under command of Abel Janz Tasman, when he discovered Van Dieman's Land, and took possession of New Holland. 1642.

Hely, Hovenden--

In charge of search party for Leichhardt. 1852.

Henty, Brothers--

Formed settlement in Portland Bay. 1835.

Hergott--

One of M'Dowall Stuart's second expedition. Discovered Hergott Springs, 1859.

Hesse and Gellibrand--

Murdered by the natives while exploring the Cape Otway country. 1837.

Hindmarsh, Captain Sir John--
In H.M.S. Buffalo founded Adelaide. 1836.
Hobson, Captain--
(Afterwards the first Governor of New Zealand.) In H.M.S. Rattle-snake; surveyed and named Hobson's Bay. 1836.
Hodgkinson, W. O.—
Commanded expedition sent by the Queensland Government to decide the amount of pastoral country existing to the Westward of the Diamantina River. Mr. Hodgkinson had been one of M'Kinlay's party when that explorer traversed the continent. This was the last exploring expedition sent out by the South Australian Government, 1876.
"Hormuzeer" and "Chesterfield"--
Under command Matthew B. Alt; through Torres Straits. 1793.
Horrocks, J. A.--
Died, soon after start of his expedition, at head of Spencer's Gulf. 1843.
Hovell, W. H.--
With H. Hume, across to Port Phillip; made the first successful trip from the eastern to the southern coast. The first white men to see the Australian Alps. 1824.
Howitt, A. W.—
In charge of relief party for Burke and Wills. King, the only survivor, found. Howitt was eventually sent back to disinter the remains of the explorers, and bring them to Melbourne, where they received a public funeral, and a statue was erected to their memory. 1861.
Hulkes and Oakden--
West side of Lake Torrens. 1851.
Hume, Hamilton--
And his brother, John Kennedy Hume, explored the country round Berrima. The first Australian born explorer. 1814.
With Meehan, surveyor. Discovered Lake George, Lake Bathurst, and Goulburn Plains. 1817.
With Messrs. Oxley and Meehan to Jarvis Bay. 1819.
With Hovell, across to Port Phillip. 1824.
Accompanied Charles Sturt on his first expedition to trace the source of the Macquarie. 1828-9.
Hunt, C. C.--
With Mr. Ridley to the De Grey River. 1863.

Jansen, Gerrit--

In command of the Zeehaan, and Abel Janz Tasman in the Heemskirk, discovered Van Dieman's Land. Afterwards took possession of New Holland. 1642.

Jardine, A.--

Police Magistrate at Rockhampton; took command of the settlement at Cape York, Somerset. 1863.

Jardine, Frank, and Alexander Jardine--

Overland with cattle from Carpentaria Downs Stationthen the farthest occupied country to the north-west--to Somerset. Cross the head of the Batavia River, probably the first white men on it since the old Dutch visits. 1864-65.

Johnson, Lieutenant, R.N.--

In the cutter Snapper, sent in search of Captain Stewart Discovered the Clyde River. 1820.

Kayzer, E. A.--

Second in charge, also surveyor and mineralogist, of the North-West Expedition, led by W.O. Hodgkinson. 1876.

Kennedy, E. B.--

Led an expedition to decide final course of Mitchell's, Barcoo (Victoria). Instead of finding on the Victoria a highway to the Gulf, they lost it in marshes. Follow the Warrego through fine grazing country. Named the Thompson. 1847.

Fatal venture up Cape York Peninsula. 1848.

Kindur, The—

A mysterious river in the unknown interior, supposed to run northwest. A runaway convict, named Clarke, brought up the story first. He said he had heard of it from the natives, so determined to make his escape and follow it, to see if it would lead him to another country. He started on his adventurous trip and said he followed the river to the sea. When at the mouth of the river he ascended a hill, and seaward saw an island inhabited, the natives told him, by copper-coloured men, who came in their canoes to the mainland for scented wood. He introduced various details of large plains which he had crossed, and a large burning mountain, but as he saw no prospect of getting away from Australia, he returned. Surveyor Mitchell took charge of an expedition to investigate the truth of his story. 1831.

King, Captain Phillip P.—

(Son of Governor King) In the Mermaid; sailed from Sydney accompanied by Mr. Allan Cunningham, botanist. His mission was to explore those portions of the coast left unvisited by previous navigators. Sailing by Cape Leeuwin, King examined the west and north-west coast, sailing from the north coast to Timor to refit. 1818. In 18iq he surveyed the lately-discovered Port Macquarie and visited Van Dieman's Land. Leaving Port Jackson, Captain King returned to the scene of his labours by way of the east coast, crossed the Gulf of Carpentaria and discovered Cambridge Gulf. In 1820 he left Port Jackson for his third voyage to the north coast; examined minutely the north-west coast. The Mermaid having sprung a leak, for the safety of the crew, Captain King had to return to Sydney. A brig was purchased, and rechristened the Bathurst. After surveying the north-west and west coast--and 'naming Dampier's Archipelago, Cygnet Bay, and Roebuck Bay, after Dampier and his vessels--he sailed to the Mauritius to refit. Returning to New Holland, he continued the survey of King George's Sound and the west coast. This concluded Captain King's fourth and last voyage round the Australian coast. 1817-20.

King, John--

The only survivor of Burke and Wills' party. Rescued by Edwin J. Welch, second in command of A. W. Howitt's relief party. 1861.

La Place, Captain--

From Toulon, visited Hobart Town and New Zealand. 1829.

Landor and Lefroy--

In Western Australia. 1843.

Landsborough, William—

Leader of the Queensland search party for Burke and Wills. journey by sea to the mouth of the Albert River, in the Gulf of Carpentaria. After exploring the country to the south, and discovering some rivers and many tributary creeks, Landsborough returned to the depôt on the Albert and heard tidings of Walker's relief party. He determined then to return overland instead of by sea. Making for the Flinders, by way of the Leichhardt, was rewarded, on following up the river, by being the discoverer of the beautiful downs country through which it runs. From thence to Bowen Downs, discovered by himself and Buchanan two years previously. The party finally proceeded to Melbourne. 1861-62.

Takes charge of the new township of Burketown, in the Gulf of Carpentaria. 1863.

Lawson, Lieutenant William-- With Wentworth and Blaxland, succeeded in crossing the Blue Mountains. 1813.

Lawson, Lieutenant William, and Scott-- Attempted to reach Liverpool Plains. Discovered the Goulburn River. 1822.

"Leeuwin" (The) (Lioness). Commander unknown--
Visited the west coast and named the Houtman Abrolhos reef after
a Dutch navigator of distinction. 1622.

Lefroy (and Party)--
Eastward of York, Western Australia; finding valuable pastoral
and agricultural land. 1863.

Leichhardt, Ludwig—
Left Jimbour Station, on the Darling Downs, in charge of an expedition to Port Essington, in the Gulf of Carpentaria. Gilbert, the
naturalist accompanying the party, killed by the blacks. 1844-45.
Last expedition, with the intention of crossing the continent.
from Mitchell's Victoria (Barcoo) River to Perth. 1848.

Leslie, Patrick--
Considered the father of settlement on the Darling Downs. Settled
on the Condamine, 1840.

"L'Esperance" (The) and "Recherche"--
With Admiral Bruni D'Entrecasteaux, to seek La Perouse. Anchored on the south coast. 1792

Lewis, J.W.--
Took charge of an expedition, sent by the Governor of South Australia, to determine the channels, directions and size of the many
rivers that flowed from Queensland through South Australia into
Lake Eyre. 1875.

Light, Colonel--
Surveyed the shores of St. Vincent's Gulf and site of the present
town of Adelaide. 1836.

"Limmen" (The) "Zeemeuw," and "De Brak"--
Under command of Abel Janz Tasman. 1644.

Lindsay, David--
Sent by the South Australian Government to complete the exploration of Arnheim's Land. On the whole the country passed over was
favourable for settlement some of it being first class sugar country.
1883.

Lockyer, Major--
Made a boat excursion up the Brisbane River. 1825.
Founded King George's Sound, which was abandoned in 1830 in
favour of the Swan River colony. 1826

Macdonald, J. G.--
With a small party, visited the Plains of Promise. Discovered a

more practicable route for cattle and sheep to the magnificent western pastoral lands on the Flinders. 1865.

Macfarlane, Thomas--

Attempted to get inland north of the Bight, but was forced to turn back after suffering great hardship. He found fairly-grassed country, but waterless. 1863.

Magalhaens--

A Portuguese navigator in the service of the Emperor of Spain, claims having touched on the Great South Landthese claims are based on the authority of an ancient map. 1520.

Malaspina, Don Alexandro--

In the Descobierta and Atrevida, Spanish discovery ships, arrived at Sydney; was imprisoned on his return to Calais. 1793.

"Mauritius" (The)--

Commanded by Captain Zeachern, touched on the west coast; discovered and named the Wilhelm's River, near the North-West Cape, probably the present Ashburton. 1818.

Meehan, Surveyor--

With Hume, discovers Lake George, Lake Bathurst, and Goulburn Plains. 1817.

With Messrs. Oxley and Hume to Jarvis Bay. 1819.

Melville Island--

Settled, 1824. Abandoned, 1829.

Miller--

With C. W. Dutton, explored the country back of Fowler's Bay. 1857.

Mitchell, Major (Sir Thomas)—

Took charge of an expedition to trace the supposed Kindur. Discovered the Drummond Range, and worked out the courses of the rivers discovered by Oxley and Cunningham. 1831-2. Accompanied by Richard Cunningham (brother to Allan Cunningham), started with his second expedition. This was more of a connecting survey than exploring the unknown. 1833.

Explores Australia Felix. 1836.

Barcoo Expedition. This was the last expedition of the Surveyor-General, and fully confirmed his reputation. 1845-46.

Died near Sydney. 1855.

Moreton Bay--

Penal settlement. 1824.

Morgan--

>With Messrs. Tench and Dawes, explored south and west of Rose Hill. Discovered the Nepean River. 1790.

Mueller, Baron Von--

>Engaged in exploring some of the still unknown portions of the south for botanical and geographical researches combined. 1847.

With A. C. Gregory's North Australian expedition. Discovery of Sturt's Creek. 1855-56.

Murray, Lieutenant John--

>Succeeded James Grant in the Lady Nelson, discovered Port Phillip, and made a further exploration of Bass's Straits. 1802.

M'Cluer, John--

>Sailed along Arnheim's Land to Cape Van Dieman. 1791.

M'Donnell, Sir Richard Graves--

>Governor of South Australia; made explorations to the Strangways and Loddon Springs, and up the Murray River to Mount Murchison. 1858.

M'Kinlay, J.--

>On the Alligator, searching for suitable site for township. His last expedition. 1864.

M'Kinlay, John--

>Started from Adelaide with a relief party in search of Burke and Wills. His trip across the continent did much to dispel the stigma that rested upon the tract known as desert, and unfit for pastoral occupation. 1861.

Died at Gawler, in South Australia. 1874.

M'Intyre, Duncan--

>From Paroo to the Gulf of Carpentaria. Found and buried the bodies of two unfortunate pioneers, Messrs. Curlewis and M'Culloch. They had been murdered in their sleep by the natives. 1864.

Took command of a search expedition for Leichhardt, organised by the ladies of Victoria, but when in the Gulf of Carpentaria died of malarial fever. 1865.

M'Millan, Angus—

>Finds his way through the Snowy Mountains on the search for country. Discovers a river running through fine grazing plains and forest. This territory was called Gipps Land. The rivers discovered by him were afterwards re-named by Count Strzelecki, and retained, whilst those given by the real discoverer were forgotten. 1840.

M'Minn, Gilbert, and A. W. Sergison--
  Equipped by the South Australian Government, to ascertain the course of the Katherine. 1876.
M'Phee--
  Explorations east of Daly Waters. May be said to have concluded the list of expeditions between the overland telegraph line and the Queensland border. 1883.
Neilson, J. and Brothers--
  From Mount Ranken, on the Darling, to Cooper's Creek, in search of pastoral country. 1861.
Nares, Sir George Strong--
  Commander of H.M.S. Salamander, surveyed the east and north-eastern part of Australia and Torres Straits. 1866-7.
Nuyts, Captain Pieter--
  In the Gulde Zeepard. Accidentally touched on the south coast. Followed it for about seven or eight hundred miles, and gave to it the name of Pieter Nuyts' Land, 1627.
Oakden and Hulkes--
  To the west of Lake Torrens. 1851.
Overlanders—
  "The first overlanders with stock from Sydney side to Port Phillip were Messrs. Ebden (afterwards treasurer), Joe Hawdon, Gardener (of Gardener's Creek), and Captain Hepburn. This was in 1837, one year before Mr. Mackinnon arrived in the colonies. In 1838 Captain Hepburn made a second overland trip, starting from Braidwood, New South Wales, with sheep purchased from Captain Coghill of that place, and in January same year (1838), Mr. Gardener started on second trip with 460 head of cattle purchased from my father, the late Dr. Reid. of Inverary Park, in Argyle; delivery of same made by myself at Yass end of January month. This trip with Mr. Gardener so far imbued me with the love for adventure that I followed with stock the June following, and formed stations on the Ovens River, near where the town of Wangaratta now stands. The first overlanders with stock to Adelaide were Joe Hawdon and Eyre, the latter afterwards celebrated as an explorer. Well can I remember the excitement caused by the then so-called race, who should be first to Adelaide, Hawdon or Eyre, but Hawdon was too good a bushman for Eyre and had more experience, and was a better judge of the season (it was a dry one). Hawdon wisely followed the course of the Murray right to Lake Alexandrina, and consequently had food and water in abundance. Eyre

crossed from Goulburn to go over the Wimmera Plains--no doubt
a shorter way had the season been propitious, but as it turned out
dry he had to retrace his steps, and follow the track of friend Hawdon. Hawdon by this time had a long start, and arrived in Adelaide
two weeks before Eyre, and had his stock disposed of. I may remark very few of us overlanders are now left, but should this meet
the eye of any such of 1837 and 1838, I make no doubt they will
remember the facts above stated."--Extract from "Answers to Cor-
respondents," from Mr. David Reid, Moorwatha, Victoria, in the
Australasian, May 4th, 1888.

Orr, John (and party)--

Expedition through Gippsland. Confirmed the previous glowing
reports. 1841.

Ovens, Major--

With Captain Curry, started on an exploring trip south of Lake
George. Discovered Morumbidgee River and Monaroo Plains.
1823.

Oxley, John—

With Lieutenant Charles Robbins, in the cutter Integrity, examined
Western Port, with a view to settlement; opinion unfavourable.
1804-5.

Surveyor-General of New South Wales. Second in command,
Mr. Evans. Accompanied by Mr. Allan Cunningham, King's botanist, and Charles Fraser, Colonial botanist, William Parr,
mineralogist, eight men, and two boats, for the purpose of tracing
the Lachlan and Macquarie. Return in 1817. The following year
again started, discovering the Castlereagh River, Liverpool Plains,
Apsley River, and the Goulburn Valley. Following down the River
Hastings, they discovered and named Port Macquarie. 1817-18.

Accompanied by Messrs. Meehan and Hume, made a short
excursion to Jarvis Bay. Oxley returned by sea his companions
overland. 1819.

In the Mermaid with Messrs. Uniacke and Lieutenant Stirling,
left Port Jackson to investigate the coast north of Sydney, with the
view of forming a penal settlement. They examine Port Curtis,
Port Bowen, and Moreton Bay. Discovered the Boyne and Brisbane Rivers. 1823.

Died near Sydney, 1828. He had been a successful explorer,
although in no case attaining the objects aimed at, had always
brought his men through in safety, and had opened up vast tracts
of country. [See Appendix.]

O'Donnell and Carr Boyd--
From the overland telegraph line to Western Australia, finding good country, but no new geographical discovery. 1883.

O'Donnell (and party)--
From the Katherine Telegraph Station, overland telegraph line to Western Australia. 1884-5.

Parry, S.--
Government Surveyor, examined the country round Lake Torrens. 1858.

Paterson, Colonel--
Intending if possible to cross the Blue Mountains, rowed up the Hawkesbury, and named the highest point reached "The Grose." 1793.

Pelsart, Francis--
In the Batavia. Wrecked on Houtman's Abrolhos. 1629.

"Pera" (The) and "Arnheim"--
Yachts commanded by Captain Jan Carstens, touched on the north coast. Pera Head in the Gulf of Carpentaria a memorial of this visit. 1623.

Perouse, Jean Francois Galup de La--
At Botany Bay with the Astrolabe and Boussole. 1778.

Phillip, Governor--
Arrived at Botany Bay with the first fleet. 1788.

Pool, Captain Gerrit Tomaz--
In the Klyn, Amsterdam, and Wezel, from Banda, was murdered on the New Guinea coast--the same spot where Captain Carstens met his death. The supercargo continued the voyage, re-visiting Arnheim's Land. 1636.

Poole--
Second in command in Sturt's Great Central Desert expedition died of scurvy; and was buried at Depôt Glen. 1845.

Port Essington--
Founded by Sir Gordon Bremer, 1824, and re-settled, 1838.

Portlock, Captain, Nathan, and Captain Bligh--
In the Providence and Assistant. Through Torres Straits. 1792.

Portuguese--
The claim to the discovery of New Holland in 1540 is doubtful.

Prout Bros.—
With one man started out from South Australia looking for country across the Queensland border. They never returned. Some months afterwards some of their horses and the bones of one of the broth-

ers were discovered by Mr. W. J. H. Carr Boyd. It was evident, from the fragments of a diary found, that they had met their death by thirst on their homeward way. 1878.

Quiros, Pedro Fernandez de—

Being second in command to Luis Vaez de Torres sailed from Callao with two wellarmed vessels and a corvette. After minor discoveries came to a land supposed by Quiros to be the continent they were in search of, and named it Australia del Espiritu Santo. 1606.

Ranken, John C. L.—

One of the Queensland pioneers. Following closely after the explorers he formed a station upon the Isaacs, and afterwards took up Afton Downs, on the Flinders. He then with a party struck northwest, and crossed the unmarked boundary of South Australia, and finally formed stations on the head of the Herbert River. 1857-70.

Receveur, Father le--

Died at Botany Bay while with La Perouse in the Astrolabe. Feb. 17th, 1778.

"Recherche" (The) and "L'Esperance"--

Under command of Admiral Bruni D'Entrecasteaux, in search of the fate of La Perouse, anchored on the south coast of Australia, 1792.

"Research" (The)--

Under command Captain Dillon; on the south coast 1826.

Ridley and 0. C. Hunt--

To the De Grey River. 1863.

Robbins, Lieutenant Charles, and John Oxley--

In the cutter Integrity, examined Western Port, with a view to settlement. Opinion unfavourable. 1804-5.

"Roebuck" (The)--

Under William Dampier, sent out by the English Government, visited the west coast of New Holland. 1688.

Roe, Surveyor-General--

Started from York; reached the Pallinup, the last stream crossed by Eyre before reaching Albany on his Great Bight expedition. After suffering great hardships, arrived at Russell Range, from there returning to Perth. 1848-49.

Roggentier, Commodore--

Started for New Holland. Discovered the Thousand Islands. 1721.

Ross and Son--

With an equipment of camels and horses, started from the

neighbourhood of Peake Station, on the overland telegraph line, to endeavour to cross the desert, but were obliged to return; a second effort being alike unsuccessful. 1874.

Ross and Harvey--

Explorations around Charlotte Waters, South Australia. 1877.

Russell, Stuart and Sydenham--

Followed the Condamine for a hundred miles from below Jimbour, the northernmost station on a Darling Downs Creek; an extensive tract of rich grazing country found; since known by the name then bestowed on it--Cecil Plains. 1841.

Russell, Stuart—

Journeyed from Moreton Bay to Wide Bay in a boat, and made an examination of some of the streams there emptying into the sea. During the same year Stuart Russell explored the country from Wide Bay to the Boyne (not Oxley's Boyne) and opened up much available pastoral country. 1842.

Saunders, Philip, and Adam, John--

Accompanied by a third man, successfully crossed from Roeburne, in Western Australia, to the overland telegraph line. 1876.

Scarr, Frank (Surveyor)—

Attempted to cross the line to the south of N. Buchanan's track, but was prevented by the waterless strip of country existing there. Finally made north, arriving at Tennant's Creek Station, and, owing to the dry season, did not extend his researches further. 1878.

Scott and Lieutenant Lawson--

Attempted to reach the Liverpool Plains. Discovered the Goulburn River. 1822.

Sergison, A. W., and Gilbert M'Minn--

Sent by the South Australian Government to ascertain the course of the Katherine River. 1876.

Sergison, A. W., and R. Travers--

Explored the country about the Daly and Fitzmaurice Rivers. 1877.

Shortland, Lieutenant--

With three ships, from Sydney to England, passed through Bougainville's Strait, north-west coast. 1788.
Discovered Hunter River. 1797.

Solander, Dr.--

Swedish botanist. Accompanied Captain Cook in the Endeavour. 1770.

Somerset--
> Settlement at Cape York. Mr. Jardine, Police Magistrate at Rock-hampton, took command, and a detachment of marines was stationed there. 1863.

Stewart, Captain--
> Sent by Governor Macquarie to search for a passage supposed to exist between Lake Bathurst and the sea. He lost his boat in Two-fold Bay, and on endeavouring to reach Sydney overland, was cut off by the natives. 1820.

Stirling, Captain--
> Accompanied by Charles Frazer, in H.M.S. Success, surveyed coast from King George's Sound to the Swan River. 1828.

Stock, Edwin (and party)--
> West of Lake Eyre. 1857.

Stockdale, Harry—
> Started on an expedition from Cambridge Gulf to explore the country in the neighbourhood with a view to settlement. Landed by steamer in Cambridge Gulf, and probably the first landing that had taken place since Captain Stokes. After a hard struggle, reached the telegraph line with one man; sending back relief to the others. 1884.

Stokes, Captain John Lort—
> Took command of the Beagle on retirement of Captain T. C. Wickham, and continued the survey, which completed our geographical knowledge of the Australian coast. The survey continued from 1837 to 1845.

Strzelecki, Count—
> Followed on M'Millan's tracks when he discovered Gipps Land, and has often been erroneously considered the discoverer. The object of this trip was to gather material for his now well-known book, "The Physical Description of New South Wales, Victoria, and Van Dieman's Land." He mounted the Alps, and named one of the highest peaks Kosciusko, from its fancied resemblance to the patriot's tomb at Cracow. 1840.

Stuart, J. M'Dowall--
> First expedition west of Lake Torrens. 1858.
>
> Made another start, discovering Hergott Springs and the Neale. His horses' shoes having given out he returned, remembering the misery he suffered on his first expedition from the want of them. 1859.

Left on his third expedition, in the vicinity of Lake Eyre, reached the centre of Australia and named a tolerable high mount Central Mount Stuart. Christened the Murchison Range and Tennant's Creek, but failed to reach the head waters of the Victoria owing to a dry strip of country. 1861.

Last expedition. Crossed the continent from shore to shore, from the south coast to the north. His health never recovered the hardships endured on this journey. 1861-62.

Died in England. 1869.

Sturt, Captain Charles (39th Regiment)—

First expedition, accompanied by H. Hume, to find the course of the Macquarie, that had baffled Oxley. Discovered the Darling, New Year's Creek (Bogan). 1828-29.

Started on his Murrumbidgee expedition. Sailed down the Murray. Found its confluence with the Darling, and followed the united streams to the lake that terminated the Murray. 1829-30.

Great Central Desert expedition, Poole second in corn mand,

M'Dowall Stuart as draftsman. 1844-45. His last expedition.

Sutherland, Captain--

On a sealing voyage, visited Port Lincoln. 181 g.

Swinden, Charles--

With others looking for pastoral country west of Lake Eyre. 1857.

Tasman, Abel Janz--

In command of the Heemskirk, and Gerrit Jansen, with the Nee-haan, discovered Van Dieman's Land. Afterwards took possession of New Holland. 1642.

With the Limmen, Zeemeuw, and De Brak. After his discov-ery of Van Dieman's Land undertook this second expedition to determine, if possible, whether Nova Guinea and New Holland were one continent; also, if Tasmania joined one or the other. His journal has never been found, but an outline copy of his chart was inlaid in the floor of the Groote Zaal in the Stadhuys in Amster-dam. Many of the names still retained in the Gulf of Carpentaria are memorials of his visit. 1644.

Tench, Captain--

Crossed the Nepean. 1789.

With Dawes and Morgan explored south-west of Rose Hill. 1790.

Testu, Guillaume Le--

Claims to early discovery of Australia, based upon a map now in the Depôt de la Guerre, at Paris, bearing his name and the date. 1542.

Thompson D. (and party)--
West of Lake Eyre searching for pastoral country. 1857.

Torres, Luis Vaez de--
With Pedro Fernandez de Quiros, sailed round Cape York and discovered Torres Straits. 1606.

Travers, R--
With A. W. Sergison, explored the country about the Daly and
Fitzmaurice Rivers. 1877.

Vancouver, Captain George--
In the Discovery and Chatham, explored the south-west coast, and
discovered and named King George's Sound. 1791.

"Vergulde Draeck" (The)--
From Batavia. Lost on Houtman's Abrolhos. 1656.

Vlaming, William de—
Came to the South Land in search of the Ridderschap, a vessel
supposed to have been wrecked on the coast of New Holland. He
found and named the Swan River. At Dirk Hartog's Roads he
found the plate left by Hartog, and added to it another inscription.
After careful examination of the coast as far as North-West Cape,
left for Batavia with his ships the Geelvink, Nyptangh, and
Wezeltje. 1695.

"Vossenbach" "Wayer", and "Nova Hollandia"--
Under command of Martin Von Delft. Sent to investigate the north
coast. The last voyage of discovery by the Dutch. 1705.

Walker, Frederick--
The leader of the Rockhampton search party for and Wills. Pushed
through from the Barcoo to the depôt found on the Gilbert. Fresh
provisioned, they returned and reached the Lower Burdekin well
nigh horseless, and quite starving. 1861-62.
Examining the country at the back of Rockingham Bay, and
marking a telegraph line from there to the mouth of the Norman
River, in the Gulf of Carpentaria. 1864.

Warburton, Major--
Investigated the country west of Lake Torrens. 1857.
Superseded Babbage. This trip established the definite size
and shape of Lake Torrens, so long the terror of the north, preventing advancement. 1858. Led an expedition to cross from the
overland telegraph line to Perth. The expedition was fitted out
with camels, but owing to their constant delays provisions fell
short and sickness came. Warburton determined to push through
the desert country he had got into, and travelled chiefly at night.

Being too much occupied in pressing through, had no time to look at the country on either side. Thus it was all pronounced desert, and of seventeen camels only two survived, the starving party being obliged to slaughter some for food. 1873.

Welch, Edwin J.—

Surveyor and second in command of A. W. Howitt's relief party for Burke and Wills. Found King, the only survivor of Burke and Wills' expedition. Since the death of his companion, King had been existing for nearly three months with the blacks. 1861. [See Appendix.]

Wentworth, Charles--

With Messrs. Lawson and Blaxland, succeeded in crossing the Blue Mountains. 1813.

Wickham, Captain John Clements—

Commander of the Beagle. Retired through ill-health. 1841. Succeeded by Captain J. L. Stokes. Left England 1837 to continue the survey of the coasts of Australia, and so minutely examined the shores that the outline of the continent was perfectly complete. The survey continued from 1837 to 1841.

Wills, William John--

Surveyor and astronomer on Burke and Wills' expedition (See Burke.) 1860-61.

Winnecke and Barclay--

Two surveyors dispatched by the South Australian Government in 1878 to reach the Queensland border from the overland telegraph line, it being a matter of moment to settle the position of the border line between the two colonies. Another attempt in 1880 proved successful. 1878-80.

Witt, Willem de--

In the Vianen, sighted the north-west coast and reported (see De Witt) it "a foul and barren shore, green fields. and very wild, barbarous inhabitants." 1628.

Zeachern, Captain--

In the Mauritius, claims to have discovered Arnheim's Land. 1618.

"Zeehaan" (The)--

Under command of Captain Gerrit Jansen, accompanied by Abel Janz Tasman in the Heemskirk. Discovered Van Dieman's Land, and took possession of New Holland. 1642.

"Zeemeuw," "Limmen," and "De Brak"--

Under Abel Janz Tasman. 1644.

"Zeewyck" (The)--

Lost on Houtman's Abrolhos. In 1839 Captain Stokes found a gun and other relics of this vessel on one of the islands. 1727.

Zouch, Lieutenant (N.S.W. Mounted Police)--

Sent in command of party to arrest the natives who murdered Richard Cunningham, the botanist to Sir Thomas Mitchell's expedition. 1835. [See Appendix.]

Appendix - CHRONOLOGICAL SUMMARY.

1503--De Gonneville visited the South Seas, and is claimed by the French to have touched on Australia.

1520--Magalhaens, the first circumnavigator, claims to have discovered Australia. (Doubtful.)

1540--The Portuguese claims to early discovery of Australia are doubtful.

1542--Guillaume le Testu. Claims based on a map now in the Depôt de la Guerre, at Paris, indicating Australia.

1601--Manoel Godinho de Eredia, a Spaniard. (Claim doubtful.)

1606--The Duyfhen entered the Gulf of Carpentaria as far as Cape Keer-Weer (Turn Again).

1606--Luis Vaez de Torres, with Pedro Fernandez de Quiros, discovered Torres Straits.

1616--Dirk Hartog, in the Endracht, visited the west coast.

1618--Zeachern, in the Mauritius, discovered Arnheim's Land.

1619--John Van Edels on the west coast.

1622--The Landt van de Leeuwin, south-west cape of Australia, named after the ship Leeuwin.

1623--Jan Carstens, with the yachts Pera and Arnheim; on the south-west coast.

1627--Pieter Nuyts, in the Gulde Zeepard; western and southern coasts.

1628--Willem de Witt, the Vianen; north-west coast named after him.

1628--Pieter Carpenter discovered the Gulf of Carpentaria.

1629--Francis Pelsart, in the Batavia; lost on Houtman's Albrolhos.

1636--Gerrit Tomaz Pool, with the Klyn, Amsterdam, and Wezel; coast of Arnheim's Land.

1642--Abel Janz Tasman and Gerrit Jansen, with the Heemskirk and Zeehaan; discovered Van Dieman's Land, and took possession of New Holland.

1644--Abel Janz Tasman, with the Limmen, Zeemeuw, and De Brak west coasts of Carpentaria.

1656--The Vergulde Draeck lost on Houtman's Albrohos.

1688--William Dampier, in the Bachelor's Delight and Cygnet, with crews of buccaneers.

1695--William de Vlaming, with the Geelvink, Nyptangh, and Wezeltje, named the Swan River.

1699--William Dampier, in the Roebuck; north-west coast of New Holland.

1705--Martin Van Delft, with the Vossenbach, Wayer, and Nova Hollandia; on the west coast. This was the last voyage of discovery by the Dutch.

1721--Commodore Roggewein started for New Holland; discovered the "Thousand Islands."

1727--The Zeewyck lost off Houtman's Abrolhos. In 1839, Captain Stokes found a gun and other relics of this visit on an island.

1768--De Bougainville discovered the Louisade Archipelago.

1770--Captain James Cook, in the Endeavour; landed at Botany Bay; explored the east coast, and took possession under the name of New South Wales.

1772--Captain Marion du Fresne and Captain Crozet, from Nance, in the Mascarin and Castres to Tasmania. The first visitors after Tasman. From thence they sailed to New Zealand, where they were murdered by the Maories.

1772--Captain Tobias Furneaux, with the Adventure; accompanied Captain Cook on his second voyage in search of Australia. Separated from the Endeavour, and afterwards, when he met Cook, gave as his opinion that Tasmania and New South Wales were joined, with a deep bay intervening. This opinion Cook thought sufficient to prevent the necessity of a further examination by himself.

1777--De St. Alouarn anchored near Cape Leeuwin.

1788--Father le Receveur, naturalist; died at Botany Bay, while with La Perouse in the Astrolabe.

1788--Lieutenant Shortland, with three ships from Sydney to England passed through Bougainville's Strait, north-west coast.

1788--Governor Phillip arrived in Botany Bay with the first fleet.

1788--Jean Francois Galup de la Perouse at Botany Bay.

1789--Hawkesbury discovered.

1789--Tench discovered the Nepean.

1790--Messrs. Tench, Dawes, and Morgan explore south and west of Rose Hill.

1791--Captain George Vancouver, in the Discovery and Chatham, explored the south-west coast, and discovered King George's Sound.

1791--Captain William Bligh passed Cape York in the Bounty's launch.

1791--Captain Edward Edwards, in search of the mutineers of the Bounty, wrecked on a reef.

1791--Captain John M'Cluer sailed along Arnheim's Land to Cape Van Dieman.

1792--Admiral Bruni D'Entrecasteaux in the Recherche and L'Esperance; to seek La Perouse.

1792--Captains William Bligh and Portlock, in the Providence and Assistant; examined Torres Straits.

1793--Matthew B. Alt and William Bampton, in the ships Hormuzeer and Chesterfield; through Torres Straits.

1793--Colonel Paterson rowed up the Hawkesbury, and named the Grose.

1793--Don Alexandro Malaspina, with the Descobierta and Atrevida, Spanish discovery ships, arrived at Sydney. Was imprisoned on his return to Calais.

1794--John Hayes, with the Duke and Duchess; visited Tasmania renamed the discoveries of D'Entrecasteaux.

1794--Quarter-master Hacking attempted to cross the Blue Mountains.

1795-96--Dr. George Bass and Matthew Flinders in the Tom Thumb.

1796--Lieutenant Bowen visited Jarvis Bay.

1796-97--Dr. George Bass; on the Blue Mountains.

1797-Dr.--George Bass's whaleboat survey of the coast to the southward.

1797--Lieutenant Shortland discovered the Hunter River.

1798--Dr. George Bass and Matthew Flinders, in the Norfolk; discovered Bass's Straits.

1798--Quarter-master Hacking revisits the Blue Mountains.

1799--Matthew Flinders, in the Norfolk; to Glass-House and Hervey Bays.

1800--Christopher Dixon, in the ship Ellegood; visited King George's Sound.

1801--James Grant, in the Lady Nelson; examined Bass's Straits and verified Bass's discovery.

1801--Ensign Barraillier; attempted exploration of the Blue Mountains.

1801-2--Matthew Flinders, in the Investigator; prosecuted his survey of the coasts of Australia.

1801-2--Captains Baudin and Hamelin, with the French ships Naturaliste and Géographe; on the Australian coasts.

1802--Lieut. John Murray and Surveyor Grimes, in the Lady Nelson discovered and surveyed Port Phillip.

1803--George Cayley, botanist; attempt to discover pass over the Blue Mountains.

1803--Lieutenant-Governor Daniel Collins, from England, in H.M.S. Calcutta, to form a penal settlement at Port Phillip, accompanied by the transport Ocean. Landed the settlement at "The Sisters," and finally decided that Port Phillip was unfit to meet the requirements of settlement. They proceeded to Tasmania, where they were all murdered at Hobart Town.

1804-5--Lieutenant Charles Robbins and John Oxley, in the cutter Integrity; examined Western Port with a view to settlement; opinion unfavourable.

1813--Messrs. Wentworth, Lawson, and Blaxland succeeded in crossing the Blue Mountains.

1814--Hamilton Hume, with his brother; explored the country round Berrima. His first trip.

1815--Deputy-Surveyor Evans discovered the first Australian inland river, the Macquarie.

1815--Cox finished a road over the Blue Mountains

1817--L. de Freycinet, in L'Uranie, touched at Sydney and Shark's Bay.

1817-20--Captain Phillip P. King, with Allan Cunningham, botanist, in the cutter Mermaid; survey of the Australian coasts.

1817--Messrs. Meehan and Hume; discovered Lake George, Lake Bathurst, and Goulburn Plains.

1817-19--John Oxley, Surveyor-General of New South Wales; Lachlan and Macquarie expeditions.

1819--Surveyor-General Oxley, accompanied by Messrs. Meehan and Hume to Jarvis Bay.

1819--Captain Sutherland, on a sailing voyage, visited Port Lincoln.

1820--Captain Stewart sent by Governor Macquarie with a small party in a boat to search for a passage supposed to exist between Lake Bathurst and the sea. He lost his boat in Twofold Bay, and on endeavouring to reach Sydney overland was cut off by the natives.

1821-22--Captain Phillip P. King, in the Bathurst; continues the survey.

1822--Messrs. Lawson and Scott attempted to reach Liverpool Plains; discover the Goulburn River.

1822-24--Captain Duperry in La Coquille; voyage amongst the Line Islands

1823--Captain Currie and Major Ovens on the Murrumbidgee

1823--Allan Cunningham found Pandora's Pass; a good stock route to the Liverpool Plains.

1823--Surveyor-General Oxley investigated Port Curtis, Port Bowen and Moreton Bay. Discovered the Brisbane River.

1824--Sir Gordon Bremer, in the Tamar; to Port Essington.

1824--Melville Island settled

1824--Hamilton Hume and W. H. Hovell journey overland to Port Phillip.

1824--Penal settlement at Moreton Bay.

1825--Allan Cunningham north of Bathurst.

1825--Major Lockyer made a boat excursion up the Brisbane River.

1826--Captain Dillon, in the Research, on the west coast,

1826--Major Lockyer, founded King George's Sound settlement.

1826--Captain Dumont D'Urville, in the Astrolabe, from touched at Bass's Strait.

1826--Fort Wellington and Raffles Bay founded.

1827-28--Captain Gould on the south coast, near Port Lincoln.

1827--Allan Cunningham discovers the Darling Downs, the Dumaresque, Gwydir and Condamine Rivers, etc.

1828--Allan Cunningham, accompanied by Charles Frazer, botanist connected the Moreton Bay settlement, with the Darling Downs by way of Cunningham's Gap.

1828--Captain James Stirling, accompanied by Charles Frazer, in H.M.S. Success; surveyed the coast of King George's Sound to the Swan River.

1828--Surveyor-General Oxley died near Sydney.

1828-29--Captain Charles Sturt's first expedition; discovered New Year's Creek (now the Bogan) and the Darling.

1829--Hay explored the country back of Parry's Inlet and discovered the Denmark River.

1829--Captain Fremantle hoisted the British flag at Fremantle.

1829--Captain la Place, from Toulon; visited Hobart Town and New Zealand.

1829--Captain R. Fitzroy, in the Beagle; visited King George's Sound.

1829--Fort Wellington and north coast settlement abandoned.

1829--Allan Cunningham explored the source of the Brisbane River his last expedition.

1839-30--Captain Charles Sturt's Murrumbidgee expedition; sailed down the Murray.

1830--Dale from the upper Swan River followed up the Avon.

1831--Major Bannister crossed from Perth to King George's Sound.

1831-32--Sir Thomas Mitchell; Kindur expedition.

1832--Captain C. Barker murdered at Lake Alexandrina by the blacks.

1833--Surveyor Dixon on the Bogan.

1833--Sir Thomas Mitchell on the Namoi.

1833--Richard Cunningham, botanist, brother to Allan Cunningham, murdered by the blacks while with Sir Thomas Mitchell's expedition.

1835--E. Henty and brother formed a settlement in Portland Bay.

1836--John Batman landed at Port Phillip, and became a permanent settler there.

1836--Captain Sir John Hindmarsh founded Adelaide; first Governor of South Australia.

1836--Colonel Light surveyed the shores of St. Vincent's Gulf, and selected site of present city of Adelaide.

1836--Captain Hobson (afterwards Governor of New Zealand), in H.M.S Rattlesnake; surveyed and named Hobson's Bay.

1836--Sir Thomas Mitchell's expedition through Australia Felix.

1837--Captain George Grey (afterwards Governor of South Australia), with Lieutenant Lushington; explorations on north-west coast.

1837-Messrs. Hesse and Gellibrand, while exploring Cape Otway country, were murdered by the blacks.

1837-45--Captains Wickham and Stokes, in the Beagle, surveyed the coasts of Australia, completing the geographical knowledge of the shores of the continent.

1838--E. J. Eyre; Port Phillip to Adelaide; discovered Like Hindmarsh.

1838--Sir Gordon Bremer re-settled Port Essington.

1839--Captain George Grey; second expedition; Western Australia.

1839--Schooner Champion examined the west coast for navigable rivers.

1839--George Hamilton and party overland from Sydney to Melbourne. (See Overlanders, page 454 [in Index of Names])

1839--Governor Gawler, South Australia; made an excursion to the Murray.

1839--E. J. Eyre to the head of Spencer's Gulf and Lake Torrens, Port Lincoln, and Streaky Bay.

1839--Allan Cunningham died in Sydney.

1840--Angus M'Millan discovered Gippsland.

1840--Patrick Leslie, called the father of Darling Downs settlement; settled on the Condamine.

1840-41--E. J. Eyre travelled the Great Bight to King George's Sound.

1841--John Orr and party explored Gippsland.

1841--Stuart and Sydenham Russell form Cecil Plains Station.

1841--Dr. Edward Barker, Edward Hobson, and Albert Brodribb were the first to walk from Melbourne to Gippsland. The present road follows their track.

1842--Stuart Russell discovered Boyne River; journeyed from Moreton to Wide Bay in a boat.

1842-45--Captain Blackwood, in the Fly; continued the surveys of Captains Wickham and Stokes; and made a minute examination of the Great Barrier Reef.

1843--Count Paul von Strzelecki followed M'Millan's tracks when he discovered Gippsland.

1843--Captain Frome, Surveyor-General of South Australia; explorations in the neighbourhood of Lake Torrens.

1843--Messrs. Landor and Lefroy; exploration in Western Australia.

1843--J. A. Horracks was killed by the explosion of his gun at the head of Spencer's Gulf soon after the start of his expedition.

1844--45-Captain Charles Sturt; Great Central Desert expedition.

1844-45--Dr. Ludwig Leichhardt; first expedition, from Jimbour Station, Darling Downs, to Port Essington; Gilbert, the naturalist, killed by natives.

1845-46--Sir Thomas Mitchell; Barcoo expedition.

1846--Dr. Ludwig Leichhardt's second expedition.

1846--A. C. Gregory and brothers; first expedition in Western Australia.

1847--E. Kennedy; to decide the final course of the Victoria, named the Thompson.

1847--Baron Von Mueller; expeditions, for botanical and geographical researches combined. in South Australia and the Australian Alps.

1848--Dr. Ludwig Leichhardt's last expedition.

1848--E. Kennedy's fatal venture up Cape York Peninsula.

1848--A. C. Gregory, with party, explore the Gascoyne.

1848--Governor Fitzgerald, of Western Australia; examined the new mineral discovery, accompanied by A. C. Gregory, and named the Geraldine Aline.

1848-49--J. S. Roe, Surveyor-General of Western Australia; from York to Esperance Bay.

1851--Messrs. Oakden and Hulkes; on west side of Lake Torrens.

1852--Hovenden Hely, in charge of search party for Leichhardt; from Darling Downs.

1854--R. Austin, Assistant Surveyor-General of Western Australia; in search of pastoral country, and to examine the interior for auriferous deposits.

1855--Sir Thomas Mitchell died near Sydney.

1855-56--A. C. Gregory and Baron von Mueller North Australian expedition, in search of Leichhardt; discover Sturt's Creek and the Elsey.

1855--B. H. Babbage; to examine country north and east of Adelaide for gold. In a second expedition the same year discovered Blanche Water.

1857--Campbell and party; west of Lake Torrens; and again, with party, looking for pastoral country west of Lake Eyre.

1857--G. W. Goyder, Deputy Surveyor-General of South Australia, to examine and survey the country about Blanche Water.

1857--Colonel Freeling, Surveyor-General of South Australia, sent to verify Goyder's report; decided that Goyder had been misled by a mirage.

1857--Stephen Hack, with Mr. Miller; examined Gawler Range and sighted Lake Gairdner.

1857--Major Warburton crossed Stephen Hack's track.

1857--Messrs. Miller and Dutton explored country back of Fowler's Bay.

1858--Sir Richard G. M'Donnel; exploration to Strangways and Loddon Springs; also up the River Murray to Mount Murchison.

1858--B. H. Babbage; third expedition from Adelaide; superseded by Major Warburton.

1858--Major Warburton, continued the expedition started by B. 11. Babbage. This trip established the definite size and shape of Lake Torrens.

1858--S. Parry, Government Surveyor, South Australia; an expedition round Lake Torrens, Lake Gregory, and Blanche Water.

1858--Frank Gregory reached the Gascoyne; discovered Mount Augustus and Mount Gould.

1858--A. C. Gregory; Barcoo expedition to search for trace of the course of Leichhardt's party. Confirmation of the supposed identity of the Barcoo and Cooper's Creek.

1858--J. M'Dowall Stuart; first expedition.

1859--J. M'Dowall Stuart; second expedition; one of his party, Hergott, discovered and named Hergott Springs.

1859--George E. Dalrymple, discovered main tributaries of the Lower Burdekin, Bowen, and Bogie Rivers.

1860--Edward Cunningham and party explored the Upper Burdekin.

1861--J. Neilson and brothers; in search of pastoral country; from Mount Ranken on the Darling to Cooper's Creek.

1860-61--Burke and Wills' expedition; death of Burke, Wills, and Gray.

1861--J. M'Dowall Stuart's third expedition; he crossed the continent after two attempts.

1861--Frank Gregory discovered the Hammersley Range, Fortescue, Ashburton, De Grey, and Oakover Rivers.

1861--Messrs. Dempster and Clarkson; Western Australia; explorations to the eastward.

1861-62--William Landsborough, in search of Burke and Wills.

1861-62--Frederick Walker, leader of the Rockhampton expedition in search of Burke and Wills.

1861--Alfred Howitt, in charge of Victorian search party for Burke and Wills.

1861--Edwin J. Welch, second in command of Howitt's search party, found King, only survivor of the Burke and Wills expedition.

1861-622.--John M'Kinlay with a relief party for Burke and Wills, from Adelaide.

1862--G. W. Goyder; explorations in the Great Bight.

1862--George E. Dalrymple on the waters of the Upper Burdekin.

1862--Messrs, Delisser and Hardwicke explore from Fowler's Bay to the edge of the Victorian Desert.

1863--Thomas Macfarlane attempted to push inland north of the Great Bight.

1863--Messrs. H. M. Lefroy and party; eastward of York, Western Australia.

1863--C. C. Hunt and Ridley to the De Grey River.

1863--Colonists landed at the De Grey River, and settled on country discovered by Frank Gregory.

447

1863--Jardine, sen., formed the settlement of Somerset, Cape York.

1863--William Landsborough; in charge of the new township, Burke-town, Gulf of Carpentaria.

1864-65--Jardine Brothers; overland to Somerset, on the west coast of Cape York.

1864--Colonel Finnis formed a settlement at Escape Cliffs.

1864--J. M'Kinlay on the Alligator River; searching for suitable site for a township; his last expedition.

1864--Duncan M'Intyre; from Paroo to the Gulf of Carpentaria; died there.

1864--C. C. Hunt; exploration east of York, Western Australia.

1865--G. W. Goyder; removed settlement of Escape Cliffs to Port Darwin.

1865--J. G. Macdonald; visited the Plains of Promise.

1864--Frederick Walker; marking a telegraph line from the back of Rockingham Bay to the Norman River, Gulf of Carpentaria.

1866-7--Sir George Strong Nares, in command of H.M.S. Salamander; surveyed the eastern and north-eastern coasts of Australia and Torres Straits.

1869--John Forrest; first expedition to Lake Barlee.

1869--J. M'Dowall Stuart; died in England.

1870--John Forrest; travelled the Great Bight, from Perth to Adelaide.

1871--A. Forrest; took charge of a private expedition in search of new pastoral country.

1872--J. W. Lewis; round Lake Eyre to the Queensland border.

1872--Ernest Giles; first expedition; discovered Lake Amadeus--a large, dry, salt lake.

1872--William Hann; explorations to Charlotte Bay.

1873--Ernest Giles; second trip; death of Gibson; Gibson's Desert named.

1873--Major Warburton; crossed from Alice Springs, overland tele-graph line, to the Oakover River, Western Australia.

1873--W. C. Gosse; in charge of Central and Western Exploration ex-pedition from Alice Springs.

1874--Ross and son started from Peake Station, but failed in their en-deavours to bridge the desert.

1874--John Forrest; from the Murchison to the overland telegraph line.

1874--John M'Kinlay; died at Gawler, South Australia.

1875--J. W. Lewis, formerly one of Warburton's party, and W. Beres-ford, were sent by the South Australian Government to survey the country about Lake Eyre.

1875-76--Ernest Giles; third and successful effort to reach Western Australia; returned to Peake Station.

1876--Gilbert M'Minn, and A. W. Sergison; to ascertain the course of the Katherine River.

1877--A. W. Sergison and R. Travers explored the country round the Daly and Fitzmaurice Rivers.

1877--Ross and Harvey; explorations in South Australia.

1876--W. 0. Hodgkinson; north-west expedition to the Diamantina and Mulligan.

1876--Phillip Saunders and Adam Johns; from Roeburn, Western Australia, to the overland telegraph line.

1878--Prout Brothers; looking for country across the Queensland border; never returned.

1878--N. Buchanan; excursion to the overland telegraph line, from Queensland border. Discovered Buchanan's Creek.

1878--Frank Scarr, surveyor, attempted to cross the line south of Buchanan's track; prevented by waterless belt of country; made north to Tennant's Creek Station.

1878-79--Ernest Favenc; in charge of the Queenslander Transcontinental Expedition, from Blackall to Powell's Creek Station, overland telegraph line.

1879--Alexander Forrest led an expedition from the De Grey River, Western Australia, to the overland telegraph line; discovered the Ord and Margaret Rivers.

1878-80--Winnecke and Barclay, surveyors; to determine the border lines of Queensland and South Australia.

1882-83--Ernest Favenc; coast rivers of the Gulf, particularly the Macarthur; then crossed to the overland telegraph line.

1883--O'Donnel and Carr Boyd; from the overland telegraph line to Kimberley District, Western Australia.

1883--M'Phee; east of Daly Waters.

1883--David Lindsay; explored Arnheim's Land.

1884-85--Harry Stockdale; from Cambridge Gulf to the Katherine Telegraph Station, overland telegraph line.

1884-5--Messrs. O'Donnel and party; from the Katherine Telegraph Station to the Kimberley District.

1888--Ernest Favenc; to examine the country on the Gascoyne and Murchison, starting from Geraldton, Western Australia.

Also from Benediction Books ...
Wandering Between Two Worlds: Essays on Faith and Art
Anita Mathias
Benediction Books, 2007
152 pages
ISBN: 0955373700

Available from www.amazon.com, www.amazon.co.uk

In these wide-ranging lyrical essays, Anita Mathias writes, in lush, lovely prose, of her naughty Catholic childhood in Jamshedpur, India; her large, eccentric family in Mangalore, a sea-coast town converted by the Portuguese in the sixteenth century; her rebellion and atheism as a teenager in her Himalayan boarding school, run by German missionary nuns, St. Mary's Convent, Nainital; and her abrupt religious conversion after which she entered Mother Teresa's convent in Calcutta as a novice. Later rich, elegant essays explore the dualities of her life as a writer, mother, and Christian in the United States-- Domesticity and Art, Writing and Prayer, and the experience of being "an alien and stranger" as an immigrant in America, sensing the need for roots.

About the Author

Anita Mathias is the author of *Wandering Between Two Worlds: Essays on Faith and Art.* She has a B.A. and M.A. in English from Somerville College, Oxford University, and an M.A. in Creative Writing from the Ohio State University, USA. Anita won a National Endowment of the Arts fellowship in Creative Nonfiction in 1997. She lives in Oxford, England with her husband, Roy, and her daughters, Zoe and Irene.

Visit Anita at http://www.anitamathias.com, and on http://theoxfordchristian.blogspot.com, her Christian blog; http://wanderingbetweentwoworlds.blogspot.com/, her personal blog, and http://thegoodbooksblog.blogspot.com, her literary and writing blog.

The Church That Had Too Much
Anita Mathias
Benediction Books, 2010
52 pages
ISBN: 9781849026567

Available from www.amazon.com, www.amazon.co.uk

The Church That Had Too Much was very well-intentioned. She wanted to love God, she wanted to love people, but she was both hampered by her muchness and the abundance of her possessions, and beset by ambition, power struggles and snobbery. Read about the surprising way The Church That Had Too Much began to resolve her problems in this deceptively simple and enchanting fable.

About the Author

Anita Mathias is the author of *Wandering Between Two Worlds: Essays on Faith and Art.* She has a B.A. and M.A. in English from Somerville College, Oxford University, and an M.A. in Creative Writing from the Ohio State University, USA. Anita won a National Endowment of the Arts fellowship in Creative Nonfiction in 1997. She lives in Oxford, England with her husband, Roy, and her daughters, Zoe and Irene.

Visit Anita at http://www.anitamathias.com, and on http://theoxfordchristian.blogspot.com, her Christian blog; http://wanderingbetweentwoworlds.blogspot.com/, her personal blog, and http://thegoodbooksblog.blogspot.com, her literary and writing blog.

www.ingramcontent.com/pod-product-compliance
Lightning Source LLC
Chambersburg PA
CBHW030908090426
42737CB00007B/127